Travel

MW00438652

This coupon entitles you to special ———
when you book your trip through the

 **TRAVEL NETWORK** ®
RESERVATION SERVICE

Hotels ♦ Airlines ♦ Car Rentals ♦ Cruises
All Your Travel Needs

Here's what you get: *

♦ A discount of $50 USD on a booking of $1,000** or more for two or more people!

♦ A discount of $25 USD on a booking of $500** or more for one person!

♦ Free membership for three years, and 1,000 free miles on enrollment in the unique Miles-to-Go™ frequent-traveler program. Earn one mile for every dollar spent through the program. Earn free hotel stays starting at 5,000 miles. Earn free roundtrip airline tickets starting at 25,000 miles.

♦ Personal help in planning your own, customized trip.

♦ Fast, confirmed reservations at any property recommended in this guide, subject to availability.***

♦ Special discounts on bookings in the U.S. and around the world.

♦ Low-cost visa and passport service.

♦ Reduced-rate cruise packages.

Visit our website at http://www.travnet.com/Frommer or call us globally at 201-567-8500, ext. 55. In the U.S., call toll-free at 1-888-940-5000, or fax 201-567-1838. In Canada, call toll-free at 1-800-883-9959, or fax 416-922-6053. In Asia, call 60-3-7191044, or fax 60-3-7185415.

* To qualify for these travel discounts, at least a portion of your trip must
   include destinations covered in this guide. No more than one coupon discount
   may be used in any 12-month period, for destinations covered in this guide.
   Cannot be combined with any other discount or program.
** These are U.S. dollars spent on commissionable bookings.
*** A $10 USD fee, plus fax and/or phone charges, will be added to the cost of
   bookings at each hotel not linked to the reservation service. Customers
   must approve these fees in advance.

Valid until December 31, 1998. Terms and conditions of the Miles-to-
Go™ program are available on request by calling 201-567-8500, ext 55.

MUN123

Frommer's® 97
1st Edition

Munich & the Bavarian Alps

by Darwin Porter and Danforth Prince

Macmillan • USA

ABOUT THE AUTHORS

Darwin Porter and **Danforth Prince** are coauthors of a number of bestselling Frommer guides, notably England, France, the Caribbean, Italy, and Spain. Porter, a bureau chief for the *Miami Herald* at 21, was the author of the first ever Frommer guide to Germany and has traveled extensively throughout the country ever since. He is joined by Prince who was formerly of the Paris bureau of the *New York Times*.

MACMILLAN TRAVEL

A Simon & Schuster Macmillan Company
1633 Broadway
New York, NY 10019

Find us online at **http://www.mgr.com/travel**

ISBN: 0-02861147-0
ISSN: 1090-2325

Editor: Alice Fellows
Production Editor: Michael Thomas
Map Editor: Douglas Stallings
Design by Michele Laseau
Maps copyright © by Simon & Schuster, Inc.

SPECIAL SALES

Bulk purchases (10+ copies) of Frommer's and selected Macmillan travel guides are available to corporations, organizations, mail-order catalogs, institutions, and charities at special discounts and can be customized to suit individual needs. For more information write to: Special Sales, Macmillan General Reference, 1633 Broadway, New York, NY 10019.

Manufactured in the United States of America

Contents

Appendix 217

Index 221

List of Maps

AN INVITATION TO THE READER

In researching this book, we discovered many wonderful places—resorts, inns, restaurants, shops, and more. We're sure you'll find others. Please tell us about them, so we can share the information with your fellow travelers in upcoming editions. If you were disappointed with a recommendation, we'd love to know that, too. Please write to:

Frommer's Munich & the Bavarian Alps, 1st Edition
Macmillan Travel
1633 Broadway
New York, NY 10019

AN ADDITIONAL NOTE

Please be advised that travel information is subject to change at any time—and this is especially true of prices. We therefore suggest that you write or call ahead for confirmation when making your travel plans. The authors, editors, and publisher cannot be held responsible for the experiences of readers while traveling. Your safety is important to us, however, so we encourage you to stay alert and be aware of your surroundings. Keep a close eye on cameras, purses, and wallets, all favorite targets of thieves and pickpockets.

SYMBOLS & ABBREVIATIONS

✪ Frommer's Favorites

Hotels, restaurants, attractions, and entertainment you should not miss.

Ⓢ Super-Special Values

Hotels and restaurants that offer great value for your money.

The following abbreviations are used for credit cards:

AE	American Express	EC	Eurocard
CB	Carte Blanche	JCB	Japan Credit Bank
DC	Diners Club	MC	MasterCard
DISC	Discover	V	Visa
ER	enRoute		

Introducing Munich

Sprawling Munich, home of some 1.3 million people, is the capital of Bavaria, and one of Germany's major cultural centers. It's one of Germany's most festive cities.

Long-time resident of Munich, Thomas Mann, wrote something about the city that might have been coined in a top-notch advertising agency: "Munich sparkles." Although the city he described was swept away by two world wars, the quote is still apt. Munich continues to sparkle, drawing temporary visitors and new residents like a magnet, from virtually everywhere.

Some of the sparkle derives from its vitality. Repleat with buzzing factories, newspapers, and television stations, service and electronics industries, and hi-tech laboratories, it's one of Europe's busiest and liveliest places. More subtle is Munich's ability to combine Hollywood-type glamour and stylish international allure and still preserve its folkloric and rustic connections.

Few other large cities are as successful as Munich in marketing folklore, rusticity, and nostalgia for the golden times of yesteryear. This rustic ambience coexists with the hip and the avant-garde and a sharp concern for what's going on, in both arts and politics, in Berlin, Moscow, and Washington, D.C.

Munich is full of non-Bavarians. More than two-thirds of the German citizens living in Munich have come from other parts of the country, and tens of thousands are expatriates or immigrants from every conceivable foreign land. Sometimes these diverse elements that make up Munich today seem unified only by the shared search for a good life. As Americans come to New York or San Francisco seeking opportunity and experience, so Germans and others migrate to Munich.

Outsiders are found in every aspect of Munich's life. The wildly applauded soccer team, FC Bayern München, is composed almost entirely of outsiders—Danes, Belgians, Swedes, Prussians—and the team was trained by a Rhinelander throughout its spate of recent successes. The city's most frequently quoted newspaper mogul (Dieter Schröder) and many of the city's artistic movers and shakers are expatriates, usually from North Germany.

What's remarkable in Munich is the unspoken collusion of the whole population in promoting Bavarian charm and rusticity, despite the fact that real dyed-in-the-wool Bavarians themselves

Munich—A city of southern European charm and central European efficiency.
                                    —Anon., but attributed to John F. Kennedy

In Munich one always has a sense that just over the mountains there is always a way of escape from all German problems, to the lands where the lemons grow.
        —Goronwy Rees, "Diary from Berlin to Munich," *Encounter,* April 1964

risk becoming a distinct minority within their own capital. This is what lends the city such a distinctive flair.

Virtually everyone has heard the city's roster of nicknames—"Athens on the Isar," "the German Silicon Valley," and "Little Paris." But none of them seem to stick. More appropriate is a label that's voiced with the most ambivalence both within and outside of Munich—"secret capital of Germany." Ironically, this label seems even more credible since the German government divided its functions between Bonn and Berlin, leading to a general all-around bureaucratic muddle.

Munich's self-imposed image is that of a fun-loving and festival-addicted city, typified by its Oktoberfest, which began as a minor sideshow to a royal wedding in 1810, and has become a symbol of the city itself. It draws more than 7 million visitors each year. Redolent with nostalgia for old-timey Bavaria, raucous hordes cram themselves into the city during a period of only 16 days.

Oktoberfest is so evocative, and so gleefully and unashamedly pagan, that dozens of sites throughout the world capitalize on Munich's success by throwing Oktoberfest ceremonies of their own. These occur even in such unlikely places as Helen, Georgia, where citizens and merchants reap tidy profits by wearing dirndls and lederhosen, playing recordings of the requisite oompah-pah music, and serving ample provisions of beer in oversized beer steins. No one has ever marketed such stuff better than Munich, but then, few other regions of Europe have had such alluring raw material from which to draw.

A somewhat reluctant contender for the role of an international megalopolis, Munich has pursued commerce, industry, and the Good Life without fanfare, downplaying its role as the car-clogged German version of Los Angeles. You get the idea that despite its economic muscle, and a roaring GNP, Munich wants to see itself as a large, agrarian village, peopled by jolly beer drinkers who cling to their folkloric roots, despite the presence on all sides of symbols of the computer age.

To many, Munich's realities don't live up to their expectations. Underneath fun-loving Munich is an unyielding conservatism and resistance to change, seasoned with strong doses of religious and political fanaticism. But as a symbol of a newly bold, recently reunited Germany forging a new identity for the 21st century, Munich simply has no parallel. As such it continues to exert a powerful appeal.

1 Frommer's Favorite Munich Experiences

- **Socializing at the Biergarten:** If you're in Munich anytime between the first sunny spring day and the last fading light of a Bavarian-style autumn, you might head for one of the city's celebrated beer gardens (Biergarten). Our favorite is Biergarten Chinesischer Turm in the Englischer Garten. Traditionally, beer gardens were tables placed under chestnut trees planted above the storage cellars to keep beer cool in summer. Naturally, people started to drink close to the source of their pleasure, and the tradition has remained. Lids on beer steins, incidentally, were meant to keep out the flies. It's estimated that today Munich has at least 400 beer gardens and cellars. Food, drink, and atmosphere are much the same in all of them.

- **Enjoying Munich's World-Class Music:** The city is the home to many outstanding classical music groups, notably the Bavarian State Opera and the Munich Philharmonic. Prices are affordable and the selection is diverse. The season of summer concerts at Nymphenburg Palace alone is worth the trip to Munich.

- **Nude Sunbathing in the Englischer Garten:** A CEO we know in Munich claims that on a summer day he has to go to this park and take off all his clothes and sunbathe naked to regain the strength necessary to work the rest of the day. Whether this is the truth or a far stretch, he is not alone. On any summery sunny day, it seems that half of Munich can be seen letting it all hang out in the Volksgarten (People's Park). The sentimental founding fathers of this park with their Romantic ideas surely had no idea they were creating a public nudist colony. If you're not much of a voyeur, and feel that most people look better with their clothes on, you can still come here to enjoy the park's natural beauty.

- **Snacking on Weisswurst:** Munich's classic "street food" is a "white sausage" made of calf's head, veal, and seasoning, about the size of a hot dog. Weisswurst must be consumed before you hear the chimes of midday, a tradition maintained even in this day of refrigeration. Smooth and light in flavor, it is eaten with pretzels and beer—nothing else. Weisswurst etiquette calls for you to remove the sausage from a bowl of hot water, cut it crosswise in half, dip the cut end in sweet mustard, then suck the sausage out of the casing in a single gesture. When you learn to do this properly, you will have become a true Münchener.

- **Getting Away from It All at the Hirschgarten:** For a glimpse of what Munich used to be like, flee from the tourist hordes and traffic to the Hirschgarten or "Deer Meadow." A "green lung" between Donnersberg Bridge and Nymphenburg Park, the area has been a deer park since 1791. In 1890 the largest beer garden in the world was built here, seating 8,000 drinkers. The Hirschgarten remains Munich's most tranquil retreat, a land of towering oaks, chestnuts, and beeches, attracting those with a love of the great outdoors—and especially those who like to pack a picnic lunch or enjoy an open-air game of chess.

- **Exploring Trendy Haidhausen:** Tourists rarely venture into this district on the right bank of the Isar River. For decades it was known as a blue-collar and low-rent district of Munich. Hippies and artists in the '70s created a cross-cultural scene that made Haidhausen, not Schwabing, the hip place to hang out. Today it is the place to see and be seen—especially if you're a *Schicki-Micki* (club-going Bavarian yuppie), a person who dresses only in black, or one of the *Müeslis* (European granolas). The place to go is one of the bars or cafés around Pariser Platz or Weissenburger Platz. Take the S-bahn to Ostbahnhof or Rosenheimerstrasse and get with it!

- **Attending Oktoberfest:** It's called the "biggest keg party" in the world. Müncheners had so much fun in 1810 celebrating the wedding of Prince Ludwig to Princess Therese von Sachsen-Hildburghausen that they've been rowdying it up ever since for 16 full days, between September 21 and October 6. The festival's tent city is at the Theresienwiese fairground, and the Middle Ages live on as oxen are roasted on open spits, brass bands oompah-pah you into oblivion, and some 750,000 kegs of the brew are tapped. There are even tents in which you can recover from your drunkenness, listening to soothing zither music.

- **R&R at Olympiapark:** Site of the 1972 Olympic Games, this 740-acre park is a city unto itself with its own mayor, post office, and elementary school. The stadium is a premier venue for various sporting events and concerts. If you like to exercise and you like the great outdoors, you can swim in one of the pools that Mark Spitz made famous in his successful pursuit of seven gold medals back in 1972. That's not all: You'll find all the jogging tracks and gyms your heart desires, even an artificial lake. To cap your visit, take the elevator to the top of the Olympiaturm for a panoramic preview of Munich and a look at the Bavarian Alps. In summer, free rock concerts blast from the amphitheater, Theatron, by Olympic Lake.

- **From vie de bohème to Schicki-Micki in Schwabing:** In fin de siècle Munich, Schwabing was the home of the avant-garde. Artists, writers, poets, and musicians of the era, including Thomas Mann, called it home. Franz Wedekind wrote the Lulu plays here that inspired the film starring Louise Brooks. Jugendstil (art nouveau) and the Blue Rider painters, and Richard Wagner, made this area the cultural capital of Europe before 1914. A revival came in 1945, with new cultural icons such as Rainer Werner Fassbinder. Schwabing lives on, although today it's gentrified and populated by fashion editors and models, along with what have been called "swinging aristocrats." Although you might come here to walk in the footsteps of Vassily Kandinsky or to see where Paul Klee or Rainer Maria Rilke lived and worked, you'll get more exposure to Schicki-Micki, or Mickey Mouse chic. Walking, strolling, shopping, and people-watching are the chief activities today. At some point find a chair at Café Roxy, 48 Leopoldstrasse, and watch the parade go by.

- **Soaking up the Wittelsbach Lifestyle:** Just northwest of the city centers lies Nymphenburg Palace, begun in 1664, an exquisite baroque extravaganza surrounded by a 495-acre park dotted with lakes, pavilions, and hunting lodges. It was the summer home of the Bavarian rulers. We prefer to visit in either summer, when outdoor concerts are presented, or from May through June, when the rhododendrons are in bloom. Go inside the palace for a look at the painted ceiling in the Great Hall. In such works as *Nymphs Paying Homage to the Goddess Flora,* Bavarian rococo reached its apogee.

- **An Afternoon in the Botanischer Garten:** If you're not a plant lover, you'll be converted here. It's one of the finest and most richly stocked botanical wonders in Europe. You can wander among the 40 acres with some 15,000 varieties of plants. Laid out between 1909 and 1914 on the north side of Nymphenburg Park, the park presents one highlight after another, especially an alpine garden with rare alpine specimens—the orange hawkweed, the dwarf alpine poppy, or the blue gentian. The flora of steeps, dunes, and moorlands thrive here, as does the heather garden, a delight in late spring.

- **Market Day at Viktualienmarkt:** The most characteristic scene in Munich is a Saturday morning here at this food market at the south end of Altstadt. Since 1807, Viktualienmarkt has been the center of Munich life, dispensing fresh vegetables, fruit from the Bavarian countryside, just-caught fish, dairy produce, poultry, rich grainy breads, moist cakes, and farm-fresh eggs. Naturally, there's a beer garden. There's even a maypole, and, as a touch of class, a statue honoring Karl Valentin (1882–1948), the legendary comic actor and filmmaker. Even more interesting than the market produce are the stallholders themselves—a few evocative of Professor Higgins's "squashed cabbage leaf," Eliza Doolittle in London's Covent Garden of yore.

- **Rafting Along the Isar:** Admittedly, it doesn't rival the Seine in Paris, but the Isar is the river of life in Munich. If you can't make it for a country walk in the Bavarian Alps, a walk along the left bank of the Isar is an alternative option. Begin at Höllriegelskreuth and follow the scenic path along the Isar's high bank. Your trail will carry you through the Römerschanze into what Müncheners call "The Valley of the Mills" (Mühltal). After passing the Bridge Inn (Brückenwirt) you will eventually reach Kloster Schäftlarn, where you'll find—what else?—a beer garden. After a mug you'll be fortified to continue along signposted paths through the Isar River Valley until you reach Wolfrathausen. Instead of walking back, you can often board a raft made of logs and "drift" back to the city, enjoying beer (what else?) and often the oompah-pah sound of a brass band as you head toward Munich.

- **A Dip at Müller's Public Baths:** Müllersches Volksbad at Rosendheimer Strasse I (S-Bahn to Isartor), is one of the most magnificent in all of Germany. This is no dull swimming pool but a celebration of grandeur fin de siècle style. Karl Hocheder designed this Moorish/Roman spectacle between 1897 and 1901, an era of opulence. When they opened they were hailed as the most modern baths in all of Europe, surpassing anything but Budapest. A local engineer, Karl Müller, donated the money to build these lavish baths. Completely renovated, the baths today have a "gentlemen's pool" with barrel vaulting and a "ladies pool" with domed vaulting. There are also sweat baths and individual baths for those who like to let it all hang out—but in private. Alas, the *Zamperlbad* or doggie bath in the basement is no more.

- **A Night at the Hofbräuhaus:** Established in 1589 by Duke Wilhelm V to satisfy the thirsts of his court, the Hofbräuhaus is not only the city's major tourist attraction, but the world's most famous beer hall, seating more than 4,000 drinkers. In 1828 the citizens of Munich were allowed to drink "the court's brew" for the first time, and it was habit-forming. A popular song, "In München steht ein Hofbräuhaus," spread the fame of the brewery. To be really authentic, you drink in the ground-floor *Schwemme* where some 1,000 beer buffs down their brew at wooden tables while listening to the sounds of an oompah-pah band. More rooms, including the *Trinkstube* for 350, are found upstairs, and in summer beer is served in a colonnaded courtyard patio with a Lion Fountain. The waitstaff in Bavarian peasant dress appears carrying 10 steins at once. Pretzels are sold on long sticks, and white *Radis* (radishes) are cut into fancy spirals. Both the radish, which is salted, and the salty pretzel seem designed to make you drink more. The Hofbräuhaus is where the good life of Munich holds forth.

2 The City Today

Today, Munich's position as the centerpiece of southern Germany conveys at least the illusion that life here is more easygoing, sunnier, and emotionally richer than life in the foggy and windswept cities along the Baltic. As such, Munich continues to captivate the German imagination.

That notion is only partially true. Despite new influences from virtually everywhere, and a proud role as high-tech capital of Germany, Munich continues to be permeated with the spirit of the bourgeoisie that helped mold it during the 18th and 19th centuries. Consequently, although some aspects of Munich are boldly innovative and experimental, the city is at the same time defiantly reactionary and proudly opposed to new ideas. Munich's avant-garde and its reactionary elements coexist, not always comfortably, and with very little of the indulgent laissez-faire and resigned world weariness that are more obviously prevalent in such places as Berlin.

At least some of Munich's modern-day smugness derives from the comforts, prestige, and economic power it has enjoyed since the end of World War II. This tends to be bitterly resented by residents of cities farther east, which have almost no hope of ever, in their lifetimes, achieving the prosperity that bourgeois and sometimes complacent Munich attracted partly as an accident of geography. In Munich, what you see is what you're likely to get. This flies in direct opposition to the more frenetic, more cerebral, more innovative, and more (dare we say it?) hysterical Berlin, where the rigors of reuniting the two Germanies occasionally borders on the surreal.

There's lots of room for economic creativity and potential profits in the dynamic tension that surrounds modern Munich. Although traditional trade patterns throughout the Cold War positioned Munich as the gateway between northern and southern Europe, the collapse of the Soviet regime in 1989 opened fertile markets in the east as well.

Unfortunately, although the role of Munich as a center of postindustrial technology and trade has been reinforced, the end of the Cold War initiated stiff competition in the touristic sphere. In the bad old days of the Cold War, Munich was the end of the line, about as far east as most mainstream tourists cared to go. Rather disturbingly in the eyes of tourist officials, Munich today seems relegated to the status of stopover on the way to more exotic cities such as the reinvented Berlin or such beauties as Budapest and Prague.

Today, Munich boasts many laurels. Its academic infrastructure, with more than 100,000 students, is the second largest in Germany, with a distinctly urbanized and cosmopolitan flavor. Greater Munich (third largest city in Germany) has more heavy industry than any other single city in Germany, and at least in theory, the possibility of more jobs. It has produced more Nobel Prize winners than any other city in Germany, and civic boosters claim, not without justification, that Munich is the most beautiful city in the country. Its museum of science and industry (the Deutsches Museum) is the largest museum of its type in the world, and its Gasteig Center, completed in 1985, is a model for other performance halls throughout Germany.

The city recognizes 14 official holidays, more than any other city in Germany, a remnant of medieval traditions when almost a third of any calendar year was devoted to religious holidays.

Cynics, many of them envious residents of Berlin, Hamburg, or the aristocratic Rhineland, claim that the only thing that really motivates a native Münchener is an aggressive pursuit of leisure time. Although that's probably not true, Munich offers more options for leisure than anywhere else in Germany, including a setting that is the most conducive in the world to beer drinking. It has some of the finest theaters (more than 60 that are legitimate, many others that are less so) and German-language repertory companies, with performances that are usually packed. By some standards, it's also the most expensive city in a reunited Germany. But despite its schizophrenic ambivalence—part class, part kitsch—and the encroachment of urban sprawl, Munich manages to retain many aspects of an alpine village. Fortunately for urban claustrophobics, there are many verdant parks, and the open spaces of the Bavarian and Austrian Alps lie within about an hour's drive.

Modern Munich contains a lot of elements designed to amuse and divert. A visitor can while away the time pursuing sports and cultural activities, or simply sit for hours in beer halls and taverns that are, on the average, more authentically folkloric than those within any other metropolis in Europe. Even if you don't happen to be Bavarian, or even German, you can still enjoy the beer-drinking tradition, and its attendant social rituals. Six major breweries are based in Munich, as well as entire industries devoted to supplying the pastime's accessories. Not least of these are rehearsal halls and recording studios for the oompah bands that help make beer-drinking rituals so delightful.

Impressions

[Munich is] A slovenly, Immoral nest,
Of fanaticism, coarseness, and cowherds,
Of holy pictures, dumplings, and women on bikes.
—Gottfried Keller (Swiss-born poet), 1840

The Bavarian people are much given to drink.
—Aventinus (15th-century humanist)

Drawbacks in Munich include the same kinds of things residents of New York or Paris complain about: impossibly high rents, urban stress, and urban anonymity. And despite the jovial facade, there's a rising incidence of urban crime and—something Munich has always seen a lot of—civil unrest.

Fortunately, Munich today offers a wider range of personal choices and different types of lifestyle options than ever before in its history. As you'll quickly learn, modern Munich offers a lot more than folkloric kitsch, although two or three steins of beer go a long way toward helping its citizens ease any pain while forging the city's new identity as Munich approaches the millennium.

3 A Look at the Past

EARLY ORIGINS   Munich is a very young city compared to some of its neighbors. Its origins derive from an unpleasant struggle between two feudal rulers who quarreled for the right to impose tolls on traffic moving along the salt road, between the then-thriving (and much older) cities of Salzburg, Hallein, Reichenhall, and Augsburg.

The spark that ignited the existence of Munich occurred in 1156, when the emperor of the Holy Roman Empire, Friedrich Barbarossa, placed all of Bavaria under the control of his cousin and ally, Guelph Heinrich der Löwe (Duke Henry the Lion). Pressed for cash, and to further his intent of building Bavaria into a network of trading centers, he ordered the destruction of a strategic bridge spanning the Isar, near the modern-day community of Oberföhring. Tolls derived from that bridge had previously gone directly into the coffers of a local clergyman, the bishop of Freising. The bishop's fully justified rage did little to influence the faraway emperor Barbarossa, who was too busy with more important problems to worry about this minor clash between church and state. This particular squabble, however, was to have far-reaching consequences.

Adding insult to injury, Henry the Lion subsequently built a new bridge a few miles upstream, adjacent to a tiny settlement of Benedictine monks, whose small community on the banks of the Isar

Dateline

- **1156** Feudal warlord Henry the Lion demolishes the local bishop's toll-collecting bridge and builds one nearby. The city of Munich is born.
- **1158** Holy Roman Emperor Barbarossa validates Henry's decision. The establishment of Munich is legitimized.
- **1173** Fortified behind walls and watchtowers, Munich's population swells to 2,500.
- **1180** Henry the Lion defies the emperor and is banished. Local governing bishop tries to destroy settlement.
- **1240** The Wittelsbach dynasty extends their influence to Munich.
- **1250–1300** Munich's population increases fivefold. New fortifications built.
- **1285** A pogrom burns 150 Jews within their synagogue.
- **1300s** Munich's population grows to 10,000, becoming the richest city of the Wittelsbachs.

continues

- **1314** Duke Ludwig IV, Munich's ruler, is elected head of the Holy Roman Empire. Munich is now the most important city in the German-speaking world.
- **1319** A Habsburg, Frederick the Handsome, attacks Munich but is taken captive. Pope's meddling backfires.
- **1322** Munich prospers because of salt trade and becomes center of loose association of German kingdoms.
- **1327** Fire devastates much of Munich's eastern district.
- 1346 Ludwig IV killed in bear hunt. New emperor strips Munich of its honors.
- **1385** Citizens of Munich rebel against Wittelsbach dynasty and execute a representative of the family.
- **1403** Power reverts back to the Wittelsbachs after their armies lay siege to Munich's walls.
- **1492** A mountain pass is carved through the Alps to expedite trade with Italy.
- **1516** Munich passes Europe's first law governing food and beverage.
- **1517** Martin Luther sparks Protestant Reformation. Munich's leaders order their city to remain Catholic.
- **1560** Wittelsbach dynasty makes Munich their official seat and launches massive rebuilding program.
- **1583** Wilhelm IV bans all religion other than Catholicism, making Munich German-speaking centerpiece of the Counter-Reformation.
- **1608** Something akin to the Spanish Inquisition persecutes non-Catholics in Munich.
- **1618–1648** The Thirty Years' War leads to siege of Munich by Swedish king who bankrupts city. Plague

continues

River was referred to as *Zu den Münichen*—at the site of the little monks. The name was later shortened to München, and the little monk, or Münichen, remains today the symbol of the city of Munich.

Henry the Lion had already had experience in the founding of trading centers. He had established the Baltic cities of Schwerin, Rostock, and Lübeck, cities that were to grow rapidly into major forces within the Hanseatic League. Repeating the patterns of his earlier successes, he granted to Munich the right to mint its own coins and to hold markets, basic tools that any city needed for survival. Tolls from his new bridge, which now funneled the lucrative salt trade across the Isar, went directly into Henry's coffers.

Within a few months, Barbarossa validated the crude but effective actions of his duke, legitimizing the establishment of Munich on June 14, 1158, the date that is commemorated as the official debut of the city. Henry, however, had to pay a price: Barbarossa ordered that a third of all tolls generated by the new bridge be paid to the bishop of Freising, whose bridge Henry had destroyed.

MEDIEVAL PROSPERITY & POLITICS   The first of the city's fortifications, a stone wall studded with watchtowers and five gates, was built in 1173 and enclosed 2,500 people. One of the most important survivals from this period (most of the wall was long ago demolished) is the Marienplatz, then and now the centerpiece of the city and the crossing point of the Salzstrasse (Salt Route), a crossroads that can still be seen on the city map today. During its early days, it was simply known as Marketplace or Grain Market.

In 1180, Duke Henry quarreled with Emperor Barbarossa, refusing to send troops to assist Barbarossa in a conquest of northern Italy. As a punishment, he was banished forever from Munich and the rest of Bavaria. Gleefully, Henry's eternal nemesis, the bishop of Freising, attempted to eradicate the upstart young city and reroute the salt trade back through his stronghold of Oberföhring. By this time, however, Munich was simply too well established to succumb.

By 1240, a new force had arisen in Munich, the Wittelsbach family. They were part of a new generation of merchant princes, and were as stern and feared and as conservative and unyielding as the Doges of Venice. Ruling through a shrewd imposition of military and economic power, their family patriarch, Otto von Wittelsbach, succeeded in having himself designated as the ruler of Bavaria shortly after the banishment of Henry the Lion in 1180. Thus began the longest and most conservative reign of any dynasty in Germany. The Wittlesbachs ruled in Munich and the rest of Bavaria until the forces of socialism swept them away during the final days of World War I. Today they are still viewed by the Bavarians with a kind of nostalgic affection.

Between 1250 and 1300, the population of Munich increased fivefold, the result of migration from the countryside and a period that was relatively free from plagues. Members of at least three religious orders established monasteries, convents, and hospitals within the city walls. The souls of Munich's faithful were segregated into a network of different parishes. The Frauenkirche, and a century later, the Marienkirche, were constructed to supplement the services of the already existing church of St. Peter.

As the population (and the resultant social tensions) grew, the city's encircling fortifications were enlarged to protect the new suburbs. Although predominantly Catholic, the city fostered a small population of much persecuted Jews as well. The worst pogrom occurred in 1285, when Munich's Jews were accused of the murder of a small child, and 150 of them were burned alive within their synagogue, which was located at the time just behind the Neues Rathaus (New Town Hall). Two years later, other groups of Jews came to Munich, but ironically, the handicaps the city imposed upon them (exclusion from all trades except moneylending) led to a modest if precarious degree of prosperity. Pogroms were repeated throughout the rest of the Middle Ages, and in 1442 the Jews were banished from Munich altogether.

Just before the dawn of the 13th century, the artisans and merchants of Munich staged a revolt against the Wittelsbach family that revolved around debased coins that were being issued by the dukes' mint. After a mob destroyed the mint and killed its overseer, the dukes exerted a form of punishment that was increasingly standard throughout the tightfisted world of medieval Bavaria—a stiff fine was imposed upon the citizenry as a means of reimbursing the loss.

IMPERIAL MUNICH During the 1300s, Munich became the richest of the several cities ruled by the Wittelsbachs, an enviable source of income derived from tolls and taxes. Grain, meats, fish, and wine were traded within specifically designated

claims a third of Munich's population.

- **1643** Wittlesbachs secure their power and strip right of Müncheners to elect their own mayor.
- **1674** Residenz catches fire but resentful Müncheners take their sweet time in putting out the flames.
- **1705** Austria invades and occupies Bavaria. Bavarian peasants marching on Munich in protest are massacred.
- **1758** Porcelain factory at Nymphenburg becomes a resounding success.
- **1759** Academy of Sciences marks the influence of the Enlightenment.
- **1771** King Max III Joseph makes some aspects of public education a legal requirement.
- **1777** Max III Joseph dies, ushering in the much hated regime of Karl Theodor, who tries to trade Bavaria for the Netherlands.
- **1799** Outbreak of French Revolution causes fear on the throne of Munich's rulers.
- **1799** Armies of Napoléon invade Munich.
- **1818** Liberal reforms as conceived by Montgelas enacted.
- **1821** Marienkirche is designed as the city's official cathedral (Dom).
- **1826** Munich gets its own university.
- **1846** Revolution leads to voluntary abdication of Ludwig I. Maximilian II ascends Bavarian throne.
- **1855** Maximilian erects the Bavarian National Museum.
- **1857** Weisswurst makes its debut in the city's beer halls.
- **1860–1890** Munich annexes a half-dozen townships.
- **1864** Maximilian dies. Mad King Ludwig II ascends to the throne at the age of 18.

continues

- **1864–65** Wagner resides in Munich, creating some of his major operas before falling out with young Ludwig.
- **1871** Bismarck, ruler of Prussia, unites the quarreling principalities of Germany. Bavarian king becomes a figurehead.
- **1882** Munich electrifies its streets and houses.
- **1886** Mad Ludwig stripped of power and shortly thereafter drowns mysteriously.
- **1892** Secession movement founded in Munich as a protest against traditional perceptions of Bavarian art.
- **1896** Art nouveau reinforces its grip on Munich thanks to *Jugend* magazine.
- **1902** Lenin spends time in Munich, publishing an incendiary magazine.
- **1911** Klee and Kandinsky found *Der Blau Reiter* school to promote modern and abstract art.
- **1914–18** World War I throws Munich into bloodshed and disillusionment, climaxed by the bitter Treaty of Versailles.
- **1918** Social unrest prevails, as 10,000 workers organize in front of the Residenz. King Ludwig III flees, marking end of Wittelsbach dynasty.
- **1919** Kurt Eisner, leader of short-lived socialist regime, is assassinated. Army sent from Berlin evicts revolutionary government.
- **1923** Hitler instigates Beer Hall Putsch in protest against Weimar government.
- **1933** Munich, along with Germany, swept by Nazi victories. Swastika flies atop city hall.
- **1934** Hitler consolidates power and crushes archrival Ernst Röhm.

continues

neighborhoods of Munich. The collection of tolls from the roads leading in and out of the city helped make whomever controlled them (in this case, the Wittelsbachs) rich.

In 1314, a Wittelsbach, Duke Ludwig IV, later to be known as Ludwig the Bavarian, was elected as the German kaiser, thanks to his status as the least threatening choice among a roster of more powerful contenders. The election suddenly threw Munich into the center of German politics and made it one of the most watched cities in Germany. Ludwig traveled to Rome for his coronation and brought back from his visit one of the treasured religious icons of medieval Munich—the severed arm of St. Anthony, which still can be seen in the church of St. Anna in Lehel.

In 1319, one of the Wittelsbachs's most vindictive enemies, the Habsburg family in the person of Frederick the Handsome, attacked Munich and laid siege to its walls. Against most of Europe's expectations, the Wittelsbachs prevailed, eventually capturing the Habsburg leader and taking him prisoner. However, the pope, residing at the time in Avignon, sided with the Habsburgs and excommunicated Ludwig. Despite this serious handicap, Ludwig retained his throne. Consequences of the excommunication were enormous and widely viewed as an example of a pope overplaying his cards. It was also the last time Rome ever again tried to directly influence the succession of a German royal line. Although Bavaria remained Catholic, and continued to be Catholic even after the Protestant Reformation, Munich positioned itself as a centerpiece of resistance to papal authority for several centuries to come. To reward Munich for its loyalty (and also to line his own pockets), Ludwig created a lucrative monopoly for the city by ordering in 1322 that all the salt mined within Hallein or Reichenhall should pass through Munich.

One of the most visible symbols of Ludwig's defiance against the popes was the shelter he offered to William of Occam. A brilliant scholar, trained in the monasteries of both England and France, and persecuted as a heretic by the pope, Occam spent the last years of his life in Munich, striving for reform of the Catholic Church. His presence helped to define Munich's image as a hard-headed Catholic city that catered only reluctantly to the whims of any faraway religious potentate.

In 1327, a fire ravaged most of the city's eastern district, and when a new encircling wall was built, it was designed with so much space that it contained the city throughout the next 400 years. Despite the city's explosive growth, and the strong temptation to alter Munich's most central core, the Marienplatz was never altered from its original form, which it more or less retains today.

Ironically, Ludwig the Bavarian's untimely death (he was killed in 1346 during a bear hunt) came at the perfect time. His unbridled ambition and successful defiance of the pope had alienated many other German princes, who were poised to attack him. As it was, the symbols of the city's sovereignty over the Holy Roman Empire—including the bejeweled Imperial orb and a valuable collection of ceremonial swords—were snatched away from the safekeeping of Munich shortly after Ludwig's death, and the city's role as headquarters of the German-speaking empire came to an abrupt end.

CIVIC MUNICH   With the demise of Ludwig, civil unrest came to Munich, and the Wittelsbachs were no longer able to present a strong united front. They fell to squabbling among themselves over the land, and territories, such as the Tyrol, formerly under Bavarian influence, were lost. The citizenry resented the close links that had formed between the Wittelsbachs and the rich patrician families that controlled the city's politics, and in 1385 armed conflicts were initiated, and Hans Impler, an official Wittelsbach representative, was publicly executed in the Marienplatz. For six years beginning in 1397, the city's prominent families abandoned Munich completely, seeking the sanctuary of their country estates, returning only after sympathetic armies had laid siege to the town, quelled the unrest, and granted a limited roster of influence to citizens of Munich in how the city's affairs were conducted.

- **1938** *Kristallnacht* descends on Munich and elsewhere—government-sanctioned vandalizing of Jewish-owned homes and businesses.
- **1939** Assassination attempt against Hitler as he sits with cronies in Munich's Bürgerbräukeller.
- **1942** Most intense Allied bombing of Munich.
- **1945** American troops enter Munich on April 30 to find 45% of the city's buildings in rubble, the population reduced.
- **1945–47** Mayor Thomas Wimmer directs massive cleanup of World War II debris.
- **1949** Munich redefined as capital of Federal *Land* of Bavaria.
- **1957** Immigrants flood Munich, bringing population to one million.
- **1972** Summer Olympics witness the murder of 11 Israeli athletes by terrorist Palestinians.
- **1985** Gasteig Center for Performing Arts opens.
- **1989** Soviet regime collapses, opening new trade zones.
- **1991** Munich becomes part of a reunified Germany.
- **1995** The Bavarian Beer Garden Revolution draws 20,000 angry protesters.

Ironically, the personal security of the Wittelsbachs was frequently compromised by the success and rapid growth of the city they governed. Their policy of living within semifortified retreats outside the city walls, so they could make a quick getaway in the case of civil unrest, was often sabotaged as Munich's boundaries continually encroached upon them. The site of the Residenz, now near the center of Munich, was originally a rocky, isolated eyrie outside the city limits, safe from rebellion and angry mobs.

Throughout the 1400s, Munich became a boom town. More than 28,000 four-wheeled carts bearing marketable goods passed through the city gates every year, besides the vast number of two-wheeled carts and people on foot. In response to this traffic, some of the town's main avenues, narrow though they were, were paved. Between 1392 and 1488, the city's increasingly prosperous merchant class built or altered into their present form many of the city's centerpieces, including the Ratsturm, the Alte Rathaus (Old City Hall), the Frauenkirche, and St. Peter's church.

By 1492, Munich had graduated from a dependence on the salt trade, and was now reaping most of its profits from trade with Italy, especially Venice. In the same year Columbus stumbled upon his landfall in the New World, the Müncheners opened a mountain pass over the Kesselberg near the hamlet of Walchensee to speed up trade routes to the "Queen of the Adriatic."

By 1500, Munich boasted a population of almost 14,000 persons, 400 of whom were beggars, and 750 of whom were priests, nuns, or monks. It also included about three dozen brewers whose products were quickly becoming associated with the name of the town. Pigs were engaged to eat the garbage strewn in the streets, and about two dozen innkeepers supplied food, drink, and lodgings to the medieval equivalent of the business traveler. The city's core (but not the surrounding fields that kept it fed) was protected from invasion by an ever-expanding ring of fortifications and towers. The most serious dangers were plagues and fires, both of which devastated the city at periodic intervals.

In 1516, the city adopted laws that later helped confirm its role as beer capital of the world. Known as the Bavarian Beer Purity Law, it was the first law in Europe regulating the production of any food or beverage.

THE REFORMATION   Although earlier religious leaders had sought the reform of the Catholic Church, Martin Luther's radical message in 1517 fell onto German soil like a torch upon dry tinder. Rome's arrogance, political meddling, and bumbling public relations, coupled with such greedy practices as the sale of indulgences for the forgiveness of sins, had alienated virtually every class of Germany's populace. Perhaps if Munich hadn't been so tightly enmeshed within the grip of the Wittelsbach dukes, the Protestant Reformation might have gained a stronger foothold in Bavaria. As it was, although Duke Wilhelm IV was initially attracted to the tenets of the Reformation, he soon drew back. Fearing a dissolution of his own power, he banned the writings of Martin Luther from his kingdom. A series of public banishments or executions of Protestants followed (most took place on everybody's favorite tourist attraction, the Marienplatz). Even the handful of the city's ruling elite who dared to embrace the new religion were banished from the kingdom. Fear and suspicion grew as rivalry between Munich (which remained Catholic) and nearby Augsburg (which became Protestant) encouraged Sunday migration between the two cities by believers who traveled to and from their respective houses of worship. As the threat of Protestantism grew more prevalent, official Munich reacted in ways that had by now grown predictable—it became more reactionary and more adamantly conservative than ever. In 1583, Wilhelm V banned all religions other than Catholicism from Bavaria, turning Munich overnight into a stronghold of the Catholic Counter-Reformation. Links were forged between the Wittelsbachs and the Jesuits, who despite their success as scholastics, were known at the time as quasi-fanatical. Catholic colleges were established, and Protestants were persecuted on sight.

THE RENAISSANCE & THE COUNTER-REFORMATION   The showy and sometimes pompous building boom associated with the Counter-Reformation marked the debut of the Renaissance in Munich. In 1560, Munich had been declared as the official seat of the Wittelsbach rulers, winning against richer and—at the time—more glamorous cities such as as Regensburg. Their lavish building programs and amusements (some feasts lasted for three weeks) became legendary, both for their grandeur and for the burdens they imposed on the citizenry who had to pay for them. In 1587, Wilhelm V weakened the power of Munich's civic authorities by removing the salt trade monopoly whose existence had been taken almost for granted since the early Middle Ages. The same year, he dipped deep into the city treasury for the construction of an elaborate palace, the Maxberg, one of the many monuments demolished during Allied bombing raids of World War II.

Simultaneously, Munich blossomed with the appearance of the Michaelskirche (St. Michael's Church) beginning in 1583. The largest Renaissance-style church north of the Alps, it was conceived as a German-speaking response to St. Peter's Basilica in Rome. Although it's one of the most grandiose monuments in Munich today, requiring 14 frenetic years to build, its construction costs almost bankrupted the Bavarian treasury. Despite the grumbling of the taxpayers who financed them, other buildings of equivalent splendor soon followed. The most visible of these included the Wittelsbach family stronghold, the Residenz.

Munich was also becoming a cultural center. Collections of books compiled by the sons of Wilhelm IV formed the basis of the city's famous libraries, including what's known today as the *Bayerischen Staatsbibliothek* (Bavarian State Library). A roster of Catholic, Munich-based composers (most notably Orlando di Lasso) became influential throughout Europe, and Munich-based painters, inspired by Mannerist models in Italy and Spain, developed a school of art referred to today as "Munich mannerism." The roots of this style were eventually developed into a baroque style unique to Munich.

By the late 16th century, Munich was regarded as an artistic beacon in an otherwise artistically barren landscape. Credit for the city's adornment must go to the reigning Wittelsbach dukes, founders of the art collection that eventually became the Alte Pinokothek. Despite the prestige these endeavors conveyed upon Munich, virtually every tradesman and merchant in town complained of the burden such acquisitions and improvements placed upon the treasury, evidence of a fundamental conservatism that has demarcated Munich ever since.

THE THIRTY YEARS' WAR   Beneath the city's newly acquired glitter, the Counter-Reformation had imposed something akin to a reign of terror. In the early years of the 17th century, witches were hunted down and burned, flagellants bloodied themselves with whips, and sermons took on foreboding tones that predicted an apocalypse. At least some of those predictions were fulfilled during the devastation of the Thirty Years' War (1618–48) between the Protestant princes and the Catholic League that followed soon thereafter.

Although that war swept most of northern Europe into its web, Munich wasn't directly affected until 1632. At that time the Protestant king of Sweden, Karl Gustav Adolf, laid siege to "the German Rome." Because an upgrading of the city's fortifications had not at the time been completed, Munich surrendered almost immediately. The terms of surrender included payment of a huge ransom (450,000 guilders, a sum guaranteed to bankrupt the weakened city), in exchange for which the city wasn't sacked and burned. The war, however, wasn't the only problem faced by the Müncheners: During its course, the Black Plague killed 7,000 people, more than a third of the population. After that stage of the disease had run its course, Maximilian I ordered the construction of the Mariensaule as a votive offering to God for having spared the city from destruction.

In 1643, the authority of the town's merchants was greatly undermined by the removal of their right to elect the mayor of Munich. The Wittlesbachs were now able to place in power anyone who would cater to their interests.

BAROQUE CASTLES & BAROQUE DREAMS   The legacy of the Thirty Years' War left a demoralized and shattered Bavaria, a Munich that was forced to rely for its identity on yesteryear's glory, and a nobility that diverted itself with fashionable but frivolous festivals based on French models. Although Bavaria was not to play a vital role in European politics during the next century, this period saw a building boom of baroque architecture. Everything from parish churches to private manor houses had to be redesigned along baroque lines imported, with subtle variations, from Italy. Bavaria retrenched itself in its self-definition as a Catholic stronghold.

The flamboyant, richly gilded, free-flowing but symmetrical baroque style developed by the city's architects was not only used to the glory of God in such churches as St. Michael's and the cloister church of St. Anna im Lehel, but also in secular construction. Notable are Nymphenburg Palace, Munich's answer to the palace at Versailles; the Green Gallery within the Residenz; ornate theaters; and countless villas, pavilions, and garden structures. Funds for the construction of these buildings were derived from sometimes crippling taxes imposed on the citizenry and the forced sale of land to wealthy aristocrats who wanted to build ever-larger palaces for their own use.

An example of the deep resentment felt by the townspeople occurred in 1674, when the seat of the Wittelsbach family, the Residenz, accidentally caught fire. Townspeople sullenly and deliberately postponed their response to calls for help for at least an hour, a vital delay that contributed to enormous rebuilding costs and an increased mistrust among the various levels of Münchener society.

Part of the public resentment against Munich's leaders lay in the aristrocracy's often disastrous meddling in international affairs. Among these were Bavaria's murky role in the War of the Spanish Succession, and the eventual occupation between 1705 and 1715 of Bavaria by Austrian soldiers. The first year of this occupation witnessed one of the most cruel massacres in 18th-century history. Led by a local blacksmith, an army of peasants, craftsmen, and burghers armed only with farm implements and scythes marched upon Munich to protest against the Austrian regime. A short march from Munich's city walls, near the hamlet of Sendling, the entire army was betrayed, then obliterated. The event has been recorded in sculptures, plays, and popular legend, the *Sendlinger Mordweihnacht (Sendling's Night of Murder)*.

In 1715, Max Emanuel was able—with the help of the French—to evict the Austrians. Aftereffects of these fruitless conflicts included countless deaths, a profound national disillusionment, and a national debt that historians assess at around 32 million guilders, a burden imposed upon an impoverished population.

POLITICAL REFORMS OF THE EARLY 1700s   To recover from the disasters initiated prior to his reign, Prince Elector Max III Joseph attempted to initiate economic reforms. Realizing that much of Bavarian industry was still fiercely protected by the medieval guild structure, he inaugurated new industries, including workshops for tapestry making and cloth making. Few of them ever generated any viable profits, but the noteworthy exception was the outfit that manufactured Nymphenburg porcelain, founded in 1758, which consistently made a profit.

The tides of liberalization slowly swept over Munich and the rest of Bavaria. Newspapers were founded in 1702 and 1750, and in 1751, some vaguely liberal reforms were made within the Bavarian legislature. An Academy of Sciences, whose discoveries sometimes opposed traditional Catholic teachings, was established in 1759.

In 1771, one of the most enlightened Bavarian rulers, Max III Joseph, revised the school system, making some aspects of public education a legal requirement. During his regime, theatrical productions abandoned their obligatory religious themes; secular dramas from northern Germany, Austria, France, and Italy were performed; and the city opened its doors to composers and conductors. Munich was the site of the inaugural performance of one of Mozart's early operas *(Idomeneo)* in 1781, but it wasn't particularly well received, and Mozart's request for an ongoing creative stipend from the Wittelsbach family was rejected.

THE REBIRTH OF CONSERVATISM   When Max III Joseph died in 1777, his branch of the Wittelsbach dynasty died with him, thereby activating the succession of a Wittelsbach from an obscure family branch in the Palatinate, a German territory outside of Bavaria. The new king, Karl Theodor, was among the least popular to date. Caring little about Bavarian national destiny, he rather amazingly negotiated to cede Munich and all of Bavaria to the Austrians in exchange for the Habsburg-dominated Netherlands. Relief for this plan came in the form of the French Revolution, which terrified every aristocrat in Europe into a more clear-eyed assessment of the power of popular opinion.

Ironically, although he was despised as a king, Karl Theodor as a builder did many things well and skillfully, adding the Karlsplatz and the Englischer Garten to the roster of Munich's attractions. Politically, however, he continued to play his hand badly, imposing stricter regimes, outlawing most personal liberties, and placing repressive measures on freethinkers at the nearby University of Ingolstadt. His death in 1799 was the cause of several days of drunken celebration throughout many neighborhoods of Munich.

THE AGE OF NAPOLÉON   Except for distant rumblings on the western horizon, and the hope it gave to Bavaria's liberals, the effects of the French Revolution of 1789 weren't immediately felt in reactionary Munich. All of that changed with the rise of Napoléon. In 1799 French troops laid siege to the capital. The Bavarian court had already fled to the safety of their villas at Amberg. The easiest way out for all parties involved the complete and immediate capitulation of the Bavarian court, which, by siding with Napoléon, were in effect committing treason against their brethren in other parts of Germany. On their first night of occupation, in June 1799, French officers enjoyed a performance in the Residenz's royal theater of Mozart's *Don Giovanni.*

To reward his vassal, Napoléon more than doubled the territory controlled by Bavaria (at the expense of Franconia and Swabia), thereby tripling the size of its population overnight. In 1806, Napoléon personally conducted the recoronation of King Max IV Joseph, enhancing the pomp and circumstance of the traditional Bavarian ritual, and renaming him King Maximilian I. (Some historians refer to him as Max I Joseph.)

The new king's son, Crown Prince Ludwig (later, Ludwig I), gets the credit for establishing the roots of what is now the most famous autumn festival in the world, *Oktoberfest.* Originally designated as a *Volksfest,* it was scheduled, along with some horse races, as a sideshow of the wedding in 1810 of the Crown Prince and Therese von Sachsen-Hildburghausen.

A final irony was this: The ancient rivalries between Munich and the bishop of Friesing (the destruction of whose bridge at Oberföhring led to the original blossoming of Munich during the 12th century) were once again reactivated. Friesing's territory was swallowed up in the new Bavarian nation created by Napoléon, and the bishop's seat moved into the heart of its old "enemy territory," downtown Munich.

Beginning around 1820, the political and constitutional status of countries throughout Europe was in flux, with the gears of the Industrial Revolution already beginning to turn. In Munich, the first foundations of a modern state were established by Freiherr von Montgelas, an expatriate from the French Alps. In a few years he built up a modern state administration and had drawn up the Bavarian constitution. It took more than a decade, but in 1818—after Montgelas had been ostracized from the court because of his ongoing arguments with members of the royal family —proposals were ratified. Munich was defined as the seat of a newly founded Bavarian Parliament, designed to afford the citizenry more clearly defined legal rights.

Despite his farsighted reforms, Montgelas was far from popular during his time in office. The reasons were petty. Müncheners had grown used to a roster of religious holidays that dominated almost a third of the calendar year, complete with complicated processions and a relief from workaday cares. Montgelas obliterated all of these, enforcing a work ethic more tuned to the priorities of hardworking Prussia than to Bavaria. Other complaints against his regime involved the inevitable influx of much resented foreigners (in this case, Franconians and Swabians) into Munich and the unwillingness on the part of the regime to continue to persecute Protestants.

Changes were enormous. The old city walls were demolished, with the exception of a small stretch that still runs parallel to the Jungfernturmstrasse. The city moat was filled in and redesignated as the Sonnenstrasse, and new neighborhoods were designed with formal parks and gardens inspired by an idealized version of ancient Rome. Crown Prince Ludwig wanted the Munich equivalent of a triumphal promenade, and thus commissioned what has been known ever since as the Ludwigstrasse.

In 1821 the Marienkirche became the official cathedral (Dom) of the archbishops of Munich and Friesing. As always, the citizens developed the art of grumbling about the expenses to a high art form. In 1826, the university was transferred from the town of Landshut to Munich, bestowing on the Bavarian capital the status of intellectual centerpiece.

BOURGEOIS MUNICH   By 1840, with a reported population of around 90,000 residents, the building boom of the early part of the century had made Munich into a well-built neoclassical gem with a distinct identity. Munich's first railway line was laid in 1846, the foundation of a network of railways that soon converged on the city from all parts of southern Germany. The same year, the city's population rose to 100,000 inhabitants.

After Crown Prince Ludwig ascended the Bavarian throne as Ludwig I, he became more conservative than anyone who knew him during his days as the arts-loving crown prince would have imagined. In 1832, he began a campaign of censoring the press, repressing student activism, and stressing his role as an absolute monarch cast in a romantic and heroic mold. All of this blew up in 1848, a year of revolts all over Europe. Although the revolt in Munich was put down, and some modest reforms were made, Müncheners considered his affair with actress and dancer Lola Montez much more odious than his rigid politics. In a series of events as lurid as anything presently publicized by the Windsor family of England, he flaunted his affair so publicly that it threatened the fabric of the Wittelsbach dynasty itself. As the scandal raged more and more out of control, Ludwig eventually abdicated the throne in favor of his son, Maximilian II.

Maximilian II continued the building programs of his father, established the Bavarian National Museum (1855), and played a role in encouraging writers to emigrate to Munich. One of these, Paul Heyse, was the first German to win the Nobel Prize for literature. Maximilian built an avenue (the Maximilianstrasse) in his own honor and held a series of competitions among architects for the design of such public buildings as the Regierung (Administrative) Building of Upper Bavaria and the Maximilianeum (Bavarian Parliament Building).

Between 1860 and 1900, at least a half-dozen once-separate villages and townships were annexed by Munich, including ones with names that today connote distinctive neighborhoods. These include Nymphenburg, Thalkirchen, Neuhausen, and Schwabing. Meanwhile, beginning around 1840, railroad lines were laid throughout Bavaria, always culminating in Munich, a fact that reinforced the city as a centerpiece of transit and commerce.

Lola Montez, Countess of Lansfeld

Lola Montez (1820–61), born in Limerick, Ireland, led a storied life resembling a plot line in a soap opera. She catapulted to sensationdom from the London stage with her evocative and scandalous spider dance. Her liaison with Bavarian King Ludwig I and his appointment of her as countess of Lansfeld compounded local dissatisfaction, leading to the Revolution of 1848 and ultimately to the king's abdication.

Eliza Gilbert (the name given her by her mother) was reared in India by her mother and enlisted fathers (both real and step). The first of her lifelong indiscretions may have been a liaison with the husband of a friend of her mother's. Exiled to Spain, there she assumed the persona of the exotic dancer and adopted the name Lola. Leap-frogging—as she might have done in an act—to London, then Munich, she turned many heads besides Ludwig's. She was called "the Bavarian Pompadour," but Richard Wagner dubbed her a "demonic beast," and Ludwig's mistress lived up to both those titles. Ludwig indulged her every whim; in return, the way she indulged him (inclusive of his foot fetish) is renowned.

Lola climbed the ranks of Bavarian hierarchy like a spiral staircase at a burlesque show. She became more than just a mistress; she was given the titles baroness of Rosenthal and countess of Lansfeld. Her enemies, among them the Jesuits, suspected that she meddled in politics and even went so far as to say she virtually ran the Bavarian government for two years, in 1847 and 1848. Public sentiment against the king's infatuation and her outlandish behavior was so powerful that Ludwig's abdication soon followed.

After a brief stint in London, Lola was forced to flee to America to avoid bigamy charges. She fled first to Mexico, then to California, where she ended her days as a cigar-smoking, stage-strutting *artiste* for the entertainment of miners during the California Gold Rush. An amazing life came to an end when she retired, found religion, and devoted her life to helping out wayward women. She died in poverty in Brooklyn. Her life, as she once boasted, was fodder for more biographies than any other woman living in her day.

The king's role in the promotion of science, industry, and education made him one of the most enlightened despots of the 19th century. When he died in 1864, the administration of many of his programs was continued by what had developed into a massive governmental bureaucracy. The new king, "Mad" King Ludwig II, unfortunately, was not so beneficial to Bavaria.

ROMANTIC BAVARIA   Rarely has the king of a nation so despised the citizens of its capital city as Ludwig II did the Müncheners. The trouble began with an early feud that evolved shortly after the new king ascended the Bavarian throne in 1864 at the age of 18. The king had become the patron of Richard Wagner, and four of his operas—*Tristan und Isolde* (1865), *Die Meistersinger von Nürnberg* (1867), *Das Rheingold* (1869), and *Die Walküre* (1870)—made their debuts in Munich. One of the many visions of the royal patron and the composer was the construction of a glittering opera house, designed by the architect of the one in Dresden. However, artistic and political imbroglios and the estimated cost of 6 million guilders led to the collapse of both the hoped-for opera house and the friendship between the king and the composer. A spate of arrogant public outbursts, and the widely publicized low regard that Wagner held for the citizens of Munich (newspapers picked up reports that he believed they were overly religious and with no artistic imagination), led to the king's command that Wagner and his lofty romantic ideals leave Munich forever.

Curiously, although viewed as hopelessly eccentric, a bizarre member of a family riddled with other mental aberrations, Ludwig's madness seemed to captivate an age obsessed with romanticism. Although his mania for the building of neo-romantic castles and palaces far from the urban bustle of Munich helped bankrupt the treasury, he rarely meddled in the day-to-day affairs of his subjects and was consequently considered an expensive-to-maintain but relatively unthreatening monarch. If, indeed, noninvolvement and absenteeism on the part of a king make him more beloved by his subjects, Mad King Ludwig enjoyed a very successful reign.

Actually, the lack of interest on the part of Ludwig II toward politics is one of the factors that helped Bismarck, from his base in Prussia, arrange the unification of Germany in 1871. The unification transformed Berlin into the capital of a united Germany, and stripped Bavaria of its status as an independent nation, a designation it had enjoyed only since 1806. Some historians maintain that the way Bismarck helped induce the mad king to give up his independent status was to secretly subsidize the building costs of his fairy-tale castles. Since such monuments as Neuschwanstein have brought billions of deutschmarks' worth of tourist dollars to the German nation ever since, they were probably wise investments.

In 1886, the Bavarian cabinet in Munich stripped the 40-year-old Ludwig II of the last vestiges of his powers. A few days later, Ludwig's death by drowning, coincidentally with a doctor and companion named Gudden, in the Starnberger Sea led to endless debate as to whether or not he was murdered before making an attempt at a royal comeback. His heir to the tattered remnants of the Bavarian throne was a mentally inept brother, Otto, whose day-to-day duties were assumed by a royal relative, Crown Prince Luitpold, who was to wear the much diminished crown until 1912. Rumors still persist around this unhappy household that the death of Mad King Ludwig was prearranged.

After the absorption of Bavaria into greater Germany, the only vestige of Bavaria's imperial past that remained was the designation of the local postal network and railways as "Royal Bavarian" (*Koeniglich-Bayerisch*). The Bavarian monarch was allowed to retain his position as figurehead during a transition period when all eyes, and most real power, slowly flowed toward Berlin.

ARTISTIC FERMENT & SOCIAL UNREST   Munich forged ahead in its role as an economic magnet within a unified Germany. In 1882, Munich had begun the process of electrifying its street lamps. Three years later, public transport was aided by a netwook of streetcars, and scientist Max von Pettenkofer discovered the source of cholera in contaminated water. His efforts led to the installation of a city water supply that was hailed as one of the best in Germany.

Although never as potent a force as Berlin, Munich became a center of creativity and artistic ferment. In 1892, the secession movement was founded as a protest against traditional aesthetics that had ruled to date. In 1896, the magazine *Jugend,* which was devoted to proselytizing the aesthetic advantages of Jugendstil, helped define Munich (along with its closest rival, Vienna) as a centerpiece of the German art-nouveau movement. In 1902, a Russian expatriate, Lenin, spent a brief stint in Munich, publishing a revolutionary magazine called *Iskra.* In 1911, Paul Klee and Wassily Kandinsky, along with several cohorts, founded Der Blaue Reiter movement to promote and define the role of abstract design within mainstream European art.

Schwabing became the center of this movement betweem 1885 and the beginning of World War I. Once a farm village, then a summer retreat for the stylishly wealthy, it became an icon for the avant-garde, the home base of satirical magazines whose contributors included Thomas Mann (who spent many years of his life in Munich), Rainer Maria Rilke, Hermann Hesse, and Heinrich Mann. Around 1890, Schwabing became a hotbed of innovative painters, architectural iconoclasts, and visionaries who, regardless of their political orientation, were invariably viewed with suspicion as dangerous to the security of the established order.

Despite the growing importance of art, freethinking, and iconoclastic literature within Munich during this period, social unrest was growing at an alarming rate. The city's population hovered around a half-million, thousands were unemployed, and the average life expectancy, thanks to such diseases as tuburculosis that were rampant within the Munich slums, was an appallingly short 25 years. Despite the privations, there remains in Munich today a nostalgic sense of loyalty to "the good old days" before the frenetic anguish of World Wars I and II.

WORLD WAR I   The entangling alliances that crisscrossed Europe on the eve of World War I (1914–1918) led to more bloodshed and greater disillusionment than Europe had ever known. Hunger was rampant in Munich even in the early years of the war, and by 1918, social unrest was so widespread that a rash of demonstrations, burnings, mob executions, and brawls between advocates of the left and right became increasingly frequent. On the gray day of November 7, 1918, more than 10,000 workers mobilized for a mass demonstration, eventually ending their unrest at the gates of the Wittelsbachs's hereditary stronghold, the Residenz. To the rulers' horror, even their guards were persuaded to join the revolutionaries, causing the dynasty's final, much weakened scion, Ludwig III, to flee from Munich under cover of darkness. The event marked the end of a dynasty that had ruled longer than any other in Europe.

The next day (November 8, 1918) Munich was declared the capital of the Free State of Bavaria (Freistaat Bayern), an independent revolutionary people's republic, led by the Revolutionary Worker's Council. The conservative, so-called "legitimate" Bavarian government went into immediate exile in nearby Bamburg. Kurt Eisner, an articulate political leader who was much less radical than many of those who elected him, ruled briefly and tempestuously, but failed to persuade the placid burghers of the Bavarian suburbs to supply the revolutionary cells in the city's center with food and supplies. Within a few months, he was assassinated on Munich's Promenadeplatz. Power shifted in a rapid series of events between coalitions of centrists and leftists whose components changed at baffling frequencies, which ended in a horrendous bloodbath when troops, sent by Berlin in 1919, lay siege to the city as a means of restoring the status quo.

THE RISE OF HITLER   Conservative reaction to the near-takeover of Munich by communists was swift and powerful, with long-ranging effects. After the events of 1919, and the humiliating terms of surrender imposed upon Germany at Versailles after the defeat of World War I, Munich became one of the most conservative cities in Germany.

In the 1920s, sociologists estimated that a full 20% of the city's population of almost three-quarters of a million residents were dependent on welfare, and the staggering rise of inflation required a wheelbarrowful of Reichsmarks to buy a loaf of bread. The disillusioned city, which retained a deep distrust of Prussian interference from the despised city of Berlin, became a kind of incubator for reactionary, anti-Semitic, and sometimes rabidly conservative political movements.

One of these was the NSDAP (National Socialist Workers Party of Germany) of which Adolf Hitler was a member, and whose meetings were often held in one of

Munich's most visited beer halls, the Hofbräuhaus. Many of Hitler's early speeches, as well as the formulation of his megalomaniacal ideas as written in *Mein Kampf* (*My Struggle*), were expressed in Munich. Ironically, many of the members of Hitler's inner circle (including Heinrich Himmler and Hermann Göring) were from the region around Munich, and thousands of the dictator's rank and file originated from the city's long-suffering, endlessly deprived slums. In 1923, Hitler's "Beer Hall Putsch," his attempt to lead a popular movement to overthrow the Weimar Republic in Berlin, was squashed, although alert observers of the social scene in Germany could quickly surmise the shape of politics to come.

Under its reactionary civic government, Munich's cultural scene degenerated into one of the least imaginative of any large metropolis in Europe. Anything racy or politically provocative was banned, and many creative persons (including Bruno Walter and Berthold Brecht) opted to change their place of residency to the more sophisticated and less reactionary milieu of Berlin.

After Hitler came to power as chancellor in Berlin, there was little opposition to the National Socialists, whose candidates swept the city's elections of March 5, 1933, and whose swastika flew above city hall by the end of the day. By July of that same year, it was painfully obvious that anyone who opposed the all-Nazi Munich city council would be deported to Germany's first concentration camp, Dachau, on Munich's outskirts.

The headquarters of the Nazi Party was established on the corner of Brienner and Arcis Streets, later to be the site of the 1938 signing by Neville Chamberlain, Daladier, Mussolini, and Hitler of the infamous Munich Agreement. Around the same time, a torture chamber was set up in the cellar of what had always been the symbol of raw power within Munich, the Wittelsbach Palace. Hitler himself even referred to Munich as "the capital of our movement," a statement heard then, as now, with great ambivalence.

Beginning in 1935, vast sums of money were spent on grandiose building projects that followed the Nazi aesthetic. In 1937, a Nazi-sponsored exhibition permeated with anti-Semitic, xenophobic references, *Entartete Kunst* (*Denatured Art*), mocked the tenets of modern art.

Jews began to be persecuted in earnest. The city's largest synagogue was closed in 1938, the same year that *Kristallnacht* (Night of Broken Glass; November 9, 1938) vandalized Jewish-owned homes and businesses across Germany. Only 200 of the city's original population of 10,000 Jews survived the war at all.

In 1939, an attempt to assassinate Hitler as he drank with cronies in a Munich beer hall (the Bürgerbräukeller) failed, and Germany (and Munich) continued the succession of aggressions that eventually led to World War II and the destruction of much of Munich.

WORLD WAR II & ITS AFTERMATH   Resistance to Hitler was fatal, and few questioned the mysterious odors emanating from around the once quiet farm community of Dachau. Nonetheless, a handful of clergymen opposed the Nazi regime. One notable opponent was Father Rupert Mayer, who was imprisoned for many years in Dachau, and who has since been beatified by the Catholic hierarchy. A heroic attempt was made by the Weisse Rose (White Rose) coalition of university students and professors to resist. Their leaders, Hans and Sophie Scholl, Willi Graf, and Hans Huber, were beheaded.

The war years brought untold misery to Munich. Almost half of the city's buildings lay in rubble by war's end, many having been blown to pieces as early as 1942. Most vestiges of Munich's Renaissance and neoclassical grandeur had been literally bombed off the map, a fact that's easy to overlook by modern tourists who admire the city's many restored monuments.

Munich paid a high price in the blood of its citizens: 22,000 of its sons died during Nazi military campaigns, and the civilian population of the city was reduced by almost a quarter-million occupants before the end of the war.

THE POSTWAR YEARS   The occupying American army fortunately retained the city's prewar mayor, Thomas Wimmer, as the city's administrator. (His once-a-week town meetings and open-door policy of listening to the problems of people in the street earned him the respect of both the Allies and the Germans.) Munich's energy between 1945 and 1947 was expended on clearing away debris from the bombings; the rubble was assembled to form decorative hillocks within the city's parks. In 1946, Munich was declared the capital of an entity whose name contained ringing implications from the Revolution of 1919: Freistaat Bayern.

Unlike many German cities, Munich was able to unearth the original plans for many of the demolished buildings, which have been restored, at often astronomical expense, to their original appearance. Today, the city's historic core of the city is surrounded by the same church steeples and towers as in the past.

In 1949 Munich was defined once again as the capital of the Federal *Land* of Bavaria within the reconfigured Federal Republic of Germany. The half-century occupation of Germany's eastern sector by the Soviets rearranged southern Germany's traditional trade routes and encouraged the development of new ones. Munich quickly emerged as the focal point for trade between northern and southern Europe. Manufacturers of computers, weapons manufacturers, publishing ventures, fashion houses, and movie studios quickly made Munich their base. The city boomed, with a population that numbered over a million before the end of 1957. Prestigious companies such as Siemens, now one of the city's most visible employers, were wooed by Munich. Munich is at least partly responsible for Germany's image as home to Europe's fastest drivers—home to BMW (Bayerisches Motoren Werke), Munich helped to reinforce the Teutonic reputation for automated excellence, efficiency, and fine craftsmanship for the perfect driving machine. Other corporations whose German operations are based in Munich include IBM and Apple.

As the city's population exploded in the 1960s, sprawling masses of concrete suburbs were thrown up hastily, all of them designed for ease of access by cars. In many cases, older buildings that might have been salvaged were demolished to make room for yet another Munich building boom.

The obsession for rebuilding and modernizing at any price was halted when the then-mayor of Munich paid an official visit to Los Angeles. Munich's press gleefully reported that the automobile-dominated society of L.A. so horrified him that a new emphasis on historical preservation thereafter became the norm. Since then, active participation by historic groups has encouraged careful renovations of older buildings.

MODERN MUNICH   For many different reasons, the 1972 Summer Olympic Games were among the most poignant in Olympic history. They were conceived as an attempt to show to all the world the bold new face of a radically rebuilt Munich, from the premises of the innovative Olympic City. The success of the event was marred by an attack of the Palestinian terrorist group Black September on the corps of Israeli athletes. Despite a police shoot-out that was publicized around the world, the collective murder of 11 of these athletes revived many past but not forgotten incidences of pogroms against Jews throughout other eras of Germany's history, and proved a massive embarrassment for all parties concerned.

In 1981, the reopening of the New Pinakothek helped elevate Munich to the status of a world-class center for art and culture. In 1985, the aesthetically controversial Gasteig Center for the Performing Arts provided Munich with world-class facilities for the presentation of symphonic music.

In 1989, the collapse of what used to be known as the Soviet Bloc allowed Munich's merchants, manufacturers, and traders to snatch a portion of the business of the newly democratized eastern zone. Simultaneously, many former residents of the eastern zone flooded into Munich to find new homes, new jobs, new ways of life, and in many cases, even more deprivation, despair, and hopelessness than they'd experienced under their original regime. They joined the ranks of tens of thousands of Turkish workers and workers from other less developed countries. The presence of these Gastarbeiter (guest workers) helped catalyze the wheels of German industry between 1950 and 1985. However, in the eyes of many native Müncheners, the Gastarbeiter have now become more of a problem than a blessing.

The latest in Munich's history of perennial civil unrest had a more trivial cause. This piece of civic disturbance occurred in the spring of 1995, and is known as "The Bavarian Beer Garden Revolution," after the city's most popular beverage. Residents in a prosperous neighborhood beside the Isar on the city's southern fringe requested that the Waldwirtschaft Biergarten be closed after 9:30pm. They were not complaining without reason—parking for the garden was woefully inadequate, and amplified music blared from the garden all over the neighborhood.

Picked up as a *cause célèbre* by thousands of often raucous fans of beer drinking, the event provoked a demonstration by 20,000 angry protesters, who feared that equivalent measures would be enacted against other beer halls throughout Munich. Although the beer hall's owners had sown the seeds for the initial protest marches, the number of participants exceeded their wildest imagination. Local politicians hastened to endear themselves to disgruntled beer drinkers by rushing through a set of laws favorable to the the beer gardens, but the issue is presently being fought through the Bavarian courts. Although the Beer Garden Revolution may have had a rather trivial cause, city residents see it as a visible sign of stress between opposing political and social forces in modern Munich.

4 Famous Müncheners

Albrecht (Albert) V (1528–1579)   This duke of Bavaria did much for regional art and culture during his reign (1550–79). Although no artist, he established the Kumquat (Cabinet of Art) and Antiquarium, Germany's first museums, making Munich a cultural center.

Egid Quirin (1692–1750) and **Cosmos Damian Asam** (1686–1739)   These painter-and-architect brothers journeyed to Rome where they were influenced by Bernini. They are known in Munich for their frescoes in such churches as St. Mary's in Thalkirchen and the Church of the Holy Ghost. They brought the flower of Bavarian rococo into full bloom.

François de Cuvilliés the Elder (1695–1768)   Although small in stature, he became the giant of Bavarian rococo architecture and decor. (See box about him in Chapter 6.) His architectural tradition was continued by his son, François, called the Younger.

Rudolf Diesel (1858–1913)   Paris born, Rudolf Christian Carl Diesel studied in Munich, patented the pressure-ignited internal combustion engine (1893), and built the first successful diesel engine (1896). Also a noted social theorist, he spent the latter part of his life in Munich in elegant Bogenhausen. The word *diesel* would become famous throughout the world. The inventor was drowned while crossing in a boat from Antwerp to Harwich.

Albert Einstein (1879–1955)   Born in Ulm, one of the greatest modern thinkers spent his formative years in Munich before becoming a Swiss citizen (1901). After the Nazi seizure of Germany he resigned his academic posts and moved to the United States, where he spent his remaining years. His theory of relativity revolutionized modern physics, garnering him the Nobel Peace Prize for physics (1916). A staunch Pacifist, he warned the world of the perils of nuclear weaponry after World War II.

Friedrich von Gärtner (1792–1847)   After a tour of Italy familiarizing him with forms of classical architecture, this Munich-trained architect succeeded Leo von Klenze as the artist responsible for the development of the Ludwigsstrasse in 1827. His synthesis of neoclassical principles of proportional and historical forms manifests itself in such major works as the Munich State Library, the University, the Siegestor, and the Feldherrnhalle.

Hubert Gerhard (1550–1620)   This sculptor trained under Giovonni da Bologna in Florence, and later worked in bronze in Augsburg, Munich, and Innsbruck. The main exponent of the Bavarian school of bronze around 1660, he led the evolution of sculpture from Mannerism to Early Baroque. The figure of St. Michael and the Dragon on the facade of St. Michael's church and the Virgin as Patroness of Bavaria on the Mariensäule in the Marienplatz facade are among his most renowned works.

Franz von Lenbach (1836–1904)   He was a major artistic figure in the 1870s, a period known in Munich as *Gründerzeit* (a major time of economic progress). He was well known for his copies of Rubens, Titian, and others commissioned for the Schack Gallery in Munich. His best known works are *The Arch of Titus, The Shepherd Boy,* and portraits of Emperor William I, Bismarck, Wagner, Liszt, and Gladstone.

Ludwig I, King of Bavaria (1796–1868)   Ludwig I became ruler of Bavaria as heir to his father Maximilian I in 1825. He supported the liberal Bavarian constitution of 1818. The reconstruction of the royal capital of Munich owes much to his determination. The provincial university was moved from Landshut to Munich by his order in 1826. He envisioned Munich as a grand metropolis. His retro-tendencies post-1830, combined with his affiliations with dancer Lola Montez, caused a crisis in the Bavarian government, ultimately leading to his abdication amid the confusion of the March revolution in 1848.

Ludwig II, King of Bavaria (1845–1886)   Fascinated by German legends since the early years of his upbringing in Schloss Hohenschwangau, King Ludwig II was destined to become a part of the lore. He became king in 1864, and by that time he was already an enthusiastic admirer and patron of romantic opera, specifically those composed by Richard Wagner for whom Ludwig's affinity can be traced back to *Lohengrin*. His well-documented dementia earned him the title "Mad King," but his shielded existence as contractor of "fairy-tale castles" in Neuschwanstein and other romantic locales did little to define the increasingly nebular line between fantasy and reality. Inevitably, he was relieved of his duty to affairs of state and drowned in Stanberg Lake at Schloss Berg amid shrouded circumstances.

Thomas Mann (1875–1955)   This famous German author moved to Munich after the death of his father. As editor of the satirical magazine *Simplicissimus* from 1898 to 1899, he sharpened his skills at scathing societal commentary. Wed in 1905, he remained in Munich until 1933, where he developed into one of the most celebrated German yarn-spinners (*Doktor Faustus*)—he won the Nobel Prize for literature in

---

"Sissi"

Elisabeth (1837–1898), "the beautiful girl from Munich," frivolous daughter of Munich's Duke Maximilian Joseph, married Emperor Franz Joseph I of Austria while still a teenager, and later proved more independent, willful, and uncooperative than anyone in Munich might have ever suspected. She was affectionately known as "Sissi" by the citizens of the Austro-Hungarian Empire. They knew few of the inner secrets of what today might be interpreted as either spoiled or hopelessly neurotic behavior. She rebelled early against the strictures imposed by her husband's straight-laced ministers, eventually escaping the marriage and empire by spending most of her time away from Vienna, her beleaguered husband, and the duties of the empire.

To everyone's surprise, her greatest success derived from her ability to soothe and placate the dour Hungarian faction of her husband's empire, efforts for which she is best and most fondly remembered. The most widely publicized of her many sorrows derived from the death, under mysterious circumstances, of her son, Rudolf, libertine and libertarian heir to the throne, whose positions on personal liberties threatened the very fabric of her husband's empire.

Tragically, the dissipated empress was one of a string of 19th-century assassinations whose deaths helped to pave the way for the later debacle of World War I. Waiting to board a pleasure craft for a ride on Lake Geneva in 1898 at the age of 60, she was fatally stabbed by an Italian anarchist. Her husband, last and longest ruler of the Austro-Hungarian Empire, never remarried.

1929. In 1933, wary of the emerging National Socialists, he embarked upon a lecture tour from which he would not soon return. After stints in southern France and Switzerland, he protested the Nazis loudly from abroad in essays entitled "Europe, Beware." Naturalized in the U.S. in 1944, he eventually returned to Europe permanently in 1952, settling two years later at Kilchberg on Lake Zurich.

Oskar von Miller (1855–1934)   This Munich engineer was a pioneer in the invention and organization of electrical power production. He became acclaimed when in 1882 he scored a major success in transmitting the first electric power in the world from Meisbach to Munich. He was the cofounder and director of German Edison Company, which developed G.E., and he contributed to the development of high-tension electric power transmission.

Carl Orff (1895–1982)   The composer spent most of his life in his native city of Munich, where he thrived as a conductor and music teacher. In 1924 he and Dorothee Günther founded Güntherschule, to teach children by his widely adopted methods stressing gymnastics and dance. As a composer he became celebrated for lavish theatrical work that combined elements of Greek theater, baroque opera, peasant life, and Christian mystery. *Carmina Burana* (1937) is his most widely recognized work.

Jan Polack (1435–1519)   The Kraków native came to Munich around 1470. His numerous frescoes and altarpieces established him as the most important Munich painter of the late Gothic period. The altarpieces in the chapel of the Blutenburg Castle, the wall paintings in the Pippinger Kirchl, and the high altar of St. Peter's are among his remaining works.

Carl Spitzweg (1808–1885)   The native Münchener and self-taught painter is the most representative of Biedermeyer artists in Germany. His humorously detailed portrayals of the small-town misfits, street musicians, postmen, and parting lovers, which were the Munich townsfolk, depicted in ironic and mocking tones their naivete and simplicity. In the Neue Pinakothek hangs *The Poor Poet,* his best-known work.

Richard Strauss (1864–1949)   Born in Munich, the composer and conductor is considered the leader of the New Romantic school. From 1886 to 1898 he was *Kapellmeister* (musical director) of the city, and later with Franz Schalk, headed the State Opera in Vienna, where he worked with all the major European orchestras. He composed both operas and symphonic works. Of his 15 operas, his most famous are *Salome* (1905), *Elektra* (1908), and *Der Rosenkavalier* (1911).

Karl Valentin (1882–1948)   A famous character performer in Munich, Valentin's sketch comedies and extemporaneous commentary are legendary in German-speaking countries. He and partner Liesl Karlstadt's performances in small theaters and cabarets bordered on absurd, but always remained comical. His twisted logic struck a chord with the common folk, and his films remain popular.

5 Architecture

ROMANESQUE   Although during the city's earliest days romanesque architecture dominated the low skyline of the town, a series of disastrous fires, the most severe of which occurred in 1327, and the destructive power of medieval rot, caused most buildings to be modified and rebuilt during later eras into whatever was fashionable at the time.

Munich's oldest parish church, St. Peters, is a good example. Built on the site of four small churches in the dim prehistory of Munich, when the town was little more than a riverside enclave of Benedictine monks, it was rebuilt in the late 1100s, then rebuilt again after the city's disastrous fire of 1327. Its foundations date from the early medieval days of Munich, although its superstructure, including a bell tower, is from around 1386. Compounding the relative newness of that church is the fact that most of its interior decor, statues, sarcophagi, and frescoes date from the 1400s and 1500s. In other words, admire this church for its Gothic splendor and venerable age, but not as a pure example of romanesque.

GOTHIC   Gothic design never established as strong a foothold in Germany as it did in France and England. Perhaps most representative of the German Gothic period is the hall-type church (*Hallenkirche*), which originated in Westphalia. It was characterized by aisles constructed at the same height as the nave, separated from the nave by tall columns. In Munich the Gothic style peaked during a period of great prosperity and civic growth. Excellent examples within the city limits include the somber brick profile of the Frauenkirche. Its cornerstone was laid by Duke Sigismund in 1468 on the site of a decrepit romanesque basilica, whose raw materials, along with the headstones from a nearby graveyard, were incorporated into the new structure. The towers were completed in 1525, as part of a rapid construction that reflected the civic muscle of Munich at the time.

RENAISSANCE   The art and architecture of the Renaissance, which began in Italy around 1520 and lasted a century, greatly influenced southern German architecture. In Munich and most of the rest of southern Germany, baroque motifs inspired directly by Italy ran rampant in a city that defined itself as the capital of the

Counter-Reformation. The movement's most spectacular example of Counter-Reformation zeal appears in the form of the massive St. Michael's Church. The largest baroque building north of the Alps, with loaded references to Catholic iconography that defied the growing power of the Protestants farther to the north, it was begun in 1583, and erected and embellished within a record-breaking 14 years. When one of its towers collapsed during the seventh year of its construction, its royal patron, Duke Wilhelm V, interpreted the accident as a sign of displeasure from God—the building wasn't impressive enough. Consequently, it was enlarged and modified into the airy and soaring interior you'll see today. A victim of intense aerial bombardment, it was laboriously rebuilt as a symbol of civic pride after the damages of World War II.

BAROQUE   Baroque style, an Italian import whose influence in Germany began around 1660 and continued into the 18th century, brought a different kind of renaissance to Germany. The baroque swept southern Germany, especially Munich and Bavaria, permeating hundreds of alpine villages with the reassuring form of onion-shaped domes thrusting skyward between snow-capped peaks.

Architectural forms no longer followed regular patterns, as individual artists and craftsmen were granted increased freedom and more variety in design. The German and Danubian baroque artists, such as those of the Vorarlberg School, sought to give an impression of movement to their florid building designs. The splendor of the period is exemplified in the work of such architects as Lukas von Hildebrandt and J. B. Fischer von Erlach. Munich, as the economic and cultural focal point of southern Germany, moved into prominence as a seat of art and architecture.

The baroque movement eventually dipped its brushes into the flippant paint of the rococo, and that movement brought even greater freedom and gaiety. Examples of architecture from this period are scattered throughout Bavaria, although within Munich, many were rebuilt after wartime damage. Examples of rococo include the Asam-Kirche (Asam Church), completed in 1746, the Mariensaule (column of the Virgin), which dominates the Marienplatz, and—inside the Residenz—the Cuvilliés Theater. Another excellent example is the Theatinerkirche, built by Prince Elector Ferdinand Maria in 1662 in gratitude for the birth of his heir, Max Emanuel. Its construction was among the most complicated in Munich because of its completion date more than a century after its inauguration.

Many of these monuments were filled with frescoes commemorating heroic, sacrificial, or transcendental deeds of martyrs, saints, and angels descending on clouds to manifest themselves to the faithful in the church below.

NEOCLASSICISM   By the 19th century, many members of the rising and prosperous middle class in Germany preferred to decorate their homes in the Biedermeier style, with its lighter designs and carefully balanced symmetry. By now the baroque and rococo styles were dead (the French Revolution, with its de-emphasis on the decorative themes of the *ancien régime,* had seen to that). Neoclassicism, with its references to the grandeur of ancient Greece and imperial Rome, became the reference of choice. Once again, the south of Germany brought a lighter touch to this style than did the north. Munich was particularly receptive. Between 1825 and 1848, Munich's transformation into a suitably royal capital became the arena for bitter conflicts between the royal patrons and their royal architects, who usually defended every nuance of their designs. At least part of Munich's neoclassical grandeur derived from the autocratic Crown Prince Ludwig's (later Ludwig I) devotion to the style. Many of the buildings erected during this era exist thanks to his direct intervention between 1825 and 1848. The Alte Pinakothek was begun in 1826, and at the time it was the largest art gallery in the world. Ludwig himself is responsible for the collection you see today of early German masters, including Dürer, and such early Italian painters as Giotto, Botticelli, and da Vinci. Other neoclassical examples are the Königsplatz, the Glyptothek, and, within the Residenz complex, the Königsbau (King's Building).

ROMANTIC   The romantic movement was full of implications for Germany's sense of national identity. Architects looked back to a rose-colored interpretation of Germany's medieval history, myth, and folklore. There was an almost obsessional rebirth of interest in Teutonic lore, myth, and legend, as rediscovered by the Brothers Grimm and reinterpreted by Richard Wagner.

Neo-medieval, or neo-romantic buildings from the era include the Staatsbibliothek (State Library), the University complex, and such focal points along the Ludwigstrasse as the Feldherrnhalle and the Siegestor, the Mariahilf-Kirche, the Church of St. Boniface, and the New Pinakothek.

The style that characterized German architecture in the latter 1800s is often termed Historicism. No one represented this flamboyant and eclectic movement better than Ludwig II of Bavaria in his palace Neuschwanstein. Outrageously ornate, with a fairy-tale decor, and later imitated in Disneyland, it's one of the major tourist attractions of modern Germany (see Chapter 11).

FROM JUGENDSTIL TO MODERNISM   By the end of the 19th century, the art-nouveau movement—called *Jugendstil* in German after the magazine *Jugend* (*Youth*)—was established in Munich in 1896. It swept the country and marked the distant beginnings of contemporary architecture. It was characterized by mass production and solid, semi-industrialized construction, as architects used such materials as glass, steel, and concrete, crafted into curved lines inspired by the sinuous forms of nature.

In the aftermath of World War I, Walter Gropius (1883–1969) founded the Bauhaus movement, whose influence was felt in Munich. Art and technique were wed at this architectural school whose primary aim was to unify arts and crafts within the context of architecture. Its appeal derived from the changing sensibilities of the Industrial Age, as well as from the need for cost-effective construction techniques during an era of rising costs and exploding demand for housing. Gropius stressed an idea of functional designs that reflected the tastes of the postindustrial revolution. Founded at Weimar and directed there by Gropius from 1919, the headquarters of the movement moved to Dessau in 1925. Gropius later fled to the United States, and the Bauhaus was dissolved in 1933.

By around 1935, the so-called National Socialist, or "Third Reich," style of architecture was the law of the land, with Munich (site of most of Hitler's earliest successes) providing the experimental background for many of its ideas. Under Hitler and such designers as Albert Speer, art and architecture became propaganda tools; pompous, monumental, innately frightening, and devoid of any real humanity.

Postwar Munich did its best to conceal the Nazi roots of some of its buildings, skillfully transforming them into more humanitarian venues. An example is the Zentralministerium (Central Ministry), a predictably pompous but anonymous building on the Von-der-Tann-Strasse, cutting through the otherwise orderly progression of the Ludwigstrasse. An even better example, recycled after the war into an art gallery, is the Haus der Kunst, which houses the Staatsgalerie Moderner Kunst (State Gallery of Modern Art). Originally erected between 1933 and 1937, its angular Fascist architecture seems curiously appropriate for the starkly modern paintings it showcases today. Ironically, virtually everything inside would have been anathema to Hitler and outlawed as "degenerate" by its original builders.

RESTORATION & RENEWAL One of the sad legacies of World War II was the virtual leveling of many of Germany's greatest architectural treasures by Allied bombing raids. Notable among these tragedies was the destruction of Dresden, until 1945 one of the most beautiful cities of Europe. Munich fared better. While 45% of its buildings were destroyed, and all the others damaged in some way, it had the economic muscle to rebuild itself after the war. Today, this is just one of the ongoing sources of envy that sparks controversy between the prosperous west and the impoverished east.

On-site witnesses claim that the first two years after the end of the war were devoted almost exclusively to clearing away the rubble. In some cases, the architectural rubble of Munich's past was swept away, never to be restored. However, many cathedrals, churches, houses, town halls, and other buildings were laboriously reconstructed in the original style.

As Munich advances through the 1990s, rebuilding continues on some structures, although architects have also turned to modernity, as shown in such sites as the stadium built for the 1972 Olympics and the new performance center at Gasteig. Regrettably (but understandably), many of Munich's postwar buildings, both domestic and commercial, were hastily erected more for convenience than for architectural grandeur. However, in the prosperous Germany of today, there is an intense concern for elegance and style in modern architecture.

6 Bavarian Cuisine

THE FOOD

Bavarians like to eat, justifying their appetites with the very reasonable assertion that any type of human interaction operates more smoothly when it's lubricated with ample amounts of food and wine, or even better, food and beer.

Calorie- and cholesterol-conscious North Americans might recoil at the sight of meals containing dumplings, potatoes, any of about a dozen different types of *Würste* (sausages), roasted meats sometimes flavored with bacon drippings, breads, and pastries. Although Munich is filled with *nouvelle* counterparts to the traditional, rather heavy-handed ministrations of old-fashioned *kuchen*, Bavarian helpings of food aren't small, and tend to be supplemented throughout the course of a day with cake and coffee breaks, which in some circles are a compulsory afternoon event.

The Bavarian affair with sausage is of ancient lineage, Würst having been a major part of the national diet almost since there were people, and livestock, in the area. Bavarians tend to view their Würst with more superstition than any other food in the alpine repertory, nostalgically adhering to such adages as "Never let the sunshine of noon shine on a Weisswurst," and the reservation of Rotwurst to (at least in traditional venues) consumption in the evening.

The emphasis in Munich on beer dates back to the misty early days of the city's origins. The city's observation of legally required adherence to publicly acknowledged standards, however, dates from 1516, prior to the establishment of standards anywhere else in Europe.

Every Bavarian professes a love for his or her favorite kind of Würst (a choice that often derives from childhood associations rather than having anything to do with taste). Many visitors' favorite is *Bratwurst*, an original derivation from nearby Nürnberg, concocted from seasoned and spiced pork. *Weisswurst*, Munich's traditional accompaniment to a foaming mug of beer, wasn't "invented" until 1857, a date remembered by Müncheners as an important watershed. The ingredients that go into it are less appetizing than the final result, but usually include a medley of veal, calf's brains, and spleen boiled in water and served hot. Modern versions contain less offal and better qualities of veal, as well as spices and lemon juice to enhance the flavor. Two are usually considered a snack. Five or six are a respectable main course. Most aficionados try not to eat the skin, but some diehards wouldn't think of removing it.

Bauernwurst (farmer's sausage) and *Knockwurst* are variations of the *Frankfurter*, which although it originated in the more westerly city of Frankfurt, achieved its greatest fame in the New World as the frankfurter. Although *Leberwurst* is a specialty of Hesse, and *Riderwurst* and *Blutwurst* (beef sausage and blood sausage) are specialties of Westphalia, all of them are widely served and enjoyed throughout Munich. Regardless of its configuration, the perfect accompaniment for wurst consists of mustard, a roll (preferably studded with pumpernickel seeds), and beer.

As savory as the wursts of Munich might be, they're considered too simple to grace the table of any truly elaborate Bavarian meal, unless accompanied by a medley of other dishes. These might include dishes from the long-ago repertoire of agrarian Bavarian cuisine, including *Züngerl* (pig's tongue) or *Wammerl* (pig's stomach), most often served with braised or boiled cabbage. Potato dumplings (*Klösse,* or *Kartoffelknödel*) also are served with many dishes, and *Leber* (liver) dumplings are considered mandatory features several times a month. *Semmelknödel* (bread dumplings) generally accompany the most famous meat dish of Bavaria, *Schweinbraten* (roast pork). Also popular, with many devotees, are *Kalbshaxen* (veal shank) and *Schweinshaxen* (roasted knuckle of pork). Carp is prized by Munich's gastronomes, as is a succulent variety of trout designated on the city's menus as *Forelle.*

Feeling hungry during your sightseeing promenades around Munich? Step into the nearest *Metzgerei* (butcher shop), and order such items as a *Warmer Leberkäs,* which has nothing to do either with liver or with cheese, but instead with ground beef and bacon, baked like a meatloaf, and sold in slices of about 100 grams each. It's best consumed with mild mustard and a roll. Another worthy choice is *Wurtzsemmel,* sliced sausage meat on a roll, or a *Schinkensemmel,* sliced ham served on a roll. You can carry it away for consumption overlooking whatever panorama you find, or carry it into a Bierkeller or Biergarten (it's been legal for centuries to bring your own food into a Münchener tavern, although it's considered polite to order at least a small beer to go with it).

AND WHAT BEER SHOULD YOU DRINK?

No self-respecting Münchener will refuse a sparkling glass of wine, and will even praise highly the light, slightly acidic versions of wines from the Rhineland. But the real glint enters a Münchener's eye when the relative merits of beer are discussed. You won't lack for choices within the beer halls of Munich, although at least part of your choice will derive from the season. Both because it's the law, and because it's a matter of ethics and pride, breweries concoct their beer with yeast, barley, hops, and water. Preservatives aren't usually added—in a city where a 200-liter cask of beer can be drained by a thirsty crowd in fewer than 12 minutes, the quantities never last long enough to really need them. Here's a rundown on what you're likely to need in your dialogues with a Münchener bartender:

"Normal" Bavarian beer, also referred to as light beer, is slightly less potent than the brew consumed in North Germany, France, or England. Its relative weakness is the main reason why many foreigners can consume a liter of it at lunch, and not feel the effect, and consume several of them in the evening before beginning to feel the least bit giddy. Don't think, however, that "normal" beer is the same as *Weiss* or (in Münchener dialect) *Weizenbeer,* which is brewed with a high concentration of fermented wheat. In springtime, along with spring lamb, fresh fruits and vegetables, and a new emphasis on green, leafy salads, Munich offers *Bock* and *Doppelbock* (Double Bock), *Märzenbier, Pils,* and any combination of the above-mentioned beers with lemonade for a drink that's less headspinning. What is the polite thing to ask for if you think you're too drunk to handle another liter of "normal" beer? Consider any of the following: A *Radlermass* (literally, "a mug for the bike") that's composed of half "normal" beer, half lemonade. There's dark beer, of which Beck's Dark is an example known to many North Americans, and even a dark Weiss beer, which happens to be wheat beer brewed in such a way as to make it smoky-looking, rather than pale. And in case you've forgotten a particularly ugly episode of Munich's civic history, there's even a beer named after the doomed socialists (the Red Guards) who forcibly took over the city's government for a few months in 1918, a *Russe,* which consists of Weiss (wheat) beer and lemonade.

The venue for the consumption of this amazing medley of fermented grains? The ideal site is any of the city's dozens of *Bierkellers* or *Biergartens,* which serve simple snack-like food items—sausages, white radishes, portions of cheese, and the kind of salted pretzels that are guaranteed to make you thirstier for what else? More beer.

Floods of suds are available throughout every season of the year. Most are served within such mega-parks as the Hirschgarten (Deer Park), the largest in Munich, and suitable for up to 8,000 revelers, the Augustiner-Keller, near the main railway staion, the Biergarten Max-Emanuel behind Munich's University, or the beer garden near the Chinesischer Turm (Chinese Tower) in the Englischer Garten. The most recently controversial of these is the Waldwirtschaft Biergarten, a not-very-prominent beer garden along the city's southern tier that managed to rally 20,000 Müncheners to its defense in 1995 when their rights as beer drinkers were at risk of being legally curtailed.

Munich drinking sites that contain the most potent memories for most foreigners include the Hofbräuhaus and the Bürgerbräukeller, both of which carry lavish associations of everyone from Adolf Hitler to the boy or girl next door.

Planning a Trip to Munich & the Bavarian Alps

This chapter is devoted to the where, when, and how of your trip—the advance-planning issues that are usually required to get it together and take it on the road.

After people decide where to go, most have two fundamental questions: What will it cost? and How do I get there? This chapter will respond to those questions and then follow with additional practical information that any visitor to Munich and the Bavarian Alps will need.

1 Information & Entry Requirements

VISITOR INFORMATION

Nearly all larger towns and all cities in the Federal Republic have tourist offices. The headquarters of the **German National Tourist Board** is at Beethovenstrasse 69, D-60325 Frankfurt am Main (☎ **069/75-72-0**).

Before you go, you'll find a German National Tourist Office in **New York** at 122 E. 42nd St., 52nd Floor, New York, NY 10168 (☎ **212/661-7200**); in **Los Angeles** at 11766 Wilshire Blvd., Suite 750, Los Angeles, CA 90025 (☎ **310/575-9799**); in **Toronto** at 175 Bloor St. E., North Tower, 6th Floor, Toronto, ON M4W 3R8 (☎ **416/968-1570**); and in **London** at Nightingale House, 65 Curzon St., London W1Y 8NE (☎ **0171/495-0081**).

You may also want to obtain **U.S. State Department** background bulletins. Contact the Superintendent of Documents, U.S. Government Printing Office, Washington, DC 20402 (☎ **202/512/1800**).

A good travel agent can also be a source of information. Make sure that the agent is a member of the **American Society of Travel Agents** (ASTA). If you get poor service, write to **ASTA Consumer Affairs Department,** 1101 King St., Alexandria, VA 22314, or you can call their direct line at **703/739-2782.**

ENTRY REQUIREMENTS

PASSPORTS & VISAS   Every U.S. traveler entering Germany must hold a valid passport. It is not necessary to obtain a visa unless you're staying longer than three continuous months. For information on permanent residence in Germany and work permits, contact the nearest German consulate. Once you gain entry into Germany, you don't have to show your passport again at the borders with Belgium,

France, Italy, Luxembourg, the Netherlands, Portugal, and Spain, according to an agreement signed among these European Union (formerly Community) countries that went into effect on January 1, 1993.

In the **United States,** you can apply for passports in person at one of 13 regional offices or by mail. To apply, you'll need a passport application form, available at U.S. post offices and federal court offices, and proof of citizenship, such as a birth certificate or naturalization papers; an expired passport is also accepted. Two identical passport-sized photographs are required. First-time applicants for passports pay $65 ($40 if under 18 years of age). Persons 18 or older who have an expired passport that's not more than 12 years old can reapply by mail. The old passport must be submitted along with new photographs and a pink renewal form (DSP-82). The fee is $55. Call **202/647-0518** at any time for information.

You can also write to Passport Service, Office of Correspondence, Department of State, 1111 19th St., NW, Suite 510, Washington, DC 20522-1075.

In **Canada,** citizens can go to one of 28 regional offices, or mail an application to the Passport Office, External Affairs and International Trade Canada, Ottawa, ON K1A 0GE (☎ **613/996-8885**). Applicants residing in a city where a passport office is located are requested to submit their application in person. Passport applications are available at passport offices, post offices, and most travel agents. All requirements for obtaining a passport are outlined on the application form. The fee is $60 Canadian. Passports are valid for five years and are not renewable. For more information, call **800/567-6868.**

In **Great Britain,** British subjects may apply to one of the regional offices in Liverpool, Newport, Glasgow, Peterborough, and Belfast, or in London if they reside there. You can also apply in person at a main post office. The fee is £18, and the passport is good for 10 years. Two photos must accompany the application. British visitors can also enter Germany with a more restricted Visitors' Passport, which is valid for one year and only for travel in Western Europe; it costs £9.

In **Australia,** citizens can apply at the nearest post office. Provincial capitals and other major cities have passport offices. Application fees are subject to review every three months. Telephone **02/13-12-32** for the latest information. An adult's passport is valid for 10 years; for people under 18, a passport is valid for 5 years.

In **New Zealand,** citizens should contact the nearest consulate or passport office to obtain an application. One can file in person or by mail. Proof of citizenship is required, and the passport is good for 10 years. Passports are processed at the New Zealand Passport Office, Documents of National Identity Division, Department of Internal Affairs, P.O. Box 10-526, Wellington, NZ (☎ **04/474-81-00**). The fee is NZ$80.

In **Ireland,** write in advance to the Passport Office, Setna Centre, Molesworth Street, Dublin 2, Ireland (☎ **01/671-16-33**). The cost is IR£45. Applications are sent by mail. Irish citizens living in North America can contact the Irish Embassy, 2234 Massachusetts Ave. NW, Washington, DC 20008 (☎ **202/462-3939**). The embassy can issue a new passport or direct you to one of the three North American consulates that have jurisdiction over a particular region; the charge is $80. If a citizen arrives in person, there's a discount of $5.

GERMAN CUSTOMS   In general, items required for personal and professional use or consumption may be brought in duty-free. No duty is levied for a private car, provided that it is reported. Gifts are duty-free up to a total value of 780 DM ($546) and can include a maximum of 115 DM ($80.50) in items that are destined for non–European Union countries.

The following items are permitted into Germany duty-free (imports from European Union countries in parentheses): 200 (300) cigarettes; 1 (1.5) liter(s) of liquor above 44 proof, or 2 (3) liters of liquor less than 44 proof, or 2 (4) liters of wine; 50 (75) grams of perfume and 0.25 (0.375) liters of eau de cologne; 500 (750) grams of coffee; 100 (150) grams of tea. All duty-free allowances are authorized only when the items are carried in the traveler's personal baggage.

2 Money

While this book documents the best hotels, restaurants, and attractions in Munich and the Bavarian Alps, we also want to show you how to stretch your buying power—to show that you don't need to pay scalper's prices for charm, top-grade comfort, and quality food. You'll generally find prices very similar to those in the United States—but sometimes you'll pay far more. As cities of the world go, Munich is rated expensive.

CASH/CURRENCY   The unit of German currency is the *deutsche mark* (DM), which is subdivided into *pfennig*. Bills are issued in denominations of 5, 10, 20, 50, 100, 200, 500, and 1,000 marks; coins come in 1, 2, 5, 10, and 50 **pfennig.** What the **deutsche mark** is worth in terms of U.S. money is a tricky question, the answer to which you determine by consulting the market quotations from day to day.

If you need a check in German marks before your trip, for example, to pay a deposit on a hotel room, or if you wish to buy traveler's checks in German marks, you can contact **Ruesch International,** 700 11th St., NW, 4th Floor, Washington, DC 20001-4507 (☎ **800/424-2923**). Ruesch performs a wide variety of conversion-related services, usually for $2 per transaction. You can also inquire at a local bank.

ATM NETWORKS   Plus, Cirrius, and other networks connecting automated-teller machines operate in Munich and throughout Germany. If your bank card has been programmed with a PIN (Personal Identification Number), it is likely that you can use your card at German ATMs to withdraw money as a cash advance on your credit card. Check to see if your PIN code must be reprogrammed for usage in Germany. Note that Discover cards are accepted only in the U.S. For Cirrius locations abroad, call **800/424-7787.** For Plus usage abroad, dial **800/843-7587.**

TRAVELER'S CHECKS   Many travelers prefer the safety and convenience of traveler's checks—they are widely accepted and can be replaced in case of theft. Most large banks sell traveler's checks, charging fees that average between 1% and 2% of the value of the checks you buy; if your bank wants more than a 2% commission, it sometimes pays to call the traveler's check issuers directly for the address of outlets where this commission will cost less.

American Express (☎ **800/221-7282** in the U.S. and Canada) is one of the largest and most immediately recognized issuers of traveler's checks. No commission is charged to members of the American Automobile Association, and to holders of certain types of American Express credit cards. The company issues checks denominated in U.S. dollars, British pounds sterling, German marks, and many other currencies. For questions or problems that arise outside the U.S. or Canada, contact any of the company's many regional representatives.

Citicorp (☎ **800/645-6556** in the U.S. and Canada, or **813/623-1709,** collect, from anywhere else in the world) issues checks in U.S. dollars, British pounds, German marks, Japanese yen, and Australian dollars.

Thomas Cook (☎ **800/223-7373** in the U.S. and Canada, otherwise call **609/987-7300,** collect, from other parts of the world) issues MasterCard traveler's checks

The U.S. Dollar & the German Mark

For American Readers At this writing, $1 = 1.42 DM (or 1 DM = 70¢), and this is the rate of exchange used to calculate the dollar values in this book.

For British Readers At this writing, £1 = approximately 2.21 DM (or 1 DM = 45p), and this is the rate of exchange used to calculate the pound sterling values in this table.

Note: The rates given here fluctuate from time to time, and may not be the same when you travel to Germany. Therefore, this table should be used only as a guide.

Deutsche Marks	U.S.$	U.K.£	Deutsche Marks	U.S.$	U.K.£
0.25	0.18	0.11	25.00	17.50	11.25
0.50	0.35	0.23	30.00	21.00	13.50
0.75	0.53	0.34	40.00	28.00	18.00
1.00	0.70	0.45	50.00	35.00	22.50
2.00	1.40	0.90	80.00	56.00	36.00
5.00	3.50	2.25	100.00	70.00	45.00
8.00	5.60	3.60	125.00	87.50	56.25
10.00	7.00	4.50	150.00	105.00	67.50
15.00	10.50	6.75	200.00	140.00	90.00
20.00	14.00	9.00	500.00	350.00	225.00

denominated in U.S. dollars and many other currencies. Depending on individual banking laws in the various states, some currencies might not be available at every outlet.

Interpayment Services (☎ **800/221-2426** in the U.S. or Canada, call **212/858-8500,** collect, from other parts of the world) sells VISA traveler's checks. Traveler's checks are denominated in U.S. or Canadian dollars, British pounds, German marks, and French francs.

MONEYGRAM If you find yourself out of money, a new wire service provided by American Express can help you tap willing friends and family for emergency funds. Through MoneyGram, 6200 S. Québec St., P.O. Box 5118, Englewood, CO 80155 (☎ **800/926-9400**), money can be sent around the world in less than 10 minutes. Senders should call AMEX to learn the address of the closest outlet that handles MoneyGrams. Cash, credit card, or the occasional personal check (with ID) are acceptable forms of payment. AMEX's fee for the service is $10 for the first $300 with a sliding scale for larger sums. The service includes a short telex message and a three-minute phone call from sender to recipient. The beneficiary must present a photo ID at the outlet where money is received.

WHAT WILL IT COST?

Germany, as well as the city of Munich, is one of the more expensive destinations in the world.

Although there are many variations in **accommodations** price structure, based on size and type of room, hotels ranked "Very Expensive" generally charge 350 DM ($245) and up for a double room. "Expensive" means that doubles cost about

What Things Cost in Munich	U.S. $
Taxi from the airport to Hauptbahnhof	63.00
Underground from the Hauptbahnhof to Schwabing	2.20
Local telephone call	.20
Double room at the Königshof (very expensive)	259.00
Double room at the Eden-Wolff (expensive)	189.00
Double room at the Adria (moderate)	126.00
Double room at the Pension Westfalia (inexpensive)	59.50
Lunch for one at Ratskeller (moderate)	21.00
Dinner for one, without wine, at Tantris (very expensive)	105.00
Dinner for one, without wine, at Zum Alten Markt (moderate)	42.00
Dinner for one, without wine, at Donisl (inexpensive)	14.00
Glass of wine	2.35
Liter of beer	6.65
Cup of coffee	2.20
Coca-Cola in a restaurant	1.75
Roll of ASA 200 color film, 36 exposures	5.00
Admission to Deutsches Museum	5.60
Movie ticket	7.50
Ticket to Nationaltheater	5.50–150.00

270 DM to 350 DM ($189 to $245); "Moderate" rooms run about 180 DM to 270 DM ($126 to $189). A double priced under about 180 DM ($126) is considered "Inexpensive." Prices are for two people occupying one room and include tax and service. All rooms are with bath unless stated otherwise. If parking is not specifically mentioned in a listing, the hotel has no garage or other parking facility. You'll need to find a place on the street or at a nearby garage. Parking rates are per day.

Munich offers a wide range of **dining,** in both cuisine and price. In the listings in this guide, a restaurant is considered "Very Expensive" if a meal costs more than about 100 DM ($70), without wine. "Expensive" dining runs about 65 DM to 95 DM ($45 to $67); "Moderate," about 35 DM to 60 DM ($25 to $42); and "Inexpensive" less than 35 DM ($25).

In the the small towns or villages of Bavaria, prices will be anywhere from 20% to 40% less than prices in Munich. A moderately priced rail pass will allow you to see a lot of Bavaria in a short time.

Although prices are high, you generally get good value for your money. The inflation rate, unlike that of most of the world, has remained low. Hotels are usually clean and comfortable, and restaurants generally offer a good Bavarian cuisine and ample portions made with quality ingredients. The trains run on time, and they're fast, and most service personnel treat you with respect.

For winter sports, the most expensive resorts are in such places as Garmisch-Partenkirchen. You can still enjoy winter fun, all at a moderate cost, if it's not important to you to be seen in chic places. You can stay in the village next to a chic resort where prices are 30% lower.

In Bavaria, many prices for children (generally defined as ages 6 to 17) are considerably lower than for adults. Children under 6 often are charged no admission or other fee.

3 When to Go—Climate, Holidays & Events

CLIMATE

In Bavaria and in the Alps, it can sometimes be very cold in winter, especially in January, and very warm in summer, but with cool, rainy days even in July and August. Spring and fall are often "stretched out"—in fact, we've enjoyed many a Bavarian-style "Indian summer" until late in October. The most popular tourist months are May through October, although winter travel to the alpine ski areas is becoming increasingly popular.

Munich's Average Daytime Temperature and Days of Rain

	Jan	Feb	Mar	Apr	May	June	July	Aug	Sept	Oct	Nov	Dec
Temp. (°F)	33	35	40	50	60	65	70	73	65	50	39	33
Day rain	19	16	19	19	21	24	18	17	18	15	17	18

HOLIDAYS

Public holidays are January 1 (New Year's Day), Easter (Good Friday and Easter Monday), May 1 (Labor Day), Ascension Day (10 days before Pentecost), Whit Monday (day after Pentecost), October 3 (Day of German Unity), November 17 (Day of Prayer and Repentance), and December 25–26 (Christmas). In addition, the following holidays are observed in some German states only: January 6 (Epiphany), Corpus Christi (10 days after Pentecost), August 15 (Assumption), and November 1 (All Saint's Day).

MUNICH CALENDAR OF EVENTS

For details on the following observances, consult the Munich Tourist Bureau, at the Hauptbahnhof (☎ **089/239-12-56**).

January

✪ Fasching (Carnival). Pre-Lenten revelry characterizes this bash with a whirl of colorful parades and masked balls. Special events are staged at the Viktualienmarkt. The celebration culminates on Fasching Sunday and Shrove Tuesday when the series of carnivals comes to a head. **Where:** The revelry spills outdoors throughout the Viktualienmarkt and in the Pedestrian Mall. **When:** From January 7 to Shrove Tuesday, usually four to six weeks later depending on the Lenten season. **How:** Anyway you please (that's the point), but for specifics, contact the Munich Tourist Bureau.

February

• **Munich Fashion Week.** The latest and often most elegant parades of fashion are staged throughout the week at various venues strewn across the city. February 12–14.

March

• **Starkbierzeit.** The "strong beer season" provides serious beer drinkers with a fresh crop to tide them over until Oktoberfest. Just one pint of one of the dense brews churned out specifically for the season (beginning the third Friday of Lent and lasting two weeks) ought to satiate most buzz seekers. A Lenten loophole from the days of strict fasting, the -ator suffix denotes the brews (e.g., Salvator).

April

✪ **Auer Dult.** A Munich tradition as old as having a beer with lunch. The Auer Dult is a colorful flea market fair where prize antiques and vintage junk await the keenest eyes and most disciplined bargain hunters. **Where:** Outdoors on the Mariahilfplatz you'll find merchants setting up shop. **When:** Auer Dult occurs three times a year for eight days—beginning the last Saturday of April (Maidult), the end of July (Jakobidult), and the end of October (Herbst Dult). **How:** Again, contact the Munich Tourist Bureau for details.

June

• **Munich Film Festival.** This festival, inaugurated in 1984, isn't as well attended as the February International Film Festival in Berlin, but it draws a serious audience. June 22–30.

• **Tollwood.** This summer music festival, originated by environmentalists, honors the free spirit of jazz, blues, and rock through the presentation of representative acts of each genre, from June 21 to July 9 in Olympiapark. Ask at the Tourist Information Bureau.

July

• **Auer Dult** (see April).

✪ **Opera Festival and Munich Summer of Music.** The Munich Philharmonic Orchestra's Summer of Music and the Bavarian State Opera Festival highlight the work of Munich's prodigal son, Wagner, and other masters including Mozart, Orff, Mahler, and Strauss. Contact the Munich Tourist Board for details.

• **Tollwood** (see June).

September

✪ **Oktoberfest.** Germany's most famous beer festival takes place principally in September, not October, as the name implies. Hotels are packed as the beer and revelry flow from tent to tent. Millions show up. **Where:** Most activities take place on Theresienwiese, where gigantic tents are sponsored by local breweries. Tents are occupied by as many as 6,000 beer drinkers. **When:** Middle of September to the first Sunday in October. **How:** Contact the Munich Tourist Bureau for particulars or just show up, with advance hotel reservations in hand, of course.

October

• **Auer Dult** (see April).
• **Oktoberfest** (see September).

November

• **Christkindlmarkt.** Every evening at 5:30pm, classic Christmas music bellows throughout the Christmas market on seasonally lit Marienplatz. You may even catch a glimpse of the *real* St. Nick. Traditionally runs from the end of November to Christmas Eve.

December

• **Christkindlmarkt** (see November).

4 Health & Insurance

HEALTH   German medical facilities are among the best in the world. If a medical emergency arises, your hotel staff can usually put you in touch with a reliable doctor. If not, contact the American embassy or a consulate, as each one maintains a list of English-speaking doctors.

Before you leave home, you can obtain a list of English-speaking doctors from the **International Association of Medical Assistance to Travelers** (IAMAT), in the United States at 417 Center St., Lewiston, NY 14092 (☎ **716/754-4883**); in Canada, at 40 Regal Rd., Guelph, ON N1K 1B5 (☎ **519/836-0102**).

It's a good idea to take with you whatever medication or drugs you'll need to avoid the time and trouble of getting a prescription filled; German, not American or British, pharmaceutical brands prevail. For some chronic conditions, a Medic Alert Identification Tag will tell a doctor about your condition and provide the telephone number of Medic Alert's 24-hour hotline so your medical records can be obtained. For a lifetime membership, the cost is a well-spent $35 for a stainless-steel bracelet. In addition, there is a $15 annual fee. Contact the **Medic Alert Foundation,** P.O. Box 1009, Turlock, CA 95381-1009 (☎ **800/432-5378**).

INSURANCE   Credit- and charge-card companies often insure users in case of a travel accident, provided the travel was paid with their card. Many homeowners' insurance policies cover luggage theft and loss of documents. Coverage is usually limited to about $500. To submit a claim, remember that you'll need police reports or a statement from a local medical authority.

Some insurance policies provide advances in cash or arrange funds transfers so you won't have to dip into your travel money to settle medical bills. Seniors should be aware that Medicare does not cover the cost of illness in Europe.

You may want insurance against trip cancellation. Some travel agencies provide coverage. Often such insurance is written into tickets paid for by credit or charge card. Insurance agents can also provide coverage.

Access America, 6600 W. Broad St., Richmond, VA 23230 (☎ **800/284-8300**), offers travel insurance and 24-hour emergency travel, medical, and legal assistance for the traveler. One call to their hotline center, staffed by multilingual coordinators, connects travelers to a worldwide network of professionals able to offer specialized help in reaching the nearest physician, hospital, or legal advisor, and in obtaining emergency cash or the replacement of lost travel documents. Varying coverage levels are available.

Mutual of Omaha (Tele-Trip Company, Inc.), Mutual of Omaha Plaza, Omaha, NE 68175, offers tour insurance packages priced from $49 to $57 per person for a tour valued at $1,000. Included in these packages are travel-assistance services and financial protection against trip cancellation, trip interruption, bankruptcy, flight and baggage delays, accident and sickness, accidental death and dismemberment, missed connection, trip delays, and medical evacuation coverages, all with the ability to waive preexisting condition limitations. Applications can be made over the phone by credit card (☎ **800/228-9792**).

Companies offering special travel insurance policies include the following: **Travel Guard International,** 1145 Clark St., Stevens Point, WI 54481 (☎ **800/826-1300** outside Wisconsin, 715/345-0505 in Wisconsin), offers a comprehensive seven-day policy that covers lost luggage, emergency assistance, accidental death, trip cancellation, and medical coverage abroad. The cost of the package is $62, but there are restrictions that you should understand before you accept the coverage.

TRAVEL ASSISTANCE   Several companies offer policies to cover travelers stranded abroad in some emergency; each maintains a toll-free 800 number for out-of-state callers.

Healthcare Abroad (MEDEX), c/o Wallach & Co., 107 W. Federal St. (P.O. Box 480), Middleburg, VA 22117-0480 (☎ **800/237-6615** or 540/687-3166), offers coverage for between 10 and 120 days at $3 per day; this policy includes accident and sickness coverage to the tune of $100,000. Medical evacuation is also included, along with a $25,000 accidental death and dismemberment compensation.

5 Tips for Travelers with Special Needs

FOR TRAVELERS WITH DISABILITIES   Many agencies provide advance data to help you plan your trip. For instance, **Travel Information Service,** Moss Rehabilitation Hospital (☎ 215/456-9603), offers caller information.

You can obtain a free copy of *Air Transportation of Handicapped Persons,* published by the U.S. Department of Transportation. Write for Free Advisory Circular No. AC12032, Distribution Unit, U.S. Department of Transportation, Publications Division, M-4332, Washington, DC 20590.

For names and addresses of operators of tours specifically for disabled visitors, and other relevant information, contact the **Society for the Advancement of Travel for the Handicapped** (SATH), 347 Fifth Ave., Suite 610, New York, NY 10016 (☎ 212/447-7284; fax 212/725-8253). Yearly membership dues in the society are $45, $25 for senior citizens and students.

The **Information Center for Individuals with Disabilities,** 29 Stanhope St., 4th Floor, Boston, MA 02116 (☎ **800/462-5015** or 617/450-9888), is another good source. It has lists of travel agents who specialize in tours for the disabled.

For the blind or visually impaired, the best source is the **American Foundation for the Blind,** 11 Penn Plaza, Suite 300, New York, NY 10001 (☎ **212/502-7600,** or 800/232-5463 for ordering of information kits and supplies). It offers information on travel and various requirements for the transport and border formalities for seeing-eye dogs.

One of the best organizations serving the needs of persons with disabilities (wheelchairs and walkers) is **Flying Wheels Travel,** 143 West Bridge St., P.O. Box 382, Owatoona, MN 55060 (☎ **800/535-6790** or 507/451-5005), offering various escorted tours and cruises internationally.

For a $20 annual fee, consider joining **Mobility International USA,** P.O. Box 10767, Eugene, OR 97440 (☎ **503/343-1284**). It answers questions on various destinations and also offers discounts on videos, publications, and programs it sponsors.

Finally, a bimonthly publication, *Handicapped Travel Newsletter,* keeps you current on accessible sights worldwide for the disabled. To order an annual subscription for $15, call **903/677-1260.**

FOR GAY & LESBIAN TRAVELERS   The gay nightlife of Munich is legendary. Violence against gays is rare, but there are some pockets of neo-Nazi skinheads. Homosexuality in southern Germany, except for the more isolated sections of the Bavarian countryside, is generally widely accepted and tolerated, especially among young people. The legal minimum age for consensual sex is 18. For information about the gay and lesbian scene in Bavaria, call **089/260-3056.**

To learn about gay and lesbian travel in Bavaria, you can secure publications or else join data-dispensing organizations before you go. Men can order *Spartacus,* the international gay guide ($32.95), or *Odysseus 1997, The International Gay Travel Planner,* a guide to international gay accommodations ($25). Both lesbians and gay men might want to pick up a copy of *Gay Travel A to Z* ($16), which specializes in general information, as well as listings of bars, hotels, restaurants, and places of interest for gay travelers throughout the world. These books and others are available from **Giovanni's Room**, 1145 Pine St., Philadelphia, PA 19107 (☎ 215/923-2960).

Our World, 1104 North Nova Rd., Suite 251, Daytona Beach, FL 32117 (☎ 904/441-5367), is a magazine devoted to options and bargains for gay and lesbian travel worldwide. It costs $35 for 10 issues. *Out and About,* 8 West 19th St., Suite 401, New York, NY 10011 (☎ 800/929-2268), has been hailed for its "straight" reporting about gay travel. It profiles the best gay or gay-friendly hotels, gyms, clubs, and other places, with coverage of destinations throughout the world. Its cost is $49 a year for 10 information-packed issues. It aims for the more upscale gay male traveler, and has been praised by everybody from *Travel & Leisure* to the *New York Times.* Both of these publications are also available at most gay and lesbian bookstores.

The **International Gay Travel Association** (IGTA), P.O. Box 4974, Key West, FL 33041 (☎ 305/292-0217, or voice mailbox 800/448-8550), encourages gay and lesbian travel worldwide. With around 1,200 member agencies, it specializes in networking travelers with the appropriate gay-friendly service organization or tour specialist. It offers quarterly newsletters, marketing mailings, and a membership directory that is updated four times a year. Travel agents, who are IGTA members, will be tied into this organization's vast information resources.

FOR SENIORS　Many discounts are available for seniors, but be advised that you have to be a member of an association to obtain some of them.

Write for a free booklet called *101 Tips for the Mature Traveler,* available from Grand Circle Travel, 347 Congress St., Boston, MA 02210 (☎ 800/221-2610 or 617/350-7500). This tour operator offers extended vacations, escorted programs, and cruises that feature unique learning experiences for seniors at competitive prices.

Golden Companions has been successful in helping travelers age 45 and older find compatible companions since 1987. It is the only travel companion network to offer personal voicebox mail service, enabling members to connect instantly with each other 24 hours a day. Membership services also include free mail exchange, a bimonthly newsletter, *Golden Gateways,* get-togethers, and tours. Annual membership costs $85, and newsletter-only subscriptions cost $17.95 for 12 months, or $26.95 for 24 months. For a free brochure, write Golden Companions, P.O. Box 5249, Reno, NV 89513 (☎ 702/324-2227; fax 702/324-2236). A sample newsletter costs $2.

Saga International Holidays is well known for its affordable all-inclusive tours for seniors, preferably those 50 years old or older. Both medical and trip cancellation insurance are included in the net price of any of their tours except for cruises. Contact SAGA International Holidays, 222 Berkeley St., Boston, MA 02116 (☎ 800/343-0273).

AARP (American Association of Retired Persons) is the best organization in the United States for seniors. It offers discounts on car rentals and hotels. For more information, contact AARP at 601 E St., NW, Washington, DC 20049 (☎ 202/434-AARP).

Information is also available from the **National Council of Senior Citizens**, 1331 F St., NW, Washington, DC 20004 (☎ 202/347-8800). A nonprofit organization, the council charges $12 per person or couple, for which you receive 11 issues annually of a newsletter that is devoted partly to travel tips. Benefits of membership include discounts on hotels, motels, and auto rentals, and also include prescription drug service, long-term-care options, and insurance programs for members.

Mature Outlook, P.O. Box 10048, Des Moines, IA 50306 (☎ **800/336-6330**), is a membership program for people 50 years old and up. Members are offered discounts at ITC-member hotels and will receive a bimonthly magazine. The annual membership fee of $14.95 entitles its members to free coupons for discounts at Sears & Roebuck Co. Savings are also offered on selected auto rentals and restaurants.

FOR SINGLES   Even though millions of adult Americans are single, the travel industry is far better geared for double occupancy of hotel rooms. One company, **Travel Companion Exchange,** has been successful in matching single travelers with like-minded companions. Jens Jurgen, the German-born founder, charges about $99 for a six-month listing. New applicants fill out a form stating their preferences and needs; then they receive a list of potential partners and travel companions. The same or the opposite sex can be requested. A bimonthly newsletter gives numerous money-saving tips of particular interest to solo travelers. A sample copy is available for $5. For an application and more information, contact Jens Jurgen, Travel Companion Exchange, P.O. Box P-833, Amityville, NY 11701 (☎ **516/454-0880**).

Since single supplements on tours carry a hefty price tag, some tour companies will arrange for you to share a room with another single traveler of the same gender. One such company that offers a "guaranteed-share plan" is **Cosmos,** featuring budget touring worldwide offices at 5310 South Federal Circle, Littleton, CO 80123 (☎ **800/ 851-0728**).

FOR FAMILIES   If you're planning to take your family abroad, you'll need to do some advance planning. You may want to discuss your vacation plans with your family doctor.

Special children's menus on airlines must be requested at least 24 hours in advance. If baby food is required, however, bring your own and ask a flight attendant to warm it to the right temperature.

Arrange ahead of time for such necessities as a crib and a bottle warmer, plus a car seat, if you're driving. Remember that in Germany small children aren't allowed to ride in the front seat. Sitters can be arranged for you at most hotels. Finding a sitter with a knowledge of English is no problem in Germany.

Family Travel Times is published quarterly by **Travel with Your Children** (TWYCH), and includes a weekly call-in service for subscribers. Subscriptions cost $40 a year and can be ordered by writing to TWYCH, 40 Fifth Ave., New York, NY 10011 (☎ **212/477-5524**).

FOR STUDENTS   Students can secure a number of travel discounts. The most wide-ranging service for students is **Council Travel,** a subsidiary of the **Council on International Educational Exchange** (CIEE), 205 E. 42nd St., New York, NY 10017 (☎ **212/661-1450**), which provides details about budget travel, study abroad, working permits, and insurance. It also publishes a number of helpful publications and issues an International Student Identity Card (ISIC) for $18 to bona-fide students. Its free copy of **Student Travels** magazine provides information on all of Council Travel's services and CIEE's programs and publications.

The **IYHF (International Youth Hostel Federation)** was designed to provide bare-bones accommodations for serious budget travelers. Regular membership costs $25 annually, only $10 for those under 18 and $15 for those 55 and up. For information, contact Hostelling Information/American Youth Hostels (HI-AYH), 733 15th St. NW, Suite 840, Washington, DC 20005 (☎ **202/783-6161**).

6 Getting There

BY PLANE

The best strategy to secure economical airfare is shopping around. Keep calling the airlines. Sometimes a cheaper ticket becomes available at the very last minute because the flight is not fully booked, so the airline discounts tickets to achieve full capacity.

Those who are unwilling to leave everything until the last minute should know certain information about airfare structures. Most airlines price fares seasonally. During peak season, the summer months, flights to Munich are most expensive. Excluding the Christmas holidays, winter months offer the lowest fares. This fits in fine with those who wish to go skiing in the Bavarian Alps. Shoulder season is in between. Most airlines also offer an assortment of fares from first class, the most expensive, through business class to economy class, the lowest "no frills" regular airfare. Most airlines also offer promotional fares with stringent requirements such as advance purchase, minimum stay, and cancellation penalties. The most common such fare is the APEX (advance purchase excursion).

Lufthansa, Germany's national airline, sometimes offers promotional fares lower than the best APEX fare. Lufthansa also offers seniors over 62 a 10% discount; the reduction applies to a traveling companion as well.

THE MAJOR AIRLINES

The only airline offering direct nonstop flights to Munich is Delta Airlines. On other airlines connections must be made through Frankfurt, Düsseldorf, or another gateway city. Airlines flying to Germany include Lufthansa, American, Delta, TWA, Continental, and United.

Of the six, **Lufthansa** (☎ **800/645-3880**) operates the most frequent service and flies to the greatest number of the country's airports. Connections with flights to Munich can be made through a number of European gateway cities. From North America, Lufthansa serves 14 gateway cities, 10 in the United States. The largest of the gateways is New York City, where flights depart from both JFK and Newark airports. From JFK daily flights depart nonstop for Frankfurt and Düsseldorf, where easy connections can be made to Munich. From Newark International, Lufthansa offers daily flights to Frankfurt. Lufthansa's other gateways include Atlanta, Boston, Chicago, Dallas/Fort Worth, Houston, Los Angeles, Miami, San Francisco, and Washington, D.C. From Canada and Mexico, Lufthansa flies to Germany from Toronto, Vancouver, Calgary, and Mexico City.

Lufthansa boasts of recent upgrades to its fleet, including the addition of four-engine Airbus A-340s. Crafted by an intra-European consortium of builders, they feature quiet rides, enhanced comfort, and greater fuel efficiency.

American Airlines (☎ **800/443-7300**) flies nonstop to Frankfurt every day from both Dallas/Fort Worth and Chicago. Nonstop flights leave several times a week from Chicago to Düsseldorf as well. There is also a nonstop daily service between Miami and Frankfurt. From Frankfurt, Düsseldorf, and—among others—London, American's flights connect easily with ongoing flights to Munich on Lufthansa or British Airways.

Despite the financial problems and frequent reorganizations of **TWA** (☎ **800/ 892-4141**), the airline offers daily nonstop service between New York's JFK and Frankfurt. At Frankfurt, it can connect passengers through Lufthansa to Munich. TWA also flies nonstop every day from New York to Paris, where connections can be made to Munich, via Air France.

Delta Airlines (☎ **800/241-4141**) is the only airline offering direct service to Munich. Delta flies out of JFK in New York, offering daily nonstop service to Munich. From its home base in Atlanta, Delta also offers daily nonstops to Munich.

United Airlines (☎ **800/538-2929**) joined the German-bound battalions in 1991 by acquiring several of Pan Am's North Atlantic routes. These include daily nonstops from Washington, D.C., to Frankfurt, and daily nonstops from Chicago to Frankfurt, where easy connections are made to Munich.

Continental Airlines (☎ **800/231-0856**) has become an important player in the transatlantic air routes into Germany with the inauguration of daily nonstop service between Newark, New Jersey, and Frankfurt. Continental maintains excellent connections between Newark and its hubs in Cleveland and Houston, and offers some of the most comfortable and affordable business-class service in the airline industry. Seats recline a full 55°, convert into sleepers, and contain individualized TV/video screens with electronic audio systems. On its transatlantic and international routes, Continental refers to the forward compartment of each of its aircraft as Business First Class. The cost of one-way passage from Newark to Frankfurt for this class of service is $1,530, about $1,000 less, each way, than comparable service on the same route in first class on many other airlines. Continental also offers discounts and other benefits to seniors 62 and over, and to their traveling companions, regardless of their age.

KLM (☎ **800/374-7747**) maintains frequent nonstop flights into Amsterdam from New York's JFK, Boston, Washington, DC's Dulles, and Atlanta; from Amsterdam, many flights on both KLM and Lufthansa fly into Munich.

British Airways offers daily nonstop flights between Munich and London.

FINDING THE BEST AIRFARE

The airlines compete in offering the most economical fares encumbered with the least number of restrictions. Any promotional fare announced without advance notice will probably be quickly matched by competitors. Insofar as airline fares go, the early bird almost always merits lower fares, since price structures are specifically geared to reward travelers who reserve and arrange payment for tickets in advance. Watch the newspapers, consult your travel agent, and remain as flexible as possible about travel dates so you can profit from last-minute price changes.

For transatlantic fares, Lufthansa divides the price structure of most of its fares into three separate categories. They include, from the least to the most expensive, nonrefundable APEX fares, instant purchase excursion fares, and full-fledged excursion fares.

The nonrefundable APEX fare requires the purchase of a ticket 21 days or more prior to departure, with payment and ticketing completed within 72 hours of finalizing the reservation. A stay of between 7 and 21 days is required prior to a passenger's use of the return flight. Lufthansa's nonrefundable APEX fares from New York to Frankfurt range from $568 round-trip on a weekday (Monday to Thursday) in winter, to a high of $878 for the same flight in summer. Flights on weekends (Friday to Sunday) cost around $60 more, round-trip, than equivalent flights on weekdays.

Flying midweek, Monday through Thursday, at presstime Delta offered a round-trip APEX fare of $934 in summer and $598 in winter, between Munich and New York.

Instant purchase excursion fares are more expensive, but more flexible, than either option listed above. Priced at $768 round-trip from New York to Frankfurt in winter, and at $1,078 for the same flight in summer, they require no advance purchase and allow returns to the passenger's point of departure after the passage of a Sunday or up to six months. One stopover en route is allowed for a surcharge of $50.

Excursion fares are the most expensive of all and least desirable except in cases of dire emergency. The fare is valid all year, has no minimum stay and a maximum stay of one year, requires no advance purchase, and permits one free stopover and one additional stopover at a charge of $50. The round-trip fare for this is $1,288 between New York and Frankfurt. Faced with such staggering differences in costs, most visitors work hard to predefine the dates and parameters of their trip to Munich within the advance time frame required for the purchase of the less expensive APEX fares.

The lowest APEX fares are available roughly from November 1 to late March, with a slight increase over Christmas. More expensive is passage during most of April, May, and mid-September to November 1, periods defined as shoulder season, when many visitors find Germany less visited and more appealing. Midsummer (June to mid-September) is the period when APEX tickets are most expensive.

There are also special discounts and promotions that airlines frequently offer. For example, travelers can save a bundle by capitalizing on airfare wars frequently staged by rival airlines. You will probably be asked to fly midweek. Other possible restrictions: payment in full within 24 hours of booking, time limits on nonrefundable return flights, and less flexibility with flight dates after booking flights on Saturday or Sunday often require a surcharge of $25 in each direction.

BUSINESS CLASS & FIRST CLASS

Business class features larger seats, upgraded food and service, and more room to spread out papers, calculators, or laptops. Since business travel is not seasonal, prices remain the same year-round. Lufthansa charges $1,529 each way for business class from New York to Munich but imposes absolutely no restrictions concerning length of stay, advance reservation, or prepayment.

First class offers extra comfort and service. The first-class Lufthansa fare from New York to Munich is $2,642 each way, and the amenities can be pleasant and refreshing. At Lufthansa (☎ 800/645-3880), first- and business-class compartments feature seats with individual TV sets, offering a choice of in-house movies and entertainment in either German or English.

The competition for first- and business-class passengers is fierce through the industry. Delta's (☎ 800/221-1212) first-class fare between Atlanta and Munich is $2,816 each way; its business fare for the same route is about $1,733 each way.

OTHER GOOD-VALUE CHOICES

BUCKET SHOPS (CONSOLIDATORS)   The name *bucket shop* originated in the 1960s in Great Britain, where mainstream airlines gave the then-pejorative name to resellers of blocks of unsold tickets consigned to them by major transatlantic carriers. Bucket shop has stuck as a label, but it might be more polite to refer to them as "consolidators." They exist in many shapes and forms. In its purest sense, a bucket shop acts as a clearinghouse for blocks of tickets that airlines discount and consign during normally slow periods of travel.

Charter operators (see below) and bucket shops once performed separate functions, but their offerings in many cases have been blurred in recent times. Many outfits perform both functions.

Tickets are sometimes, but not always, priced at up to 35% less than full fare. Terms of payment can vary—anywhere from 45 days prior to departure to last-minute sales offered in a final attempt by an airline to fill a craft. Tickets can be purchased through regular travel agents, who usually mark up the ticket 8% to 10%, maybe more, thereby greatly reducing your discount. A survey conducted of fliers who use consolidator tickets voiced only one major complaint: Use of such a ticket doesn't qualify you for an advance seat assignment, and you are therefore likely to be assigned a "poor seat" on the plane at the last minute.

The survey revealed that most fliers estimated their savings at around $200 per ticket off the regular price. Nearly a third of the passengers reported savings of up to $300 off the regular price. But—and here's the hitch— many people who booked consolidator tickets reported no savings at all, as the airline will sometimes match the consolidator ticket by announcing a promotional fare. The situation is a bit tricky and calls for some careful investigation on your part to determine just how much you're saving, if anything.

800-FLY-4-LESS is a nationwide airline reservation and ticketing service that specializes in finding the lowest fares. For information on available consolidator airline tickets for last-minute travel, call **800/359-4537.** When fares are high and advance planning time is low, such a service is invaluable.

One of the biggest U.S. consolidators is **Travac,** 989 Sixth Ave., 16th Floor, New York, NY 10018 (☎ **800/TRAV-800** or 212/563-3303 in New York), which offers discounted seats throughout the U.S. to most cities in Europe on airlines that include TWA, United, and Delta. Another Travac office is at 2601 E. Jefferson St., Orlando, FL 32803 (☎ **407/896-0014**).

In New York, try **TFI Tours International,** 34 W. 32nd St., 12th Floor, New York, NY 10001 (☎ **800/745-8000** or 212/736-1140 in New York). This tour company offers services to 177 cities worldwide.

In the Midwest, explore the possibilities of **Travel Avenue,** 10 S. Riverside Plaza, Suite 1404, Chicago, IL 60606 (☎ **800/333-3335**), a national agency whose headquarters are here. Its tickets are often cheaper than most shops, and it charges the customer only a $25 fee on international tickets, rather than taking the usual $10 commission from an airline. Travel Avenue rebates most of that back to customers.

In New England, a possibility is **TMI** (Travel Management International), 3617 Dupont Ave. South, Minneapolis, MN 55409 (☎ **800/245-3672**), which offers a wide variety of discounts, including youth fares, student fares, and access to other kinds of air-related discounts as well. Among others, its destinations include Munich.

UniTravel, 1177 N. Warson Rd., St. Louis, MO 63132 (☎ **800/325-2222**), offers tickets to Europe at prices that may or may not be reduced from the price a client would get if he or she phoned the airlines directly. UniTravel is best suited to providing discounts for passengers who decide (or need) to get to Munich on short notice.

One final option suitable only for clients with flexible travel plans is available through **Airhitch,** 2641 Broadway, 3rd Floor, New York, NY 10025 (☎ **212/864-2000** or 800/326-2009). Prospective travelers inform Airhitch of any five consecutive days in which they're available to fly to Europe. Airhitch agrees to fly its passengers within those five days from a particular region in the U.S. (these regions include the Northeast, Southeast, Midwest, West Coast, or Northwest). Attempts will be made to fly passengers to and from the cities of their choice, such as Munich, but no guarantees are made. One-way fares range from $169 to $269.

STANDBY FARES   Another cheap alternative for flights to Germany is Air-Tech Ltd., 584 Broadway, Suite 1007, New York, NY 10012 (☎ **212/219-2190**); it is a "space-available" travel service, offering standby fares mainly to Europe. All travelers need do is register with Air-Tech, specify preferred destination, give a two- to five-day travel window, and call Air-Tech the Wednesday before their travel window begins. Travelers are then informed of flights and seating available. Passengers unable to book a flight within their chosen travel window are given the option to reschedule or receive a full refund.

CHARTER FLIGHTS   Strictly speaking, a charter uses an aircraft reserved months in advance for one-time-only transit to some predetermined point. Before paying for a charter, check the restrictions on your ticket or contract. You may be asked to purchase a tour package and pay far in advance. You'll pay a stiff penalty (or forfeit the ticket entirely) if you cancel. Charters are sometimes canceled when the plane doesn't fill. In some cases, the charter-ticket seller will offer an insurance policy for a cancellation for good cause (hospital confinement or death in the family, for example).

Some charter companies have proved unreliable in the past. One reliable charter-flight operator is **Council Charter,** run by the Council on International Educational Exchange, 205 E. 42nd St., New York, NY 10017 (☎ **800/800-8222** or 212/661-0311), which arranges charter seats on regularly scheduled aircraft.

REBATORS   Rebators are firms that pass along part of their commission to the passenger, although many assess a fee for their services. They are not the same as travel agents but can sometimes offer similar services. Most rebators offer discounts averaging 10% to 25%, plus a $25 handling charge.

Specializing in clients within the Midwest, **Travel Avenue,** 10 S. Riverside Plaza, Suite 1404, Chicago, IL 60606 (☎ **800/333-3335** or 312/876-1116), is one of the oldest agencies of its kind. They offer up-front cash rebates on every airfare over $300. In a style similar to a discount brokerage firm, they pride themselves on *not* offering travel counseling. Instead, they sell airline tickets to independent travelers who have already worked out their travel plans. Also available are tour and cruise fares, plus hotel reservations, usually at prices less expensive than if you have reserved them on your own.

Another major rebator is **The Smart Traveller,** 3111 S.W. 27th Ave. (P.O. Box 330010), Miami, FL 33133 (☎ **800/448-3338** or 305/448-3338). The agency also offers discounts on package tours, which include hotels, car rentals, and Danube cruises for which easy connections can be made from Munich.

TRAVELING AS A COURIER   Couriers are hired by overnight air-freight firms hoping to skirt Customs hassles and delays on the other end. With a courier, the checked freight sails through Customs as quickly as regular luggage.

Don't worry—the courier service is absolutely legal and can lead to a greatly discounted airfare; sometimes you can even fly free. You're allowed one piece of carry-on luggage only (your baggage allowance is used by the courier firm to transport its cargo). As a courier, you don't actually handle the merchandise you're "transporting" to Europe; you just carry a manifest to present to Customs.

Upon your arrival, an employee of the courier service will reclaim the cargo. Incidentally, you fly alone, so don't plan to travel with anybody. Most operate from Los Angeles or New York, but some operate out of Chicago or Miami. Courier services are often listed in the *Yellow Pages* or in advertisements in travel sections of newspapers.

You might contact **Halbart Express,** 147-05 176th St., Jamaica, NY 11434 (☎ **718/656-8189,** 10am to 3pm daily), or **Now Voyager,** 74 Varick St., Suite 307, New York, NY 10013 (☎ **212/431-1616,** 10am to 5pm daily).

The **International Association of Air Travel Couriers,** P.O. Box 1349, Lake Worth, FL 33460 (☎ **407/582-8320**), publishes *Shoestring Traveler,* a newsletter, and *Air Courier Bulletin,* a directory of courier bargains around the world. The annual membership fee is $45. The fee also includes access to their 24-hour fax-on-demand system and computer bulletin board, which are updated daily with last-minute flights and bulletins.

TRAVEL CLUBS   Another possibility for low-cost air travel is the travel club, which supplies an unsold inventory of tickets offering discounts usually in the range of 20% to 60%.

After you pay an annual fee, you're given a "hotline" number to call to find out what discounts are available. Many of these discounts become available several days in advance of actual departure, sometimes as long as a week or even a month. Of course, you're limited to what's available, so you have to be fairly flexible.

Moment's Notice, 7301 New Utrecht Ave., New York, NY 11228 (☎ **718/ 234-6295**), charges $25 per year for membership, which allows spur-of-the-moment participation in dozens of tours. Each is geared for impulse purchases and last-minute getaways, and each offers air and land packages that often represent substantial savings over what you'd have paid through more conventional channels. Although membership is required for participation in the tours, anyone can call the company's hotline (☎ **212/750-9111**) to learn what options are available. Most of the company's best-valued tours depart from New Jersey's Newark airport.

Sears Discount Travel Club, 3033 South Parker Rd., Suite 900, Aurora, CO 80014 (☎ **800/433-9383** in the U.S.), offers a $50 membership that includes a catalog (issued four times a year), maps, discounts at select hotels, and a limited guarantee that equivalent packages will not be undersold by any other travel organization. It also offers a 5% rebate on the value of all airline tickets, tours, hotels, and car rentals purchased through them (paperwork, including receipts and itineraries required).

FLYING WITH FILM, CAMCORDERS & LAPTOPS

All luggage, including carry-on articles, is subject to X-ray inspection at airport security counters. The machines won't hurt most conventional film, but if you prefer, ask for a hand inspection, and avoid passing your film or videotapes through the X-ray machines. Don't rely on lead-lined bags as insurance against X-ray exposure: Most security staffs compensate for the presence of such safeguards by simply increasing the intensity of X rays beamed onto your luggage.

Videotape is not, as stated above, usually damaged by X rays, but it can be damaged by the magnetic field of a walk-through metal detector, so ask, once again, for a hand check. This might involve taking a picture with your camera, or turning on the camcorder to prove that the machine isn't a disguise for something more sinister.

Camcorders are usually powered by rechargeable batteries that can be replenished with a universal (worldwide) AC adaptor. These can be plugged into either a 110-volt (North American) or 220-volt (German) electrical outlet. (You'll need to supply the appropriate plug, but these are usually sold as part of the rig when the machine is purchased.)

Passing a laptop computer through a security X-ray machine won't harm the hard disk of a laptop computer, but to be safe, ask for a hand check anyway. If you do this, you'll be asked to switch on your computer (the security force wants to see the DOS prompt and the memory check) to prove that nothing is amiss. In such circumstances, it's usually easier to operate your laptop from its battery source, as there might not be a convenient place to plug in the machine close to the security checkpoint, so ensure in advance that your laptop's batteries are charged.

On virtually any international flight, a percentage of seats will be occupied by travelers peering into the screens of their laptops. Most airlines allow use of these machines anytime except during takeoff and landings, as their magnetic fields can interfere with navigational equipment. To avoid customs-related unpleasantness, it's wise to carry a photocopy of the receipt you obtained when you bought your laptop originally, to avoid the insinuation that you might have purchased the device abroad and haven't paid sales or import tax on it. Above all, make sure you understand the voltage your laptop requires. Some operate on either North American (11-volt) current or German (220-volt) current; others are much more fussy.

MUNICH'S AIRPORT

Franz Josef Strauss Airport, inaugurated in 1992, is among the most modern, best equipped, and most efficient airports in the world. The $5.3-billion facility handles more than 100 flights a day, serving 60 cities worldwide. It lies 18 miles northeast of central Munich at Erdinger Moos. Facilities include parking garages; car-rental centers; restaurants, bars, and cafés; money-exchange kiosks; lockers; and luggage-storage facilities. For flight information, call the airline of your choice.

S-Bahn (☎ **089/55-75-75**) trains connect the airport with the Hauptbahnhof (main railroad station) in downtown Munich. Departures are every 30 minutes for the 40-minute trip. The fare is 13.20 DM ($9.25); Eurailpass holders ride free. A taxi into the center costs about 90 DM ($63). Airport buses, such as those operated by Lufthansa, also run between the airport and the center.

If you're going to rent a car, refer to "Getting Around" in Chapter 3 for more information.

BY TRAIN

Many passengers, especially holders of the Eurailpass, travel to Germany by train, since it lies in the heart of Europe and has connections with major capitals. British Rail, for example, runs four trains a day to Germany from London. Of course, many travelers will want to take the Eurostar service running between London and Brussels direct via the Channel Tunnel. **Rail Europe** (☎ **800/94-CHUNNEL** for information) sells tickets on the Eurostar direct train service between London and Paris or Brussels. Tickets are purchased through British Rail travel centers in London (☎ **0171/834-2345** for a location near you). Four daily trains leave from Victoria Station in London, going by way of the Ramsgate–Ostend ferry or jetfoil. If you go by jetfoil, Cologne is just $9^1/_2$ hours away; it's $12^1/_2$ hours with the Dover–Ostend ferry. Most trains change at Cologne for destinations elsewhere in Germany. Travel from London to Munich—depending on the connection—can mean a trip of 18 to 22 hours. Most visitors find it cheaper to fly from London to Munich than to take the train.

From Paris, the Orient Express (☎ **0171/928-6000**) leaves from Gare de l'Est at 7:43pm daily and arrives in Munich at 4:26am. If you're in Rome, you can take the Michelangelo Express daily at 8:15am. It arrives in Munich at 6:30pm. The Bavaria leaves Zurich at 7:41am daily, reaching Munich at 11:51am.

Munich's main rail station, the **Hauptbahnhof,** on Bahnhofplatz, is one of Europe's largest. Located near the city center and the trade fairgrounds, it contains a hotel, restaurants, shopping, car parking, and banking facilities. All major German cities are connected to this station, most with a train arriving and departing almost every hour. Some 20 daily trains connect Munich to Frankfurt, and there are about 23 daily rail connections to Berlin.

The rail station is connected with the S-Bahn rapid-transit system, a 260-mile network of tracks, providing service to various city districts and outlying suburbs. The major subway serving Munich (the U-Bahn) is also centered at the rail station. In addition, buses fan out in all directions. Long-distance buses arrive and depart in the section of the station known as Westwing–Starnberger Bahnhof. For information about long-distance trains, call **089/194-19;** for S-Bahn trains, call **089/55-75-75.**

BY BUS

Bus travel to Germany's major cities, including Munich, is available from London, Paris, and many other cities in Europe. The continent's largest bus operator, **Eurolines,** operates out of Victoria Coach Station in central London, and within a 35-minute subway ride from Central Paris, at 28 avenue du Général-de-Gaulle, 93541 Bagnolet. Metro: Gallieni. For information about Eurolines in Britain, call **0582/40-45-11** or 0171/730-8235, or contact any National Express bus lines or travel agent. For information about Eurolines in France, call **01-49-72-51-51.** Buses on long-haul journeys are equipped with toilets and partially reclining seats. They stop for 60-minute breaks every four hours for rest and refreshment, although in case of emergencies, they stop more frequently. Passage from Paris to Munich costs 380 F ($76) one way or 600 F ($120) round-trip. In methods similar to APEX fares on airlines, discounts are available to passengers who pay for and predetermine their exact itineraries several weeks in advance, and discounts of around 20% are offered in some instances for passengers under age 26.

The price of bus transport between London and Munich is £61 ($91.50) one-way, or £99 ($148.50) round-trip. Discounts of about 20% are sometimes offered to qualifying passengers under age 26. Buses from London to Munich depart three times a week. For information about Eurolines in Germany, contact **Deutsche Touring** (Eurolines Stadtbüro), Mannheimerstrasse 4, D-60329 Frankfurt am Main (☎ **069/ 790-32-81**).

Eurolines does not maintain a U.S.-based sales agent, although any European travel agent can arrange for a ticket on the bus lines that link Europe's major cities.

In Munich buses depart from the section of the Hauptbahnhof called West-wing-Starnberger Bahnhof. For information about connections, tariffs, and schedules, contact **Deutsche Touring GmbH,** Arnulf Strasse 3 (☎ **089/59-18-24**). It covers many major cities and also runs buses to the Romantic Road. **Bayern Express Reisen,** Arnulf Strasse 16–18 (☎ **089/55-30-74**), offers daily service to Berlin via Nürnberg. Excursions to such popular Bavarian destinations as Berchtesgaden, Schwangau-Neuschwanstein, Garmisch-Partenkirchen, and Chiemsee (see Chapter 10) are offered by several local bus companies, including **Panorama Tours,** at a number of locations (call **089/59-15-04** for more information).

BY CAR & FERRY

If you're driving to Munich from England, you face a choice of ports from where to begin your Germany odyssey. P&O Ferries (☎ **0990/98098** in London) maintain between 20 and 25 ferryboat crossings a day, depending on the season, between the busy harbors of Dover and Calais, in northeastern France. The crossing can take as little as 1 hour and 15 minutes, depending on the craft. Other options involve passage through the Netherlands from Harwich, in the east of England, to the Hook of Holland, for a sea crossing of about eight hours. For information, call Sealink (☎ **0990/707-070** in England). Some other possibilities exist for ocean crossings between England and ports in Belgium or on the mainland of Europe, but the best source of information for many of these routes, as well as for new developments regarding the Channel Tunnel, is BritRail. For information about timetables and departures, contact a travel agent on either side of the Atlantic. In the U.S. or Canada, call **800/677-8585** or 212/575-2667.

Germany also has Autobahn (express highway) links to its neighbors. Motorists from Brussels take the E5 into Cologne. From Innsbruck (Austria), the E17, E86, and E11 lead directly to Munich. From Italy, most motorists go from Bolzano in the north along the E6 to Innsbruck, where the road continues north to Munich.

It's slow going from France. From Paris, you must take the Autoroute du Soleil to Switzerland and then take Swiss expressways until you reach the German frontier. For Munich, you can continue east from Zurich, heading for Innsbruck in the east, where you can then make Autobahn connections to Munich.

PACKAGE TOURS

Many questions arise for people planning their first European trip. How do I plan my trip so as not to miss the most outstanding sights of the destination? Will I have a problem moving from place to place, complete with luggage? Am I too old to embark on such a journey? How will I cope with a foreign language?

Our advice to first-time travelers is simple: Take a tour during which your needs are looked after from arrival at a European airport to departure back to the United States. Taking a tour is often cheaper than exploring a country on your own.

Leading tour operators include the following: **Lufthansa** (☎ **800/645-3880** in the U.S.), the major German airline.

American Express Vacations, P.O. Box 1525, Fort Lauderdale, FL 33302 (☎ **800/446-6234** in the U.S. and Canada), is the most instantly recognizable tour operator in the world. Its offerings in Germany and the rest of Europe are more comprehensive than those of many other companies. If **American Express Vacations** doesn't offer what you want, and if you're clear enough in your vision, it will arrange an individualized itinerary through specified regions for you.

DER Tours, 11933 Wilshire Blvd., Los Angeles, CA 90025 (☎ **800/782-2424** or 310/479-4411), offers discounted airfares, car rentals, hotel packages, short regional tours, and German Rail, Eurail, and other rail passes.

Delta Airlines (☎ **800/221-6666**) offers both fly/drive and fly/rail packages for touring Germany, including Bavaria. For tourists with limited time, it features three-day "city sprees" in metropolises like Munich.

U.K. residents can go to any travel agent for an array of package tours to Germany. They can also telephone the German national carrier, **Lufthansa** (☎ **0181/750-3500** in London), for the latest details on fly/drive and fly/rail tour packages of Germany.

Getting to Know Munich 3

Munich is a lively place all year—fairs and holidays seem to follow one on top of the other. But this is no "oompah" town. Here you'll find an elegant and tasteful city with sophisticated clubs and restaurants, the best theaters, and the finest concert halls.

One of Europe's most visited cities, Munich is full of monuments and fabulous museums. A place with memories of yesterday, both good and bad, it is very much a city living in its present. Today, with some 1.3 million inhabitants, 16% of which are foreigners, Munich is the third largest city in Germany. It is also the German's first choice as a place to live, according to various polls. It is a major economic center for north–south European trade and for high-tech microelectronics and other industries. It also has a huge publishing center and a burgeoning number of film studios.

A city of art and culture, it is Germany's largest university town. Munich is mainly a city for having fun and enjoying the relaxed lifestyle, the friendly ambience, and its wealth of activities, nightlife, sights, and cultural events.

1 Orientation

Munich is just slightly smaller than Berlin or Hamburg. Trying to see all of it would be a major undertaking; however, you can explore the heart of Munich on foot. Many attractions are in the environs, so for these, you'll have to rely on a car or public transportation.

VISITOR INFORMATION

Tourist information can be obtained at the Franz Josef Strauss Airport in the central area (☎ **089/9759-2815**), open Monday through Saturday from 8:30am to 10pm and on Sunday from 1 to 9pm, and at the Hauptbahnhof. The main tourist office, **Fremden-verkehrsamt,** at the Hauptbahnhof (☎ **089/2333-0256**), is found at the south exit opening onto Bayerstrasse. Open Monday through Saturday from 9am to 9pm and on Sunday from 11am to 7pm, it offers a free map of Munich and will also reserve rooms.

CITY LAYOUT

Munich's **Hauptbahnhof** lies just west of the town center and opens onto Bahnhofplatz. From the square you can take Schützenstrasse to one of the major centers of Munich, **Karlsplatz** (nicknamed

Munich Orientation

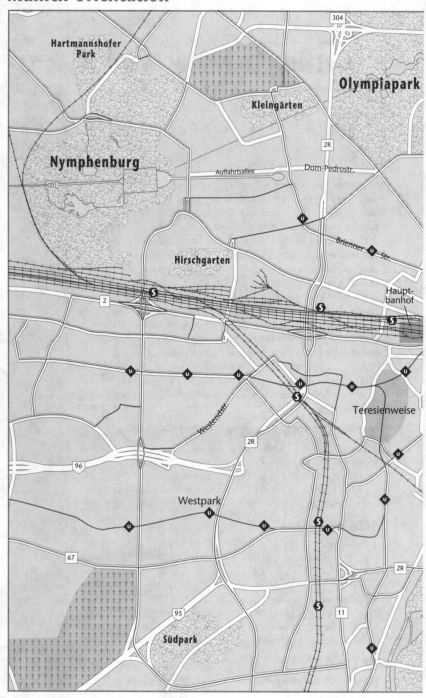

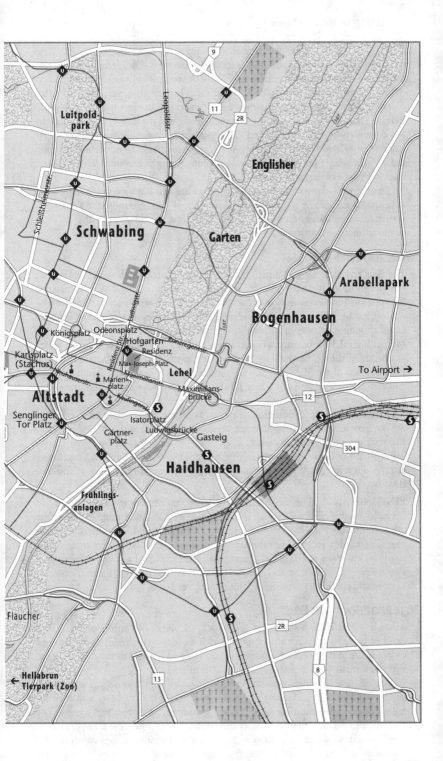

Stachus). Many tram lines converge on this square. From Karlsplatz, you can continue east along the pedestrians-only Neuhauserstrasse and Kaufingerstrasse until you reach Marienplatz, where you'll be deep in the **Altstadt** (old town) of Munich.

From **Marienplatz,** with its daily glockenspiel performance, you can head north on Dienerstrasse, which will lead you to Residenzstrasse and finally to **Max-Joseph-Platz,** a landmark square, with the Nationaltheater and the former royal palace, the Residenz. Between Marienplatz and the Nationaltheater is the **Platzl** quarter, where you'll want to head for nighttime diversions, as it's the seat of some of the finest (and some of the worst) restaurants in Munich, along with the landmark Hofbräuhaus, the most famous beer hall in Europe.

North of the old town is **Schwabing,** a former bohemian section whose main street is Leopoldstrasse. The large, sprawling municipal park grounds, the Englischer Garten, are found due east of Schwabing. Northeast of Schwabing is the Olympic complex (more about that later).

MAIN ARTERIES & STREETS

The best known street in Munich is the **Maximilianstrasse,** the most fashionable shopping and restaurant avenue, containing the prestigious Hotel Vier Jahreszeiten Kempinski München. It is one of the city's busiest east–west arteries. Other major east–west thoroughfares include **Kaufingerstrasse** and **Neuhauserstrasse.** Both are major shopping avenues in the core of the pedestrian zone in Old Town. Two of Munich's great 19th-century avenues, **Ludwigstrasse** and **Brienner Strasse,** stretch toward the district of Schwabing. Brienner Strasse was originally planned as part of the expansion of the Maxvorstadt. Ludwigstrasse, which was designed to display the greatness of the kingdom of Ludwig I, is bordered on both sides by impressive neoclassical and neo-Romanesque buildings.

Odeonsplatz, on the southern end of Ludwigstrasse, was established to celebrate the Bavarian kingdom. **Leopoldstrasse** begins on the northern side of Ludwigstrasse and continues through Schwabing. The last of the 19th-century boulevards to be constructed was **Prinzregentstrasse,** lying between Prinz-Carl-Palais and Vogelweideplatz. Along the Prinzregentstrasse at no. 7 is the residence of the prime minister of Bavaria.

FINDING AN ADDRESS/MAPS   Locating an address is relatively easy in Munich, as even numbers run up one side of a street and odd numbers down the other. In the Altstadt, "hidden" squares may make it a little difficult; therefore, you'll need a detailed street map, not the more general maps handed out free by the tourist office and many hotels. The best maps are published by Falk, and they're available at nearly all bookstores and at many newsstands. These pocket-size maps are easy to carry and contain a detailed street index at the end.

NEIGHBORHOODS IN BRIEF

Altstadt   This is the historic part of Munich, the site of the medieval city. Three gates remain to indicate the original town borders: the Sendlinger Tor and Odeonsplatz to the north and south, the Isar Tor and Karlstor to the east and west. You can virtually walk across the district in 15 minutes.

The hub is Marienplatz, with its Rathaus (town hall), the town's primary square. In the Middle Ages, Marienplatz was the scene of many jousts and tournaments. Today it is brimming with mimes, musicians, and street performers. The square is also the site of many festivals and political rallies and is the traditional stopping and starting place for parades and processions. Included in the Alstadt district is the Fussgänger (pedestrian) Zone, home to many of Munich's department stores and elegant shops. Here Müncheners may wander at leisure without dodging busy city traffic.

Gasteig This is the city's primary cultural, educational, and conference center. This modern building in the Haidhausen district houses the city library and the Munich Philharmonic Orchestra. Its various theaters and lecture halls play host to a variety of events, principally musical and theatrical performances.

Lehel This district, just east of Old Town, is part of the original planned expansion of the city that occurred in the latter years of the 19th century. The area is mainly residential and is noted for its fine neo-Renaissance architecture.

Ludwigstrasse One of Munich's great monumental avenues, it was originally designed for King Ludwig I as a street worthy of his kingdom. The buildings in the southern section of the street adhere to a strict neoclassical style, whereas the architecture in the northern sector is neo-Romanesque. The overall effect is that of uniformity.

Maxmilianstrasse The equivalent of New York's Fifth Avenue, Maxmilianstrasse is Munich's Golden Mile. Planned as a showcase for the king's dominion, it has architecture in what is known as Maximilianic style, an eclectic combination of styles, with an emphasis on Gothic. Here you find the city's most elegant and expensive boutiques, restaurants, and hotels. Visitors can browse through stores like Armani, Hermès, and Bulgari. Along with numerous chic hotels and restaurants, the street is also home to the Museum of Ethnology and the overpowering monument to the king, the Maxmonument. The street is the primary connector from Old Town to the suburbs of Lehel and Haidhausen.

Olympiapark This residential and recreational area was the site of the 1972 Olympics, which is remembered for the terrorist attack against the Israeli athletes. Located northwest of the city center, this enormous development is practically a city unto itself. It has its own post office, railway station, elementary school, and even its own mayor. On weekends it hosts rock and pop concerts, and its many auditoriums and stadiums are now venues for performances and events of all kinds. The enormous television tower houses a restaurant and the top level affords the finest views in Munich.

Nymphenburg Located just northwest of the city center, this district is home to the Nymphenburg Palace and Park. Built in 1664, the baroque palace was the original home of the Wittlesbach rulers. The palace is also home to the Nymphenburg porcelain museum and factory. Adjoining the palace is a vast expanse of lakes and gardens. The original plan in 1671 for a small Italian garden has been greatly augmented over the years.

Schwabing Located in the northern sector of the city, this area was once the center of bohemian life in Munich, much like New York's Greenwich Village, and much like Greenwich Village, it has gentrified into a locale for lawyers, producers, and other professionals, and a hangout for university students. At the turn of the century, it soared to popularity as the artists' quarter, where the city's leading artists, actors, poets, musicians, and writers lived or gathered. Many famous literary figures have called Schwabing home, including Thomas Mann. The area houses the city's finest examples of art-nouveau architecture.

Arabellapark This is the city's commercial and industrial quarter. Located just northeast of the city center, this ultramodern region is home to several large international companies. The glass and concrete buildings offer little architectural beauty, but have become an outstanding feature of Munich's skyline.

Bogenhausen   Located just northeast of the city center, near Arabellapark, lies the Bogenhausen district. Like Schwabing, the area has many excellent examples of art-nouveau architecture. Once the preferred neighborhood by the prosperous citizens of Munich, the district is now the center of numerous galleries, boutiques, and restaurants.

Brienner Strasse   Designed as part of the development of the Maxvostadt during the reign of Maximilian I, this street was home to the aristocratic families and wealthy citizens of Munich. Today it is the location of many galleries and luxury shops.

Maxvorstadt   Launched as a planned expansion of the city by Maximilian I, today the area draws its character from the many facilities of the University of Munich. The area is teeming with student bars, book shops, and galleries.

Westpark   This 178-acre park, laid out for the fourth International Garden Show, is full of extensive lawns, playgrounds, and ponds. The park is complete with two beer gardens, several cafés, and a lakeside theater that hosts outdoor concerts during the summer months. Also located in the park is the Rudi Sedlmayer Sports Hall, one of Munich's premier venues for large rock concerts.

2 Getting Around

BY PUBLIC TRANSPORTATION

The city's rapid-transit system is preferable to streetcars and certainly to high-priced taxis. The underground network contains many convenient electronic devices, and the rides are relatively noise-free. The same ticket entitles you to ride the **U-Bahn** and the **S-Bahn,** as well as **trams** (streetcars) and **buses**. The U-Bahn, or Untergrundbahn, is the line you will use most frequently; the S-Bahn, or Stadtbahn, services suburban locations.

At the transport hub, Marienplatz, U-Bahn and S-Bahn rails crisscross each other. It's possible to use your Eurailpass on S-Bahn journeys, as it's a state-owned railway. Otherwise, you must purchase a single-trip ticket or a strip ticket for several journeys at one of the blue vending machines positioned at the entryways to the underground stations. These tickets entitle you to ride both the S and U lines, and they're also good for rides on trams and buses. If you're making only one trip, a **single ticket** will average 3 DM ($2.10), although it can reach as high as 16 DM ($11.20) to an outlying area.

Costing less per ride is the **strip ticket,** called *Streifenkarte* in German. It's good for several rides and sells for 13 DM ($9.10). A short ride requires only one strip. A **day ticket** for 8 DM ($5.60), called *Tageskarte,* is also a good investment if you plan to stay within the city limits. If you'd like to branch out to Greater Munich (that is, within a 50-mile radius), you can purchase a day card for 16 DM ($11.20). A trip within the metropolitan area costs you two strips, which are valid for two hours. In that time, you may interrupt your trip and transfer as you like, traveling in one continuous direction. When you reverse your direction, you must cancel two strips again. Children 4 to 14 use the red *Kinderstreifenkarte,* costing 8.50 DM ($5.95) for eight strips; for a trip within the metropolitan area, they cancel only one strip. Children above the age of 15 pay adult fares. For **public transport information,** dial 089/23-80-30. For S-Bahn information dial 089/55-75-75.

Where the U-Bahn comes to an end, buses and trams take over; you can transfer as many times as you need to reach your destination, using the same ticket.

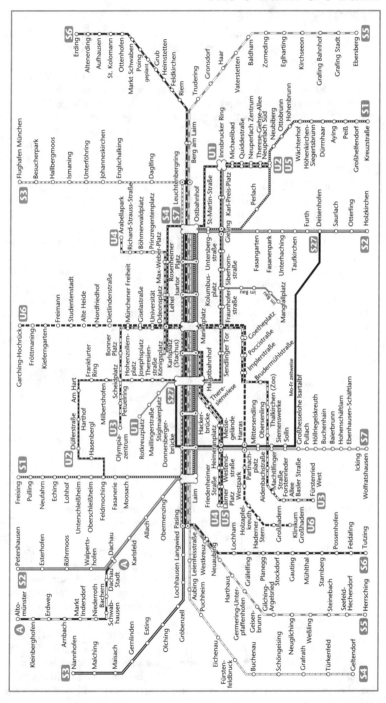

ON FOOT & BY BICYCLE

Of course, the best way to explore Munich is on foot, since it has a vast pedestrian zone in the center. Many of its attractions can, in fact, be reached only on foot. Pick up a good map and set out.

The tourist office also sells a pamphlet called *Radl-Touren für unsere Gäste,* costing only .50 DM (35¢). It outlines itineraries for touring Munich by bicycle.

One of the most convenient places to rent a bike is **Lenbach & Pöge,** Hans-Sachs-Strasse 7 (☎ 089/26-65-06), near the U-Bahn station at Frauen-hoferstrasse. It's open Monday through Friday from 9am to 1pm and 2 to 6:30pm, and on Saturday from 9am to 1pm. Charges are 18 DM ($12.60) for a full day.

BY CAR

Competition in the European car-rental industry is almost as fierce as in the transatlantic airline industry. All the big U.S. car-rental companies, including Avis, Budget, and Hertz, are represented in Germany. You can make reservations and do comparison shopping by calling their toll-free numbers in the United States: **Avis** (☎ 800/331-2112), **Budget** (☎ 800/472-3325), and **Hertz** (☎ 800/654-3001).

You can rent cars in the city center as well. Companies include **Avis,** Nymphenburger Strasse 61 (☎ **089/1260-0020**), and **Sixt/Budget Autovermietung,** Seitzstrasse 9–11 (☎ **089/22-33-33**). It's wise to call a number of agencies as prices can vary widely. Rental companies are found under *Autovermietung* in the yellow pages of the Munich phone book. Rental rates may vary by company and type of car. For instance, Avis rents cars ranging from an Opel to a BMW for 119 DM–399 DM ($83.30–$279.30) daily, and Budget rents daily for 69 DM–359 DM ($48.30–$251.30) for a range of cars spanning from an Opel to a Mercedes. Cars at most major rental companies can usually be rented at one Germany city and returned at another for no additional charge.

An understanding of insurance and its many legal and financial implications is all-important during your initial paperwork. A collision-damage waiver (CDW) is an optional insurance policy that can be purchased when you sign a rental agreement. For an extra fee, the rental agency agrees to eliminate all but a small percentage of your financial responsibility for liability and collision damage in case of an accident. If you don't have a CDW and do have an accident, you'll usually pay for all damages, up to the cost of actually replacing the vehicle if the accident is serious enough.

Certain credit- and charge-card companies, usually including American Express and Diners Club, agree to reimburse card users for the deductible in the event of an accident. Because of that, many renters have chosen to waive the cost of the extra CDW. However, although the card issuers will usually (several weeks after the accident) reimburse the renter for the cost of damages, payments have sometimes been delayed with such coverage until after the completion of certain documents. Unless there's enough of a credit line associated with your particular credit or charge card, some car renters involved in an accident will be required to pay cash on the spot (sometimes a large sum).

To avoid misunderstandings, the large car-rental companies offer clients the option of either automatically including the CDW as part of the rental price or forgoing it completely in favor of the insurance that sometimes applies automatically through your credit- or charge-card company. Although this confusion has sometimes resulted in "double coverage," it has nonetheless prevented hundreds of renters from having to shell out cash while waiting for reimbursement.

Regardless of the insurance-related options you select, all three of the companies maintain competitive rates that tend to be more attractive if you reserve your car from North America between one day and two weeks in advance of your departure. Currently, the most spectacular bargain is offered by Hertz, where a promotional rental of a small but peppy Ford Fiesta, with manual transmission, rents for only $100 a week, plus payment of 15% government tax and—when applicable—a one-time airport pickup surcharge of $9. Equivalent cars at Avis and Budget rent for $150 and $101 respectively, plus tax and airport surcharges. Promotional rates offered by car-rental corporations should be researched to ensure the best value.

Be alert that cars with automatic transmission, which is viewed as a luxury in Europe, cost more ($100 or more) than cars without it. Budget's least expensive car with an automatic (a Ford Escort or VW Golf) rents for $230 per week, plus tax, airport surcharge ($9), and (the optional) CDW ($24). Although all three of the above-mentioned companies allowed dropoffs within Germany at no extra charge, Budget offers the most reasonable rates for dropoffs outside of Germany. For example, if you pick up your car in Munich but request permission to return the car in, say, Paris, it will cost you a supplemental fee of only $99 at Budget, as opposed to around $112 at Avis, and $210 at Hertz.

Some passengers prefer the convenience of prepaying their rental in dollars before leaving the United States. In such circumstances, an easy-to-understand net price (which includes the CDW, all taxes, airport surcharges, and—in some cases—additional personal accident insurance) is quoted and prepaid at least 14 days before departure by credit or charge card. The main benefit to those who opt for this is a somewhat more streamlined rental process, a price structure that is easier to understand, and an ability to avoid unpleasant surprises caused by sudden unfavorable changes in currency exchange rates. Remember, however, that if you opt to prepay, and if your plans change, you'll have to go through some rather complicated paperwork (and in some cases, the payment of a penalty of around $25) for changes or cancellation of any of these prepaid contracts.

Don't overlook the possibility of renting any of Germany's sleekly styled sports cars or luxury sedans. All three of the companies inventory these cars in abundance, usually at correspondingly elaborate prices.

Because of heavy traffic, don't attempt to see Munich by car. If you're driving into Munich, call your hotel and ask if parking is available on site. Hotel recommendations (see "Accommodations," in Chapter 4) indicate if parking is available at the hotel. Otherwise, drive to your hotel, unload your luggage, and ask one of the staff to direct you to the nearest parking garage. Charges tend to be high in most of these garages, often 20 to 30 DM ($13.20 to $19.80) per night.

DRIVING RULES   In Germany, you drive on the right. Easy-to-understand international road signs are posted throughout Germany. Road signs are in kilometers, not miles. In congested areas the speed limit is about 50 kmph, or around 30 mph. On all other roads except the Autobahns the speed limit is 100 kmph, or about 60 mph. In theory, there is no speed limit on the Autobahns (in the left, fast lane), but many drivers reportedly going too fast have written that they have been stopped by the police and fined on the spot. So reasonable precaution is recommended here, for safety if not other reasons. A German driver on the Autobahn can be a ferocious creature, and you may prefer the slow lane. The government nevertheless recommends an Autobahn speed limit of 130 kmph, or 80 mph. Both front-seat and back-seat passengers are required to wear safety belts.

Note: Drinking and driving is a very serious offense in Germany. Therefore, be sure to keep any alcoholic beverages in the trunk or some other storage area. Avoid even the appearance of drinking alcohol while driving.

BREAKDOWNS/ASSISTANCE   There are two major automobile clubs in Germany: the **DTC** (**Deutscher Touring Automobile Club**), Amalienburgstrasse 23, D-81247 Munich 60 (☎ **089/891-133-0**), and AvD (**Automobilclub von Deutschland**), Lyoner Strasse 16, D-60329 Frankfurt (☎ **069/66-060**). If you don't belong to an auto club and have a breakdown, call from an emergency phone on the Autobahn. These are spaced about a mile apart. On secondary roads, go to the nearest phone and call **01309/09-911.** In English, ask for "road service assistance." Emergency assistance is free, but you pay for parts or materials.

MAPS   The best driving maps, available at all major bookstores throughout Germany, are published by Michelin, which offers various regional maps. Other good maps for those who plan to do extensive touring are published by Hallweg.

DRIVER'S LICENSES   If you or your car is from an EU country, all you need is a domestic license and proof of insurance. Otherwise, an international driver's license is required.

For an international driver's license, apply at a branch of the **American Automobile Association** (**AAA**). You must be at least 18 years old and have two 2-by-2-inch photographs, a $10 fee, and a photocopy of your U.S. driver's license with an AAA application form. AAA's nearest office will probably be listed in the local telephone directory, or you can contact AAA's national headquarters at 1000 AAA Dr., Heathrow, FL 32746-5063 (☎ **407/444-4300**). Remember that an international driver's license is valid only if physically accompanied by your original driver's license. In Canada, you can get the address of the **Canadian Automobile Club** closest to you by calling its national office at ☎ **613/226-7631.**

Both in Germany and throughout the rest of Europe, you must have an international insurance certificate, known as a green card (*carte verte*) to legally drive a car. Any car-rental agency will automatically provide one of these as a standard part of the rental contract, but it's a good idea to double-check the documents the counter attendant gives you at the time of rental just to be sure that you can identify it if asked by a border patrol or the police.

BY TAXI

Cabs are relatively expensive—the average ride costs 8 DM–12 DM ($5.60–$8.40). In an emergency, call ☎ **089/21-611.**

FAST FACTS: Munich

American Express   Your lifeline back to the States might be American Express, Promenadeplatz 6 (☎ **089/29-09-00**), which is open for mail pickup and check cashing Monday through Friday from 9am to 5:30pm and on Saturday from 9:30am to noon. Unless you have an American Express card or traveler's checks, you'll be charged 2 DM ($1.40) for picking up your mail.

Area Code   The telephone area code for Munich is 089.

Bookstores   Try Anglia English Bookshop, Schellingstrasse 3 (☎ **089/28-36-42**), in the Schwabing district, which sells English-language titles and travel books. It's open Monday through Friday from 9am to 6:30pm and on Saturday from 10am to 1:30pm.

Business Hours Most **banks** are open Monday through Friday from 8:30am to 12:30pm and 1:30 to 3:30pm (many banks stay open until 5:30pm on Thursday). Most **businesses** and **stores** are open Monday through Friday from 9am to 6pm and on Saturday from 9am to 2pm. On *langer Samstag* (the first Saturday of the month) stores remain open until 6pm. Many stores in Munich observe a late closing on Thursday, usually 8 or 9pm.

Car Rentals See "Getting Around" earlier in this chapter.

Climate See "When to Go" in Chapter 2.

Consulates See "Embassies and Consulates" below.

Currency See "Money" in Chapter 2.

Currency Exchange You can get a better rate at a bank than at your hotel. American Express traveler's checks are best cashed at the local American Express office (see above). On Saturday and Sunday, or at night, you can exchange money at the Hauptbahnhof exchange, Bahnhofplatz, which is open daily from 6am to 11:30pm.

Dentists For an English-speaking dentist, go to Universitäts-Kieferklinik, Lindwurmstrasse 2A (☎ 089/5160-2911), the dental clinic for the university. It deals with emergency cases and is always open.

Doctors The American, British, and Canadian consulates keep a list of recommended English-speaking physicians.

Driving Rules See "Getting Around" earlier in this chapter.

Drugstores See "Pharmacies" below.

Electricity In most places the electricity is 220 volts AC, 50 cycles. Therefore, a transformer will be needed for your U.S. appliances. Many leading hotels will supply one.

Embassies and Consulates Offices representing various foreign governments are located in Munich. A **United States** Consulate is at Königstrasse 5, D-80539 München (☎ 089/28-880). A Consulate General Office for the **United Kingdom** is located at Burkleinstrasse 10, D-80538 (☎ 089/21-10-90). **Canada** maintains a consulate at Tal 29, D-80331 (☎ 089/29-06-50). The **Australian** government does not maintain an office in Munich, but if you should need assistance, contact their consulate in Berlin at Uhlandstrasse 181–183 D-10623 (☎ 030/880-08-80). The embassy of **New Zealand** is at Bundeskanzlerplatz 2–10, D-53113 Bonn (☎ 0228/22-80-70).

Emergencies For emergency medical aid, phone **089/55-77-55.** Call the police at **089/110.**

Eyeglasses German optics are among the most precise in the world, and dozens of opticians in central Munich quickly prepare new eyeglasses or contact lenses. Hertie Department Store, Bahnhofplatz 7 (☎ 089/55-120), has a department selling both eyeglasses and cameras. A different selection of frames and contact lenses is available from Söhnges Optik, Kaufingerstrasse 34 (☎ 089/29-00-550) and Brienner Strasse 7 (☎ 089/29-07-100).

Holidays See "When to Go" in Chapter 2.

Hospitals Munich has many hospitals. Americans, British, and Canadians can contact their consulates for a recommendation of a particular hospital. For emergency medical service, call **089/55-77-55.**

Language Many Germans speak English. English is usually spoken at major hotels and restaurants and in the principal tourist areas. A good phrase book to carry with you is the *Berlitz German for Travellers,* available in most big bookstores in the United States.

Liquor Laws   As in many European countries, the application of drinking laws is flexible. Laws are enforced only if a problem develops or if decorum is broken. Officially, someone must be 18 to consume any kind of alcoholic beverage in Germany, although at family gatherings wine or schnapps might be offered to underage imbibers. For a bar or café to request proof of age of a prospective client is very rare. Drinking and driving, however, is treated as a very serious offense.

Lost Property   Go to the local lost-and-found office at Arnulfstrasse 31 (☎ 089/ 12-40-80), open Monday through Friday from 8:30am to noon; on Tuesday it's also open from 2 to 5:30pm. If you should lose an item on the S-Bahn or one of the German trains, then go to the lost-and-found office at Track 25 in the Hauptbahnhof (☎ 089/128-66-64); it's open daily from 6:30am to 3:30pm.

Luggage Storage/Lockers   Facilities are available at the Hauptbahnhof on Bahnhofplatz (☎ 089/1223-5047), which is open daily from 5am to 12:30am.

Mail   To post a letter on the street, look for a mailbox painted yellow. The cost to send an airmail letter to the United States or Canada is 3 DM ($2.10) for the first 5 grams (about a fifth of an ounce) and 2 DM ($1.40) for postcards. To mail a package, go to one of the larger post offices in Munich (see below). All letters to the United Kingdom cost 1 DM (70¢) or .60 DM (40¢) for postcards.

Newspapers/Magazines   The *International Herald Tribune* is the most widely distributed English-language newspaper in the city. You can also find copies of *USA Today* and the European editions of *Time* and *Newsweek.*

Pharmacies   For an international pharmacy where English is spoken, go to International Ludwig's Apotheke, Neuhauserstrasse 11 (☎ 089/26-03-021), in the pedestrian shopping zone. It's open Monday through Friday from 9am to 6:30pm and on Saturday from 9am to 2pm. There's always a pharmacy open 24 hours in every neighborhood. Every *Apotheke* has a sign in its window indicating where to find the nearest one staying open (it changes from night to night).

Police   Throughout the country, dial **110** for emergencies.

Post Office   The Postamt München (main post office) is across from the Hauptbahnhof, at Bahnhofplatz 1 (☎ 089/5454-2732). It's open days and into the night, and you can also make long-distance calls here (far cheaper than at your hotel, where you'll be charged for service). If you want to have your mail sent to you, mark it *Poste Restante* for general delivery (take along your passport to reclaim any mail and go to Counter 8, 9, or 10). Have your mail addressed D-80074 München. The office is open Monday through Friday from 6am to 10pm and on Saturday, Sunday, and holidays from 7am to 10pm.

Radio   The BBC World Service broadcasts to Munich, as does the American Forces Network (AFN), which you can hear on 1107 AM. English news broadcasts are presented frequently on the Bavarian Radio Service (Bayerischer Rundfunk).

Rest Rooms   Use the word *Toilette* (pronounced twa-*leht*-tah). Rest rooms may be labeled WC or H (for *Herren,* men) and F (for *Frauen,* women). In the center of Munich are several public facilities that you should not hesitate to use. You can also patronize the facilities at terminals, restaurants, bars, cafés, department stores, hotels, and pubs.

Safety   Munich, like all big cities of the world, has its share of crime. Major crimes are pickpocketing and purse- and camera-snatching. If necessary, store valuables in a hotel safe. Most robberies occur in the much-frequented tourist areas, such as the areas around the Hauptbahnhof, which can be dangerous at night, and the Marienplatz, where tourists gather. Many tourists lose their valuables when they carelessly leave clothing unprotected as they join the nude sunbathers in the Englischer Garten.

Taxes   As a member of the European Union, the Federal Republic of Germany imposes a tax on most goods and services known as a **value-added tax** (VAT), or in German, *Mehrwertsteuer.* Nearly everything is taxed at 15%. That includes vital necessities such as gas and luxury items such as jewelry. Note that the goods for sale, such as German cameras, have the 15% tax already factored into the price; whereas services, such as paying a garage mechanic to fix your car, will have the 15% added to the bill. Stores that display a "Tax Free" sticker work with the **Tax Free Shopping Service.** They will issue you a Tax Free Shopping Check at the time of purchase. When leaving the country before you check your baggage (Customs will want to examine what you purchased), have your check stamped by the German Customs Service as your proof of legal export. You may then be able to obtain a cash refund at one of the Tax Free Shopping Service offices in the major airports and many train stations, even at some of the bigger ferry terminals. Otherwise, you must send the checks to Tax Free Shopping Service, Mengstrasse 19, D-23552 Lübeck, Germany. If you want the payment to be credited to your bank card or your bank account, mention this.

Taxis   See "Getting Around" earlier in this chapter.

Telephone/Telex/Fax   Local and long-distance calls may be placed from all post offices and coin-operated public telephone booths. The unit charge is 0.30 DM or three 10-pfennig coins. More than half the phones in Germany require an advance-payment telephone card from Telekom, the German telephone company. Phone cards are sold at post offices and newsstands, costing 12 DM ($8.40) and 50 DM ($35). The 12-DM card offers about 40 minutes and the 50-DM card is useful for long-distance calls. Rates are measured in units rather than minutes. The farther the distance, the more units are consumed. For example, a three-minute call to the United States costs 41 units. All towns and cities in Germany may be dialed directly by using the prefix listed in the telephone directory above each local heading. Telephone calls made through hotel switchboards can double, triple, or even quadruple the charge. Therefore, try to make your calls outside your hotel at a post office where you can also send telexes and faxes. Credit cards are generally not accepted, but some of the international hotels accept the AT&T calling card. USA Direct can be used with all telephone cards and for collect calls. The number from Germany is **01-30-00-10.** Canada Direct can be used with the Bell Telephone card and for collect calls. This number from Germany is **01-30-00-14.** Telephone calls to Germany from the U.S. and Canada can be made by dialing **0-11-49.**

Television   There are two national TV channels, ARD (Channel 1) and ZDF (Channel 2). Sometimes these stations show films in the original language (most often English). The more expensive hotels often have cable TV, with such programs as CNN.

Time Zone   Germany operates on central European time (CET), which places it six hours ahead of eastern time (ET) in the United States and one hour ahead of Greenwich mean time. Summertime in Germany begins in April and ends in September—there's a slight difference in the dates from year to year—so there may be a period in early spring and in the fall when there's a seven-hour difference between U.S. ET and CET. Always check if you're traveling at these periods, especially if you need to catch a plane.

Tipping   If a restaurant bill says *Bedienung,* that means a service charge has already been added, so just round up to the nearest mark. If not, add 10% to 15%. Round up to the nearest mark for taxis. Bellhops get 2 DM ($1.40) per bag, as does the doorman at your hotel, restaurant, or nightclub. Room-cleaning staffs get small tips in Germany, but tip concierges well who perform some special favor such as obtaining hard-to-get theater or opera tickets. Tip hairdressers or barbers 5% to 10%.

Water   Tap water is safe to drink in Munich.

Accommodations 4

Finding a room in Munich is comparatively easy, but tabs tend to be high. Bargains are few and hard to find—but they exist.

If you arrive without a reservation, go to the **Munich Tourist Information Office** on Platform 12 at the Hauptbahnhof (☎ **089/2333-0256**), where general information is also available; it's open daily from 8am to 10pm. There, Bavarian personnel (most speak English), with some 34,000 listings in their files, will come to your rescue. Tell them what you can afford, pay a fee, and get a receipt— as well as a map with instructions on how to reach the accommodation that they've booked for you. You pay a fee of 5 DM ($3.50) per room. Keep your receipt. If you don't like the room, go back to the tourist office and they'll try to find you another lodging at no extra charge. Correspondence, however, should be addressed to Landeshauptstadt München, Fremdenverkehrsamt, D-80313 München. These offices are open Monday through Friday from 9am to 3pm.

Advance Reservations Citi Incoming, Mullerstrasse 11 (Postfach 140163), D-80451 München (☎ **089/260-69-14;** fax 089/260-6484), is the best place in Munich if you'd like to book hotel rooms in whatever price range you desire, and also arrange for Avis rental cars and Grey Line sightseeing tours. The service is free to the traveler and, although this company works with hotels on a commission basis, it guarantees that travelers never pay more than if they had made the bookings themselves. In some cases, Citi Incoming can even get you a better rate than off-the-street bookings because hotels make special offers to travel agencies. Guaranteed bookings can easily be made by phone or fax. The company provides this service not only for Munich but also for other areas of Germany as well, even for neighboring countries such as Austria and Switzerland. They'll even provide you with road maps. Both long-term bookings and last-minute requests are handled. There are no fixed open hours; prospective clients can call or fax at any time. If no one is in the office, an answering machine takes requests.

All hotels raise their prices for Oktoberfest and various trade fairs. Some hotels announce their tariffs in advance (see below); others prefer to wait until the last minute to see what the market will bear.

1 Best Bets

- **Best Historic Hotel: Kempinski Hotel Vier Jahreszeiten München** (☎ **800/ 426-3135** in the U.S., or 089/221-50) is one of the most famous hotels in the world—the lineage of this hostelry stretches back to 1858. Maximilian II himself took a personal interest in the hotel's establishment, even going so far as to aid its founder financially. The Walterspiel family brought it to worldwide prominence, and over the years it's entertained the greats and near-greats.

- **Best for Business Travelers: München Park Hilton** is a modern 15-story structure, completely geared to welcome the business traveler, and providing all needed services. It is close to many corporate headquarters, and has the best conference facilities of any hotel in the city. Actually the hotel was once an office block until pressed into service as a hotel for the 1972 Olympics. After business is concluded you can unwind at the hotel's health club.

- **Best for a Romantic Getaway: Romantik Hotel Insel Mühle,** constructed around a 16th-century mill, is a romantic choice with its antique decor and its rooms with sloping garretlike ceilings. It also has an old-world restaurant with massive beams and a wine cellar. Though far removed from the hustle and bustle, it's only 6 miles west of Munich's Marienplatz.

- **Best Trendy Hotel: Rafael,** small and deluxe, in a neo-Renaissance building, this hotel dates only from 1990 but has quickly established itself as a choice of visiting celebrities, including fashion models, dress designers, and the media elite. Its discreet style and formal elegance make it the right address for those who don't want to be "too obvious"—that is, by staying at one of the lavish, bigger hotels.

- **Best Lobby for Pretending You're Rich: Bayerischer Hof & Palais Montgelas** (☎ **800/223-6800** in the U.S., or 089/2-12-00; fax 089/21-20-906) is a real old-fashioned European formal hotel with a deluxe lobby filled with English and French furniture and Oriental rugs. It's been called the "living room" of Munich. "Meet you in the lounge of the Bayerischer Hof" is often heard. As hotels go, there's no more impressive lobby in which to have a drink.

- **Best for Families: Arabella Olympiapark Hotel München** is right at Europe's biggest sports and recreation center, and rents many triple rooms that are ideal for families. It's among the most modern and best-kept places in the city, and your kid will enjoy meeting some of the sports heroes who often stay here. At Olympiapark the entire family can use the sports facilities, including a large Olympic-size swimming pool.

- **Best Moderately Priced Hotel: Splendid,** an old-world hotel, is graced with antiques, Oriental rugs, and chandeliers, and many rooms are decorated in a style known as "Bavarian baroque" and evoke the aura of a country home. Not all accommodations in this little hotel have private baths, so if you opt for sharing a bathroom, the price becomes budget level.

- **Best Budget Hotel: Pension beim Haus der Kunst** is one of Munich's better pensions. Ideally located near the Englischer Garten, it has decent and comfortable rooms with shared baths. Its low cost, along with warm hospitality and copius breakfasts, make this little entry a winning choice among those who are watching their deutsche marks.

- **Best B&B: Gästehaus Englischer Garten,** close to the Englischer Garten and its summer nudes, is an oasis of charm and tranquility in fashionable Schwabing. An ivy-covered former private villa, it offers attractively furnished rooms; those in the annex are really small apartments with tiny kitchenettes. When the weather's right, breakfast is served in the rear garden.

- **Best Service: Eden-Hotel-Wolff** employs one of the most thoughtful staffs in Munich. Although such hotels as the Bayerischer Hof offer state-of-the-art service, the attentive, efficient, unhurried yet down-to-earth English-speaking staff here gets the job done—and well, anticipating all your needs.
- **Best Location: An der Oper** is in the virtual heart of Munich. You're just steps away from the central core, the Marienplatz. Moments after leaving the hotel you can be shopping along the Maximilianstrasse or exploring the traffic-free malls just steps from the Bavarian National Theater, and all for a reasonable price.
- **Best Health Club: München Marriott Hotel** has the finest fitness center of any hotel in Munich. In the hotel's cellar, it contains a swimming pool almost 45 feet long, whirlpools, hydrojets, a solarium, and state-of-the-art exercise equipment. There's also a *Kosmetik-Kabine* for beauty treatments and massages, plus separate saunas for men and women. Residents of the Marriott use the club for free; nonresidents pay 30 DM ($21) for a day pass.
- **Best Hotel Pool: Arabella Hotel Bogenhausen**'s state-of-the-art indoor pool is on the 22nd floor, offering not only views but its own waterfall. Although many hotels in Munich have swimming pools, none competes with this choice, in the verdant suburb of Bogenhausen only seven subway stops from the center of town. That's not all—you get five whirlpools, along with saunas and a trio of steamrooms inspired by ancient Rome, each ideal for après-swim.
- **Best Views: Holiday Inn Crowne Plaza Munich,** near the Olympic Stadium on the northern perimeter of Schwabing, has not only the best view of Munich, but the added treat of a view of the distant Bavarian Alps. The hotel was constructed with two eight-story towers to house guests for the 1972 Olympics; for the view, ask for a room on an upper floor, facing south.

2 In Central Munich

VERY EXPENSIVE

✪ Bayerischer Hof & Palais Montgelas

Promenadeplatz 2–6, D-80333 München. ☎ **800/223-68-00** in the U.S., or 089/21-200. Fax 089/21-20-906. 440 rms, 45 suites. MINIBAR TV TEL. 430 DM–510 DM ($301–$357) double; from 730 DM–1,950 DM ($511–$1,365) suite. Rates include buffet breakfast. AE, DC, MC, V. Parking 28 DM ($19.60). Tram: 19.

A Bavarian version of New York's Waldorf-Astoria, the Bayerischer Hof & Palais Montgelas is in a swank location, opening onto a little tree-filled square. After zillions of marks were spent on it, it is now better than ever, a rival even of the frontranking Kempinski Hotel Vier Jahreszeiten München. The tastefully decorated central lounge is known as the meeting place of Munich (see "Best Bets" above). Integrating the sumptuously decorated Palais Montgelas into the hotel brought deluxe suites and double rooms, as well as a number of conference and banqueting rooms. Only 80 of the guest rooms are air-conditioned.

Dining/Entertainment: The major dining room, the Garden-Restaurant, evokes the grandeur of a small palace, with an ornate ceiling and crystal chandeliers. Generous drinks and charcoal specialties from the rôtisserie are served in the clublike bar, where the tables are lit by candles and the reflected glow from octagonally paned stained-glass windows. There's also the Kleine Komödie Theater, a Trader Vic's, and the best nightclub in Munich, recommended separately.

Services: Room service, laundry, baby-sitting.

Facilities: Rooftop pool and garden with bricked sun terrace, sauna, massage rooms.

Central Munich Accommodations

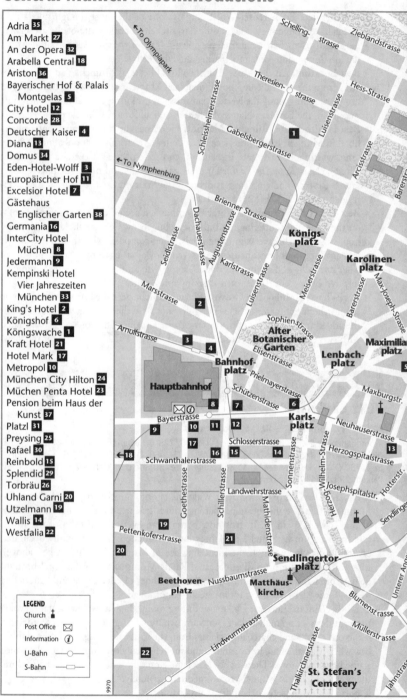

Adria 35
Am Markt 27
An der Opera 32
Arabella Central 18
Ariston 36
Bayerischer Hof & Palais
  Montgelas 5
City Hotel 12
Concorde 28
Deutscher Kaiser 4
Diana 13
Domus 34
Eden-Hotel-Wolff 3
Europäischer Hof 11
Excelsior Hotel 7
Gästehaus
  Englischer Garten 38
Germania 16
InterCity Hotel
  Müchen 8
Jedermann 9
Kempinski Hotel
  Vier Jahreszeiten
  München 33
King's Hotel 2
Königshof 6
Königswache 1
Kraft Hotel 21
Hotel Mark 17
Metropol 10
München City Hilton 24
Müchen Penta Hotel 23
Pension beim Haus der
  Kunst 37
Platzl 31
Preysing 25
Rafael 30
Reinbold 15
Splendid 29
Torbräu 26
Uhland Garni 20
Utzelmann 19
Wallis 14
Westfalia 22

LEGEND
Church ✝
Post Office ✉
Information ⓘ
U-Bahn ──○──
S-Bahn ──□──

9970

68

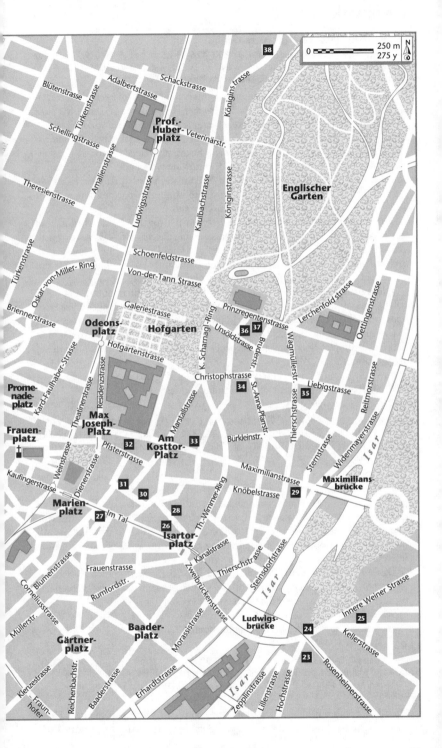

69

○ Kempinski Hotel Vier Jahreszeiten München

Maximillianstrasse 17, D-80539 München. ☎ **800/426-31-35** in the U.S., or 089/221-50. Fax 089/212-52-000. 316 rms, 48 suites. A/C MINIBAR TV TEL. 480 DM–780 DM ($336–$546) double; from 950 DM ($665) suite. AE, DC, MC, V. Parking 30 DM ($21). Tram: 19.

The most elegant place to stay in Munich is this grand hotel with a tradition stretching back to 1858. Rivaled only by the Bayerischer Hof, it is one of Germany's most famous and distinctive hostelries—actually among the finest in the world. For a fine old-world experience, you can do no better. Maximilian II took a personal interest in the establishment of the original hotel and financially helped the founder, restaurateur August Schimon. The hotel gained worldwide fame under the ownership of the Walterspiel family, who still owned it when it was mostly destroyed in a 1944 air raid. They rebuilt the hotel and returned it to its number-one position, selling it in 1970 to its present proprietors, Kempinski Hotels.

The guest rooms and suites, which have hosted royalty, heads of state, and famed personalities from all over the world, combine the charm of days gone by with modern amenities. The windows opening onto Maximilianstrasse are double glazed, and quiet is assured in the units facing the three inner courts. The hotel is not connected to other Vier Jahreszeiten hotels found throughout Germany.

Dining/Entertainment: Vier Jahreszeiten Restaurant, its finest dining spot (open daily), is recommended separately. The Four Seasons is under a magnificent glass roof above the lobby. Guests like to linger in the Jahreszeiten Bar, where piano music is played nightly during the cocktail hour, with an international trio performing until 2am. The completely refurnished Bistro Eck surprises guests with its modern yet classical atmosphere.

Services: Room service, laundry facilities, baby-sitting, massages.

Facilities: Indoor pool and sauna, solarium, sun terrace.

Königshof

Karlsplatz 25, D-80335 München. ☎ **800/44-UTELL** in the U.S., or 089/55-13-60. Fax 089/55-13-61-13. 103 rms, 9 suites. A/C MINIBAR TV TEL. 370 DM–450 DM ($259–$315) double; 520 DM–995 DM ($364–$696.50) suite. AE, DC, MC, V. Parking 20 DM ($14) in 180-car underground garage. S-Bahn: S3, S7, or S8 to Karlsplatz. Tram: 19.

In the heart of Munich, the lively, personlized Königshof overlooks the famous Stachus (Karlsplatz) and the old part of the city, where it opened in 1862. The proprietors, the Geisel family, maintain its legend. As a mansion hotel it attracts an extremely upmarket clientele, but does not match the Rafael (see below) in this type of premier address. The hotel offers traditional comfort plus up-to-date facilities. All its sleekly styled rooms have soundproofing and picture windows, and there are interesting shopping and sightseeing streets nearby.

Dining/Entertainment: On the second floor is the well-known Restaurant Königshof, serving French and international cuisine. A piano bar provides entertainment. The lobby houses an intimate club bar, the Königshof-Bar.

Services: Room service, laundry, baby-sitting.

Facilities: Car-rental facilities, shopping boutiques.

○ Rafael

Neuturmstrasse 1, D-80331 München. ☎ **089/29-09-80**, or 212/744-4300 in New York City, 0171/431-7916 in London. Fax 089/22-25-39. 74 rms, 20 suites. A/C MINIBAR TV TEL. 490 DM–690 DM ($343–$483) double; 820 DM–2,220 DM ($574–$1,554) suite. AE, DC, MC, V. Parking 30 DM ($21). U-Bahn or S-Bahn: Marienplatz. Tram: 19.

One of Munich's small hotels is also one of its most posh. Only the Kempinski Hotel Vier Jahreszeiten München and the Bayerischer Hof outclass this sophisticated and luxurious winner. A wedge-shaped neo-Renaissance building within sight of the Frauenkirche at Marienplatz, this hotel was inaugurated in 1990 in a marble-fringed format of style and elegance with neoclassical and Biedermeier touches. A marble staircase sweeps upward to the very comfortable guest rooms, each with a richly appointed bathroom and specially crafted furniture or original antiques.

Dining/Entertainment: The culinary showplace is Mark's Restaurant, very intimate, with 75 seats and a piano bar.

Services: Concierge, 24-hour room service, laundry, baby-sitting, valet parking. The service staff is among the most professional in southern Germany.

Facilities: Rooftop pool (May to October) with a view over the historic district, boutiques.

EXPENSIVE

Arabella Westpark-Hotel

Garmischer Strasse 2, D-80339 München. ☎ **089/51-960.** Fax 089/519-6100. 248 rms, 10 suites. MINIBAR TV TEL. 233 DM–295 DM ($163.10–$206.50) double, 340 DM ($238) suite. During Oktoberfest and trade fairs, 285 DM–345 DM ($199.50–$241.50) double, 470 DM ($329) suite. Breakfast 25 DM ($17.50) extra. AE, DC, MC, V. Parking 16 DM ($11.20). U-bahn: U4 or U5 to Heimeran Platz.

A 10-story, four-star member of the conservative Arabella chain, this hotel is more personalized and more intimate and has a bit less drama and flair than the Arabella Hotel Bogenhausen recommended below. The bedrooms were completely renovated in 1996, with new carpets and draperies and a general upgrade of amenities. On the premises is a stylish and impeccably maintained restaurant, Ambiente, and two bars. One of these is an adjunct to the hotel's swimming pool and saunas.

Concorde

Herrnstrasse 38, D-80539 München. ☎ **089/22-45-15.** Fax 089/22-83-282. 71 rms, 4 suites. MINIBAR TV TEL. 235 DM–265 DM ($164.50–$185.50) double Mon–Thurs, 180 DM ($126) Fri–Sun; 220 DM–285 DM ($154–$199.50) suite daily. Rates include buffet breakfast. AE, DC, MC, V. Closed Dec 22–Jan 7. Parking 18 DM ($12.60). U-Bahn: U3 or U6 to Isartor Platz; then a three-minute walk to the hotel.

It's set on a quiet side street, a few minutes' walk from some of the most frequently visited attractions in town. This efficiently managed hotel has six floors, an elevator, and was renovated in 1996. Its desirable location and its proximity to both the British and American consulates draws a large number of diplomats. Each bedroom has a modern, somewhat bland styling, with a large, comfortable bed and angular contemporary furnishings. Although there are no dining or bar facilities on-site, many restaurants are in the neighborhood, and drinks can be served in the lobby on request.

Deutscher Kaiser

Arnulfstrasse 2, D-80335 München. ☎ **089/54-530.** Fax 089/545-32-255. 174 rms. MINIBAR TV TEL. 270 DM ($189) double, including breakfast. AE, DC, MC, V. Parking 21 DM ($14.70). U-Bahn or S-Bahn: Hauptbahnhof.

The hotel caters to a high-turnover roster of European business travelers who appreciate its efficiency, its relative anonymity, and its position across the street from the entrance to Munich's main railway station. Rising 15 stories above the congested neighborhood, it contains comfortable, culturally neutral bedrooms that, on the higher floors, offer views over the Alps and the city's distant outskirts. It is similar to the InterCity Hotel München (which we prefer to this one). There is no restaurant on the premises. However, this is a hotel that, depending on room availability, might be willing to grant a discount if you ask for one.

Eden-Hotel-Wolff

Arnulfstrasse 4–8, D-80335 München. ☎ **089/55-11-50.** Fax 089/551-15-555. 214 rms, 4 suites. MINIBAR TV TEL. 260 DM–450 DM ($182–$315) double; from 370 DM–500 DM ($259–$350) suite. One child up to age 6 stays free in parents' room. Rates include buffet breakfast. AE, DC, MC, V. Parking 19 DM ($13.30). U-Bahn or S-Bahn: Hauptbahnhof.

Opposite the Hauptbahnhof, the stone-clad Eden-Hotel-Wolff misleads with its sedate exterior. The interior is decorated in a richly traditional style, and if you must stay in the railroad station area, this is your best bet. In the main dining room the theme is Bavarian—a natural-pine ceiling, gleaming brass lantern sconces, and thick stone arches—and excellent Bavarian dishes and a savory international cuisine are served. On a cold night, the fireplace makes the bar a snug and cozy retreat. The guest bedrooms are both traditional and modern, with a rather fashionable decor, often with marble-clad baths.

Excelsior Hotel

Schutzenstrasse 11, D-80335 München. ☎ **089/55-13-70.** Fax 089/55-137-121. 113 rms, 4 suites. A/C MINIBAR TV TEL. 295 DM–325 DM ($206.50–$227.50) double; 380 DM–450 DM ($266–$315) suite. AE, DC, MC, V. Parking 16 DM ($11.20). U-bahn: Hauptbahnhof.

This solidly comfortable four-star hotel near the city's main railway station prides itself on its restored facade, a pale gray exterior that replicates its original design from 1905 that was destroyed in wartime bombings. Last renovated in 1991, it's under the same management as the Königshof, a few steps away, and is not a member of any chain. Bedrooms are quite spacious, outfitted in a tasteful and conservative style. There's a piano bar and a restaurant, Vinothek, on the premises. Overall, this is a low-key, discreet, highly Europeanized hotel with a resolute lack of glitter. Clients are welcome to use the sauna, exercise equipment, and whirlpool facilities on the nearby premises of the Königshof.

InterCity Hotel München

Bayerstrasse 10, D-80335 München. ☎ **089/54-55-60.** Fax 089/54-55-6-610. 203 rms, 8 suites. A/C MINIBAR TV TEL. 245 DM–398 DM ($171.50–$278.60) double; 285 DM–460 DM ($199.50–$322) suite. AE, DC, MC, V. Parking 22 DM ($15.40). U-Bahn or S-Bahn: Hauptbahnhof.

This four-star hotel was once a late-19th-century *Jugendstil* showplace that rose from the southern precincts of Munich's main railway station. Blasted apart during World War II and rebuilt in the 1950s in a bland angular style, it retains hints of its art-nouveau origins in an otherwise internationally modern interior. Part of its attraction is that a porter with your luggage can escort you from the railway sidings directly to the hotel's lobby without crossing any streets. You'll be disappointed if you're a railway buff, since you won't be able to watch trains arriving or departing, but that's overcome by the fact that bedrooms are soundproofed against urban noise, and are comfortable, contemporary, and suited to the needs of international travelers. As a concession to Munich's unending obsession with folklore, a few of the hotel's bedrooms celebrate the Bavarian style with deliberately rustic furnishings. There's a leather-trimmed bar on the premises, as well as a comfortable restaurant one floor above street level, in a culturally neutral setting, with an otherwise continental menu peppered with a scattering of Bavarian dishes.

King's Hotel

Dachauer Strasse 13, D-80335 München. ☎ **089/55-18-70.** Fax 089/55-18-73-00. 96 rms, 14 suites. MINIBAR TV TEL. 255 DM ($178.50) double; 380 DM ($266) suite. Some weekends, depending on bookings (Fri–Sun), 165 DM ($115.50) double. During Oktoberfest and trade fairs, 285 DM ($199.50) double; 445 DM ($311.50) suite. AE, DC, MC, V. U-Bahn: Hauptbahnhof.

The interior of King's Hotel sports the most traditional Bavarian decor of any of the many four-star hotels in Munich. The comfortable, seven-story hotel looks from the outside like a modern townhouse, but inside the carved headboards, flowered fabrics, and rich paneling offer a pleasant contrast to the 20th-century anonymity of the area around the city's main railway station. Built in 1987, the hotel was named after a German family that prides itself on the English spelling of its name. No meals are served other than breakfast, although the in-house bar offers a limited selection of pizzas, soups, and snack items. Some of the suites have tiny kitchens. It's a four-minute walk from the Hauptbanhof.

München Park Hilton

Am Tucherpark 7, D-80538 München. ☎ **800/445-86-67** in the U.S., or 089/3-84-50. Fax 089/384-51-845. 477 rms, 21 suites. A/C MINIBAR TV TEL. 370 DM ($259) double; 810 DM– 910 DM ($567–$637) suite. 50 DM ($35) supplement for room on executive floor, where breakfast and use of a resident's lounge are included. AE, DC, MC, V. Parking 23 DM ($16.10). Bus: E54 from Schwabing. U-Bahn: U3 or U6 to Giselastrasse.

This building in verdant Trivoli Park was transformed into a hotel from an office complex in time for the 1972 Olympics. A sleek, 15-story tower whose access is sometimes a bit difficult for motorists to find, it lies between the Englischer Garten and the Isar River, in a neighborhood that's close to the headquarters of many giant corporations. A five-star hotel, it's one of Munich's two Hiltons (the other, the four-star City Hilton, is less plush and has no swimming pool). Bedrooms here have floor-to-ceiling picture windows, balconies affording a distant view of the Alps, and monochromatic color schemes inspired by the earth tones of autumn.

Dining/Entertainment: Overlooking the pool is the Isar Terrassen, which combines a rollicking beer garden with a middle-of-the-road restaurant. Fine dining is offered at the Hilton Grill on the ground floor, and at a Chinese restaurant, Tse Yang. The Piano Bar features a pianist and the best martinis in town.

Services: 24-hour room service, baby-sitting, laundry, dry cleaning, hairdresser.

Facilities: Health club (renovated in 1996) facing the Englischer Garten, with heated outdoor pool, sauna, Turkish bath, solarium.

München Penta Hotel

Hochstrasse 3, D-81669 München. ☎ **089/48-020.** Fax 089/448-8277. 582 rms, 12 suites. A/C MINIBAR TV TEL. 300 DM–380 DM ($210–$266) double; 600 DM ($420) suite. During weekend periods of low demand, promotional rates of 195 DM ($136.50) sometimes available Fri–Sun. Parking 28 DM ($19.60). AE, DC, MC, V. S-Bahn: Rosenheimer Platz.

After the Sheraton, this is Munich's largest hotel. It's two subway stops east of the Marienplatz, in a congested neighborhood near the Isar River, not far from the Gasteig Center and the Deutsche Museum. An 11-story concrete structure built in 1973, it offers a busy, handsome, and cosmopolitan environment much favored by airline personnel and business travelers. Rated four stars by the government, it's the kind of place that shows bustling international Munich at its most efficient, but not necessarily at its most charming.

Dining/Entertainment: The hotel contains three restaurants, the most formal of which is the Gasteig Taverne. Less formal and expensive are the Bierstube and the brasserie-style Münchener Kindl Stuben with a likable bar.

Services: Room service, baby-sitting, laundry, dry cleaning.

Facilities: Indoor pool, sauna, and a network of kiosks and shops.

Platzl

Sparkassenstrasse 1, D-80331 München. ☎ **089/23-70-30.** Fax 089/23-70-3800. 167 rms, 2 suites. TV TEL. 290 DM–410 DM ($203–$287) double; 450 DM ($315) suite. Rates include buffet breakfast. AE, DC, MC, V. U-Bahn: U3 or U6 to Marienplatz.

In the historic Altstadt, this restored hotel stands opposite the world-famous Hofbräuhaus and close to Marienplatz in the very core of Munich. It's one of the best choices in Munich for a real taste of *Gemutlichkeit*. Obviously, it's the beer-drinker's favorite, as more beer is consumed in and around this hotel than at any other place in Europe. The Aying brewery owns the hotel and has decorated the bedrooms—many of which are quite small—in a rustic Bavarian motif. The furnishings are both traditional and modern, and the location is unbeatable if you'd like to be within walking distance of the major attractions. The hotel's restaurant, Pfistermühle, serves a Bavarian cuisine. Next door is the folk theater, Platzl's Theaterie.

Torbräu

Tal 41, D-80331 München. ☎ **089/22-50-16.** Fax 089/22-50-19. 86 rms. TV TEL. 265 DM–320 DM ($185.50–$224) double. Breakfast included. AE, DC, MC, V. Closed one week at Christmas. Parking 15 DM ($10.50). U-Bahn: Isartor.

The foundations of this four-star hotel in the heart of historic Munich date from the 15th century. Although many vestiges of its folkloric exterior attest to the hotel's distinguished past, the bedrooms are more modern and reasonably comfortable. In all, the place is a lot more charming than many of its bandbox-modern competitors. The hotel's restaurant, Firenze, is open daily for lunch and dinner, featuring a festive selection of Italian specialties favored by merchants and office workers from the surrounding district. There's also a café-conditorei on the premises.

MODERATE

Adria

Liebigstrasse 8a, D-80538 München. ☎ **089/29-30-81.** Fax 089/22-70-15. 47 rms. MINIBAR TV TEL. 180 DM–250 DM ($126–$175) double. Rates include buffet breakfast. AE, MC, V. Closed Dec 23–Jan 6. U-Bahn: U4 or U5. Tram: 20.

The Adria has an inviting, friendly atmosphere. The lobby sets the stylish contemporary look, and guest rooms are furnished with armchairs or sofas, small desks, and hair dryers. Breakfast, a buffet with waffles, cakes, homemade rolls, health-food selections, and even sparkling wine, is served in the garden room. On Sunday smoked salmon is an added treat. Services include money exchange, laundry, theater tickets, and arrangements for sightseeing tours. For 50 DM ($35) the hotel will give you a "license" allowing you to park free in the neighborhood; when you return the license at checkout time, the fee is returned.

Ⓢ An der Oper

Falkenturmstrasse 11, D-80331 München. ☎ **089/290-02-70.** Fax 089/290-02-729. 55 rms. TEL. 195 DM–220 DM ($136.50–$154) double. Rates include buffet breakfast. AE, MC, V. Tram: 19.

Located just off Maximilianstrasse, near Marienplatz, this hotel is superb for sightseeing or shopping in the traffic-free malls, just steps from the Bavarian National Theater. In this price category it is better run and more comfortable than the Adria, described above. In spite of its basic, clean-cut modernity, there are elegant touches, such as the crystal chandeliers in the little reception area. The guest rooms offer first-class amenities; each contains a small sitting area with armchairs and tables for breakfast. The rooms have been renovated in a light contemporary style with soft and subdued colors. A restaurant with a menu tinged with French cuisine, Bosuirth, occupies space in the same building.

Arabella-Central Hotel

Schwanthalerstrasse 111, D-80339 München. ☎ **089/51-08-30**. Fax 089/51-08-32-49. 102 rms. MINIBAR TV TEL. 205 DM–265 DM ($143.50–$185.50) double. AE, DC, MC, V. Closed two weeks at Christmastime. Parking 16 DM ($11.20). Tram: 18 or 19.

Managed by a well-respected middle-bracket German hotel chain, this three-star hotel was built in the 1960s in a five-floor format that's been renovated many times since then. It lies about a five-minute walk from the Messegelände and the Oktoberfest grounds. Everything is modern, often attractively so, and convenient. Some rooms are equipped with balconies, there's a sauna, whirlpool, and solarium on the premises, and the hotel provides both laundry and baby-sitting services. Other than simple bar snacks and a generous morning buffet, there's no food served on the premises, but there are many dining options nearby.

Ariston

Unsöldstrasse 10, D-80538 München. ☎ **089/22-26-91.** Fax 089/291-35-95. 58 rms. TV TEL. 200 DM ($140) double. Rates include buffet breakfast. AE, DC, MC, V. Parking 20 DM ($14). U-Bahn: U4 or U5 to Lehel.

A modern hotel in the center of Munich, not too far from the Haus der Kunst and the Bavarian National Museum, the Ariston is a straightforward, no-frills place in a central but safe location, an option when the Adria and An der Oper are fully booked. Rooms are furnished very simply, but a small entryway to each unit allows for greater quiet and privacy.

City Hotel

Schillerstrasse 3a, D-80336 München. ☎ **089/55-80-91.** Fax 089/550-3665. 65 rms. A/C MINIBAR TV TEL. 198 DM ($138.60) double during "normal" periods, 240 DM ($168) double during Oktoberfest and trade fairs. AE, DC, MC, V. U-Bahn: Hauptbahnhof.

This six-story hotel was built in 1972, not far from Munich's main railway station. Positioned midway between three- and four-star status by the local tourist authorities, it manages to combine a modern and efficient design with a discreet coziness that's a pleasant alternative to the congestion that's the norm all around it. Bedrooms are unfussy, uncomplicated, and blandly but comfortably outfitted in a modern international style. No meals are served other than a buffet breakfast, although there's a simple beer-hall–style restaurant on the building's street level that's patronized by many clients of the many offices and businesses nearby.

Hotel Domus

St.-Anna-Strasse 31, D-80538 München. ☎ **089/22-17-04.** Fax 089/228-53-59. 45 rms, 2 suites. MINIBAR TV TEL. 220 DM–250 DM ($154–$175) double; 280 DM ($196) suite. Breakfast included. Parking 15 DM ($10.50). U-Bahn: U4 or U5 to Lehel.

This sleekly modern, five-story hotel from the 1970s might sound like a university dormitory, but it isn't. Although it's rather large, it has some of the aspects of a private home. Near the Englischer Garten, it's not as close to Munich's medieval core, as, for example, the Torbräu (see below), but parking is easier, a fact that endears it to many of its regular clients. On weekends the clientele might include couples from other parts of Europe in Munich on a sightseeing binge; on weekdays the place has a high percentage of business travelers. Guest rooms are tastefully furnished in appealing monochromatic earth tones, and to help with an undisturbed night's sleep, the hotel pays special attention to the quality of its carpeting and doors. If you ask that breakfast be served in your room, you'll miss out on an exceptionally well-presented buffet.

Hotel Germania

Schwanthalerstrasse 28, D-80336 München. ☎ **089/59-04-60.** Fax 089/59-11-71. 92 rms. MINIBAR TV TEL. 175 DM–250 DM ($122.50–$175) double. Breakfast included. AE, MC, V. U-Bahn or S-Bahn: Hauptbahnhof.

This is a well-administered three-star contender built after wartime damage reduced the vicinity of the railway station to rubble. The boxy, sedate building is not a

🏨 Family-Friendly Hotels

Gästehaus Englischer Garten *(see p. 81)* An oasis of calm and tranquility near the Englischer Garten, this ivy-covered villa provides old-fashioned family atmosphere.

Arabella Olympiapark Hotel München *(see p. 81)* Right at Europe's biggest sports and recreation center, this hotel rents many triple rooms—ideal for families.

Hotel Jedermann *(see p. 78)* This hotel, which is family run, also caters to families on a budget, and makes cribs or cots available for them.

particularly inspired architectural statement, and this is very much a functional, three-star hotel geared to busy traffic from business travelers and sightseers. The cost is relatively reasonable and the accommodations, although not plush, are superior to many other three-star hotels charging comparable prices within the same neighborhood. There's an Italian restaurant, Salioni, on the premises, open daily for lunch and dinner.

Hotel Mark

Senfelderstrasse 12, D-80336 München. ☎ **089/55-98-20.** Fax 089/559-82-333. 90 rms. MINIBAR TV TEL. 190 DM–220 DM ($133–$154) double. Rates include buffet breakfast. AE, DC, MC, V. Parking 15 DM ($10.50). U-Bahn or S-Bahn: Hauptbahnhof.

This hotel near the Hauptbahnhof's south exit should be considered for its comfort and moderate prices. Rebuilt in 1956, it offers serviceable amenities and up-to-date plumbing. The guest rooms are modern and functionally furnished, although a bit cramped. Breakfast is the only meal served.

Hotel Metropol

Bayerstrasse 43, D-80335 München. ☎ **089/53-07-64.** Fax 089/53-28-134. 260 rms (223 with bath). TV TEL. 132 DM ($92.40) double without bath, 185 DM–215 DM ($129.50–$150.50) double with bath. Supplements of about 15% are charged during Oktoberfest and trade fairs. Rates include breakfast. AE, DC, MC, V. U-Bahn or S-Bahn: Hauptbahnhof.

Large and commercially minded, this durable, well-maintained hotel was built in the 1960s in a spot near the city's main railway station. The design includes an important concession to cost-conscious clients—the entire sixth (uppermost) floor is devoted to bedrooms without shower or toilet, an arrangement that has attracted many students who later, as business travelers to Munich, became patrons of the more expensive rooms with bath on the lower floors. Bedrooms are soundproofed against noise from the busy neighborhood outside, and there's a restaurant on the premises, so guests need not wander around the not-always-safe railway station area at night in search of a meal. After breakfast has been served, warm platters are available continuously from noon to 9:30pm.

Hotel Reinbold

Adolf-Kolping-Strasse 11, D-80336 München. ☎ **089/59-79-45.** Fax 089/59-62-72. 61 rms, 2 suites. A/C MINIBAR TV TEL. 184 DM ($128.80) double; 274 DM ($191.80) suite. Breakfast included. Rates about 30% higher at Oktoberfest and during trade fairs. AE, DC, MC, V. Parking 20 DM ($14). U-Bahn or S-Bahn: Hauptbahnhof.

A no-nonsense, no-frills hotel, within a three-minute walk from the railway station, the Reinbold delivers what it promises: a clean, decent room and efficient and polite service. Designed with six concrete and glass stories, it's a boxy-looking structure built in the early 1970s and renovated several times since, most recently in 1996.

Bedrooms are compact, monochromatic, and comfortably (but not lavishly) furnished. Baby-sitting is available, and laundry services are provided on weekdays, but not on weekends. No meals other than breakfast are served, but many restaurants are in this busy neighborhood.

Königswache

Steinheilstrasse 7, D-80333 München. ☎ **089/52-20-01.** Fax 089/52-32-114. 39 rms. MINIBAR TV TEL. 179 DM ($125.30) double, 150 DM ($105) on Sat–Sun with reservation. Rates include buffet breakfast. AE, MC, V. Parking garage (reservation required) 12 DM ($8.40). U-Bahn: U2 to Königsplatz.

Although not as regal as its name, the Königswache has much to recommend it, in spite of its sterile facade. The location, about a 10-minute ride from the Hauptbahnhof and only 2 minutes from the technical university, is between the Stachus and Schwabing. The staff speaks English. The relatively lackluster rooms are modern and comfortable, with writing desks. The hotel bar is decorated in a cozy, rustic style.

Kraft Hotel

Schillerstrasse 49, D-80336 München. ☎ **089/59-48-23.** Fax 089/550-3856. 39 rms. MINIBAR TV TEL. 180 DM ($126) double, 240 DM ($168) double during Oktoberfest and trade fairs. AE, DC, MC, V. U-Bahn: Sendlingertorplatz.

One of the most appealing things about this simple, three-star hotel is its location in the heart of the Altstadt, within a few minutes' walk of the Sendlingertorplatz, and a five-minute walk from the railway station. Architecturally, its seven stories are less appealing, based on the style of boxy architecture so widespread in Munich after World War II. Bedrooms are streamlined, and efficiently designed, usually with some built-in furniture. There's no restaurant on the premises, but many dining options are within a short walk from the hotel.

✪ Splendid

Maximilianstrasse 54, D-80538 München. ☎ **089/29-66-06.** Fax 089/29-131-76. 40 rms (32 with bath), 1 suite. TV TEL. 135 DM–240 DM ($94.50–$168) double without bath, 195 DM–335 DM ($136.50–$234.50) double with bath; from 390 DM–680 DM ($273–$476) suite. Rates include buffet breakfast. AE, DC, MC, V. Free parking. U-Bahn: U4 or U5. Tram: 19 or 20.

The Splendid is one of the most attractive old-world hotels in Munich, with public rooms decorated with antiques, Oriental rugs, and chandeliers. Each room reflects the owner's desire to evoke the aura of a country home. Most rooms are in a style known as "Bavarian baroque," although two recently remodeled ones are in the Louis XVI style. Room prices are scaled according to time of year, size, furnishings, and plumbing, with the highest prices charged at fair and festival times. On sunny mornings many guests prefer to breakfast on the trellised patio. Baby-sitting can be arranged, and room service is provided.

INEXPENSIVE

⑨ Am Markt

Heiliggeistrasse 6, D-80331 München. ☎ **089/22-50-14.** Fax 089/22-40-17. 32 rms (13 with bath). TEL. 110 DM ($77) double without bath, 160 DM ($112) double with bath. Rates include continental breakfast. No credit cards. Parking 12 DM ($8.40). S-Bahn: From the Hauptbahnhof, take any S-Bahn train headed for Marienplatz, a two-stop ride from the station.

This popular Bavarian hotel stands in the heart of the older section. The hotel is not luxurious, but owner Harald Herrler has wisely maintained a nostalgic decor in the lobby and dining room. Behind his reception desk is a wall of photographs of former guests, including the late Viennese chanteuse Greta Keller. As Mr. Herrler points out, you're likely to find yourself surrounded by opera and concert artists at breakfast, who stay here because they're close to where they perform. The guest rooms are basic modern—small but trim and neat. All units have hot and cold running water, with free use of the corridor baths and toilets.

Europäischer Hof

Bayerstrasse 31, D-80335 München. ☎ **089/55-15-10.** Fax 089/55-15-12-22. 153 rms (139 with bath or shower and toilet). TV TEL. 130 DM ($91) double without bath or shower and toilet, 164 DM–188 DM ($114.80–$131.60) double with bath or shower and toilet. AE, DC, MC, V. Parking 12 DM ($8.40). U-Bahn or S-Bahn: Hauptbahnhof.

This nine-story hotel opposite the Hauptbahnhof was originally built in 1960 by an order of Catholic nuns (order of the Holy Family) who added a chapel that's still in place today. Now run by the Sturzer family, the establishment offers simple but clean accommodations, some of which overlook an inner courtyard. Most rooms have some built-in furniture; all have double-glazed windows for soundproofing, radios, and closets that are usually positioned near each room's entrance. Some contain minibars. Despite its dreary location, the hotel is clean and well managed, with cozy touches. Breakfast is the only meal served, although a likable Italian restaurant, Ca d'Oro, occupies part of the building's street level.

Hotel Jedermann

Bayerstrasse 95, D-80335 München. ☎ **089/53-32-67.** Fax 089/53-65-06. 55 rms (34 with shower and toilet). TEL TV. 95 DM–140 DM ($66.50–$98) double without shower and toilet, 130 DM–220 DM ($91–$154) double with shower and toilet; 120 DM–185 DM ($84–$129.50) triple without shower and toilet, 155 DM–265 DM ($108.50–$185.50) triple with shower and toilet. Rates include buffet breakfast. Parking 8 DM ($5.60). Ten-minute walk from Hauptbahnhof (turn right on Bayerstrasse from south exit).

This pleasant, cozy spot has been deftly run by the Jenke family since 1961. Renovated and enlarged in 1990, its central location and good value make it a desirable choice. It has a wood-paneled interior and Bavarian furnishings, and is an apt choice for families; cribs or cots are available. A generous breakfast buffet is served in a charming room; Bavarian fare can be arranged for lunch or dinner from one of the restaurants in the vicinity.

Hotel Wallis

Schwanthalerstrasse 8, D-80336 München. ☎ **089/59-16-64.** Fax 089/550-3752. 54 rms. A/C TV TEL. 149 DM ($104.30) double. During trade fairs and Oktoberfest, 269 DM ($188.30) double. AE, DC, MC, V. U-Bahn: Karlsplatz.

Unpretentious, uncomplicated, and comfortable, this three-star hotel's Bavarian-inspired interior is warmer and cozier than you'd imagine after a look at its angular postwar exterior. Bedrooms are relatively small, but each was renovated in 1995 and furnished with simplified reproductions of the kind of furnishings found in alpine villages to the south. Only breakfast is served, although there's a bar on the premises, and many worthwhile restaurants lie within a short walk. The staff is polite and helpful to newcomers navigating their way around the city's historic core. Don't even think of checking in here during Oktoberfest, as its proximity to the Hofbräuhaus almost guarantees it being fully booked.

⑨ Pension beim Haus der Kunst

Bruderstrasse 4, D-80802 München. ☎ **089/22-21-27.** Fax 089/834-8248. 9 rms (none with bath), 1 apt (with bath). 90 DM ($63) double; 200 DM ($140) apt for four. Rates include breakfast. AE. U-Bahn: Lehel.

Noted for an ideal location near the Englischer Garten, copious breakfasts, and warm hospitality, this inexpensive and well-run small pension is one of Munich's best. It's low-key and decent, and early reservations are important here. The establishment's apartment contains the only private bath; guests in the other rooms (all doubles) must share the facilities in the hallways. Parking, when available, is free on the street.

Pension Diana

Altheimer Eck 15, D-80331 München. ☎ **089/260-31-07.** Fax 089/263-934. 17 rms (none with bath). 90 DM ($63) double; 130 DM ($91) triple; 170 DM ($119) quad. Rates include breakfast. AE, MC, V. Parking 18 DM ($12.60). U-Bahn: Karlsplatz.

Set behind a grand stone facade, the Diana occupies a section of what used to be a grand palace in an interesting central district of Munich. There's no elevator, so you'll have to climb a wide baroque staircase to the third floor. There you'll find bright, sunny guest rooms, each with simple but comfortable pinewood furnishings, plus hot and cold running water.

⑤ Pension Westfalia

Mozartstrasse 23, D80336 München. ☎ **089/53-03-77.** Fax 089/54-39-120. 19 rms (11 with bath). TEL. 85 DM ($59.50) double without bath, 130 DM ($91) double with bath. Rates include buffet breakfast. AE, V. U-Bahn: U3 or U6 to Goetheplatz. Bus: 58 from the Hauptbahnhof.

Facing the meadow where the annual Oktoberfest takes place, this four-story town house near Goetheplatz is one of Munich's best pensions, offering immaculately maintained guest rooms, many with TVs. Owner Peter Deiritz speaks English. Parking is free on the street, when available.

Uhland Garni ✳

Uhlandstrasse 1, D-80336 München. ☎ **089/54-33-50.** Fax 089/54-33-5250. 27 rms. MINIBAR TV TEL. 150 DM–270 DM ($105–$189) double. Rates include buffet breakfast. DC, MC, V. Free parking. Bus: 58.

This family-owned (since 1955) hotel in a residential area offers friendly, personal service, and could easily become your home in Munich. The stately art-nouveau–style mansion stands in its own small garden. Its bedrooms are soundproof, and all are snug, traditional, and cozy. Only breakfast is served. The hotel is just a 10-minute walk from the Hauptbahnhof.

Utzelmann

Pettenkoferstrasse 6, D-80336 München. ☎ **089/59-48-89.** Fax 089/59-62-28. 11 rms (4 with shower and toilet). 95 DM ($66.50) double without bath, 110 DM ($77) double with shower only, 145 DM ($101.50) double with shower and toilet. Rates include breakfast. No credit cards. U-Bahn: Sendlingertorplatz.

A 12-minute walk south of Munich's center, this pension was established in 1965 in a stripped-down house originally built about a century ago. The atmosphere inside is familylike. Its owners, Hermann Ernst and his hardworking wife, have freshened everything with furniture, carpeting, and modern toilets.

3 In Schwabing

EXPENSIVE

München Marriott Hotel

Berliner Strasse 93, D-80805 München. ☎ **800/228-92-90** or 089/36-00-20. Fax 089/36-00-22-00. 348 rms, 12 suites. A/C MINIBAR TV TEL. 225 DM–285 DM ($157.50–$199.50) double; from 485 DM ($339.50) suite. During selected nonpeak weekends, 210 DM ($147) double, including breakfast. AE, DC, MC, V. Parking 22 DM ($15.40). U-Bahn: U6 to Nord Friedhof.

Marriott's usual postmodern style fits appropriately into this verdant setting along the northern tier of Schwabing. Built in 1990, about 2¹/₂ miles north of Munich's historic core, it offers a well-designed, Americanized venue whose German staff welcomes travelers from throughout Europe. The lobby is one of the most appealing in Schwabing, with blond wood, marble, potted plants, and sunlight streaming in from all sides. A cafe and bar serve simple platters, and the California Grill interprets Pacific coast cuisine into a culinary oddity (at least in Munich) that has enjoyed great success. Many of the clients check in as parts of groups and conventions, although individual travelers aren't ignored. Bedrooms are identical, and the staff seems highly motivated. On the premises is a business center, a health club with sauna and exercise equipment, and a hardworking concierge.

Residence München

Artur-Kutscher Platz 4, D-80802 München. ☎ **089/38-17-80.** Fax 089/381-78-951. 165 rms. MINIBAR TV TEL. 238 DM–370 DM ($166.60–$259) double. AE, DC, MC, V. Parking 10 DM ($7). U-Bahn: U3 to Münchner Freiheit.

In the center of artsy Schwabing, this is an eight-story, angularly modern hotel that's used by business travelers as well as performers at many of Munich's theaters and concert halls. Originally built in 1969, and renovated progressively throughout the years, it's a four-star hotel with almost no emphasis on historical charm, but with lots of modern comfort. There's an attractive lounge, with vibrant colors and lots of wood paneling, and bedrooms that are relatively spacious and usually have balconies. Prices are set according to the floor to which you're assigned, and the season.

Dining/Entertainment: Breakfast is served in Le Pavillon Restaurant, where globe lighting and bentwood furniture evoke *la belle époque*. Other than room service, there are no facilities for lunch, but dinner is presented in a cosy bar-restaurant, Die Kutsche, a tribute to folkloric Munich.

Facilities: There's an indoor pool, with walls and ceilings of varnished pine, lots of subtropical plants, and lounge chairs.

MODERATE

Holiday Inn Crowne Plaza Munich

Leopoldstrasse 194, D-80804 Munich. ☎ **800/465-43-29** in the U.S., or 089/38-179-0. Fax 089/38-179-888. 394 rms, 3 suites. A/C MINIBAR TV TEL. 190 DM–230 DM ($133–$161) double; 550 DM ($385) suite. During Oktoberfest and trade fairs, 295 DM ($206.50) double, 650 DM ($455) suite. During selected weekends, 208 DM ($145.60) double, with breakfast included. AE, DC, MC, V. Parking 21 DM ($14.70). U-Bahn: U3 or U6 to Münchner Freiheit.

Set near the Olympic Stadium, on the northern perimeter of Schwabing about 3 miles north of Munich's historic core, this hotel was built in anticipation of the 1972 Olympics in a format that included two eight-story towers. As a member of the deluxe upper tier of the Holiday Inn chain, it offers lots of incentives for a stay here, including a lobby comfortable and stylish enough to want to spend time in, and bedrooms outfitted with big, carefully soundproofed windows and contemporary, uncontroversial furnishings. Those on the upper floor, facing south, benefit from views of the city and the faraway Alps; others overlook the suburbs and the urban sprawl surrounding Munich's northern tier.

On the premises are two restaurants, one a folksy Bavarian eatery whose name, *Omas Küche or* "Grandmother's Kitchen," conveys the style of cuisine it serves; another focuses on Italian cuisine. There is also a health club with exercise equipment and a heated indoor pool, a disco with live entertainment on weekends, and a full roster of business services. Because of the hotel's easy access from the Autobahns funneling into Munich from points north (including Autobahn Nürnberg–Berlin–Frankfurt), it's especially convenient for motorists.

Hotel Leopold
Leopoldstrasse 119, D-80804 München–Schwabing. ☎ **089/36-70-61.** Fax 089/360-43-150. 78 rms. TV TEL. 175 DM–198 DM ($122.50–$138.60) double. Breakfast included. AE, DC, MC, V. Parking 9 DM ($6.30). U-Bahn: U3 or U4 to Münchner Freiheit.

The core of this unusual hotel is a Jugendstil villa that was originally built as a private home in 1924. In the 1970s, a modern annex, connected to the original house with a glass-sided passageway, was added, and the remaining garden area was upgraded and made more lavish. The setting is close to an exit road of the Autobahn Nürnberg–Würzburg–Berlin, which gives the place the atmosphere of a suburban motel with plentiful parking. Despite the verdant setting, however, the hotel lies only four subway stops from Munich's Marienplatz, and the Englischer Garten is only a few minutes away by foot. Public areas have traditional Bavarian motifs. Rooms in the old section have been modernized to make them equivalent to rooms in the new section, and all have been made as soundproof as possible.

INEXPENSIVE

✪ Gästehaus Englischer Garten
Liebergesellstrasse 8, D80802 München–Schwabing. ☎ **089/39-20-34.** Fax 089/39-12-33. 12 rms (6 with bath), 15 apts. MINIBAR TV TEL. 130 DM ($91) double without bath, 138 DM– 168 DM ($96.60–$117.60) double with bath. No credit cards. Parking 10 DM ($7). U-Bahn: U3 or U6 to Münchner Freiheit.

This oasis of charm and tranquility, close to the Englischer Garten, is one of our preferred stopovers in the Bavarian capital. The ivy-covered villa was once the site of a mill. It later became a private villa, but for some two decades now Frau Irene Schlüter-Hubscher has operated it as a hotel. All the rooms are attractively furnished. Across the street is an annex with 15 small apartment units, all with bath and tiny kitchenettes. Try for Room 16, 23, 26, or especially 20. In fair weather, breakfast is served in a rear garden.

4 In Olympiapark

Arabella Olympiapark Hotel München
Helene-Mayer-Ring 12, D-80809 München. ☎ **089/351-60-71.** Fax 089/35-43-730. 105 rms. MINIBAR TV TEL. 205 DM–370 DM ($143.50–$259) double. Rates include buffet breakfast. AE, DC, MC, V. Free parking. U-Bahn: U2 or U3 to Olympia Centrum.

Right at Europe's biggest sports and recreation center stands the Arabella Olympiapark Hotel München. The hotel is near the stadium, site of many major sports events, and appeals to fitness-minded people who want to be near all the sports action. Its guest rooms are among the most modern and best kept in the city, and sports heroes, both European and American, casually stroll through the lobby. There's no need to drive into the city center: The U-Bahn will whisk you there in minutes. If you want to unwind after a tough night in the beer halls, you'll find a refreshing pool, a sauna, and a massage room at the nearby Olympiapark.

5 In Haidhausen

VERY EXPENSIVE

München City Hilton
Rosenheimerstrasse 15, D81667 München. ☎ **800/455-86-67** in the U.S. and Canada, or 089/ 48-04-0. Fax 089/4804-4804. 479 rms, 20 suites. A/C MINIBAR TV TEL. 390 DM–560 DM

($273–$392) double; from 600 DM ($420) suite. AE, DC, MC, V. Parking 28 DM ($19.60). S-Bahn: S1, S2, S3, S4, S5, S6, or S7 to Rosenheimer Platz.

When it opened in 1989, the München City Hilton became the second Hilton to grace the city skyline. Owned by a Dutch pension fund, it lies beside the Deutsches Museum and the Gasteig performing arts center. The low-rise hotel was designed with red brick, shimmering glass, and geometric windows divided by white bands of metal reminiscent of a Mondrian painting. Munich's historic center is an invigorating 25-minute walk across the river. On the premises are a pair of well-designed restaurants, a lobby-level cafe, a bar, and a staff sensitive to visitor needs. The traditional guest rooms contain modern adaptations of Biedermeier furniture, plush carpeting, and cable.

Dining/Entertainment: The Hilton offers good drinking and dining facilities, including Zum Gasteig, a Bavarian restaurant decorated in a typical style; Löwen-Schanke, a Bavarian pub; and Café Lenbach, where you can order a leisurely breakfast or afternoon tea.

Services: 24-hour room service, laundry, dry cleaning, baby-sitting.

Facilities: Flower shop, newsstand.

EXPENSIVE

Preysing

Preysingstrasse 1, D-81667 München. ☎ **089/45-84-50.** Fax 089/458-454-44. 76 rms, 5 suites. A/C MINIBAR TV TEL. 328 DM ($229.60) double; 375 DM–540 DM ($262.50–$378) suite. Rates include breakfast. AE, DC, V. Closed Dec 23–Jan 6. Parking 18 DM ($12.60). Tram: 18.

If you don't mind a hotel on the outskirts and you want a quiet location, one of the best places to stay is the Preysing, across the Isar near the Deutsches Museum (a short tram ride will whisk you into the center of the city). When you first view the building, a seven-story modern structure, you may feel we've misled you. However, if you've gone this far, venture inside for a pleasant surprise.

The family who runs the hotel has one of the most thoughtful staffs in Munich, and the hotel's style is most agreeable, with dozens of little extras to provide home-like comfort. Fresh flowers are everywhere, and the furnishings, traditional combined with modern, have been carefully selected. Rooms have many amenities.

Dining/Entertainment: Preysing's restaurant is one of the finest in Munich (see Chapter 5).

Services: Room service, laundry, baby-sitting.

Facilities: Indoor pool, sauna, solarium, whirlpool.

MODERATE

Habis

Maria-Theresia-Strasse 2A, D-81675 München-Haidhausen. ☎ **089/470-50-71.** Fax 089/47-05-101. 25 rms. TV TEL. 190 DM ($133) double. Rates include buffet breakfast. AE, DC, MC, V. U-Bahn: U4 or U5 to Max-Weber-Platz.

This small hotel of special character is across from Isarpark, overlooking the river; on the other side of the bridge are some of Munich's leading museums. The renovated hotel, built on a corner, has five floors of individualized guest rooms, and a wine restaurant. The hotel's general decor, especially the entrance with its curving staircase, is modified art nouveau. The bedrooms have strong earth colors, with painted built-in pieces, trim beds, and casual wicker armchairs.

6 In Bogenhausen

EXPENSIVE

München Sheraton

Arabellastrasse 6, D-81925 München. ☎ **089/92-640.** Fax 089/91-68-77. 637 rms, 16 suites. A/C MINIBAR TV TEL. 265 DM–495 DM ($185.50–$346.50) double; 970 DM–2,000 DM ($679–$1,400) suite. AE, DC, MC, V. Parking 19 DM ($13.30). U-Bahn: U4 to Arabellapark.

This is the largest hotel in Munich, set in the northern suburb of Bogenhausen, about seven subway stops from downtown Munich. A sprawling, giant, somewhat anonymous place built in 1972, it's well accustomed to welcoming groups of sightseers, salespeople from around the world, and businesspeople from international corporations. This is a hotel that's hard to ignore, towering as it does, 22 stories above the surrounding northern suburbs. Although the hotel has a lot to offer, it's beginning to look just a bit worn, as the last renovations, around 1991, left some parts of the hotel unchanged. But with so many facilities, and a willingness to discount rooms based on occupancy, it's still a worthy choice.

Dining/Entertainment: In addition to its bars, the hotel has two restaurants, the Atrium, whose design corresponds to modern, intra-European pizzazz, and the rustic and *gemütlich* Alt Bayern Stube. There's also a nightclub under separate management that features Brazilian music, the Amazona.

Services: 24-hour room service, laundry, concierge.

Facilities: Health club, 65-foot indoor pool, solarium, fitness room, sauna, massage parlor, shopping arcade, and an in-house branch of Avis Rent-a-Car.

MODERATE

Arabella Hotel Bogenhausen

Arabellastrasse 5, D-81925 München. ☎ **089/92-320.** Fax 089/923-24-449. 467 rms, 32 suites. A/C MINIBAR TV TEL. 235 DM–245 DM ($164.50–$171.50) double; 385 DM–635 DM ($269.50–$444.50) suite during "normal" times. During Oktoberfest and trade fairs, 285 DM–345 DM ($199.50–$241.50) double; 685 DM–935 DM ($479.50–$654.50) suite. AE, DC, MC, V. Parking 16 DM–25 DM ($11.20–$17.50). U-Bahn: U4 to Arabellapark.

Set in the verdant suburb of Bogenhausen, seven subway stops north of the Odeonsplatz, this is one of the largest hotels in Munich, and one of the most stylish and imaginatively designed in the Arabella chain. Originally built between 30 and 40 years ago, it benefitted from a lavish renovation that was concluded in 1995, when all but the cheapest category of rooms were reaccessorized and upgraded. Some accommodations imitate the Bavarian *Landhaus* style, with replicas of the kind of solid and dignified furniture you might have found in the home of a prosperous and conservative Bavarian burgher early in the century. Top-category rooms are outfitted in burgundy with lots of paneling, an international style that echoes the feel of the glossy public areas.

Dining/Entertainment: Restaurants include The Brasserie and Capriccio, the more formal of the two. Both serve Bavarian, continental, and international cuisine.

Services: Room service, laundry, baby-sitting.

Facilities: Indoor pool on the 22nd floor, with its own waterfall, five whirlpools, three steam rooms with a decor inspired by ancient Rome, two saunas, solariums, exercise equipment, a poolside bar, and a grove of indoor palm trees.

7 At Neu-Perlach

Novotel München

Rudolf-Vogel-Bogen 3, D-18739 München. ☎ **800/221-4542** in the U.S., or 089/63-80-00. Fax 089/635-1309. 253 rms. A/C MINIBAR TV TEL. Mon–Thurs 240 DM ($168) double, Fri–Sun 158 DM ($110.60) double. During trade fairs and Oktoberfest, weekday rate applies throughout the weekend. Children up to 16 stay free in parents' room. AE, DC, MC, V. U-Bahn: Neuperlach Sud.

Set in a suburb, 3 miles southeast of Munich's center, this hotel is accessible after a 15-minute (eight-stop) subway ride from the Marienplatz. Originally built in 1985, it's a comfortable uncharacteristically large member of a worldwide French chain, a well-established favorite with business travelers and families who appreciate the Novotel formula of standardized modern bedrooms, no-nonsense efficiency, pan-European anonymity, and easy access to motorways. There's an indoor pool, a bar that does a brisk business with an international crowd of clients, and a restaurant that serves well-prepared, albeit formulaic, food in generous portions.

8 At Untermenzing

Romantik Hotel Insel Mühle

Von-Kahr-Strasse 87, D-80999 München-Untermenzing. ☎ **089/8-10-10.** Fax 089/812-0571. 39 rms, I suite. TV TEL. 300 DM ($210) double; 410 DM ($287) suite. Breakfast included. DC, MC, V. Free parking. S-Bahn: Pasing, then bus 76.

Until 1985, this 16th-century stone-sided mill was left to decay in its isolated position beside the Würm (a tributary of the Isar), 6 miles west of Munich's Marienplatz. The restoration has retained part of the mill's 1506 construction. Although a large part of the hotel's income, as well as its reputation, derives from its atmospheric restaurant, it also provides a charming alternative to the roster of large modern hotels that comprise the majority of Munich's overnight accommodations. There's a plank-covered wharf where parasols shield diners from the midday sun; the decor and design of each bedroom is different—some have sloping garretlike ceilings and contain thick carpets and well-designed upholsteries and stylish accessories.

The real beauty of the place can be seen in the massive beams of the dining room, and in the mellow brick vaults of the wine cellar. Meals are served Monday to Saturday from noon to 2pm and 6 to 10pm, and feature a roster of well-prepared Bavarian and continental dishes. Down-on-the-farm menu items include medallions of veal in a mushroom-flavored cream sauce with fresh vegetables, rack of venison, roasted goose with black-currant dressing, and a selection of fish that usually includes sole and halibut.

9 Near the Airport

Kempinski Hotel Airport München

Terminalstrasse 20, D-85356 München. ☎ **800/426-3135** in the U.S., or 089/97-820. Fax 089/978-21-513. 343 rms, 46 suites. A/C MINIBAR TV TEL. 240 DM–350 DM ($168–$245) double; 650 DM–1,200 DM ($455–$840) suite. AE, DC, MC, V. Parking 12.50 DM ($8.75). U-Bahn: Airport.

When it was built between the runways of Munich's airports in 1993, it was noted as the most architecturally innovative and discreetly avant-garde airport hotel in Europe. Partially owned, like other members of the Kempinski chain, by Lufthansa, it was designed by a Chicago-based architect of German descent, Helmet Jahn, with a four-story shimmering glass and steel exterior and an interior design whose colorful, postmodern accents ward off the monochromatic landscape of the surrounding airport. Despite its nearness to runways, the hotel's interior is soothing and silent, the result of careful attention to soundproofing. A soaring hotel lobby contains a subtropical garden with palms and views over one of Europe's busiest airports.

Dining/Entertainment: The Charles Lindbergh restaurant, with its bar, serves a well-prepared repertoire of both international and Bavarian dishes.

Services: Business center, 24-hour room service.

Facilities: Sauna, steam bath, solarium, fitness center.

10 Gay Hotels

Die Deutsche Eiche

Reichenbackstrasse 13, D-80469 München. ☎ **089/23-11-660.** 48 rms (23 with bath). MINIBAR TV TEL. 130 DM ($91) double without bath; 155 DM ($108.50) double with bath. Rates include breakfast. AE, MC, V. Parking in public garage (a 3-minute walk) 25 DM ($17.50) per night. U-Bahn: Marienplatz.

This is the oldest and most deeply entrenched gay hotel in Munich. It's about 80% gay, with a hardworking staff that claims gay-friendly policies to have been the norm at this hotel since it was built in 1894. Rooms are comfortably but simply outfitted in earth tones; those on the two lower floors have private baths, and those on the upper floors have shared facilities in the corridors. Under separate management, at street level, is a mostly gay French/Italian restaurant, Die Deutsche Eiche, recommended separately. Clients of the hotel receive a 5 DM ($3.50) discount at the men's sauna (Bäderhaus) behind the hotel, under separate management. The hotel's name, incidentally, translates as "the German Oak."

Hotel König Ludwig

Hohenzollernstrasse 3, D-80801 München. ☎ **089/33-59-95.** Fax 089/39-46-58. 48 rms, 1 suite. TV TEL MINIBAR. Fri-Sun 190 DM ($133) double, 250 DM ($175) suite. Mon-Thurs 210 DM ($147) double, 300 DM ($210) suite. Rates include breakfast. AE, DC, MC, V. Parking 50 DM ($35). U-Bahn: Giselastrasse.

Set near Munich's university, this 1980s building rises six floors above a busy urban landscape. Its gay-friendly reputation became deeply entrenched shortly after its construction, when a former director placed advertisements in most of Europe's gay guides, defining the establishment as a mostly gay organization. Now under new management, the hotel has assumed a more restrained point of view, but still makes a point of welcoming the dozens of gay clients that continue to show up as a result of trickle-down effect of many years of gay promotion. The staff, some of whom admit privately to sympathy for the advancement of gay causes, is invariably tactful, polite, and helpful. Bedrooms are monochromatic and rather blandly international in style.

5 Dining

Munich is one of the few European cities that has more than one "three-star" restaurant, and some of its sophisticated eating places are among the finest anywhere. This is the place to practice *Edelfresswelle* ("high-class gluttony"). As well as international cuisine, there are many local specialties. The classic local dish is, of course, Weisswurst, herb-flavored white veal sausages blanched in water and traditionally consumed before noon.

It is said that Müncheners consume more beer than people in any other German city. Bernd Boehle once wrote: "If a man really belongs to Munich he drinks beer at all times of the day, at breakfast, at midday, at teatime; and in the evening, of course, he just never stops." The place where every first-time visitor heads for at least one eating and drinking fest is the Hofbräuhaus am Platzl. It's described later in Chapter 9.

1 Best Bets

- **Best Spot for a Romantic Dinner: Grünwalder Einkehr** lets you escape from the urban sprawl of Munich to a "green lung" retreat 8 miles south of the center. A trio of dining rooms has been installed in a 200-year-old former private home. Today in a rustic setting you can feast on French-inspired dishes that include many Gaelic favorites such as roast rack of lamb with rosemary sauce. It's the best place to get away from it all.

- **Best Spot for a Business Lunch: Mark's Restaurant,** in the deluxe hotel Rafael, is the chic business luncheon stopover of Munich. The movers and shakers of the Bavarian capital gather in the informal lobby level setting of Mark's corner to make the big deal. Menu items change according to the season and the inspiration of the chef, and, as you dine, you can practically feel deutsche marks changing hands.

- **Best Spot for a Celebration: Kay's Bistro** is the number one spot on the see-and-be-seen circuit. Kay's Bistro is sophisticated and chic—and also lots of fun. It's filled nightly with a glamorous clientele who like not only good food but a festive restaurant in which to celebrate their latest deal, marriage, or divorce (whatever). The decoration is always changing based on the season, but the French and international cuisine remains eternally alluring.

- **Best Decor:** The **Garden Restaurant,** in the Bayerischer Hof Hotel, evokes the interior of a small, pastel-colored palace with references to gardening and blooming plants. Serving upscale food to a cosmopolitan crowd, it offers completely fresh ingredients—flown in from virtually everywhere—that complement the soothing decor.

- **Best Wine List: Geisel's Vinothek,** in the Hotel Excelsior, is the best spot in Munich for a taste of the grape. Dedicated to Bacchus, this deliberately unpretentious choice has one of the city's finest collections of Italian, French, Austrian, and German wines—all sold by the glass. You can also order Italian cuisine.

- **Best Value: Palais Keller** offers great value, although it's housed in the cellar of one of the most elegant hotels in Munich. Its well-prepared cuisine of Bavarian and German dishes is priced about the same as far less desirable beer halls and *Weinstuben* nearby. Let a smiling waitress in a frilly apron introduce you to *Tafelspitz,* the fabled boiled beef dish of the Teutonic world.

- **Best for Kids: Mövenpick Restaurant** is right in the heart of Munich and decorated with a whimsical theme; various rooms are devoted to various venues, everything from the Longhorn Corner for Texas-style steaks to Grandma's Kitchen for some old-fashioned cookery. Some kids come here for a full meal just of *Rösti,* those fabled Swiss fried potatoes.

- **Best Continental Cuisine: Tantris,** in Schwabing, serves the city's most refined cuisine, a treat to the eye as well as the palate. Chef Hans Haas is one of the top chefs of Germany, and is forever sharpening his culinary techniques as he wines and dines the celebrated people of Europe. Nothing in Munich equals the flavors, service, and delight of the dishes found here.

- **Best French Cuisine: Bistro Terrine**'s food tastes so authentically French you'll think you're back in Lyon. Menu items are often more inventive than the fin de siècle atmosphere of this art-nouveau bistro in Schwabing implies. The menu changes with the seasons—for example, in autumn nuggets of venison might appear with a hazelnut-flavored gnocchi and port wine sauce.

- **Best Italian Cuisine: El Toulà** is an elegant choice for Italian haute cuisine, the best in Munich where the competition grows increasingly stiff. The setting is rich and evocative, and the cookery is mainly inspired by the Piedmont and Lombardy districts, with some Venetian delectables thrown in as well. The pasta dishes—each homemade and succulent—are meals unto themselves.

- **Best Seafood: Austernkeller,** the best oyster cellar in Munich, prepares not only the freshest oysters in town but also an array of delectable seafood selections that range from mussels to clams and sea snails. The lobster Thermidor is worth the drive into Munich. The kitsch collection of plastic lobsters shouldn't put you off: the food is far worthier than the decor.

- **Best Bavarian Cuisine: Nürnberger Bratwurst Glöckl Am Dom** is Munich's coziest restaurant: Here you can enjoy a Bavarian cuisine so authentic that it's hardly changed since the turn of the century. (The restaurant opened first in 1893 and was rebuilt after a World War II bombing raid.) Bavarians, who often look as stern as one of the Dürer prints on the wall, come here for all their favorite dishes—just like grandmother made a hundred years ago.

- **Best Late-Night Dining: Käfer's Am Hofgarten** is good and yuppie oriented, and the dining scene goes on on weekends until three in the morning. It's a fashionable French bistro with amazingly reasonable prices, and you can enjoy an international array of food, inspired by every place from America to Thailand.

- **Best Outdoor Dining: Locanda Picolit,** an Italian restaurant in the heart of Schwabing, offers an outdoor terrace in summer with a view over a garden that's

Munich Dining

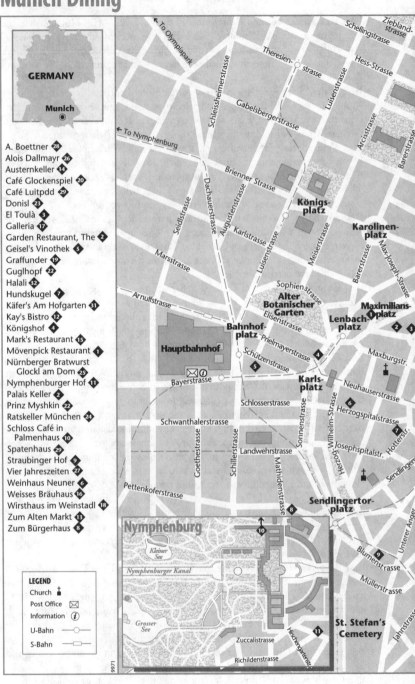

A. Boettner 28
Alois Dallmayr 26
Austernkeller 14
Café Glockenspiel 20
Café Luitpdd 29
Donisl 23
El Toulà 3
Galleria 17
Garden Restaurant, The 2
Geisel's Vinothek 5
Graffunder 19
Guglhopf 22
Halali 32
Hundskugel 7
Käfer's Am Hofgarten 31
Kay's Bistro 12
Königshof 4
Mark's Restaurant 15
Mövenpick Restaurant 1
Nürnberger Bratwurst
   Glockl am Dom 25
Nymphenburger Hof 11
Palais Keller 2
Prinz Myshkin 22
Ratskeller München 24
Schloss Café in
   Palmenhaus 10
Spatenhaus 29
Straubinger Hof 9
Vier Jahreszeiten 27
Weinhaus Neuner 6
Weisses Bräuhaus 16
Wirsthaus im Weinstadl 18
Zum Alten Markt 13
Zum Bürgerhaus 8

LEGEND
Church ⛪
Post Office ✉
Information ⓘ
U-Bahn ──○──
S-Bahn ──▭──

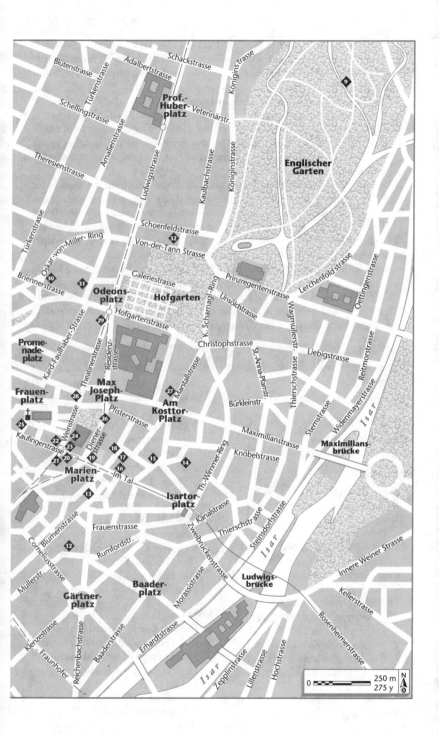

one of the most evocative in Munich. The place suggests a Mediterranean world. Menu items change with the season, and you can enjoy the agrarian bounty of Italy while doing some people-watching and soaking up the fresh breezes blowing across Munich at the same time.

- **Best People-Watching: Graffunder** is on Marienplatz, the virtual heart of Munich, and here you can take in the passing parade while enjoying a selection of French and Italian wines sold by the glass. Platters of food ranging from simple snacks to more elaborate concoctions are also served. But it's the landmark square of Marienplatz itself that distracts from the cuisine, the very center of the festive life of the city.
- **Best for Pretheater Dinner: Spatenhaus,** across the street from the opera house on Max-Joseph-Platz, is the ideal dining venue if you're going to the opera or one of the theaters nearby. It's Munich's best-known beer restaurant but definitely not a beer hall. It's handsomely appointed and rather conservatively decorated, and has excellent Bavarian and international fare. Since the restaurant is open in the afternoon, you can drop in quite early for a meal before culture.
- **Best Picnic Fare: Alois Dallmayr** offers not only the best picnic fare in Munich, but the best in Germany. With the food you can gather up here, you could even invite the queen of England for lunch in the Englischer Garten. One of the world's most renowned delis, this supermarket of goodies has elegant picnic fare such as foie gras, but it also offers more democratically priced fare.

2 Restaurants by Cuisine

ALPINE
Zum Bürgerahaus (Central Munich, *I*)

AUSTRO-HUNGARIAN
Nymphenburger Hof
(Nymphenburg, *E*)

BAVARIAN
Asam Schlössel (South of Center, *I*)
Bamberger Haus (Schwabing, *I*)
Biergärten Chinesischer Turm
(Schwabing, *I*)
Chesa Rüegg (Central Munich, *M*)
Donisl (Central Munich, *I*)
Gaststätte zum Flaucher
(South of Center, *I*)
Halali (Central Munich, *M*)
Hirschgarten (Nymphenburg, *I*)
Hundskugel (Central Munich, *I*)
Nürnberger Bratwurst Glöckl Am
Dom (Central Munich, *I*)
Palais Keller (Central Munich, *I*)
Ratskeller München
(Central Munich, *M*)
Spatenhaus (Central Munich, *M*)

Straubinger Hof (Central Munich, *I*)
Weinbauer (Schwabing, *I*)
Weinhaus Neuner
(Central Munich, *M*)
Weisses Brauhaus
(Central Munich, *I*)
Zum Alten Markt
(Central Munich, *M*)
Zum Aumeister (Freimann, *I*)

BEER GARDENS
Bamberger Haus
Biergärten Chinesischer Turm
Gaststätte zum Flaucher
Hirschgarten
Zum Aumeister

CAFES
Die Alte Boerse (Central Munich)
Cafe Glockenspiel (Central Munich)
Cafe Luitpold (Central Munich)
Guglhopf (Central Munich)
Ruffini (Rotkreuzplatz)
Schlosscafé im Palmenhaus
(Nymphenburg)

Key to abbreviations: *VE* = Very Expensive, *E* = Expensive, *M* = Moderate, *I* = Inexpensive

CONTINENTAL

Alois Dallmayr (Central Munich, *M*)
Bar-Restaurant Moritzz
(Central Munich, *M*)
Gastehaus Glockenbach
(Südbahnhof, *E*)
Mark's Restaurant (Central
Munich, *M*)
Park Hilton Grill (Central
Munich, *VE*)
Tantris (Schwabing, *VE*)

FRENCH

Bistro Terrine (Schwabing, *E*)
Gastätte die Deutsche Eiche
(Central Munich, *M*)
Graffunder (Central Munich, *E*)
Grünwalder Einkehr (Grünwald, *M*)
Kay's Bistro (Central Munich, *E*)
Prielhof (Bogenhausen, *E*)
Tantris (Schwabing, *VE*)

GERMAN

Käfer-Schänke (Bogenhausen, *E*)
Palais Keller (Central Munich, *I*)
Preysing-Keller (Haidhausen, *E*)
Wirsthaus im Weinstadl
(Central Munich, *I*)

INTERNATIONAL

A. Boettner (Central Munich, *VE*)
Donisl (Central Munich, *I*)
Garden Restaurant
(Central Munich, *VE*)
Kafer's Am Hofgarten
(Central Munich, *I*)
Tantris (Schwabing, *VE*)
Käfer-Schänke (Bogenhausen, *E*)
Kay's Bistro (Central Munich, *E*)

Königshof (Central Munich, *VE*)
Mövenpick Restaurant
(Central Munich, *M*)
Preysing-Keller (Haidhausen, *I*)
Spatenhaus (Central Munich, *E*)
Vier Jahreszeiten
(Central Munich, *VE*)
Zum Alten Markt
(Central Munich, *M*)

ITALIAN

Al Pino (Solln, *I*)
Casale (Denning, *I*)
El Toulà (Central Munich, *E*)
Galleria (Central Munich, *E*)
Gastätte die Deutsche Eiche
(Central Munich, *M*)
Geisel's Vinothek (Central Munich, *I*)
Graffunder (Central Munich, *I*)
Der Katzlmacher (Schwabing, *M*)
La Mucca (Schwabing, *M*)
La Vigna (Englschalking, *I*)
Locanda Picolit (Schwabing, *M*)
Spago (Schwabing, *M*)

MEDITERRANEAN

Garden Restaurant
(Central Munich, *VE*)

SEAFOOD

Austernkeller (Central Munich, *M*)

SWISS

Chesa Rüegg (Central Munich, *M*)
Mövenpick Restaurant
(Central Munich, *M*)

VEGETARIAN

Prinz Myshkin (Central Munich, *I*)

3 In Central Munich

VERY EXPENSIVE

✪ A. Boettner

Theatinerstrasse 8, off Marienplatz. ☎ **089/22-12-10.** Reservations required. Main courses 50 DM–66 DM ($35–$46.20); fixed-price lunch 87 DM ($60.90). AE, DC, MC, V. Mon–Fri 11:30am–11pm, Sat 11:30am–2:30pm. Tram: 19. INTERNATIONAL.

Although not in the same league as Tantris (see below), Boettner is a citadel of fine taste, good food, and impeccable service—all wrapped in a discreet and distinguished ambience. One of the choicest special restaurants of Munich is tiny and totally intimate—at times everybody seems to know everybody else. It has been run by the same family since 1901. You're assured such savory fare as saddle of venison and fried goose liver on a bed of green beans. Lobster is a specialty, sometimes appearing in a soufflé of pike or in an exquisite lobster stew Boettner. In season, fresh venison attracts the aficionado of game. For dessert, the velvety chocolate mousse is a particularly good choice. The restaurant is for the discriminating gourmet only. You'll find it in a pedestrian zone, a five-minute walk from the opera.

Garden Restaurant

In the Bayerischer Hof Hotel, Promenadeplatz 2–6. ☎ **089/21-200.** Reservations recommended. Main courses 38 DM–56 DM ($26.60–$39.20). Fixed-price lunch 54 DM ($37.80); fixed-price dinners 90 DM–100 DM ($63–$70). AE, DC, MC, V. Tram: 19. MEDITERRANEAN/ INTERNATIONAL.

Evocative of the interior of a small, pastel-colored palace loaded with blooming plants, this is the showcase restaurant within one of the showcase hotels of Munich. Set in a solemnly hushed room off the otherwise bustling lobby of the hotel, it serves up-scale food to a cosmopolitan crowd. Menu items are about as cultivated and esoteric as you're likely to find in Munich, completely based on fresh ingredients flown in from virtually everywhere. In some cases there's an emphasis on flavors and textures of the Mediterranean. Examples include fresh lobster folded into an herb-flavored green risotto, a succulent version of goose-liver terrine whipped with sauterne into a mousse, the best mashed potatoes in Munich accented with caviar in the style of French chef Michel Guerard, butter-braised filet of sole with parslied new potatoes, and (not to everyone's taste) filet of turkey dredged in pulverized cornflakes. Desserts are appropriately lavish, and wine choices are among the most varied in Munich.

✪ Park Hilton Grill

In the Park Hilton Hotel, Am Tucherpark 7. ☎ **089/38-450.** Reservations recommended. Fixed-price lunch 53 DM ($37.10); fixed-price dinners 90 DM–120 DM ($63–$84). Main courses 42 DM–65 DM ($29.40–$45.50). AE, DC, MC, V. Sun and Tues–Fri noon–2:30pm; and 7–10:30pm. U-Bahn: U3 or U6 to Giselastrasse, then bus 54. CONTINENTAL.

Realizing the stiff competition they faced from other restaurants on the northern outskirts of Munich, the developers of the Hilton used their imagination in transforming a corner of its modern premises into one of the most sophisticated and well-conceived restaurants in town. The impressive result is a replica of a richly paneled private club that just happens to be open to the public, and just happens to be a place with charm, panache, and flair. Tables are elaborately decorated in this civilized venue; dishes combine both traditional and modern European and North American cuisine. Despite the set luncheon's elegance, management offers a free bottle of champagne if the meal is not completed within an hour of a patron's arrival. A meal might include salmon carpaccio with a white asparagus vinaigrette, spaghettini with morels in an herb sauce, monkfish on lentils with crispy Parma ham, or one of Munich's best Bavarian-style duck dishes, on white cabbage with dumplings. Dinners are even more elaborate, including the pièce de résistance, wood pigeon with foie gras and artichokes set in Madeira-flavored aspic, followed by a lavish array of desserts that usually ends in coffee with petits-fours.

✪ Restaurant Königshof

In the Hotel Königshof, Karlsplatz 25 (Am Stachus). ☎ **089/55-13-60.** Reservations required. Main courses 44 DM–64 DM ($30.80–$44.80); fixed-price menus 128 DM–148 DM ($89.60– $103.60). AE, DC, MC, V. Daily noon–2:30pm and 7–11pm. S-Bahn: S3, S7, or S8 to Karlsplatz. Tram: 19. INTERNATIONAL.

The owners of this deluxe hotel want the Königshof to surface near the top in culinary delights. While this hotel dining room is no longer the finest in Munich—

that honor has passed on to the Hilton Grill—it still surfaces near the top. The Geisel family renovations have produced a room with oyster-white panels of oak, polished bronze chandeliers, silver candelabra, and porcelain. The black-jacketed waiters in their long white aprons are polite and skilled. Chef Martin Bräuer is both inventive and creative. His "culinary masterpieces" depend on his whim, and, almost as important, on what's available in season. He likes extremely fresh ingredients, and the food here reflects his passion. Perhaps you'll get to try his foie gras with sauterne, lobster soufflé, loin of lamb with fine herbs, lobster with vanilla butter, or sea bass suprême.

Restaurant Vier Jahreszeiten

In the Kempinski Hotel Vier Jahreszeiten München, Maximilianstrasse 17. ☎ **089/21-25-0.** Reservations required. Main courses 42 DM–56 DM ($29.40–$39.20); seven-course fixed-price menu 120 DM ($84). AE, DC, MC, V. Daily noon–3pm and 6–11pm. Closed Aug. Tram: 19. INTERNATIONAL.

The Restaurant Vier Jahreszeiten is in a quiet and elegant location within walking distance of the opera house. The atmosphere is dignified and refined, the service extremely competent, and the food prepared along classic French lines, with many imaginative variations. The menu changes every four to six weeks, but appetizers are likely to include mushroom soufflé served with artichoke-cream sauce, freshly made vegetable soup flavored with pesto, or turbot encased in basil-flavored crust. For a main course, you might try breast of Bresse chicken with scampi, flavored with a ginger sauce, or roast medallions of venison with cherry-pepper sauce. Another main-dish specialty is blanquette of veal and lobster. Desserts include such specialties as strawberries Walterspiel, or, for two, tangerine soufflé served with foamy vanilla sauce.

EXPENSIVE

El Toulà

Sparkassenstrasse 5. ☎ **089/29-28-69.** Reservations required. Main courses 35 DM–42 DM ($24.50–$29.40). AE, DC, MC, V. Tues–Sat noon–2pm and 7–11pm. Closed first three weeks in Aug. U-Bahn: U2 or U3 to Marienplatz. S-Bahn: All trains. Bus: 52. ITALIAN.

This elegant restaurant is one of the finest links in a chain that stretches from Rome to Tokyo. It not only serves the most refined Italian haute cuisine in the Bavarian capital but is one of the city's top dining choices, competing with such well-established places as Boettner. The turn-of-the-century decor, with wickered bentwood chairs, features a work called *Woman with Hound* by well-known artist Dudovic. All pasta is homemade on the premises, and the fish and meat specialties use only the freshest ingredients. The cookery style ranges from the cuisine of Piedmont to Lombardy, with a stopover in Venice. Care is taken with the vegetables, and the desserts are luscious. Prices are a bit luscious as well.

Galleria

Ledererstrasse 2 at Sparkassenstrasse. ☎ **089/29-79-95.** Reservations recommended. Main courses 35 DM–44 DM ($24.50–$30.80); fixed-price lunch 50 DM ($35); fixed-price dinner 80 DM ($56). AE, DC, MC, V. Mon–Sat noon–3pm and 6pm–midnight. U-Bahn: Marienplatz. ITALIAN.

This is one of the most appealing of the several Italian restaurants within Munich's historic core, and the one that takes the greatest risks with experimental versions of Italian cuisine. A few blocks east of the Marienplatz, with a modern and brightly colored setting and modern paintings, it provides gracious service and a roster of dishes that change with the availability of ingredients and the inspiration of the chefs. Examples include poached seawolf with fresh vegetables in fennel sauce; an aromatic guinea fowl scented with lavender; filet of sole with a velvety eggplant mousse and basil; herb-flavored risotto with chunks of lobster and braised radicchio (the best such dish we've ever had in Munich); and roasted soft-shell crabs with a light onion sauce. Dessert might include a smooth zabaglione served with pears marinated in port wine.

Kay's Bistro

Utzschneiderstrasse 1. ☎ 089/260-35-84. Reservations required. Main courses 38 DM–45 DM ($26.60–$31.50). AE, MC. Daily 7pm–1am. U-Bahn: U2 or U3 to Marienplatz. FRENCH/ INTERNATIONAL.

Munich's most sophisticated dining rendezvous, Kay's is off the historic Viktualien-markt. It's filled nightly with a glamorous (sometimes media related) clientele that wants to be seen in the right places. The decoration is changed often—perhaps you'll be there when the walls are covered with Hollywood souvenirs. Not only the interior design but the staff outfits and even the food reflect the restaurant's decorative motif. French and international cuisine is light, nouvelle, and avant-garde; many ingredients are bought fresh daily. Kay Wörsching, a magazine columnist, personally greets his guests with a gracious welcome.

MODERATE

✪ Alois Dallmayr

Dienerstrasse 14–15. ☎ 089/213-51-00. Reservations required. Main courses 28 DM–46 DM ($19.60–$32.20). AE, DC, MC, V. Mon–Wed and Fri 9am–6:30pm, Thurs 9am–8:30pm, Sat 9am–3pm. Tram: 19. CONTINENTAL.

The Fauchon's of Munich is Alois Dallmayr, whose history goes back to 1700. Near the Rathaus, it is Germany's most famous delicatessen, of world renown. After looking at its tempting array of delicacies from around the globe, you'll think you're lost in a millionaire's supermarket. Dallmayr has been a purveyor to many royal courts. Here you'll find Munich's most elegant consumers, looking for that "tinned treasure," perhaps Scottish salmon, foie gras, English biscuits, wines, and spirits, as well as out-of-season fresh produce.

The upstairs dining room serves a subtle German version of continental cuisine, owing a heavy debt to France. The food array is dazzling, ranging from the best herring and sausages we've ever tasted to such rare treats as perfectly vine-ripened tomatoes flown in from Morocco, and papayas from Brazil. The famous French poulet de Bresse, believed by many gourmets to be the world's finest, is also shipped in. The smoked fish is a taste sensation and the soups are superbly flavored, especially one made with shrimp. If you're dining alone, you might prefer to sit at the counter instead of a table. The bustling restaurant is crowded at lunchtime.

Austernkeller

Stollbergstrasse 11. ☎ 089/29-87-87. Reservations required. Main courses 22 DM–46 DM ($15.40–$32.20). AE, DC, MC, V. Tues–Sun 6pm–1am. Closed Dec 23–26. U-Bahn: Isartorplatz. SEAFOOD.

The "oyster cellar" is a delight to both visitors and the local trade. You get the largest selection of the finest oysters in town; many gourmets make an entire meal of raw oysters. Others prefer them elaborately prepared—for example, oysters Rockefeller. A delectable dish to start is the shellfish platter with fresh oysters, mussels, clams, scampi, and sea snails. Or you might begin with a rich fish soup or cold hors d'oeuvre. French meat specialties are offered, but most guests prefer the fish dishes—no other chef in Munich can make a lobster thermidor as good as the one served here. The decor, under a vaulted ceiling, is a kitsch collection of everything from plastic lobsters to old porcelain.

Chesa Rüegg

Wurzerstrasse 18. ☎ **089/29-71-14.** Reservations recommended. Main courses 25 DM–45 DM ($17.50–$31.50); fixed-price lunch 25.50 DM ($17.85). AE, DC, MC, V. U-Bahn: Odeonsplatz or Marienplatz. BAVARIAN/SWISS.

Set in the historic core of Munich, adjacent to the Vier Jahreszeiten Hotel, this restaurant recreates the warm coziness of a gemütlich inn high in the Bavarian or Swiss Alps. Within a setting accented with roughly textured plaster, wood paneling, oversized cow bells, and kerosene lamps, you can pretend you're far from the urban setting of Munich's Altstadt. Menu items include Zurich-style strips of veal in cream sauce with *Rösti,* braised filet of pork with Ticino-style polenta, and filet of beef with truffles and red wine sauce. *Hint:* By the time of your visit, look for an increased emphasis on Bavarian dishes, as the menu here goes through transitions based on the chef's vision of the moment.

✪ Halali

Schönfeldstrasse 22. ☎ **089/28-59-09.** Reservations recommended. Main courses 29 DM– 39 DM ($20.30–$27.30); fixed-price lunch 35 DM ($24.50); fixed-price dinner 85 DM ($59.50). AE, MC, V. Mon–Sat noon–3pm; Mon–Fri 4pm–1am. U-Bahn: Odeonsplatz. BAVARIAN.

Few aspects of the decor have changed here since it was established around 1900, and very few of the staff or clients would ever want it to change. The setting is baronial, and devoted to a Teutonic version of The Hunt, as even its name (which translates into something akin to "Tally-Ho") would suggest. Amid high ceilings, solid archways, and a collection of stag's horns, you can order a flavorful array of traditional dishes that include terrine of venison and Blutwurst (blood sausage), both of which are specialties of the house. Either of these might be followed with filet of venison in wine sauce, grilled Bavarian duck, guinea fowl, or pheasant. Also recommended are ravioli stuffed either with goosemeat and mushrooms, or with ricotta and truffles; pan-fried trout with parsley butter and new potatoes; and a warm apple tart with vanilla sauce. These dishes are prepared with a certain style and flair; you get very good value here.

Mark's Restaurant

In the Hotel Rafael, Neuturmstrasse 1. ☎ **089/29-09-80.** Reservations recommended. Fixed-price lunch in Mark's Corner 45 DM ($31.50); dinner main courses 38 DM–54 DM ($26.60–$37.80). AE, DC, MC, V. Daily noon–2pm and 6:30–10pm. U-Bahn: Marienplatz. CONTINENTAL.

The restaurant, in the prestigious Hotel Rafael, is appropriately elegant, outfitted with the requisite porcelain, silver, and impeccably trained service. If you opt for a meal here, don't ask to meet a chef named Mark (the place was named after the owner's son), and expect different venues at lunch and dinner. Lunch is served in a small, cozy enclave off the lobby, Mark's Corner, and is usually limited to a set-price menu favored by businesspeople. Dinners are swankier and more elaborate, served one floor above street level in a formal dining room that overlooks a monumental staircase and the lobby below. On Monday night the formal dining room is closed, and evening meals are served in the relatively informal lobby level setting of Mark's Corner.

Menu items change according to the season and the inspiration of the chef and might include dishes that succeed beautifully despite their sometimes experimental nature. Examples include kohlrabi soup with strips of ham; guineau fowl in mustard sauce with herbs; wild salmon with red and green lentils; halibut with fennel sauce; a ragoût of fish in puff pastry with balsamic vinegar and herbs; and breast of free-range chicken with curried vinaigrette, sometimes served as a salad.

Mövenpick Restaurant

Im Künstlerhaus, Lenbachplatz 8. ☎ **089/545-94-90.** Main courses in upstairs dining room 22 DM–48 DM ($15.40–$33.60); main courses in street-level dining room 12 DM–36 DM ($8.40–$25.20). AE, DC, MC, V. Daily 8:30am–11pm. U-Bahn: U4 or U5 to Stachus. SWISS/ INTERNATIONAL.

The *Jugendstil* building (Künstlerhaus) that contains it was originally constructed in 1898 as a publicly subsidized community of artists, most of whom studiously avoided politically or socially controversial subjects. In 1971, in anticipation of Munich's Olympic Games, the site was transformed into a network of atmospheric dining rooms, each with a different historic or whimsical theme. In the Venezia dining room, on the ground floor, turn-of-the-century murals have been painstakingly refurbished after the World War II bombings. Other venues include rooms with names like Rosenzimmer, the Pub, and (upstairs) the garden-style Pastorale, Omas Küche (Grandma's Kitchen), and a corner inspired by the plains of Texas, Longhorn Corner.

Regardless of the room you select, service and cuisine are more formal and prices more expensive upstairs than on the ground floor. There, no one will mind if you order just coffee, beer, or a dish of ice cream, although ordering only a snack might be frowned upon upstairs. Regardless of where you sit, however, one especially fine choice is Zurich-style veal strips in cream sauce, served with *Rösti* potatoes. Vegetarians might opt for a savory platter of Steinpilz mushrooms served in cream sauce and accompanied by Bavarian dumplings.

Ratskeller München

Im Rathaus, Marienplatz 8. ☎ **089/22-03-13.** Reservations required. Main courses 15 DM–33 DM ($10.50–$23.10). AE, MC, V. Daily 10am–midnight. U-Bahn: U2 or U3 to Marienplatz. BAVARIAN.

Throughout Germany you'll find Ratskellers, traditional restaurants in Rathaus (city hall) basements (note that *Rat* means "counsel," not the animal) serving good, inexpensive food and wine. Munich is proud to possess one of the best Ratskellers in Germany. The decor is typical: lots of dark wood and carved chairs. The most interesting tables, often staked out by in-the-know locals, are the semiprivate dining nooks in the rear, under the vaulted painted ceilings. Bavarian music adds to the ambience. The menu, a showcase of regional fare, includes some international dishes, many of them vegetarian, which is unusual for a Ratskeller. A freshly made soup of the day is featured, and you can help yourself from the salad bar. Some of the dishes are a little heavy and too porky—best left for your overweight Bavarian uncle—but you can find lighter fare if you search the menu carefully.

Spatenhaus

Residenzstrasse 12. ☎ **089/290-70-60.** Reservations recommended. Main courses 24.50 DM–42.50 DM ($17.15–$29.75). AE, DC, MC, V. Daily 10:30am–12:30pm. U-Bahn: U3, U4, or U6 to Odeonsplatz or Marienplatz. BAVARIAN/INTERNATIONAL.

One of Munich's best-known beer restaurants has wide windows overlooking the opera house on Max-Joseph-Platz. Of course, to be loyal, you should accompany your meal with the restaurant's own beer, called Spaten-Franziskaner-Bier. You can sit in an intimate, semiprivate dining nook or at a big table. The Spatenhaus has old traditions, offers typical Bavarian food, and is known for generous portions and reasonable prices. If you want to know what all this fabled Bavarian gluttony is all about, order the "Bavarian plate," which is loaded down with pork, sausages, and other meat. After that, you'll have to go, not to a nunnery, but to a spa.

Weinhaus Neuner

Herzogspitalstrasse 8. ☎ **089/260-39-54.** Reservations recommended. Main courses 24 DM–33 DM ($16.80–$23.10); fixed-price menus 34 DM–58 DM ($23.80–$40.60). AE, MC, V. Mon–Sat 11:30am–3pm and 6:30pm–midnight. U-Bahn: U4 to Stachus. S-Bahn: All trains to Stachus. BAVARIAN.

This is an *Ältestes Weinhaus Münchens,* one of the city's landmark taverns. It dates to the late 15th century and is the only building in Munich that has its original Tyrolean vaults. The place brims over with warmth and charm. Once young priests were educated here, but after secularization by Napoléon the place became a wine tavern and a meeting place for artists, writers, and composers, including Richard Wagner. Its rooms have been renovated and its paintings restored.

It's divided into two parts. The less expensive place to dine is the casual Weinstube, with lots of local atmosphere, where you can order typical Bavarian dishes such as home-smoked beef. The restaurant, on the other hand, is elegant, with candles and flowers. The chef happily marries cuisine moderne and regional specialties.

⊛ Zum Alten Markt

Am Viktualienmarkt, Dreifaltigkeitsplatz 3. ☎ **089/29-99-95.** Reservations recommended. Main courses 30 DM–40 DM ($21–$28). No credit cards. Mon–Sat noon–2pm and 6–10pm. U-Bahn: U2 or U3 to Marienplatz. Bus: 52. BAVARIAN/INTERNATIONAL.

Snug and cozy, Zum Alten Markt serves beautifully presented fresh cuisine at a good price. Located on a tiny square just off Munich's large outdoor food market, the restaurant has a mellow charm and a welcome from its owner, Josef Lehner. The interior decor with its intricately coffered wooden ceiling were taken from a 400-year-old Tyrolean castle. In summer there are outside tables. Fish and fresh vegetables come from the nearby market. You might begin with a tasty homemade soup, such as cream of carrot, or perhaps black-truffle tortellini in cream sauce with young onions and tomatoes. The chef makes some of Munich's best Tafelspitz (the elegant boiled-beef dish so beloved by Emperor Franz Josef of Austria). You can also order classic dishes such as Bavarian goose and a savory roast suckling pig.

INEXPENSIVE

⊛ Donisl

Weinstrasse 1. ☎ **089/22-01-84.** Reservations recommended. Main courses all 11.95 DM ($8.35). AE, DC, MC, V. Daily 9am–midnight. U-Bahn: U2 or U3 to Marienplatz. S-Bahn: All trains. BAVARIAN/INTERNATIONAL.

Donisl is Munich's oldest beer hall, dating from 1715. Some readers praise this Munich-style restaurant's relaxed and comfortable atmosphere. The seating capacity is about 550, and in summer you can enjoy the hum and bustle of Marienplatz while dining in the garden area out front. The restaurant has two levels, the second of which is a gallery. English is spoken. The standard menu offers traditional Bavarian food as well as a weekly changing specials menu. Specialties include the little white sausages, Weisswurst, a decades-long tradition of this place. The chef also prepares a good duck. Select beers from Munich's own Hacker-Pschorr Brewery top the evening. A zither player at noon and an accordion player in the evening entertain guests.

Graffunder

Tal 1. ☎ **089/29-24-27.** Snack items and platters 10 DM–19 DM ($7–$13.30); glasses of wine 6 DM–7.80 DM ($4.20–$5.45). No credit cards. Mon–Fri 6pm–midnight, Sun 5pm–midnight. U-Bahn: Marienplatz. ITALIAN/FRENCH.

Don't expect the grace notes and service rituals of a full-fledged restaurant at this informal place. It specializes in the presentation of French and Italian wines, usually sold by the glass, and configured into a breezy, easygoing venue that's been the rage in London for almost a decade now. Food, while not actually conceived as an after-thought to the wine, is nonetheless considered an accompaniment. Platters range from the very simple (tomato, basil, and mozzarella salads or a platter of carpaccio) to the more elaborate (pastas, escalopes of veal, chicken with morels or chanterelles, or Mediterranean ratatouille). In all, it's an excellent French/Italian alternative to the predictable regime of beer-hall-style suds and wursts that accompany so many other meals served in Munich's folkloric core.

Geisel's Vinothek

In the Hotel Excelsior, Schützenstrasse 11. ☎ **089/55-13-71-40.** Reservations recommended for dining, not necessary for wine tasting. Main courses 10 DM–28 DM ($7–$19.60); fixed-price meals 14 DM ($9.80). Glasses of wine 4 DM–12 DM ($2.80–$8.40). AE, DC, MC, V. Warm food daily noon–8:30pm; wine daily noon–1am. U-Bahn: Hauptbahnhof. ITALIAN.

The four-star Excelsior hotel made a deliberate choice when it decided not to compete with the *grand chic* restaurants of its competitors: for example, the Bayerischer Hof with its super-upscale Garden Restaurant. Instead, the hotel opted for a cozy, consciously Gemütlich enclave of rustic charm that evokes an unpretentious trattoria high in the Italian Alps. It's known for its assortment of Italian, French, Austrian, and German wines, dispensed by the glass to clients who can just sit or eat at the bar. There are also about a dozen tables scattered throughout the room for those who want a full-fledged meal. Menu items include savory cuisine from Italy, mostly conceived as a tasty foil for the wine. Examples include carpaccio, mozzarella with fresh basil and tomatoes, *vitello tonnato,* platters containing an assortment of mixed grilled fish, veal, and chicken dishes, and pastas whose composition changes with the seasons and mood of the chef. All this is routine Italian fare, but with the wine as a backup, almost everything tastes good.

Hundskugel

Hotterstrasse 18. ☎ **089/26-42-72.** Reservations required. Main courses 14 DM–37 DM ($9.80–$25.90). No credit cards. Daily 10am–midnight. U-Bahn: U2 or U3 to Marienplatz. BAVARIAN.

The city's oldest tavern, Hundskugel dates back to 1440, and apparently serves the same food as it did back then. If it was good a long time ago, why mess with the menu? Built in an alpine style, it's within easy walking distance of Marienplatz. Perhaps half the residents of Munich at one time or another have made their way here to be wined and dined in style. The cookery is honest Bavarian with no pretensions. Although the chef makes a specialty of Spanferkel (roast suckling pig with potato noodles), you might prefer Tafelspitz (boiled beef) in dill sauce or roast veal stuffed with goose liver. To begin, try one of the hearty soups, made fresh daily.

Käfer's Am Hofgarten

Odeonsplatz 6. ☎ **089/2-90-75-30.** Reservations recommended for dinner. Main courses 27 DM–35 DM ($18.90–$24.50); fixed-price menus 19 DM–35 DM ($13.30–$24.50). AE, MC, V. Mon–Thurs 10:30am–1am; Fri 10:30am–3am; Sat 9:30am–3am; Sun 9:30am–1am. U-Bahn: U3, U4, U5, or U6 to Odeonsplatz. Bus: 54. INTERNATIONAL.

Even its staff (most of them are under 30) make jokes about the affluent and youthful clientele that hangs out at this French bistro at the beginning of the Ludwigstrasse. Almost everyone you're likely to see inside—at least until the fickle fashions of yuppie-dom change—range in age from 27 to 35. Part of the place's allure derives from the building, a 200-year-old historic monument; the decor, which might have

🐣 Family-Friendly Restaurants

Nürnberger Bratwurst Glöckl Am Dom *(see p. 99)* Hot dogs will never taste the same again after your child has tried one of those delectable little sausages from Nürnberg.

Mövenpick Restaurant *(see page 96)* The food at this Swiss-run restaurant is so wide and varied, and the settings are so different, that your kid will surely agree on one room or the other. Dining options range from a garden-style Pastorale to Grandma's Kitchen, with even a corner inspired by the plains of Texas. You can order only a light meal or else a big spread—whatever you want. It's all very informal and moderately priced.

Ratskeller München *(see page 96)* All parents eventually take their kids to the centrally located Marienplatz in Munich. Once there, there is no better place for dining than the architectural interesting Ratskeller, one of the finest in Germany. It's got everything needed to fill your kid up, ranging from vegetarian dishes to a freshly prepared salad bar. The hearty soups served here make a complete lunch unto themselves.

been lifted directly from gaslight-era Paris; and an ambience eminently suited for relaxing for gossiping and convivial chitchat. Another powerful allure is the food—it's the most self-consciously eclectic in Munich, combining Thai curries with dim sum and spring rolls with Bavarian duckling, American rib-eye steaks, English lamb chops, and Italian tagliatelle with asparagus. There's additional seating upstairs, and a staff that thinks nothing is at all strange about serving breakfast to recovering night-owls at 3pm.

🟢 Nürnberger Bratwurst Glöckl Am Dom

Frauenplatz 9. ☎ **089/29-52-64.** Reservations recommended. Main courses 15 DM–29 DM ($10.50–$20.30). No credit cards. Daily 9am–midnight. U-Bahn: U2 or U3 to Marienplatz. S-Bahn: All trains. BAVARIAN.

In the coziest and warmest of Munich's local restaurants, you sit in chairs that look as if they were made by a Nuremberg carver. The restaurant first opened in 1893 but had to be rebuilt after World War II. Upstairs, reached through a hidden stairway, is a dining room decorated with reproductions of Dürer prints. The homesick Nürnberger comes here just for one dish: Nürnberger Schweinwurstl mit Kraut—those delectable little sausages. The restaurant has a strict policy of shared tables, and service is on tin plates. Last food orders go in at midnight. A short walk from Marienplatz, the restaurant faces the cathedral, the Frauenkirche.

🟢 Palais Keller

In the Hotel Bayerischer Hof (Palais Montgelas), Promenadeplatz 2. ☎ **089/21-20-990.** Reservations recommended. Main courses 15 DM–35 DM ($10.50–$24.50), platter of the day 15 DM–25 DM ($10.50–$17.50). AE, DC, MC, V. Daily 11am–midnight. Tram 19. BAVARIAN/GERMAN.

Massive, with a high turnover and a sense of bustling energy, this richly folkloric restaurant lies deep in the cellar of one of Munich's finest hotels, down a flight of stone steps. Despite its elegant associations, its prices are easily competitive with those of Munich's many beer halls and Weinstuben. Waitresses speak English and wear frilly aprons and genuine smiles. There is a tempting array of such German dishes as veal in sour cream sauce with glazed turnips, cabbage, and carrots; pike balls on buttery leaf spinach with shrimp sauce; and Tafelspitz (boiled beef) with horse radish and vinaigrette sauce. Some diners, especially those who make the place a regular stopover, order whatever Tagesteller (platter of the day) is being served, accom-panied by one of the restaurant's broad selections of German wines. These are sold by the bottle or glass, along with foaming mugs of beer.

Prinz Myshkin

Hackenstrasse 2. ☎ **089/26-55-96.** Reservations recommended. Main courses 16 DM–30 DM ($11.20–$21); fixed-price meals 13.80 DM–28.50 DM ($9.65–$19.95). AE, MC, V. Daily 11am– 11:30pm. U-Bahn: U2 or U3 to Marienplatz. VEGETARIAN.

One of the best known and most popular vegetarian restaurants in Munich, it's set near Marienplatz, with hanging plants and a window view. Freshly made salads with names like "Aphrodite" and "Barbados," vegetarian involtini and casseroles, soups, and nine zesty pizzas are some of the choices, many of which are excellent. This is not a buffet—rather, it's a full-fledged restaurant with table service from a helpful staff. Wine and beer are available.

Straubinger Hof

Blumenstrasse 5. ☎ **089/260-84-44.** Reservations necessary only for six or more. Main courses 18 DM–27 DM ($12.60–$18.90). AE, MC, V. Mon–Fri 9am–8:30pm (last order), Sat 9am–3pm (last order). U-Bahn: Marienplatz. BAVARIAN.

This is one of the most recommendable and consistently crowded restaurants in the Altstadt, a well-managed, unpretentious, folkloric place sponsored by the brewers of Paulaner beer. No one will mind if you stop in just for a brew throughout the morn-ing and afternoon, although during peak lunch and dinner hours, it's good form to order at least a small platter of cheese, Blutwurst, Weisswurst, or Rotwurst, if not a the steaming platter of Tafelspitz (boiled beef with horseradish), Sauerbraten, or roasted knuckle of pork. In something approaching an orgy of Teutonic nostalgia for the kind of food old-time Bavarians were served as children, you're likely to see in the menu the term *Grossmutter Art,* or "in the style of grandmother." A large stein of beer costs from 5.20 DM ($3.65) to 5.50 DM ($3.85), depending on the type you order. This restaurant's position close to the Viktualienmarkt guarantees—at least in theory—the use of ultra-fresh produce. Portions are ample, prices are reasonable, and in summer, your seating options will spill out onto the pavement. Looking for a traditional Bavarian dessert? The deliberately old-fashioned specialty of the house is Apfelschmarrn, an apple-laced pastry. The restaurant also has all-vegetarian options.

Weisses Bräuhaus

Tal 7. ☎ **089/29-98-75.** Reservations recommended, especially for the back room. Main courses 20 DM–32 DM ($14–$22.40). No credit cards. Daily 8am–midnight. U-Bahn: U2 or U3 to Marienplatz. BAVARIAN.

In the heart of the city, the Weisses Bräuhaus is big, bustling, and Bavarian with a vengeance. Not for the pretentious, this informal place does what it has done for cen-turies: serves home-brewed beer. At one time the famous salt-trade route between Salzburg and Augsburg passed by its door, and salt traders were very thirsty back then.

In a world of smoke-blackened dark-wood paneling and stained glass, the front room is for drinking and informal eating; the back room has white tablecloths and black-outfitted waiters. You can begin with smoked filet of trout or rich-tasting potato soup, then try roast pork with homemade potato dumplings and cabbage salad, or Viennese veal goulash with mushrooms and cream sauce. You'll invariably share your table, but that's part of the fun here.

Wirtshaus im Weinstadl

Burgstrasse 5. ☎ **089/290-40-44.** Reservations required. Main courses 12 DM–30 DM ($8.40–$21). AE, MC. Mon–Sat 10:30am–1am. U-Bahn: U2 or U3 to Marienplatz. GERMAN.

A Weinhaus since 1850 and reputedly the oldest in Munich, Weinstadl was built in 1551 for use as a municipal wine cellar. Real old-world charm is found here: vaulted ceilings, a *trompe l'oeil* facade, and wrought-iron sconces. Dining is on three levels. Hearty Bavarian food and Palatinate wines are served; especially invigorating is the bean soup with ham. A typical main dish is roast pork with potato dumplings and mixed salad. Watch for the daily specials. In summer the activities spill over into an outdoor beer garden, where the ambience is heightened by the view of the neighborhood's medieval buildings.

Zum Bürgerhaus

Pettenkoferstrasse 1. ☎ **089/59-79-09.** Reservations recommended. Lunch platter 16.50 DM ($11.55); fixed-price menu 24 DM ($16.80); main courses 24 DM–32 DM ($16.80–$22.40). AE, MC, V. Mon–Fri 11:30am–2:30pm and Mon–Sat 7:30pm–midnight. U-Bahn: Sendlinger Tor. ALPINE.

Originally built in 1827, and outfitted with the dark-stained wood paneling and all the Gemütlich accessories you'd expect, this is one of the few restaurants in the old town that escaped relatively unscathed from the devastation of World War II. Appropriate for its rustic, nostalgic charm, it places culinary emphasis on Europe's mountainous heartland, including foothills and summits throughout the French, Italian, Swiss, German, and Austrian Alps. Menu choices change with the seasons, but at one time or another might include a Burgerhaus salad (garnished with herbed croûtons and bacon); lamb with rosemary sauce; filet of venison with red wine sauce; Zurich-style veal with Rösti and cream sauce; Viennese-style pork schnitzels; Bavarian duck with orange sauce; Angus steak bordelaise, and a cold-weather favorite, a *Burgerhaus Pfanne* that combines cutlets of turkey, veal, and pork in one well-seasoned pan. This restaurant's homemade version of noodles with cream sauce, herbs, and mushrooms sounds a little bland but is actually one of the more savory dishes.

4 Near the Südbahnhof

✪ Gastehaus Glockenbach

Kapuzinerstrasse 29, corner of Maistrasse. ☎ **089/53-40-43.** Reservations recommended. Main courses 35 DM–50 DM ($24.50–$35), fixed-price menus 60 DM–125 DM ($42–$87.50). DC, MC, V. Tues–Fri noon–1:30pm (last order); Tues–Sat 7–9:30pm (last order). Closed three weeks in Aug, one week at Christmas. U-Bahn: U3 or U6 to Goetheplatz. CONTINENTAL.

Despite a deliberately low-key approach, this unpretentious restaurant has emerged as one capable of holding its own against the more expensive, more imperious *grand bourgeois* icons. The setting is a 200-year-old building, close to a tributary (the Glockenbach) of the nearby Isar. Originally conceived as a brewery, it was transformed into its present incarnation in 1983. The dignified country-baroque interior is accented with vivid modern paintings, and the most elegant table settings in town, including a lavish array of porcelain by a company not well known in the New World, Hutchenreuther. Cuisine changes with the season and according to the inspiration of the chef, Karl Ederer.

Examples include imaginative preparations of venison and pheasant in autumn, lamb and veal dishes in springtime, seasonal shellfish, and a medley of ultra-fresh vegetables from local farms and exotica imported from sophisticated purveyors throughout the world. Wines are mostly European, with goodly representatives from Italy, France, and Austria.

5 Near the Isar, South of Center

Asam Schlössel

45 Maria-Einsiedel-Strasse. ☎ **089/723-6373**. Main courses 15 DM–30 DM ($10.50–$21). No credit cards. Daily 11am–1pm. U-Bahn: Talkirchen (zoo). BAVARIAN.

It offers a relaxed, relatively informal hideaway from the congestion of Munich, within a historic setting. The building was conceived in 1724 as a private villa for a pair of artists. Any residual holdovers—including its pastel-colored neofeudal design—from the original, castlelike structure have been emphasized, within the standardized traditional format of all the Augustiner brewery restaurants. Several brews, all products of Augustiner, are offered, including both pale and dark versions fermented from wheat (*Weissebier*). Menu items include roasted shoulder of pork (*Schweinsschulterbraten*) basted with (what else?) beer and served with braised red cabbage, and potato dumplings; beef braised in red wine (*Böfflamott*) with bread dumplings (*Semmelknödel*); and a dish beloved by the last of Austria's Habsburg emperors, a savory form of boiled beef with horseradish (*gesottener Tafelspitz mit frischen Kren*).

6 In Schwabing

This district of Munich, which used to be called "bohemian" in the 1940s, overflows with restaurants, many of which are awful, although there is an array of good places that attract a youthful clientele. The evening is the best time for a visit.

VERY EXPENSIVE

✪ Tantris

Johann-Fichte-Strasse 7, Schwabing. ☎ **089/36-20-61**. Reservations required. Fixed-price five-course lunch 148 DM ($103.60); fixed-price dinner 192 DM ($134.40) for five courses, 218 DM ($152.60) for eight courses; special five-course dinner Tues–Thurs (including red and white wine) 215 DM ($150.50). AE, DC, MC, V. Tues–Fri noon–3pm; Tues–Sat 6:30pm–1am. Closed public holidays; annual holidays in Jan and May. U-Bahn: U6 to Dietlindenstrasse. FRENCH/INTERNATIONAL/CONTINENTAL.

Tantris serves Munich's finest cuisine—it's simply the best. Chef Hans Haas was voted the top chef in Germany in 1994, and, if anything, he has refined and sharpened his technique since winning that honor. His penchant for exotic nouvelle carries him into ever greater achievements. There is no restaurant in Munich that comes close to equaling this place, not even Preysing-Keller, Boettner, or Gastehaus Glockenbach. The setting is unlikely—but once you're inside, you're transported into an ultramodern atmosphere with fine service. Leading Munich businesspeople like to entertain here.

The food is a treat to the eye as well as to the palate, and the beautiful interior adds to your enjoyment. The cooking is both subtle and original. Choice of dishes is wisely limited: There's an eight-course menu that changes daily, plus a five-course table d'hôte, served at noon. You might begin with one of the interesting soups, or a terrine of smoked fish served with green cucumber sauce, then follow with classic roast duck on mustard-seed sauce, or a delightful concoction of lobster medallions on black noodles. These dishes show a refinement and attention to detail, plus a quest for technical perfection, that is found nowhere else in Munich.

EXPENSIVE

Bistro Terrine
Amalienstrasse 89. ☎ **089/28-17-80.** Reservations recommended. Main courses 27 DM–38 DM ($18.90–$26.60); fixed-price lunch 42.50 DM ($29.75); fixed-price dinner 85 DM ($59.50). AE, MC, V. Mon–Sat noon–1:45pm and 6:30–10:30pm. U-Bahn: U3 or U6 to Universität. FRENCH.

It's one of the closest approximations in Munich to an authentic art-nouveau bistro. Its nouvelle cuisine is based on traditional recipes as authentic and savory as anything you'd find in Lyon, as intriguing and creative as what you'd expect in a chic experimental restaurant in Paris. There's room for up to about 50 diners at a time, but because the way the dining room is arranged, with banquettes and wood and glass dividers, it seems bigger than it actually is. During clement weather, there's additional seating on an outdoor terrace.

Menu items are often more innovative than the restaurant's turn-of-the-century setting would imply, and might include tartar of herring with fresh-made potato chips and salad; watercress salad with sweetbreads; cream of paprika soup; an autumn fantasy that includes nuggets of venison served with hazelnut-flavored gnocchi and port wine sauce; zander fish baked in an herb-and-potato crust; or an alluring specialty salmon with a chanterelle-studded risotto. After all this novelty, the most satisfying desserts might include a traditional tarte tatin or even an old-fashioned crème brûlée that's jazzed up with Tahitian-style vanilla sauce.

MODERATE

Der Katzlmacher
Kaulbacherstrasse 48. ☎ **089/34-81-29.** Reservations recommended. Main courses 28 DM–39 DM ($19.60–$27.30); fixed-price lunches 40 DM–50 DM ($28–$35); fixed-price dinners 60 DM–90 DM ($42–$63). AE, MC, V. Tues–Sat noon–3pm and 6:30pm–1am. U-Bahn: Universität. ITALIAN.

Few other Italian restaurants would have had the nerve to deliberately adopt a pejorative German word referring to Italians as their name. This one did, however, as whimsical proof of a sense of humor that's made them beloved by loyal local fans. The setting is a postwar building whose two dining rooms are evocative of a mountain lodge high in the Italian Alps. Starched white napery contrasts pleasantly with the rustic setting. Menu items derive from the culinary traditions of the Italian Marches, Friulia, and Emilia-Romagna, northerly agrarian provinces known for their fine cuisines and bounty. Menu specialties might include calzone stuffed with spinach and pine nuts, ravioli with ricotta and herbs, a commendable grilled swordfish with red wine vinaigrette, eel with champagne sauce, John Dory in saffron sauce, and a succulent version of *fritto misto del pesce* based on whatever is seasonal.

La Mucca
Georgenstrasse 105. ☎ **089/271-6742.** Reservations recommended. Main courses 24 DM–34 DM ($16.80–$23.80). DC, MC, V. Tues–Sun noon–2:15pm and 6–11:30pm. U-Bahn: U2 to Josephsplatz. ITALIAN.

This is an unpretentious and charming Italian restaurant in the heart of Schwabing, run by Italian expatriates who manage to infuse the ambience here with touches of Mediterranean humor, Mediterranean charm, and—when things get busy—Mediterranean hysteria. Small and convivial, with only 55 seats scattered between two different dining rooms, it prepares such well-received dishes as *lotte* (sea bass) baked in a salt crust, arguably the most delectable item on the menu. The chef shows flair with his carpaccio of lamb with olive oil and white beans, and also prepares that famous dish of Rome, *saltimbocca* (literally "jump-in-your-mouth," with ham and veal). You have to be born and bred in Italy, or else a true devotee of Italian cuisine as we are, to opt for a platter of grilled sardines in arugula. Both the antipasti and pasta selections are excellent, especially rigatoni with zucchini strips.

Locanda Picolit

Siegfriedstrasse 11. ☎ **089/39-64-47.** Reservations recommended. Main courses 29 DM–36 DM ($20.30–$25.20); fixed-price menu 79 DM ($55.30). AE, DC, MC, V. Sun–Fri noon–2:30pm and 6–11pm. Closed in June. U-Bahn: U3 or U6 to Münchener Freiheit. ITALIAN.

It occupies a modern building from the 1960s that's studded with streamlined, uncontroversial furnishings and dramatic oversized modern paintings. In summer, because of an outdoor terrace with a view over a garden, it's easy to believe that you've suddenly been transported to the Mediterranean world. Set in the heart of Schwabing, the restaurant's existence is the result of the imagination and hard work of Danillo Munisso and his Munich-born wife, Ingrid. Although menu items come from throughout Italy, you might suspect that those Sr. Munisso appreciates the most derive from his native Friuli district, near Venice. Even the locanda's name, Picolit, comes from one of that region's well-known wines.

The menu is influenced by whatever is seasonal at the time. Examples include a lavish use of asparagus, arugala, shellfish, rabbit, wild mushrooms, and venison, configured into such alluring dishes as ravioli stuffed with lobster, tagliatelle, rotini, or linguini with braised radicchio and shellfish, and, when available, saltimbocca (veal with ham).

Spago

Neureutherstrasse 15 at Arcisstrasse. ☎ **089/271-2406.** Reservations recommended. Main courses 25 DM–39 DM ($17.50–$27.30). Fixed-price lunch 39 DM ($27.30); fixed-price dinner 59 DM ($41.30). AE, MC, V. Mon–Fri noon–2:30pm; Sun–Fri 6–11:30pm. U-Bahn: U2 to Josephsplatz or U3 to Universität. ITALIAN.

The venue isn't as overwhelmingly successful, or as self-conscious and self-promotional, as its Los Angeles namesake, but nonetheless, this amiable and multilingual Italian restaurant in Schwabing serves some extremely good food. Opened in 1992, it offers lots of Italian pizzazz as well as modern and upscale Italian food. Some of the dishes are tagliatelle with porcini mushrooms; braised breast of chicken stuffed with herbs and spinach; ravioli with artichoke hearts or with potatoes and chanterelles; an especially delectable fish baked with herbs in a salt crust and wild mushrooms, sautéed with herbs and arugala; a perfectly prepared suckling lamb prepared with mint and balsamic vinegar; and an array of desserts that are as beautiful as they are tasty.

INEXPENSIVE

Weinbauer

Fendstrasse 5. ☎ **089/39-81-55.** Reservations recommended. Main courses 10.50 DM–26.50 DM ($7.35–$18.55). No credit cards. Daily 11am–midnight. U-Bahn: U3 or U6 to Münchner Freiheit. BAVARIAN.

Just off Leopoldstrasse is this small, relatively untrammeled budget restaurant. Despite a complete renovation in 1993, it retains many traditional Bavarian accessories, evoking an unglossy dining room in a small town somewhere in the Alps. Menu items include Wiener schnitzel, Nürnberger wurst'l with sauerkraut, sirloin steak with an herb-butter sauce, goulash soup, and Blutwurst and Leberwurst platters. The food is reliable but hardly spectacular. Any of these might be washed down with a half liter of tap beer.

7 In Haidhausen

◆ Preysing-Keller

Preysingstrasse 1. ☎ **089/45-84-50.** Reservations recommended. Main courses 32 DM–46 DM ($22.40–$32.20); fixed-price menus 89 DM–125 DM ($62.30–$87.50). AE, DC, V. Mon–Sat 6pm–1am. Tram: 18. GERMAN/INTERNATIONAL.

Preysing-Keller is a "find," but you have to cross the Isar to discover its superb cookery and wines. It's connected to the Hotel Preysing (see Chapter 4). You'll dine in a 300-year-old cellar with massive beams and high masonry arches; the decor is simple, with wooden tables and chairs. Daily market excursions are made by the staff, who select only the freshest ingredients. The fresh fish and seafood are kept in aquariums on the premises prior to cooking. The goose-liver pâté is a specialty, as is lobster in butter sauce and steak tartar of venison. Everything on the menu appears seductively fresh. The cuisine is derived from classic Bavarian dishes made new by the innovative chef.

8 In Bogenhausen

Käfer-Schänke

Prinzregentenstrasse 73. ☎ **089/416-82-47.** Reservations required. Main courses 34.50 DM–69 DM ($24.15–$48.30); fixed-price lunch 43 DM ($30.10). AE, DC, MC, V. Mon–Sat 11:30am–midnight. Closed holidays. U-Bahn: U4 to Prinzregentenplatz. Bus: 55. GERMAN/INTERNATIONAL.

For casual dining prepared with elegant style, this spot on the second floor of a famous gourmet shop, Käfer, is one of the best in Munich. The setting resembles a chalet, and the cuisine roams the world for inspiration—everywhere from Lombardy to Asia. You select your hors d'oeuvres from the most dazzling display in Munich and are billed according to how many pâtés or croûtes you choose. Waiters serve the main dishes. Often Käfer-Schänke devotes a week to a particular country's cuisine. On one visit, we enjoyed the classic loup (sea bass) with fennel as presented on the French Riviera. The salads have what one reviewer called "rococo splendor." From a cold table, you can choose smoked salmon or smoked eel. Venison, quail, and guinea hen are regularly featured. There's a deluxe gourmet shop on the main floor.

Prielhof

Oberföhringer Strasse 44. ☎ **089/98-53-53.** Reservations necessary. Fixed-price lunch 38 DM ($26.60); fixed-price dinner 78 DM ($54.60). Main courses 35 DM–50 DM ($24.50–$35). DC, MC, V. U-Bahn: U4 to Arabellapark. FRENCH.

It's one of the most glamorous French restaurants in town. The decor is more Austrian and urbane than that of its many Bavarian competitors. A green ceramic Kachelofen (porcelain stove) dominates one side of the main dining room. Menu items are influenced by modern French cuisine, and are written in an amiable (and very French) scrawl on the frequently changing menu. They include cream of potato soup with chanterelles; sautéed sweetbreads with asparagus and fresh tomatoes; a heavenly braised guinea fowl with wild greens and shiitake mushrooms; vegetable risotto with braised goose liver; gratin of saltwater fish with leafy salad and chive sauce; braised hen with rosemary, tomatoes, and parslied potatoes; and our favorite, rack of lamb in an herb crust with creamed potatoes, ratatouille, and green beans. Dessert might be an amaretto parfait with marinated berries. The restaurant is named, incidentally, after the upscale neighborhood where it's located.

9 In Denning

Casale

Ostpreussenstrasse 42. ☎ **089/93-62-68.** Reservations recommended. Main courses 36 DM–63 DM ($25.20–$44.10). Fixed-price menus 65 DM–98 DM ($45.50–$68.60). AE, DC, MC, V. Daily noon–2:30pm and 6–11pm. U-Bahn: U4 to Arabellapark. ITALIAN.

It's one of the more restrained, discreet, upscale, and formal of Munich's many Italian restaurants, with a decor more self-consciously "expensive" than many others of its competitors. Set in Denning, near the mega-hotels of the Bogenhausen district, north of Munich's center, it works hard on such tours de force as a nine-course *menu dégustazione* that requires several hours to consume gracefully. Menu items are savory and stylish, and usually served with flair. They include sea bass prepared with rosemary in a salt crust, filet of beef with Barolo sauce, and an array of pastas that include ravioli stuffed with pulverized veal and spices and an excellent linguine with fresh asparagus or exotic seasonal mushrooms.

10 In Englschalking

✪ La Vigna

Wilhelm-Diess-Weg 2, at the Englschalkinger Strasse, in Bogenhausen. ☎ **089/93-14-16.** Reservations recommended. Fixed-price menu 89 DM ($62.30); main courses 34 DM–41 DM ($23.80–$28.70). AE, DC, MC, V. Sun–Fri noon–2:30pm and 6:30–11pm. U-Bahn: U4 to Arabellapark. ITALIAN.

This is our favorite Italian restaurant in Munich. It's popular with business travelers staying at the mega-hotels nearby, and with residents of the upscale suburb of Bogenhausen. Its cuisine is among the top; it ranks with Gastehaus Glockenbach and A. Boettner. Within a postmodern and monochromatic gray and white setting that has room for only 35 diners, you can enjoy specialties that subtly reflect the traditional cuisine of Naples and Apulia. Dishes are succulent and sophisticated, and usually include osso buco with risotto, carpaccio of beef or thinly sliced marinated salmon, lamb baked in an herb crust, bonito with potato salad and artichokes, tortellini with fontina cheese and herbs, and—if you ask for it—a savory version of bean soup. The staff is Italian, smart, briskly efficient, and humorous, and very, very good at catering to a wide spectrum of nationalities.

11 In Solln

Al Pino

Frans-Hals-Strasse 3, Solln. ☎ **089/79-98-85.** Reservations recommended for dinner. Main courses 28 DM–38 DM ($19.60–$26.60). AE, MC. Sun–Fri noon–2:30pm, daily 6–8:30pm (last order). S-Bahn: S7 to Solln. ITALIAN.

Set in the southern suburb of Solln, seven subway stops from Munich's main railway station, this is a likable and unpretentious restaurant with well-prepared food. It's busier in the evening than at lunch, and although diners are welcome to linger at the table as long as they want, management prefers that they be seated before 8:30pm, a fact that might cramp your style if you're a night owl. The venue evokes the ambience of a comfortable, upscale trattoria in a bustling northern Italian city like Milan (though some Sicilian items appear on the menu). Especially delectable is freshly made pasta with fresh chanterelles or salmon, ravioli stuffed with herbs and mozzarella, platters of perfectly grilled fresh fish, and desserts that might include mascarpone. These can be accompanied by a bottle of Italian wine from the establishment's well-stocked cellar.

12   In Grünwald

Grünwalder Einkehr

Nördlicher Münchner Strasse 2, in Grünwald. ☎ **089/6-49-23-04.** Reservations recommended. Fixed-price lunch 30 DM ($21); main courses 23 DM–40 DM ($16.10–$28). AE, DC, MC, V. Wed–Mon noon–3pm and 6pm–midnight. U-Bahn: U2 to Silberhornstrasse, then tram 25. FRENCH.

This restaurant, 8 miles south of the city, was once the home of a prosperous landowner around 200 years ago. Its trio of dining rooms are outfitted in a cozy and elegantly rustic Bavarian style that a temporary refugee from city streets might find very appealing. The cuisine, however, reflects a different tradition—menu items are conservative and French, featuring such dishes as a succulent roast rack of lamb with rosemary sauce, bouillabaisse that's a long way from the French Riviera, filet of beef with green peppercorn sauce, pistou, and a satisfying, old-fashioned version of *tarte tatin.*

13   Nymphenburg

Nymphenburger Hof

Nymphenburger Strasse 24. ☎ **089/123-3830.** Reservations recommended in summer. Fixed-price lunch 33 DM ($23.10); fixed-price dinner 76 DM–95 DM ($53.20–$66.50). Main courses 28 DM–40 DM ($19.60–$28). AE, DC, MC. Mon–Sat noon–3pm and 6–11pm. U-Bahn: U1 to Steiglmaierplatz. AUSTRO-HUNGARIAN.

Many Müncheners consider an outing to its verdant outdoor terrace, 6 miles west of the Marienplatz and 3 miles from Schloss Nymphenburg, the next best thing to a week in the country. Although the modern blue and white interior is attractive in any season, the place is especially appealing in summer when the beautiful outdoor terrace, separated from the busy avenue by a screen of trees, is open.

Don't expect even a hint of traditional nostalgia, as everything is streamlined and modern. The only nostalgic thing about the place is the courtly but amused service and the cuisine, inspired by what used to be known as the Austro-Hungarian Empire. Examples include a succulent form of paprika-laden crêpes, palatschinken Hortobagy; about the best Wiener schnitzel in Bavaria; Tafelspitz (the boiled-beef favorite of Austrian Emperor Franz Josef); Kaiserschmarr (a sweet dessert made with apples); a variety of Czechoslovakian pastries made with honey and plums; and the gooey sticky dessert beloved across the border, Salzburger knockerl.

14   Gay Restaurants

Bar-Restaurant Moritzz

Klenzestrasse 43. ☎ **089/20-16-776.** Reservations recommended weekends. Main courses 20–27 DM ($14–$18.90). No credit cards. Sun–Thurs 7pm–12:30am; Fri–Sat 7pm–1:30am. U-Bahn: Fraunhoferstrasse. CONTINENTAL/THAI.

This is the most stylish and hip gay restaurant in Munich. As estimated by the staff, it has a 70% gay male clientele; lesbian women and gay-friendly hetrosexuals make up the rest of the clients. Part of the space is devoted to a sprawling and attractive bar with a private club–like atmosphere, where red leather chairs, mirrors, and an impeccably trained staff emulate a Paris hotel bar of the 1920s. No one will mind if you decide to eat at the bar, or never move from its premises. You can enjoy at least 40 single malt whiskies, a dozen single-barrel bourbons, and a wide array of unusual wines. The adjacent dining room, however, offers an appealing combination of Thai and continental food, prepared by a central-European staff (mostly from the Czech

Republic), whose interpretation of Thai cuisine is usually applauded. Examples include a *vorspeisen-teller* of mixed Thai specialties, and some fans find the lemon-grass soup almost addictive. Continental cuisine includes veal preparations, fresh fish, pastas, and salads (including a platter-size version garnished with strips of confit of duckling).

Restaurant-Gastätte die Deutsche Eiche

In the Hotel Deutsche Eiche, Reichenbackstrasse 13. ☎ **089/23-11-660.** Reservations recommended. Main courses 10–28 DM ($7–$20.30). No credit cards. Mon–Sat 11:30am–3pm and 6pm–midnight. U-Bahn: Marienplatz. ITALIAN/FRENCH

This restaurant in the historic center of Munich thrives with a largely gay clientele (estimated at around 85%). The decor mimics that of a sophisticated, modern high-tech interior in Milan, and the menu offers a repertoire of northern Italian specialties. The menu changes every month or so; staples include a zesty penne a l'arrabiata (tomato sauce with red-hot peppers), veal scallops with Marsala sauce, scampi in garlic sauce, and salads that are large enough to comprise a main course in their own right.

15 Cafes

The cafe is still going strong in Munich, and many Müncheners take a break to relax over coffee or a beer, read the newspaper, or meet friends. For afternoon coffee and pastry, also see the cafes listed in Chapter 9.

Cafe Glockenspiel

Marienplatz 28. ☎ **089/26-42-56.** Mon–Sat 10am–6pm. U-Bahn or S-Bahn: Marienplatz.

This is the most frequented cafe in Munich, lying in the exact center of Altstadt. A crowd gathers here at 10:30am to watch the miniature tournament staged each day by the clock on the Rathaus facade. In addition to the view, the cafe has good coffee costing from 4 DM to 5 DM ($2.80 to $3.50), with pastries beginning at 4.80 DM ($3.35). It also makes a fine place to end your day tour of Munich and fortify yourself for Munich after dark. Arrive around 5pm for a drink and watch the square change its stripes as it goes from daytime to night. It's ideal for people-watching.

Cafe Luitpold

Briennerstrasse 11. ☎ **089/29-28-65.** Mon–Fri 9am–8pm and Sat 8am–7pm. U-Bahn: Königsplatz or Odeonplatz.

Opened in 1888, and rebuilt in a blandly modern style after the ravages of World War II, this cafe once attracted such notables as Ibsen, Kandinsky, Johann Strauss the Younger, and other great musicians, artists, authors, as well as members of the royal court of Bavaria. What you'll find today, however, is a mainstream workaday Munich stopping in for a pastry, a platter of food, coffee, or a mug of beer. There's a more formal restaurant associated with the place, but we tend to prefer the cafe section instead. A large beer costs 5.40 DM ($3.80); coffee costs from 4.25 DM ($2.95).

Die Alte Boerse

Maffeistrasse 3. ☎ **089/22-67-95.** Mon–Fri 8am–6:30pm and Sat 8am–4pm. U-Bahn: Marienplatz.

It's one of the oldest and most nostalgia-laden cafes in Munich, a battered, evocative holdover from the city's days as the center of an independent kingdom. It occupies an annex room of what was once a stock exchange. Regular patrons bring in their newspapers and other reading matter, recalling the leisurely cafe life of another era. Coffee costs 4 DM ($2.80) a cup, and there's also a short menu of daily platters priced from 13.80 DM to 26 DM ($9.65 to $18.20).

Guglhopf

Kaufingerstrasse 5. ☎ **089/260-88-68.** Mon–Wed and Fri 7am–8pm; Thurs 7am–10pm; Sat 8am–7pm; Sun 10am–7pm. U-Bahn: Marienplatz.

Though it opened in the 1970s, this cafe's ambience of old-fashioned nostalgia and Bavarian rusticity will make you think it's older than it really is. It's named for the closest thing to a Bavarian "national pastry," the Guglhopf. Made with flour, eggs, and sugar, the pastry comes in at least four different variations, including chocolate and/or nuts. You can borrow any of a half-dozen newspapers while you eat your pastry and drink your coffee or beer. A slice of the namesake pastry costs 3.30 DM ($2.30), beer or Weissbeer is 4.90 DM ($3.45), and platters are 9.90 DM to 16 DM ($6.95 to $11.20).

Ruffini

Orffstrasse 22. ☎ **089/16-11-60.** Tues–Sat 10am–midnight and Sun 10am–6pm. U-Bahn: U1 to Rotkreuzplatz.

Müncheners head for this place, at the end of the U-bahn line 1, for a respite from the pressures of the inner city. It offers everything you'd expect from a traditional cafe. You can relax over your coffee or beer with the most recent edition of several different newspapers, or view the cafe's current painting exhibition (most are for sale). The cafe maintains its own bakery in the cellar, and a wine shop and delicatessen on a corner nearby. Coffee costs 4.30 DM ($3); snacks such as cheese platters go for 11 DM ($7.70). The cafe offers natural food, free from artificial fertilizers, flavors, or coloring. Warm platters are 19 DM to 25 DM ($13.30 to $17.50).

Schlosscafé im Palmenhaus

In the gardens of Schloss Nymphenburg, near entrance 43 and the rose gardens. ☎ **089/ 17-53-09.** Daily 9:30 am–6:30pm. Closed on Mon from Nov to Mar. Tram: 17.

The cafe is in a historical reconstruction of a 17th-century building that once functioned as a conservatory for palm trees. The original building, older than the Schloss itself, was destroyed in World War II. Here you can have your coffee capped with whipped cream, or drink your beer in the garden, weather permitting. Coffee costs 3.80 DM ($2.65), and beer goes for 5.20 DM ($3.65). Luncheon platters of unpretentious food include rice curries, schnitzels with french fries, and salads, and cost from 15.80 DM to 25 DM ($11.05 to 17.50).

16 Beer Gardens

If you're in Munich anytime between the first sunny spring day and the last fading light of a Bavarian-style autumn, you might head for one of the city's celebrated beer gardens. Traditionally, beer gardens were simple tables, placed under chestnut trees that were planted above the storage cellars to keep the beer cool in summer. People, naturally, started to drink close to the source of their pleasure, and the tradition has remained. Lids on beer steins, incidentally, were meant to keep out flies. It's estimated that today Munich has at least 400 beer gardens and cellars. Food, drink, and atmosphere are much the same in all of them.

Bamberger Haus

Brunnerstrasse 2. ☎ **089/308-89-66.** Main courses 15.50 DM–32 DM ($10.85–$22.40); large beer 4.50 DM ($3.15). Restaurant, daily noon–midnight; beer hall, daily 5pm–1am. AE, MC, V. U-Bahn: U3 or U6 to Scheidplatz.

The Bavarian Brew

Few cities in the world cling to a beverage the way Munich clings to beer. Müncheners consume a per-capita world's record of the stuff: 280 liters a year, as opposed to a wimpy 150 liters a year, per capita, throughout other parts of Germany. Mention of this kind of heroism usually prompts a cynical, and perhaps witty, response from wine drinkers in Berlin or the Rhineland—they say that Bavarians never open their mouths except to ingest more beer. The response of Müncheners is that politics, as well as art, music, poetry, commerce, finance, short-term planning, long-term planning, and the affairs of the human heart, require plenty of beer and lots of good, unfussy food. Over your stein of beer, you can complain about anything and everything—linguists have even coined a word for the local habit of mumbling into a stein of beer—*guanteln*. And why not? It's a therapeutic, relatively inexpensive way to let off steam, and loaded with nostalgic overtones of what is rather inaccurately perceived as a more lenient age.

Some of the most significant events within Munich's history have begun in the beer halls, and the platforms of several different revolutions have floated on the suds within steins of lager. There was Hitler's Beer Hall Putsch (Hofbräuhaus, 1923); a bungled attempt to assassinate Hitler (in the Burgerbräukeller, 1939); and most recently, the Beer Garden Revolution, a 1995 event where a threat to the civil liberties of beer drinkers prompted mass rallies of infuriated Müncheners. These, along with dozens of smaller, but still very sudsy tempests, have trained Munich's politicians to view the effects of the brew on their constituents with considerable respect.

Statistics regarding Oktoberfest are daunting indeed, although there's always a lager lout from Britain or Austrailia trying to prove that he can best any Bavarian in the consumption of suds. Seven million visitors flood into the city in less than 16 days, surging into every beer hall in town, and into the network of sprawling tents set up in the Theresienweise specifically for the event. The festival promoted the consumption of millions of liters of beer during the two drink-sodden weeks of its duration.

But beer drinking isn't confined to a celebration of the bounty of the autumn harvest. It continues throughout the year. As proof, the invention in 1857 of Weisswurst (which everyone knows is the perfect accompaniment for beer, especially if it happens to be consumed before noon) is celebrated as something of a national holiday. *Prost!*

In a century-old house northwest of Schwabing at the edge of Luitpold Park, Bamberger Haus is named after the city of Bamberg, most noted for the quantity of its beer drinking. Most visitors head for the street-level restaurant. Bavarian and international specialties include well-seasoned soups, grilled steak, veal, pork, and sausages. If you want only to drink, you might visit the rowdier and less expensive beer hall in the cellar.

✪ Biergärten Chinesischer Turm

Englischer Garten 3. ☎ **089/38-38-730.** Meals from 15 DM ($10.50); large beer 9.50 DM ($6.65). Daily 10am–midnight. MC V. U-Bahn: U3 or U6 to Giselastrasse.

Our favorite is in the Englischer Garten, the park lying between the Isar River and Schwabing. The biggest city-owned park in Europe, it has several beer gardens, of which the Biergärten Chinesischer Turm is the best. The largest and most popular of its kind in Europe, it takes its name from its location at the foot of a pagodalike tower, a landmark that's easy to find. Beer and Bavarian food, and plenty of it, are what you get here. For a large glass or mug of beer, ask for *ein mass Bier,* which is enough to bathe in. It will likely be slammed down, still foaming, by a server carrying 12 other tall steins. The food is very cheap. Homemade dumplings are a specialty, as are all kinds of tasty sausage. You can get a first-rate Schweinbraten (braised loin of pork served with potato dumpling and rich brown gravy), which is Bavaria's answer to the better-known Sauerbraten of the north. Leberknödl (liver noodles) is classic, served in a broth with fresh chives. Huge baskets of pretzels are passed around, and they're eaten with radi, the large, tasty white radishes famous from these parts. Oompah bands often play, and it's most festive. It's open May to October until midnight, but from November to April, its closing depends on the weather and the number of guests.

Gaststätte zum Flaucher

Isarauen 8. ☎ **089/72-32-677.** Meals 16 DM–28 DM ($11.20–$19.60); large beer 9.50 DM ($6.65). May–Oct, daily 10am–10pm; Nov–Apr, Thurs–Sun 10am–8pm. Bus: 52 from Marienplatz.

If you're going to the zoo, which we'll recommend later, you might want to stop over for fun and food at the Gaststätte zum Flaucher, which is close by. The word *Gaststätte* tells you that it's a typical Bavarian inn. This one is mellow and traditional, with tables set in a tree-shaded garden overlooking the river. Here you can order the local specialty, Leberkäse, a large loaf of sausage eaten with freshly baked pretzels and plenty of mustard, a deli delight. The most expensive food platter goes for 16.50 DM ($11.55).

Hirschgarten

Hirschgartenstrasse 1. ☎ **089/17-25-91.** Meals 9.50 DM ($6.65); large beer 9.20 DM ($6.45). No credit cards. Daily 9am–midnight. S-Bahn: Laim. Tram: Romanplatz.

In the Nymphenburg Park sector (near one of Munich's leading sightseeing attractions, Schloss Nymphenburg), west of the heart of town, this beer garden is part of a 500-acre park with hunting lodges and lakes. The largest open-air restaurant in Munich, it seats some 8,000 beer drinkers and Bavarian merrymakers. A 1-liter stein of Augustiner tap beer goes for 9.20 DM ($6.45).

Zum Aumeister

Sondermeierstrasse 1. ☎ **089/32-52-24.** Main courses 16 DM–29 DM ($11.20–$20.30); large beer 5.40 DM ($3.80). Tues–Sun 10am–10pm. No credit cards.

If you're motoring, you might visit a hunting lodge that was once owned by the kings of Bavaria. It's Zum Aumeister, which lies off the Frankfurter Ring at München-Freimann, a 20-minute drive north of the center. It offers a daily list of seasonal Bavarian specialties, and you might enjoy cream of cauliflower soup or perhaps a rich oxtail.

6 What to See & Do in Munich

Munich is a city of art and culture, one of Europe's most visited. Munich has innumerable monuments, and more museums than any other city in Germany. In quality, its collections even surpass those of Berlin. The Wittelsbachs were great collectors—some might say pillagers—and have left behind a city full of treasures.

Go to Munich to have fun and to enjoy the relaxed lifestyle, the friendly ambience, and the wealth of activities, sightseeing, and cultural events. You'll never be at a loss for something to do or see here, and on a short trip, you'll only be able to sample the city's offerings.

SUGGESTED ITINERARIES

If You Have 1 Day

Local tourist tradition calls for a morning breakfast of Weisswurst (little white sausages). Head for Donisl (see Chapter 5), which opens at 9am. A true Münchener downs them with a mug of beer. Then walk to Marienplatz (see "Exploring the City Center," below), with its glockenspiel and Altes Rathaus (town hall). Later stroll along Maximilianstrasse, one of Europe's great shopping streets.

In the afternoon, visit the Alte Pinakothek and catch at least some exhibits at the Deutsches Museum. Cap the evening with a night of Bavarian food, beer, and music at the Hofbräuhaus am Platzl (see Chapter 9).

If You Have 2 Days

Spend Day 1 as detailed above. In the morning of Day 2, visit the Staatsgalerie Moderner Kunst and, if the weather's right, plan a lunch in one of the beer gardens of the Englischer Garten. In the afternoon, visit Nymphenburg Palace, summer residence of the Wittelsbachs.

If You Have 3 Days

Spend Days 1 and 2 as outlined above. Occupy your third day exploring the sights you've missed so far: the Residenz, the Städtische Galerie im Lenbachhaus, and the Bavarian National Museum. If you have any more time, return to the Deutsches Museum. Have dinner, or at least a drink, at the Olympiapark Tower, enjoying a panoramic view of the Alps.

What's Special About Munich

Museums & Galleries
- Alte Pinakothek, a royal art collection that grew into one of the most important museums in Germany.
- Deutsches Museum, the largest technological museum in the world, with priceless holdings, including the first automobile.
- Bavarian National Museum, the rich display of Bavaria's historical treasures.

Architectural Highlight
- Cuvilliés Theater, from the mid-1700s, the grandest small rococo theater in the country.

Castles & Palaces
- Schloss Nymphenburg, summer residence of the Wittelsbach dynasty.
- The Residenz, the official home of Bavaria's rulers from 1385 to 1918.

Top Attractions
- Olympiapark, site of the 1972 Olympic Games, now a residential and recreational area.
- Beer gardens and halls, dozens of them, including the most famous in the world: the state-owned Hofbräuhaus am Platzl.

Special Events
- Fasching or Carnival, a joyous season extending from just after Epiphany right up to Shrove Tuesday.
- Oktoberfest, the world's greatest beer-drinking blast (actually mostly in September).

If You Have 5 or More Days

Spend Days 1–3 as outlined above. As fascinating as Munich is, tear yourself away for a day's excursion to one of the Royal Castles built by the "mad king," Ludwig II (see Chapters 10 and 11). On Day 5, take an excursion to Dachau, the notorious World War II concentration camp (see Chapter 10), or visit Garmisch-Partenkirchen for a taste of the Bavarian Alps (see Chapter 11).

1 Exploring the City Center

Marienplatz, dedicated to the patron of the city, whose golden statue stands on a huge column in the center of the square (the Mariensaüle), is the heart of the Altstadt. On its north side is the **Neues Rathaus** (New City Hall) built in 19th-century Gothic style. Each day at 11am, and also at noon and 5pm in the summer, the glockenspiel on the facade performs a miniature tournament, with enameled copper figures moving in and out of the archways. Since you're already at the Rathaus, you may wish to climb the 55 steps to the top of its tower (an elevator is available if you're conserving energy) for a good overall view of the city center. The **Altes Rathaus** (Old City Hall), with its plain Gothic tower, is to the right. It was reconstructed in the 15th century, after being destroyed by fire.

South of the square you can see the oldest church in Munich, St. Peter's. The **Viktualienmarkt,** just off Marienplatz and around the corner from St. Peter's church, has been a gathering place since 1807. Here people buy fresh country produce, wines, meats, and cheese as well as gossip, browse, and snack.

Munich Attractions

LEGEND
Church ✝
Post Office ✉
Information ⓘ
U-Bahn ─○─
S-Bahn ─▭─

9972

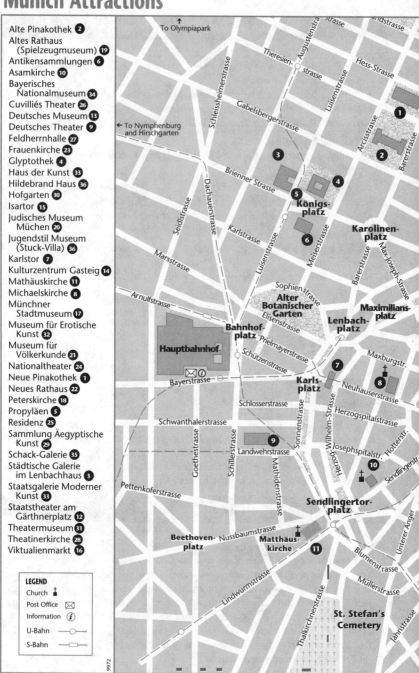

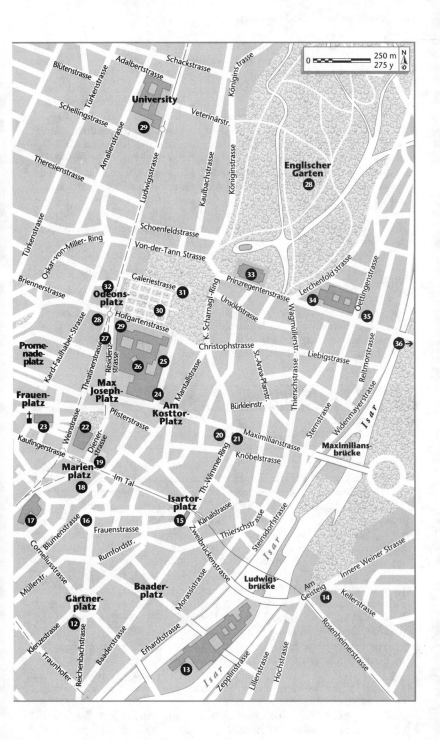

To the north lies **Odeonsplatz,** Munich's most beautiful square, surrounded by the Residenz (Royal Palace) and the **Theatinerkirche.** Adjoining the Residenz is the restored **Nationaltheater,** home of the acclaimed Bavarian State Opera and the Bavarian National Ballet.

Running west from Odeonsplatz is the wide shopping avenue, Briennerstrasse, leading to **Königsplatz.** Flanking this large Grecian square are three classical buildings constructed by Ludwig I—the **Propyläen,** the **Glyptothek,** and the **Antikensammlungen.** Returning to Odeonsplatz, note the **Feldherrnhalle,** a loggia designed after a Florentine model, at the south end of the busy Ludwigstrasse. The Ludwigstrasse leads north to the section of Munich known as **Schwabing.** This is the Greenwich Village or Latin Quarter of Munich, proud of its artistic and literary heritage, numbering among its own such writers as Ibsen and Rilke. The Blue Rider group, which influenced abstract art in the early 20th century, originated here. Today Schwabing's sidewalk tables are filled with young people from all over the world.

The **Isartor** (Isar Gate) is one of the most photographed Munich landmarks. Take the S-Bahn to Isartor. This is the only tower left from the wall that once encircled Munich, forming part of the city's fortifications against invaders.

The other major gate of Munich is the **Karlstor,** once known as Neuhauser Tor, lying northeast of Karlsplatz (nicknamed Stachus). Take the S-Bahn to Karlsplatz. The Karlstor lies at the end of Neuhauser Strasse, which formed part of the town's second circuit of walls, dating from the 1500s. It takes its present name from Elector Charles Theodore in 1791. Unlike the Isartor, the Karlstor lost its main tower (built 1302) in an 1857 explosion.

2 Museums & Palaces

✪ Alte Pinakothek

Barer Strasse 27. ☎ **089/2380-5215.** Scheduled to reopen in 1997. Check with tourist board for hours and admission prices. U-Bahn: U2 to Königsplatz. Tram: 18. Bus: 53.

This is not only Munich's most important art museum, but one of the most significant collections in Europe. The nearly 900 paintings on display (many thousands more are in storage) in this huge neoclassical building represent the greatest European artists from the 14th through the 18th centuries. Begun as a small court collection by the royal Wittelsbach family in the early 1500s, the collection grew and grew. There are only two floors with exhibits, but the museum is immense, and we do not recommend that you try to cover all the galleries in one day, but try to see the works below.

The landscape painter *par excellence* of the Danube school, Albrecht Altdorfer, is represented by no fewer than six monumental works. The works of Albrecht Dürer include his greatest—and final—*Self-Portrait* (1500). Here the artist has portrayed himself with almost Christlike solemnity. Also displayed is the last great painting by the artist, his two-paneled work called *The Four Apostles* (1526).

Several galleries are given over to works by Dutch and Flemish masters. The *St. Columbia Altarpiece* (1460–62), by Roger van der Weyden, is the most important of these, in size as well as significance. Measuring nearly 10 feet across, it is a triumph of van der Weyden's subtle linear style, and one of his last works (he died in 1464).

A number of works by Rembrandt, Rubens, and Van Dyck include a series of religious panels painted by Rembrandt for Prince Frederick Hendrick of the Netherlands. A variety of French, Spanish, and Italian artists are found in both the larger galleries and the small rooms lining the outer wall. The Italian masters are well represented by Fra Filippo Lippi, Giotto, Botticelli, Raphael (*Holy Family*), and Titian.

You'll also see a *Madonna* by da Vinci, a famous self-portrait by the young Rembrandt (1629), and a number of works by Lucas Cranach, including his *Venus*. In the *Land of Cockaigne*, Pieter Brueghel has satirized a popular subject of European folk literature: The place where no work has to be done and where food simply falls into one's mouth. Note the little egg on legs running up to be eaten, and the plucked and cooked chicken laying its neck on a plate. In the background you'll see a knight lying under a roof with his mouth open, waiting for the pies to slip off the eaves over his head.

Important works are always on display, but exhibits also change. You'd be wise to buy a map of the gallery to guide you through the dozens of rooms. The museum was closed for renovation in 1994, and scheduled for reopening in 1997. Call for information.

○ Residenz

Max-Joseph-Platz 3. ☎ **089/29-06-71.** Museum and Treasure House, 5 DM ($3.50) adults, 3 DM ($2.10) students and seniors; Theater, 3 DM ($2.10), adults, 2.50 DM ($1.75) students and seniors. Children under 15 admitted free. Museum and Treasure House, Tues–Sun 10am–4:30pm (last tickets sold at 4pm); Theater, Mon–Sat 2–5pm, Sun 10am–5pm. U-Bahn: U3, U5, or U6 to Odeonsplatz.

When a member of the royal Bavarian family said that he was going to the castle, he could have meant any number of places, especially if he was Ludwig II. But if he said that he was going home, he could only be referring to the Residenz. This enormous palace, with a history almost as long as that of the Wittelsbach family, was the official residence of the rulers of Bavaria from 1385 to 1918. Added to and rebuilt over the centuries, the complex is a conglomerate of various styles of architecture. Depending on how you approach the Residenz, you might first see a German Renaissance hall (the western facade), a Palladian palace (on the north), or a Florentine Renaissance palace (on the south facing Max-Joseph-Platz).

The Residenz has been completely restored since its almost total destruction in World War II and now houses the Residenz Museum, a concert hall, the Cuvilliés Theater, and the Residenz Treasure House.

The **Residenz Museum,** Max-Joseph-Platz 3, comprises the southwestern section of the palace, some 120 rooms of art and furnishings collected by centuries of Wittelsbachs. To see the entire collection, you'll have to take two tours, one in the morning and the other in the afternoon. You may also visit the rooms on your own.

The Ancestors' Gallery is designed like a hall of mirrors, with one important difference: Where the mirrors would normally be, there are portraits of the members of the Wittelsbach family, set into gilded, carved paneling. The largest room in the museum section is the Hall of Antiquities, possibly the finest example of interior Renaissance secular styling in Germany. Frescoes, painted by dozens of 16th- and 17th-century artists, neatly adorn every inch of space on the walls and ceilings. The room is broken into sections by pilasters and niches, each with its own bust of a Roman emperor or a Greek hero. The central attraction is the two-story chimneypiece of red stucco and marble. Completed in 1600, it's adorned with Tuscan pillars and the coat-of-arms of the dukes of Bavaria.

On the second floor of the palace, directly over the Hall of Antiquities, the museum has gathered its enormous collection of Far Eastern porcelain. Note also the fine assemblage of oriental rugs in the long, narrow Porcelain Gallery.

François Cuvilliés

In the 17th and 18th centuries, Bavaria's rulers were determined to rival Rome itself by adorning their city with churches and abbeys and monuments. In the cutthroat competition for commissions that followed, an unlikely candidate emerged for the role of Munich's most brilliant master of the rococo style.

François Cuvilliés (1695–1768) was born in Belgium, a dwarf. Few roles were open to those like himself, and he became, like many of his peers, first a page boy and later court jester to Max Emanuele, elector of Bavaria. When the elector was exiled, François accompanied him, and in St-Cloud near Paris, he first encountered the structure and form of the French baroque, absorbing his patron's interest in French aesthetics. Ambitious and witty, with a charm that transcended his stature, he won his patron's friendship and support, and when the elector was reinstated with pomp and ceremony as ruler of Bavaria, he became a draftsman for the court's chief architect.

Cuvilliés proved himself so talented that in 1720 the elector sent him for a four-year apprenticeship to one of the leading architects of Paris, Jacques-François Blondel, but when he returned to Munich, his work soon eclipsed that of his master. By 1745, the former jester had been elevated to the title of chief architect to the Bavarian court.

Commissions he received between 1726 and his death in 1768 include some of southern Germany's most important rococo monuments. Noted for a flamboyant sinuousness, they include the interior of the Amalienburg Pavilion in the park of Nymphenburg Palace and the facade of the Theatinerkirche. His most famous work is, of course, the remarkable Altes Residenztheater, familiarly called by his name.

Cuvilliés's son, François Cuvilliés the Younger (1731–77), also became an architect, although he never achieved the greatness of his father. Most notably, he put the finishing touches on the facade of the Theatinerkirche that his father had left unfinished at his death.

If you have time to view only one item in the **Schatzkammer** (Treasure House), make it the 16th-century Renaissance statue of *St. George Slaying the Dragon.* The equestrian statue is made of gold, but you can barely see the precious metal through the thousands of diamonds, rubies, emeralds, sapphires, and semiprecious stones embedded in it.

Both the Residenz Museum and the Schatzkammer are entered from Max-Joseph-Platz on the south side of the palace. From the Brunnenhof, you can visit the Alte Residenztheater, better known as the **Cuvilliés Theater,** whose rococo tiers of boxes are supported by seven bacchants. Directly over the huge center box, where the royal family sat, is a crest in white and gold topped by a jewel-bedecked crown of Bavaria held in place by cherubs in flight. In summer this theater is the scene of frequent concert and opera performances. Mozart's *Idomeneo* was first performed here in 1781.

The Italianate **Hofgarten,** or Court Garden, is one of the special "green lungs" of Munich. To the north of the Residenz, it's enclosed on two sides by arcades; the garden dates from the time of Duke Maximilian I and was laid out in 1613–17. In the center is the Hofgarten temple, a 12-sided pavilion dating from 1615.

Residenz

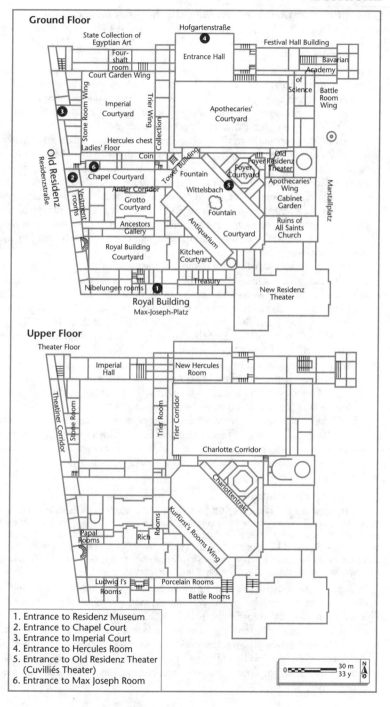

Ground Floor

Hofgartenstraße

State Collection of Egyptian Art

Four-shaft room

Entrance Hall

Festival Hall Building

Bavarian Academy of Science

Court Garden Wing

Battle Room Wing

Stone Room Wing

Trier Wing

Imperial Courtyard

Apothecaries' Courtyard

Collection

Hercules chest

Ladies' Floor

Coin

Old Residenz

Residenzstraße

Chapel Courtyard

Tower Building

Fountain

Foyer Courtyard

Foyer

Old Residenz Theater

Antler Corridor

Wittelsbach

Apothecaries' Wing

Cabinet Garden

Vestment rooms

Grotto Courtyard

Fountain

Ruins of All Saints Church

Ancestors Gallery

Antiquarium

Courtyard

Marstallplatz

Royal Building Courtyard

Kitchen Courtyard

Nibelungen rooms

Treasury

New Residenz Theater

Royal Building
Max-Joseph-Platz

Upper Floor

Theater Floor

Imperial Hall

New Hercules Room

Theatiner Corridor

Stone Room

Trier Room

Trier Corridor

Charlotte Corridor

Charlottentrakt

Kurfürst's Rooms Wing

Rooms

Papal Rooms

Rich

Ludwig I's Rooms

Porcelain Rooms

Battle Rooms

1. Entrance to Residenz Museum
2. Entrance to Chapel Court
3. Entrance to Imperial Court
4. Entrance to Hercules Room
5. Entrance to Old Residenz Theater (Cuvilliés Theater)
6. Entrance to Max Joseph Room

0   30 m / 33 y   N

✪ Bayerisches Nationalmuseum (Bavarian National Museum)

Prinzregentenstrasse 3. ☎ **089/21-12-41.** Admission 3 DM ($2.10) adults, 2 DM ($1.40) students and seniors, free for children under 15. Tues–Sun 9:30am–5pm. U-Bahn: U4 or U5 to Lehel. Tram: 20. Bus: 53.

King Maximilian II in 1855 began an institution to preserve Bavaria's artistic and historical riches. So rapidly did the collection grow in the past 100 years that the museum moved to larger quarters several times. Its current building, near the Haus der Kunst, contains three vast floors of sculpture, painting, folk art, ceramics, furniture, and textiles, as well as clocks and scientific instruments.

Entering the museum, turn right and go into the first large gallery (the Wessobrunn Room). Devoted to early church art from the 5th through the 13th centuries, this room holds some of the oldest and most valuable works. The desk case contains medieval ivories, including the so-called Munich ivory, from about A.D. 400. The carving shows the women weeping at the tomb of Christ while the resurrected Lord is gingerly stepping up the clouds and into heaven. At the crossing to the adjoining room is the stone figure of the *Virgin with the Rose Bush,* from Straubing (ca. 1300), one of the few pieces of old Bavarian church art to be influenced by the spirit of mysticism.

The Riemenschnneider Room is devoted to the works of the great sculptor and carver Tilman Riemenschneider (ca. 1460–1531) and his contemporaries. Characteristic of the sculptor's works is the use of natural, unpainted wood. Note especially the 12 apostles from the Marienkapelle in Würzburg (1510), St. Mary Magdalene, the central group from the high altar in the parish church of Münnerstadt (1490–92), and the figure of St. Sebastian (1490). Also on display are famous collections ofarms and armor from the 16th to 18th centuries.

On the second floor is a fine collection of stained and painted glass—an art in which medieval Germany excelled. Other rooms on this floor include baroque ivory carvings, Meissen porcelain, and ceramics. One novelty addition to the museum is the collection of antique clocks, some dating from the 16th century.

In the east wing of the basement level are many Christmas cribs from Germany, Austria, Italy, and Moravia. The variety of materials competes with the variety of styles—wood, amber, gold, terracotta, and even wax were used in making these nativity scenes. Also on this level is a display of Bavarian folk art, including many examples of wood carving.

✪ Schloss Nymphenburg

Schloss Nymphenburg 1. ☎ **089/17-90-86-68.** The 8 DM ($5.60) ticket includes the palace, Marstallmuseum (carriages), museum of porcelain, and the pavilions in the park; children 6–14 pay 5 DM ($3.50). For Nymphenburg palace, Amalienburg, Marstallmuseum, and museum of porcelain only, 6 DM ($4.20) for adults, 4 DM ($2.80) for children. Apr–Sept, Tues–Sun 9am–5pm; Oct–Mar, Tues–Sun 10am–4pm. Parking beside the Marstallmuseum. U-Bahn: U1 to Rotkreuzplatz, then tram 12 toward Amalienburgstrasse. Bus: 41.

In summer, the Wittelsbachs would pack up their bags and head for their country house, Schloss Nymphenburg. A more complete, more sophisticated palace than the Residenz in Munich, it was begun in 1664 by Elector Ferdinand Maria in Italian villa style and took more than 150 years and several architectural changes to complete. The final palace plan was the work of Elector Max Emanuel, who in 1702 decided to enlarge the villa by adding four large pavilions connected by arcaded passageways. Gradually the French style took over, and today the facade is in a subdued baroque style.

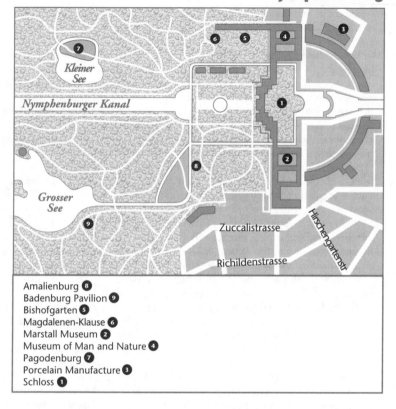

Amalienburg **8**
Badenburg Pavilion **9**
Bishofgarten **5**
Magdalenen-Klause **6**
Marstall Museum **2**
Museum of Man and Nature **4**
Pagodenburg **7**
Porcelain Manufacture **3**
Schloss **1**

The palace interior is less subtle, however. Upon entering the main building, you're in the great hall, decorated in rococo colors and stuccos. The frescoes by Zimmermann (1756) depict incidents from mythology, especially those dealing with Flora, goddess of the spring, and her nymphs, for whom the palace was named. This hall was used for both banquets and concerts during the reign of Max Joseph III, elector during the mid-18th century. Concerts are still presented here in summer. The smaller rooms are devoted to tapestries, paintings, and period furniture.

From the main building, turn left and head for the arcaded gallery connecting the northern pavilions. The first room in the arcade is the Great Gallery of Beauties, painted for Elector Max Emanuel in 1710. More provocative, however, is Ludwig I's Gallery of Beauties in the south pavilion (the apartments of Queen Caroline). Ludwig commissioned no fewer than 36 portraits of the most beautiful women of his day. The paintings by J. Stieler (painted from 1827 to 1850) include the *Schöne Münchenerin* (lovely Munich girl) and a portrait of Lola Montez, the dancer whose "friendship" with Ludwig I caused a scandal that factored into the Revolution of 1848.

To the south of the palace buildings, in the rectangular block of low structures that once housed the court stables, is the **Marstallmuseum.** In the first hall, look for the glass coronation coach of Elector Karl Albrecht, built in Paris in 1740. From the same period comes the elaborate hunting sleigh of Electress Amalia, adorned with a statue of Diana, goddess of the hunt; even the sleigh's runners are decorated with shellwork and hunting trophies.

The coaches and sleighs of Ludwig II are displayed in the third hall. His constant longing for the grandeur of the past is reflected in the ornately designed state coach, meant for his marriage to Duchess Sophie of Bavaria, a royal wedding that never came off. The fairy-tale coach wasn't wasted, however, since Ludwig often rode in it through the countryside to one of his many castles, creating quite a picture. The coach is completely gilded, inside and out; rococo carvings cover every inch of space except for the panels, faced with paintings on copper. In winter the king would use his state sleigh, nearly as elaborate as the Cinderella coach.

Nymphenburg's greatest attraction is the **park.** Stretching for 500 acres in front of the palace, it's divided into two sections by the canal that runs from the pool at the foot of the staircase to the cascade at the far end of the English-style gardens.

Within the park are a number of pavilions. The guided tour begins with the **Amalienburg,** whose plain exterior belies the rococo decoration inside. Built as a hunting lodge for Electress Amalia (in 1734), the pavilion carries the hunting theme through the first few rooms and then bursts into salons of flamboyant colors, rich carvings, and wall paintings. The most impressive room is the Hall of Mirrors, a symphony of silver ornaments on a faint blue background.

The **Badenburg Pavilion** sits at the edge of the large lake of the same name. As its name implies, it was built as a bathing pavilion, although it's difficult to visualize Ludwig dashing in from the water in a dripping swimsuit, across those elegant floors. A trip to the basement, however, will help you appreciate the pavilion's practical side. Here you'll see the unique bath, surrounded by blue and white Dutch tiles. The ceiling is painted with frescoes of mythological bathing scenes.

The octagonal **Pagodenburg,** on the smaller lake on the other side of the canal, looks like a Chinese pagoda from the outside. The interior, however, is decorated with pseudo-Chinese motifs, often using Dutch tiles in place of Chinese ones.

The **Magdalenenklause** may look like a ruin, but that was the intention when it was built in 1725. Also called the Hermitage, it was planned as a retreat for prayer and solitude. The four main rooms of the one-story structure are paneled with uncarved stained oak, with simple furnishings and a few religious paintings. It's really a drastic change from the other buildings.

✪ Deutsches Museum (German Museum of Masterpieces of Science and Technology)

Museumsinsel 1. ☎ **089/217-91.** Admission 9 DM ($6.30) adults, 6 DM ($4.20) seniors, 3 DM ($2.10) students, 2.50 DM ($1.75) children 6–12, free for children 5 and under. Daily 9am–5pm (closes at 2pm the second Wed in Dec). Closed major holidays. S-Bahn: Isartor. Tram: 18.

On an island in the Isar River, in the heart of Munich, this is the largest technological museum of its kind in the world. Its huge collection of priceless artifacts and historic originals includes the first electric dynamo (Siemens, 1866), the first automobile (Benz, 1886), the first diesel engine (1897), and the laboratory bench at which the atom was first split (Hahn, Strassmann, 1938). There are hundreds of buttons to push, levers to crank, and gears to turn, as well as a knowledgeable staff to answer questions and demonstrate how steam engines, pumps, or historical musical instruments work.

Munich's Art Scene

Ever since Franz Marc (1880–1916), Wassily Kandinsky (1866-1944), and August Macke (1887-1914) founded the art movement Der Blaue Reiter in 1911 to free art from rigid constraints, Munich has had a lively art scene. Later joined by Paul Klee (1879-1940), the Blue Rider movement stood for experimentation and originality, and became the high point of German Expressionism. Kandinsky, the most influential member of the group, is often credited with having produced the first "abstract" painting.

Lovis Corinth (1858-1925), also a Munich-based painter, took a different road. He was a disciple of Max Lieberman and Max Slevogt, and his abstract impressionist paintings dealt with themes derived from history and theology.

Art developed during the postwar era with what critics described as a frenzy of energy, a creative outburst that produced dozens of young artists, so many, in fact, that the hundreds of art openings that happenened every year became a popular venue for meeting one's friends, and spawned the rather derogatory epithet, *kir royale* (actually a bubbly drink composed of currant juice and champagne), to refer to supposed art lovers more interested in the parties and *vernissages* of the art than the paintings themselves.

Among contemporary artists with Bavarian roots to look out for are Johannes Muggenthaler (b. 1954), whose cheerful canvases predict a futuristic but rosy and romantic picture. Stefan Hunderstein (b. 1957), a long-time resident of Munich, is a master of photorealistic techniques with subtle distortions and a searing politicized edge.

A personal favorite is Matthias Wähener (b. 1953), an intensely politicized artist whose idiosyncratic technique involves computer-generated photo distortions. No other artist has succeeded so well in mingling the symbols of postwar Europe with a German-born baby-boomer's reactions to those events. His work is simultaneously nostalgic, stimulating, and enigmatic. Throughout his genre, the artist's image is transposed Forrest Gump–style atop images of the great and mighty; for example, the artist stands looking skeptically at JFK as he delivers his "Ich bin ein Berliner" speech during the Cold War.

For late-breaking developments in the world of art in Munich, you might want to visit the Mosel and Tschechow Gallery, Winterstrasse 7 (089/651-56-21).

Among the most popular displays are those on mining, with a series of model coal, salt, and iron mines, as well as the electrical power hall, with high-voltage displays that actually produce lightning. There are also exhibits on transportation, printing, photography, textiles, and many other activities, including glass-blowing and paper-making demonstrations. The air-and-space hall is the largest in the museum. The new hall for high-tech exhibits, computer science, automation, microelectronics, and telecommunications is also very intriguing. The museum's astronomy exhibition shows how this science developed from its earliest beginnings to its current status, and is the largest permanent astronomy exhibition in Europe. A good restaurant and a museum shop are on the premises.

Neue Pinakothek
Barer Strasse 29. ☎ **089/2380-5195.** Admission 6 DM ($4.20) adults, 3.50 DM ($2.45) students and seniors, free for children 15 and under. No admission fee on Sun. Tues and Thurs 10am–8pm, Wed and Fri–Sun 10am–5pm. U-Bahn: U2 to Königsplatz. Tram: 27. Bus: 53.

The Neue Pinakothek offers a survey of 18th- and 19th-century art. Across Theresienstrasse from the Alte Pinakothek, the museum was reconstructed after its destruction in World War II; it reopened in 1981.

The museum has paintings by Gainsborough, Goya, David, Manet, van Gogh, and Monet, and many modern works. Among the more popular German artists represented are Wilhelm Leibl and Gustav Klimt; you'll encounter a host of others whose art is less well known. Note particularly the genre paintings by Carl Spitzweg.

✪ Staatsgalerie Moderner Kunst (State Gallery of Modern Art)

Haus der Kunst, Prinzregentenstrasse 1. ☎ **089/21-27-37.** Staatsgalerie, 5 DM ($3.50) adults, 3 DM ($2.10) students and seniors. No admission fee on Sun. Tues–Wed and Fri–Sun 10am–5pm, Thurs 10am–8pm. Closed some holidays. U-Bahn: Odeonsplatz. Bus: 53.

Munich's State Gallery of Modern Art is housed in the west wing of the massive Haus der Kunst, which was constructed in 1937. Some art critics claim that it has one of the 10 finest modern art collections in the world. It shows about 400 paintings, sculptures, and art objects from the 20th century. The largest exhibit is devoted to modern German art. You'll see paintings by Klee, Marc, Kirchner, Beckmann, and Lovis Corinth as well as Italian art, with stars such as Marino Marini and Renato Guttoso; American abstract expressionism; minimalist art; and a host of the younger modern artists, including Anselm Kiefer. There are 14 works by Picasso, the earliest dating from 1903.

The east wing of the Haus der Kunst, Prinzregentenstrasse 1 (☎ **089/ 211-27-115**), is entered separately and requires a separate ticket. It's devoted to changing exhibitions, which often feature exciting new artists whose canvases are for sale as well as on display. Many traveling exhibitions of worldwide importance stop here.

3 Churches

In addition to the historic churches described below, visitors might also want to visit the **Matthäuskirche,** Nussbaumstrasse 1 (U-Bahn: Sendlinger-Tor-Platz), an Evangelical cathedral built from 1953 to 1955.

✪ Frauenkirche (Cathedral of Our Lady)

Frauenplatz 12. Free admission. Daily 7am–7pm. U-Bahn and S-Bahn: Marienplatz.

When the smoke cleared from the 1945 bombings, only a fragile shell remained of Munich's cathedral. Workmen and architects who restored the 15th-century Gothic cathedral used whatever remains they could find in the rubble. The overall effect of the rebuilt Frauenkirche is strikingly simple, yet dignified.

The twin towers, which remained intact with their strange early Gothic onion domes, have been the city's landmark since 1525. Instead of the typical flying buttresses, huge props on the inside support the edifice and separate the side chapels. The Gothic vaulting over the nave and chancel is borne by 22 octagonal pillars.

Entering the main doors at the cathedral's west end, you first notice no windows (actually, except for the tall chancel window, they're hidden by the enormous pillars). According to legend, the devil was delighted at the notion of hidden windows and stamped in glee at the stupidity of the architect—you can still see the strange footlike mark called "the devil's step" in the entrance hall.

In the chapel directly behind the high altar is the cathedral's most interesting painting: *The Protecting Cloak,* a 1510 work by Jan Polack, showing the Virgin holding out her majestic robes to shelter all humankind. The collection of tiny figures beneath the cloak includes everyone from the pope to peasants.

Peterskirche (St. Peter's Church)

Rindermarkt 1. ☎ **089/260-48-28.** Church, free; tower, 2.50 DM ($1.75) adults, 1.50 DM ($1.05) students, .50 DM (35¢) children. Apr–Oct, daily 9am–7pm (or even longer); Nov–Mar, daily 9am–6pm. U-Bahn: Marienplatz.

Munich's oldest church (1180) has turned over a new leaf, and it's a gold one at that. The white and gray interior has been decorated with painted medallions of puce and gilded baroque. It contains a series of murals by Johann Baptist Zimmermann, but nothing tops the attraction of the bizarre relic in the second chapel on the left: the gilt-covered and gem-studded skeleton of St. Mundita. It stares at you with two false eyes in its skull, which rests on a cushion. Jewels cover the mouth of rotten teeth, quite a contrast to the fresh roses usually kept in front of the black and silver coffin.

Near the Rathaus, St. Peter's, known locally as Old Peter, also has a tall steeple, although you may be discouraged from going up since it lacks an elevator. Colored circles on the lower platform tell you whether the climb is worthwhile: If the circle is white, you can see as far as the Alps.

Theatinerkirche

Theatinerstrasse 22. Free admission. Church, daily 6am–7:30pm; crypt, May–Nov 1, Mon–Fri 10am–1pm and 2–4:30pm, Sat 10am–3pm. U-Bahn: Odeonsplatz.

Named for a small group of Roman Catholic clergy (the Theatines), this church, dedicated to the scholar-saint Kajetan, is Munich's finest example of Italian baroque. Two Italian architects, Barelli and Zucalli, began building it in the mid-17th century. It was completed in 1768 by the son of the court architect, François de Cuvilliés.

The arched ceiling of the nave is supported by fluted columns that line the center aisle. Above the transept, dividing the nave from the choir, the ceiling breaks into an open dome with an ornate gallery decorated with large but graceful statues. Nothing detracts from the whiteness of the interior, except the dark wooden pews and the canopied pulpit.

Michaelskirche

Neuhauser Strasse 52. ☎ **089/2317-060.** Free admission. Guided tour, 5 DM ($3.50) at Wed 2pm. Church daily 9am–8pm. Crypt Mon–Fri 10am–1pm and 3–4:45pm, Sat 10am–3pm. U-Bahn or S-Bahn: Karlsplatz, Stachus, or Marienplatz.

The largest Renaissance church north of the Alps, it was constructed by Duke Wilhelm the Pious in 1583. Seven years into construction, the tower collapsed. The duke took this as divine portent that the church was not large enough. During the second phase of construction, the size of the church was dramatically increased, making it not only the largest Renaissance church north of the Alps, but the possessor of the world's second largest barrel vaulted roof. Among those who have been laid to rest in the crypt are Duke William himself, more than 40 Wittelsbachs, and, perhaps the family's most notorious member, Mad King Ludwig II.

Asamkirche

Sendlingerstrasse 62. Free admission. Daily 9am–8pm. U-Bahn: Sendlinger Tor.

St.-Johann-Nepomuk-Kirche, commonly referred to as the Asamkirche after its builders, was constructed by the Asam brothers, Cosmas Damian and Egid Quirin. Although modest on the outside, the interior of this small 18th-century church is a baroque fantasy. Above the entrance stands the statue of St. Nepomuk (the church's patron), a 14th-century monk who drowned in the Danube. Upon entering the chapel, visitors are greeted with a burst of frescoes surrounded by rich red stucco and lavishly gilded woodwork, a superb illustration of the Bavarian passion for ornamentation.

4 More Attractions

Antikensammlungen (Museum of Antiquities)

Königsplatz 1. ☎ **089/59-83-59.** Admission 5 DM ($3.50) adults. Joint ticket to the Museum of Antiquities and the Glyptothek, 8 DM ($5.60) adults, free for children under 14, free for everyone on Sun. Tues and Thurs–Sun 10am–4:30pm, Wed noon–8:30pm. U-Bahn: U2 to Königsplatz.

After 100 years of floating from one museum to another, the Museum of Antiquities finally found a home in the 19th-century neoclassical hall on the south side of Königsplatz. The collection grew around the vase collection of Ludwig I and the Royal Antiquarium, both of which were incorporated after World War I into a loosely defined group called the Museum Antiker Kleinkunst (Museum of Small Works of Ancient Art). Many pieces may be small in size but not in value or artistic significance.

Entering the museum, you're in the large central hall. The five main-floor halls house more than 650 Greek vases, collected from all parts of the Mediterranean. The pottery has been restored to near-perfect condition, although most of it dates as far back as 500 B.C. The oldest piece is "the goddess from Aegina" from 3000 B.C. Technically not pottery, this pre-Mycenaean figure, carved from a mussel shell, is on display with the Mycenaean pottery exhibits in Room I. The upper level of the Central Hall is devoted to large Greek vases discovered in Sicily and to Etruscan art.

Returning to the Central Hall, take the stairs down to the lower level to see the collection of Greek, Roman, and Etruscan jewelry. Note the similarities with today's design fashions. Included on this level, as well, are rooms devoted to ancient colored glass, Etruscan bronzes, and Greek terracottas.

Glyptothek

Königsplatz 3. ☎ **089/28-61-00.** Admission 5 DM ($3.50) adults. Joint ticket to the Museum of Antiquities and the Glyptothek, 6 DM ($4.20) adults, free for children under 14, free for everyone on Sun. Tues–Sun 10am–4:30pm. U-Bahn: U2 to Königsplatz.

The ideal neighbor for the Museum of Antiquities, the Glyptothek supplements the pottery and smaller pieces of the main museum with an excellent collection of ancient Greek and Roman sculpture. Included are the famous pediments from the temple of Aegina, two marvelous statues of *kouroi* (youths) from the 6th century B.C., the colossal figure of a *Sleeping Satyr* from the Hellenistic period, classical masterpieces of sculpture from ancient Athens, and a splendid collection of Roman portraits. In all, the collection is the country's largest assemblage of classical art. King Ludwig I, who had fantasies of transforming Munich into another Athens, ordered it built.

Münchener Stadtmuseum (Municipal Museum)

St. Jakobsplatz 1.☎ **089/233-22-370.** Admission 5 DM ($3.50) adults, 2.50 DM ($1.75) children. Tues and Thurs–Sun 10am–5pm, Wed 10am–8:30pm. U-Bahn or S-Bahn: Marienplatz.

Munich's Municipal Museum is to the city what the Bavarian National Museum is to the whole state. Housed in the former armory building, the museum offers insight into the city's history and the daily lives of its people. Special exhibitions about popular arts and traditions are frequently presented. A wooden model shows Munich in 1572. The extensive furniture collection is changed annually so that visitors have a chance to see various periods from the vast storehouse.

The museum's most important exhibit is its Moorish Dancers (*Moriskentanzer*) on the ground floor. These 10 figures, each two feet high, carved in wood and painted in bright colors by Erasmus Grasser in 1480, are among the best examples of secular Gothic art in medieval Germany. In the large Gothic hall on the ground floor you can admire an important collection of armor and weapons from the 14th to 18th centuries.

The second-floor photo museum traces the early history of the camera back to 1839. Every day, at 6 and 9pm, the film museum shows two films from its extensive archives. The historical collection of musical instruments on the fourth floor is one of the greatest of its kind in the world. It includes an ethnological collection.

Enter the Municipal Museum through the main courtyard, where there's a cafeteria.

Stadtische Galerie im Lenbachhaus

Luisenstrasse 33. ☎ **089/2333-2000.** Admission 8 DM ($5.60) adults, 4 DM ($2.80) children 6–12, free for children 5 and under. Tues–Sun 10am–6pm. U-Bahn: U2 to Königsplatz.

This gallery, in the ancient villa of painter Franz von Lenbach (1836–1904), exhibits works by von Lenbach and others. Entering the gold-colored mansion through the gardens, you'll be greeted by a large collection of early works by Paul Klee (1879–1940)—mainly those predating World War I. There's an outstanding group of works by Kandinsky, leader of the Blue Rider movement, and many 19th- and 20th-century paintings throughout the villa. The enclosed patio is pleasant for a coffee break.

Staatliche Sammlung Ägyptischer Kunst (Egyptian Museum)

Hofgartenstrasse 1. ☎ **089/29-85-46.** Admission 4.50 DM ($3.15) adults, 2.50 DM ($1.75) children. Free on Sun and holidays. Tues 9:30am–4pm and 7–9pm, Wed–Sun 9:30am–4pm. U-Bahn: Odeonsplatz. S-Bahn: Marienplatz.

The State Collection of Egyptian Art is located in the Residenz. The museum evolved from the collections of Duke Albrecht V and King Ludwig I, and contains pieces from every period of Egyptian history, from the predynastic period (4500–3000 B.C.) to the Coptic period (A.D. 4th–9th centuries). On exhibit are sculptures, reliefs, jewelry, tools, weapons, as well as sarcophagi.

Stuck-Villa (Jugendstil Museum)

Prinzregentenstrasse 60. ☎ **089/4555-5125.** Free admission. Daily 10am–5pm, Thurs until 9pm. U-Bahn: U4 to Prinzregentenplatz.

This splendid house was designed by painter Franz von Stuck (1863–1928) for himself, and mingles art-nouveau style with elements of late neoclassical. The ground-floor living rooms contain frescoes by the artist himself, and many of his paintings are on display. On the first floor is a permanent collection of Jugenstil.

Volkerkundemuseum (Ethnology Museum)

Maximilianstrasse 42. ☎ **089/228-55-06.** Admission 2 DM ($1.40). Tues–Sun 9:30am–4:30pm. Tram: 19 or 20.

The museum, housed in an imposing building completed in 1865, has an extensive collection of art and artifacts from all over the world, and is one of the principal museums of its kind in Europe. Particularly interesting is the Peruvian collection; the museum also has exhibitions from other parts of South America, East Asia, and West and Central Africa. Part of the museum is closed for renovation and is scheduled to reopen in spring of 1997. The hours and the admission charge may change at that time.

5 Parks, Gardens & the Zoo

Bordering Schwabing on the east and extending almost to the Isar River is Munich's city park, the 18th-century **Englischer Garten,** one of the largest and most beautiful city parks in Germany. It was the idea of Sir Benjamin Thompson, the English scientist who spent most of his life in the service of the Bavarian government, and was laid out in 1785. You can wander for hours along the walks and among the trees, flowers, and summer nudes, stopping for tea on the plaza near the Chinese pagoda, or having a beer at the nearby beer garden. You might also take along a picnic put together at the elegant shop of Alois Dallmayr, or less expensive fare from **Hertie,** across from the Hauptbanhof, Kaufhof at Marienplatz, or from Munich's famous open-air market, the Viktualienmarkt.

Bordering Nymphenburg Park to the north is the **Botanischer Garten.** The garden is composed of 49 acres of land, teeming with more than 15,000 varieties of flora. Each subdivision is devoted to a particular variety of plant. The highlight of the Botanischer Garten is the alpine garden, laid out according to geographic region and altitude. It's at its peak during the summer months. Another favored attraction is the heather garden. Visitors to the garden during the late summer months are treated to an explosion of vibrant violets and purples. Other attractions include the rose garden, fern gorge, and the series of hothouses that are home to numerous exotic tropical plants. To reach the Botanischer Garten (☎ 089/17-86-13-10), take the U-Bahn to Rotkreuzplatz, then tram 12. The garden is open November through January daily from 9am to 4:30pm; February and March daily from 9am to 5pm; April through September daily from 9am to 6pm; and May through August daily from 9am to 7pm. The hothouses close half an hour before the garden does. During the day, the garden closes from 11:45am to 1pm. Admission is 3 DM ($2.10) for adults and 1.50 DM ($1.05) for children.

In west Munich, between Schloss Nymphenburg and the main railway line, stands the **Hirschgarten.** Designated by elector Karl Theodor as a deer park in 1791, this 67-acre tract of land is home to one of Munich's most tranquil stretches of greenery. In the 19th century, Müncheners would visit the meadow to view the protected game as they grazed. The head huntsman secured the right to sell beer, which prompted the Hirschgarten to soar in popularity. Eventually a beer garden was established, now the largest in the world, with a capacity for 8,000 thirsty patrons. To reach the park, you can take the S-Bahn to Laim; or you can catch bus 32 or 83 from Steubenplatz. Although no longer a wildlife preserve, the Hirschgarten still draws the citizens of Munich for picnics, barbecues, or an afternoon game of chess.

About 4 miles south of the city center, the **Hellabrunn Zoo** stands in the Tierpark Hellabrunn, Tierparkstrasse 30 (☎ 089/62-50-80). It's one of the largest zoos in the world, and may be visited daily from 8am to 6pm (in winter, daily from 9am to 5pm) for an admission of 9 DM ($6.30) for adults, 6 DM ($4.20) for students and seniors, and 4 DM ($2.80) for children. To reach the park, you can take bus no. 52, leaving the Marienplatz, or U-Bahn U3 to Thalkirchen. Hundreds of animals roam in a natural habitat. A walk through the park is so attractive that it's recommended even if you're not a zoo buff. There's also a big children's zoo, as well as a large aviary.

6 The Olympic Grounds

The **Olympiapark** (☎ 089/30-67-24-14), site of the 1972 Olympic Games, is 740 acres at the city's northern edge. More than 15,000 workers from 18 countries transformed the site into a park of nearly 5,000 trees, 27 miles of roads, 32 bridges, and a lake, containing Germany's greatest sports complex, and one of the greatest in Europe.

Olympiapark is a city in itself: It has its own railway station, U-Bahn line, mayor, post office, churches, and elementary school. It broke the city skyline by adding a 960-foot television tower in the center of the park.

The showpiece of this city is a huge stadium, capable of seating 69,200 spectators, and topped by the largest tent-style roof in the world—nearly 90,000 square yards of tinted acrylic glass. The supports for the stadium are anchored by two huge blocks, each capable of resisting 4,000 tons under stress. The roof serves the additional purpose of collecting rainwater and draining it into the nearby Olympic lake.

Olympia Tower, Olympiapark (☎ **089/3067-2705**), is open daily from 9am to midnight. A ticket for a ride up the tower, the speediest elevator on the continent, costs 5 DM ($3.50) for adults and 2.50 DM ($1.75) for children under 15.

The most expensive dining spot in the tower is the **Tower Restaurant,** featuring a selection of French and German dishes. Food is served daily from 11am to 5:30pm and 6:30pm to midnight. A complete dinner costs 65 DM–78 DM ($45.50–$54.60). Before or after dinner, you'll want to take in the extraordinary view, which reaches to the Alps. Four observation platforms look out over the Olympiapark. The Tower Restaurant revolves around its axis in 36, 53, or 70 minutes, giving the guests who linger a changing vista of the entire Olympic ground. Credit cards: AE, DC, MC, V.

At the base of the tower is the **AM Olympiasee,** Spiridon-Louis-Ring 7 (☎ **089/308-10-00**), serving genuine Bavarian specialties, with meals costing 18.50 DM ($12.95) and up. Favored items include half a roast chicken and various hearty soups, and food is served daily from 9:30am to 7pm (until 9pm in summer). The restaurant is popular in summer because of its terrace. No credit cards are accepted. Take U-Bahn U3 or U8 to Olympiazenturm.

Near Olympiapark, you can visit the **BMW Museum,** Petuelring 130 (☎ **089/3822-3307**), where the history of the automobile is stunningly displayed in an atmosphere created by Oscar winner Rolf Zehetbauer, a "film architect." The exhibition "Horizons in Time," housed in a demisphere of modern architecture, takes you into the future and back to the past. You can view 24 video films and 10 slide shows (an especially interesting one shows how people of yesterday imagined the future). The museum is open daily from 9am to 5pm, charging 5.50 DM ($3.85) for adults and 4 DM ($2.80) for children. While there, you might also ask about BMW factory tours. Take U-Bahn U3 or U8 to Olympiazentrum.

7 Especially for Kids

From the Deutches Museum to the Marionetten Theater, to the Bavarian Film Studio, kids love Munich.

Take your children to the **Münchener Stadtmuseum,** St. Jakobsplatz 1 (☎ **089/2332-2370**). On the third floor is an array of puppets from around the world, with star billing going to the puppeteer's art. The comical and grotesque figures include both marionettes and hand puppets. Like a Lilliputian version of the world of the stage, the collection also includes detailed puppet theaters and miniature scenery. A special department is devoted to fairground art, including carousel animals, shooting galleries, roller-coaster models, and wax and museum figures. The main exhibit contains the oldest-known carousel horses, dating from 1820. For hours and admission fees, see "More Attractions," above.

If children have a favorite museum in Munich, it's the **Deutsches Museum,** Museumsinsel 1 (☎ **089/21-791**), which has many interactive exhibits. For details, see "Museums," above.

The **Spielzeugmuseum,** in the Altes Rathaus, Marienplatz 15 (☎ **089/29-40-01**), is a historical toy collection. It is open daily from 10am to 5:30pm. Admission is 5 DM ($3.50) for adults, 1 DM (70¢) for children, and 10 DM ($7) for a family.

At the **Münchener Marionetten Theater,** Blumenstrasse 32A (☎ **089/26-57-12**), you can attend puppet shows and the *théâtre de marionnettes.* Adults as well as children are delighted with the productions; many are of Mozart operas. Performances are on Wednesday, Thursday, Saturday, and Sunday at 3pm. Performances Saturday at 8pm cost 15 DM ($10.50). Admission is 8 DM ($5.60) for adults and 6 DM ($4.20) for children. To reach the theater, take the U-Bahn to Sendlinger Tor.

The **Bavaria Film Studio,** Bavariafilmplatz 7, Geiselgasteig (☎ **089/6499-2304**), is Europe's largest filmmaking center. Children will enjoy the film presentations and the Bavaria Action Show. See "Special-Interest Sightseeing," below, for details.

The **Hellabrunn Zoo** has a large children's zoo where children can pet the animals. For details, see "Parks, Gardens & the Zoo," above.

Not to be ignored is the **Circus Krone,** Marstrasse 43 (☎ **089/55-81-66**). It might be compared to London's Albert Hall, since its productions are so varied. From December 25 to March 31 a circus show is presented. There are matinee performances on Wednesday, Friday, Saturday, and Sunday. See Chapter 9 for details.

8 Special-Interest Sightseeing

FOR CINEMA FANS

Bavaria Film Studio

Bavariafilmplatz 7, Geiselgasteig. ☎ **089/6499-2304**. Admission 14 DM ($9.80) adults, 12 DM ($8.40) students and senior citizens, 9 DM ($6.30) children 4–14, free for children 3 and under. Tours: Mar–Oct daily 9am–4pm, Nov–Feb daily 10am–3pm. Tram: 25.

The Bavaria Film Studio is Europe's largest filmmaking center, a blend of the traditions from the great days of black-and-white German cinema in the 1920s and the excesses of modern Hollywood. In its showcase theater, visitors can watch clips from German-made Steven Spielberg–style thrillers such *Adventure in the Devil's Mine* and *Space Race.* Guided 90-minute tours of the studio are offered daily throughout the year.

Another attraction is the Bavaria Action Show, where stunt teams demonstrate fistfights, escapes from burning buildings, falls down staircases, and even a plunge off a 92-foot-high building. The show lasts about 30 minutes, and is priced at 9 DM ($6.30) per person. It's performed only from March through October, daily at 11:30am and 1:30pm, with additional shows on Saturday and Sunday at 2:30pm.

FOR THEATER BUFFS

Theatermuseum

Galeriestrasse 4. ☎ **089/22-24-49**. Free admission. Tues 10am–noon, Thurs 2–4pm. U-Bahn: Odeonsplatz.

Founded in 1910, the German Theatermuseum is a haven for theater fans from all over the world. The museum boasts a multitude of relics connected with the history of theater. Its collection includes theater plans, stage sets, as well as various props, costumes, and masks used in productions around the world. The archive contains thousands of manuscripts, programs, and revues. The museum's library houses additional manuscripts, scores, and journals. Available at the museum is the *Münchener Spielplan,* a service providing information on all theatrical performances currently being performed in the Munich area.

AN EROTIC MUSEUM

Museum für Erotische Kunst

Odeonsplatz 8. ☎ **089/228-35-44.** Admission 8 DM ($5.60) adults, 6 DM ($4.20) students. Tues–Sun 11am–7pm. U-Bahn: Odeonsplatz.

The Museum of Erotic Art houses a hodgepodge of sexual art and accoutrements from all over Europe, America, and Japan. This is not a visit for puritans. The collection houses, among other curiosities, a chastity belt with jagged openings, assorted phallic paraphernalia, and numerous other kinky contraptions.

FOR JEWISH HISTORY

Jüdisches Museum München

Maximilianstrasse 36. ☎ **089/29-74-53.** Free admission. Tues–Wed 2–6pm and Thurs 2–8pm. U-Bahn: Isartor. Tram: 18.

This small private museum portrays the history of Jews in Nazi Germany through photographs, letters, and exhibits. The horrors suffered during Nazi occupation are startingly illuminated through powerful portraits of daily life. The yellow stars that Jews were forced to wear continuously are on display, as well as an exhibit that chronicles the hunt for Raoul Wallenburg, the Swedish diplomat who spirited hundreds of Jews to safety during World War II.

FOR THE LITERARY ENTHUSIAST

Hildebrand Haus

Maria-Theresia Strasse 23. ☎ **089/419-47-20.** Free admission. Mon–Wed 8am–4pm, Thurs 10am–7pm, Fri 8am–2:15pm. U-Bahn: Prinzregentenplatz. Tram: 18.

The Hildebrand Haus, former home and studio to sculptor Adolf von Hildebrand, now houses the Monacensia Library. Hildebrand, who is best known for designing the Wittelsbach Fountain, designed and built the house in 1897. The library's collection is comprised of numerous manuscripts and unpublished works by various Bavarian writers and artists such as Frank Wedekind, Klaus Mann, and Ludwig Ganghofer.

9 Organized Tours

CITY TOURS   Blue buses, with sightseeing tours conducted in both German and English, leave from the square in front of the Hauptbahnhof, at Hertie's, all year round. Tickets are sold on the bus and no advance booking is necessary.

A one-hour tour, costing 15 DM ($10.50) for adults and 8 DM ($5.60) for children 6 to 12, leaves at 10am, 11:30am, and 2:30pm daily from May to October. Winter departures, November to April, are daily at 10am and 2:30pm.

A 2¹/₂-hour tour, including the Olympic Tower, costs 27 DM ($18.90) for adults and 14 DM ($9.80) for children. Departures are at 10am and 2:30pm from May to October and at 10am and 2:30pm from November to April.

A second 2¹/₂-hour tour, costing 27 DM ($18.90) for adults and 14 DM ($9.80) for children, visits the famous Neue Pinakothek (painting gallery), Liebfrauendom (landmark of Munich), and the chiming clocks at Marienplatz. It departs Tuesday through Sunday at 10am.

A third 2¹/₂-hour tour, costing 27 DM ($18.90) for adults and 14 DM ($9.80) for children, visits Nymphenburg Palace and the Schatzkammer, departing Tuesday through Sunday at 2:30pm.

FARTHER AFIELD　If you'd like to visit some of the Bavarian attractions outside of Munich, you can sign up with **Panorama Tours,** an affiliate of Gray Line. Their office is at Arnulfstrasse 8 (☎ **089/59-15-04** daytime, **0177/203-30-37** after hours), to the north of the Hauptbahnhof. Hours are 7:30am to 6pm on Monday through Friday, 7:30am to noon on Saturday, and 7:30am to 10am on Sunday and holidays. The firm offers about a half-dozen tours of the region around Munich, usually priced at 75 DM ($52.50) per adult and 38 DM ($26.60) per child.

If you want to visit Ludwig's castles, there's an 8¹/₂-hour tour to the royal castles at Neuschwanstein, Hohenschwangau, and Linderhof that includes a brief stopover in the hamlet of Oberammergau. A 9-hour tour focuses exclusively on Oberammergau and Linderhof. An 8¹/₂-hour tour takes you to Ludwig's castle at Herremchiemsee. You can also take a tour to Salzburg in Austria that includes a boat ride on the Wolfgangsee, and takes about 11¹/₂ hours. Another 8¹/₂-hour tour travels to Berchtesgaden and the site of Hitler's once luxurious retreat at Obersalzburg. The last of these full-day tours is an 8¹/₂-hour trek along the Romantic Road, with stops at the well-preserved towns of Nördlingen, Dinkelsbühl, and Rothenburg.

Farther afield and more expensive, at 138 DM ($96.60), is a 9-hour visit to Garmisch-Partenkirchen that includes a funicular ride to the top of Bavaria's tallest mountain, the Zugspitze, from which you can look down on four different countries. This tour departs between 8:30 and 10:30am.

On a darker note is a 4¹/₂-hour excursion to Dachau, departing every Saturday at 1:30pm. Priced at 40 DM ($28) for adults and 21 DM ($14.70) for children, the tour incorporates a visit to the notorious concentration camp, and also a tour through the historic town of Dachau itself and the medieval Schloss Dachau. During the visit to the death camp, participants are requested to respect the dignity of the site by wearing appropriate attire.

TOURING BY BICYCLE　Pedal pushers will want to try Mike Lasher's **Mike's Bike Tour,** St. Bonifatiusstrasse 2, (☎ **089/651-82-75**). His bike-rental services for 25 DM ($17.50) include maps, locks, helmets, and child and infant seats at no extra charge. Tours in English and bilingual tours of central Munich run from March through November at a cost of 28 DM ($19.60). Tours leave at 11:30am and 4pm daily (call to confirm). This unique enterprise has been praised widely by its clients, thanks in part to the charm of its American owner. Participants meet under the tower of the old town hall, a gray building on the east end of Marienplatz. Mike, the consummate guide, will be there—whistle in mouth—letting everyone know who he is. The tour veers from the bike paths only long enough for a lunch stop at a biergarten. Fear not faint-hearted, the rides are nonstrenuous with plenty of photo opportunities, historical explanations, and Q&A sessions.

10　Outdoor Activities

The best place to enjoy the great outdoors is not in Munich itself, but just outside the city limits. Munich is surrounded by mountains and alpine lakes. The Bavarian Alps afford some of the finest skiing and hiking in the world. Avid skiers will want to make an excursion to the Zugspitze, the highest mountain peak in Germany. Ski slopes begin at an elevation of 8,700 feet. For information on ski resorts and other snow-related activities in the Munich area, contact **Bayerischer Segler-Verband,**

Munich's Soccer Craze

Like Italy, England, and Brazil, Germany is crazed on soccer. Munich's equivalent of the Chicago Bulls is its famous soccer team, **Bayern München.** One of Europe's most outstanding teams, Bayern München has won the German National Championship 13 times since 1932. Most recently, they won the European Football Federation championship in 1995, and in 1996 the *Welttokalsieger* championship, an event that designated the team as the best non-national team in the world (national teams play in the World Cup).

However, it's a matter of civic pride to many Müncheners, especially when they're soaked with beer, to root enthusiastically for a less-well-rated local team, **T.S.V. 1860 München.** This team was around about 40 years before Bayern München was founded, and it still arouses local loyalty—something like the less-well-rated Chicago Cubs as opposed to the better-rated Chicago White Sox. Both teams call the Olympic Stadium in Olympiapark their home.

Georg-Brauchle-Ring 93 (☎ **089/1570-2366**). The mountains are a haven for hikers and nature lovers during the summer months. Trails abound for all levels of experience. See Chapter 11 for details. The alpine lakes around Munich are excellent locales for swimming and other water sports. The Ammersee and Starnbergersee, both a short drive from the city, are favorite locales for sailing, windsurfing, and other water sports. See Chapter 10 for more information. Visitors can also go for a dip in the frigid, snow-fed waters of the Isar River.

BIKING   Ever conscious of the enivironment, Munich is a very bike-friendly city. The city is full of bike paths, and most major streets maintain bike lanes. The many parks and gardens scattered throughout Munich offer hours of riding. The tourist office provides suggested tours in its *Radi Touren.* Although printed in German, the maps are excellent and easily followed. You can rent bikes at the entrance to the **Englischer Garten,** Königstrasse and Veterinästrasse (☎ **089/52-99-43**); **Radius Touristik,** Arnulfstrasse 9 (☎ **089/59-61-13**); **City Hopper Tours,** Hohenzollern Strasse 95 (☎ **089/272-11-31**); and **Mike's Bike Tour,** St. Bonifatiusstrasse 2 (☎ **089/651-82-75**). Many S-Bahn stations also rent bikes and allow them to be returned at other S-Bahn stations.

BOATING   Rowboats add to the charm of the lakes in the **Englischer Garten.** (There's also a kiosk located at the edge of the Kleinhesselcher See for rentals during clement weather.) There are rowboat rentals on the southern bank of the **Olympiasee,** in the Olympiapark.

Raft trips on the Isar River are conducted between the town of Wolfrathausen and Munich between early May and late September. A raft may contain up to 60 other passengers, but if the idea appeals to you, one company that usually has space is **Franz and Sebastian Seitner,** Heideweg 9, D-82515 Wolfrathausen (☎ **08171/18-320**).

GOLF   Visitors who are members of golf clubs in their own countries are permitted to play on two courses in Munich. For a complete round of golf, go to the Munich Golf Course (☎ **08170/450**) located in Grünwald, about 15¹/₂ miles from the city center. The course is open daily from 8am to 8pm. The greens fee is 100 DM ($70), and visitors must arrange a tee time in advance. Munich also has a nine-hole course in Thalkirchen (☎ **089/723-13-04**), closer to the city center. The course is open daily from 8am to 8pm. The greens fee is 70 DM ($49). Guests do not need a reservation.

HIKING & HILLCLIMBING   Bavaria is packed with well-marked hiking trails. For information about nearby terrains and itineraries, contact the **Deutscher Alpenverein,** Van-Kahr-Strasse 2–4 (☎ **089/14-00-30**).

ICE-SKATING   During the winter's coldest months, a lake in the Englischer Garten freezes over and is opened to ice skaters. Also blocked off for skaters is a section of the Nymphenburger Canal. Be alert to the GEFAHR (Danger) signs that are posted whenever temperatures rise and the ice becomes too thin. The **Olympic Icestadium,** Spiridon-Louis-Ring 3 (☎ **089/3067-2414**), in the Olympiapark, is the indoor rink. Information on hockey matches and other ice-skating events is available from **Bayerischer Eissportverband,** Georg-Brauchle-Ring 93 (☎ **089/15-40-27**).

JOGGING   Regardless of the season, the most lushly landscaped place in Munich is the **Englischer Garten** (U-Bahn: Münchener Frieheit), which has a 7-mile circumference and an array of dirt and asphalt tracks. Also appropriate are the grounds of the **Olympiapark** (U-Bahn: Olympiazentrum), or the park surrounding **Schloss Nymphenburg.** More convenient to the center of the city's commercial district is a jog along the embankments of the Isar River.

SWIMMING   Although most Müncheners head to the lakes to swim, there are several excellent facilities within the city. The largest public swimming pool is the giant competition-size pool in the Olympiapark, the **Olympia-Schwimmhalle** (☎ **089/30-67-20-15**).

TENNIS   At least 200 indoor and outdoor tennis courts are scattered around greater Munich. Many can be booked in advance through **Sport Scheck** (☎ **089/9928-7460**). For information on Munich's many tennis tournaments and competitions, contact the **Bayerischer Tennis Verband,** Georg-Brauchle-Ring 93, D-80992 München (☎ **089/157-02-640**).

SPECTATOR SPORTS

If you want to attend a soccer match between opposing teams from different ends of Europe, chances are good that there'll be one in Munich's enormous **Olympiapark** (☎ **089/3067-2424**). Originally built for the 1972 Olympics, Olympiapark is the largest recreational and sports venue in Europe, and has facilities for competitions of virtually every kind. To get tickets for any sports event, call **089/5418-1818,** Monday through Friday from 9am to 6pm and on Saturday from 10am to 3pm.

Munich Strolls 7

A walk through the city is the only true way to get to know it. The city of great beer halls intoxicates in many other fashions. Altstadt (Old Town) is a traditional walking tour for most visitors, but more seasoned travelers may find a new appreciation for the capital of Bavaria by visiting some of the city center's lesser known but equally merited sights. Those wishing to experience a more offbeat locale should try the walk through Schwabing where free thought is a longstanding tradition.

1 Walking Tour 1: Central Altstadt

Start: Frauenkirche.
Finish: Königsplatz.
Time: 2¹/₂ hours, not counting visits to interiors or shopping.
Best Times: Daylight hours during clement weather.
Worst Times: Monday through Friday from 7:30 to 9am and 4:30 to 6pm, because of heavy traffic.

With a history spanning centuries of building and rebuilding, Munich is one of Europe's most interesting cities architecturally.

Begin your tour at the dignified cathedral with its impressive brickwork, the:

1. **Frauenkirche.** Built in a mere 20 years, beginning in 1468 on the site of a much older church, the majestically somber building is capped with twin towers, the symbol of Munich.

After admiring their design, walk for about a block southeast along any of the pedestrian alleyways radiating away from the rear of the church. In about two minutes you'll find yourself in the most famous medieval square of Munich:

2. ✪ **Marienplatz,** in whose center a golden statue of St. Mary (the Mariensäule) rises above pavement that was first laid in the 1300s when the rest of the city's streets were a morass of mud and sewage. On the square's northern boundary sits the richly ornamented bulk of the Neues Rathaus (New City Hall), built between 1867 and 1908 as a neo-Gothic symbol of Munich's power. The building's mechanical clock with its glockenspiel performance is one of Munich's most carefully preserved monuments. At the square's eastern border, beyond a stream of traffic, is the simpler

and smaller Altes Rathaus (Old City Hall), which was rebuilt in its present form in 1470 after fire destroyed an even earlier version.

From the square, walk south along Rindermarkt, encircling the masonry bulk of the:

3. Peterskirche. Its foundations date from 1000, and the interior is a sun-flooded fantasy of baroque stucco and gilt. Walk to the back of this church, where you'll see the sprawling premises of one of the best-stocked food emporiums in Europe, the:

4. Viktualienmarkt. Known as "Munich's stomach," it's packed with opportunities for snacking, picnicking, beer drinking, or watching the ritual of European grocery shopping. At the northern end, at the corner of the streets Rosen Tal and Im Tal, rise the richly ornate baroque walls of the:

5. Heiliggeist (Holy Ghost) Church. Its foundations were laid in the 1100s, but the form in which you see it today was completed in 1730.

From here, cross the busy boulevard identified as Im Tal and walk north along Maderbraustrasse (which within a block will change its name to Orlandostrasse and then to Am Platz). There, look for the entrance to the most famous beer hall in Europe, the state-owned:

6. Hofbräuhaus. For a description, see Chapter 9. For the moment, note its location for an eventual return. Now, walk east along Pfisterstrasse. To your left are the walls of the:

7. Alter Hof, originally built in 1255, and once the palace of the Wittelsbachs, although eclipsed later by grander palaces. Since 1816 it has housed the rather colorless offices of Munich's financial bureaucracies. On the opposite (northern) edge of Pfisterstrasse rise the walls of the:

8. Münzhof (built 1563–67). During its lifetime it has housed the imperial stables, the first museum north of the Alps, and (between 1809 and 1986) a branch of the government mint. Today it's the headquarters for Munich's Landmark Preservation office (Landesamt für Denkmal-schutz). If it's open, the double tiers and massive stone columns of the building's Bavarian Renaissance courtyard are worth a visit.

Pfisterstrasse funnels into a broader street, Hofgraben. Walk west for one block, then turn right (north) along Residenzstrasse. The first building on your right will be the city's main post office (Hauptpost) and a few paces farther you'll reach:

9. Max-Joseph-Platz. Designed as a focal point for the monumental avenue (Maximilianstrasse) that radiates eastward, the plaza was built during the 19th century on the site of a Franciscan convent in honor of Bavaria's first king. At the north edge of the plaza lies the vast exhibition space and labyrinthine corridors of one of Munich's finest museums, the:

10. ✪ Residenz. Constructed in different stages and styles from 1500 to 1850, it served as the official home of the rulers of Bavaria. Rebuilt after the bombings of World War II, in a design recreating its labyrinthine floor plan, it contains seven semiconcealed courtyards, lavish apartments that have housed foreign visitors such as Elizabeth II and Charles de Gaulle, and museums that include the Residenz Museum, the Treasure House of the Residenz, the Cuvilliés Theater (a richly gilded rococo theater built in 1753), and the Herkulessaal, a baroque concert hall noted for its decorations.

If you haven't already done so, walk from Max-Joseph-Platz north along Residenzstrasse. Make the first left and walk west along Salvatorstrasse; then, within

Walking Tour 1: Altstadt

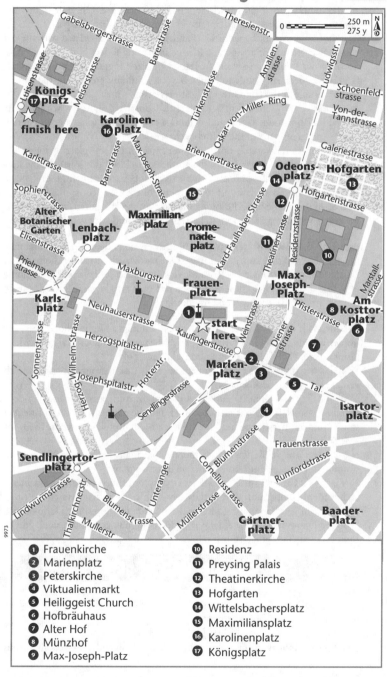

1. Frauenkirche
2. Marienplatz
3. Peterskirche
4. Viktualienmarkt
5. Heiliggeist Church
6. Hofbräuhaus
7. Alter Hof
8. Münzhof
9. Max-Joseph-Platz
10. Residenz
11. Preysing Palais
12. Theatinerkirche
13. Hofgarten
14. Wittelsbachersplatz
15. Maximiliansplatz
16. Karolinenplatz
17. Königsplatz

137

another block, turn right (north) along Theatinerstrasse. On your right you'll immediately notice the imposing walls of Munich's first baroque palace, the:

11. **Preysing Palais.** Built between 1723 and 1728, it's still associated with the oldest surviving family of aristocratic lineage in Bavaria today. Next to the Palais's northern wall, and faced with an Italian-inspired loggia, is the Felhernhalle (1841–44), originally built to honor Bavaria's military greats. On the western (opposite) side of the same street (Theatinerstrasse) is the:

12. **Theatinerkirche** (Church of St. Kajetan). Completed in 1690, with a triple-domed Italian baroque facade added about a century later, it has a crypt containing the tombs of many of the Wittelsbachs.

Now, continue walking north passing through Odeonsplatz, below which several subway lines converge. On the northeastern side of this square lie the flowers, fountains, and cafés of one of Munich's most pleasant gardens, the:

13. **Hofgarten.** Originally laid out for members of the royal court in 1613, it was opened to the public in 1780. Along the edges of the Hofgarten, as well as along the avenues radiating away from it, lie many opportunities for your much awaited:

☕ **TAKE A BREAK**   Do as the Müncheners do and enjoy the panorama of Odeonsplatz and the nearby Hofgarten. One particularly attractive choice is **Cafe Luitpold,** Briennerstrasse 11. Rebuilt in a streamlined design after the bombings of World War II, it has in the past welcomed such cafe-loving habitués as Ibsen, Johann Strauss the Younger, and Kandinsky.

Now, walk westward along Briennerstrasse, through a neighborhood lined with impressive buildings. On your right, notice the heroic statue of Maximilian I, the Great Elector (1597–1651), rising from the center of:

14. **Wittelsbachersplatz.** In a short time, the gentle fork to your left leads into the verdant and stylish perimeter of:

15. **Maximiliansplatz.** Shop at your leisure or plan to return later for a more in-depth sampling of this prestigious neighborhood. For the moment, return to Briennerstrasse, turn left (west), and head toward the 85-foot obelisk (erected in 1833) that soars above:

16. **Karolinenplatz.** Its design commemorates Bavarians killed in the Napoleonic invasion of Russia. Continuing west, you'll come upon:

17. **Königsplatz.** Crown Prince Ludwig selected its formal neoclassical design after an architectural competition during the early 19th century. Its perimeter is ringed with some of Germany's most impressive museum buildings, the Doric-inspired Propyläen monument (west side), the Antikensammlungen (south side), and the Ionic-fronted Glyptothek (north side).

2 Walking Tour 2: Altstadt—West of Marienplatz

Start: Marienplatz.
Finish: Viktualienmarkt.
Time: 2 hours.
Best Times: Daylight hours during clement weather.
Worst Times: Monday through Friday from 7:30 to 9am and 4:30 to 6pm, because of heavy traffic.

Marienplatz is an easy, logical starting place for this second discovery of the Altstadt. Walk down the shop-lined Koffingerstrasse to Liebfrauenstrasse and stop to gaze at Frauenkirche (visited in the previous tour). Continue westward to:

Walking Tour 2: West of Marienplatz

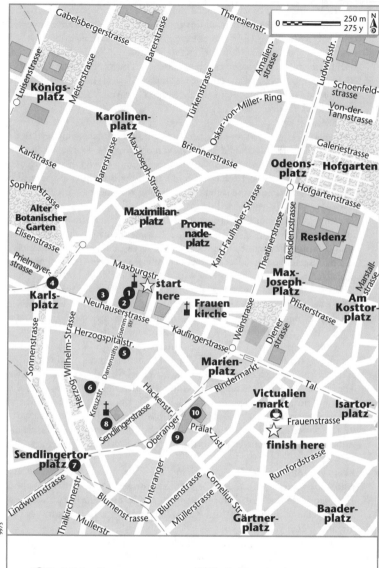

① St. Michael's
② Richard Strauss Fountain
③ Bürgersaal
④ Karlplatz-Stachus
⑤ St.-Anna-Damenstift

⑥ Allerheiligenkirche am Kruez
⑦ Sendlinger-Tor-Platz
⑧ Asam Kirche and Haus
⑨ Ignaz-Günther-Haus
⑩ Münchner Stadtmuseum

1. ✪ **St. Michael's.** Hubert Gerhard's larger-than-life creation. The figure of St. Michael slaying the dragon adorns the church's rich Renaissance facade. The church, constructed in 1597, possesses an interior that merits a glance as well. The barrel vault room is second in size only to St. Peter's in Rome. King Ludwig II's final resting place, it also houses other Wittelsbach rulers. Continue west to:

2. **Richard Strauss Fountain.** Scenes from Strauss's *Salome* (1905) are incorporated in bas-reliefs on the fountain's central column. The Munich composer's opera is interpreted with decorative flair.
   Then walk by:

3. **Bürgersaal.** The two-story church completed in 1710 has an appealing front featuring the Virgin and Child in a crescent moon over the doorway. The bottom floor was once the worship hall of a Jesuit community called the Marion congregation. You'll eventually reach the fountain of the little boy, at the medieval Karlstor, and the end of the pedestrian mall. You've come to:

4. **Karlplatz-Stachus,** engineered upon demolition of the old town walls in 1791. The unpopular Elector Karl Theodor lent his name to the square only to suffer the indignity of having the alternate, *Stachus,* become the common reference of the local citizenry. The name Stachus dates back to an 18th-century local eatery, or to a marksman who practiced nearby, depending on which story you deem most plausible.
   Diagonally and to the right is the 19th-century Palace of Justice. Directly in front of you, at a distance, is the main train station. Turn 180°, walking back to the Strauss fountain. Enjoy one of the finest views in town—the Cathedral that ascends before the walker. Turn right at Eisenmannstrasse and head for:

5. **St.-Anna-Damenstift** (1735), a large church on the corner. Rebuilt in the 1950s, it replicates the old church that was collapsed by bombs during World War II. The attached building, which is now a secondary school for girls, was once a convent. The church, built by Johann Baptist Gunetzrhhainer in 1732–35, features stucco work and frescoes by the brothers Asam, Egid Quirin, and Cosmas Damian.
   The street name changes to Damenstiftstrasse for the duration of the block as we pass a pretty, old house numbered 4 and the 18th-century Palais Lerchenfeld. Although we've not made a turn, the street is now named Kruezstrasse, home of the:

6. **Allerheiligenkirche am Kruez.** Built around 1478 by Ganghofer, the same builder who constructed the cathedral, All Saints, formerly St. Peter's, now houses Ukranian Catholics. The Gothic building features baroque touches such as the apse from a remodeling in 1620 and Renaissance altarwork in the pattern of J. B. Strauss (1770).
   The street merges into Herzog-Wilhelm-Strasse, which veers left and ends at:

7. **Sendlinger-Tor-Platz,** the 1318 edifice, once a medieval fortification. Built about the same time as the Karlstor, the two side towers of the gates are the only original survivors. Sendlinger Strasse, a lengthy, brightly colored avenue of small commercial outlets, leads us back into town. Stay on the right side of the street as you walk back and you will encounter:

8. **Asam Kirche and Haus.** The aforementioned brothers created the building in 1746 as a sort of monument to themselves. The Bavarian rococo school dominates the interior, courtesy of Egid Quirin, along with frescoes and paintings by brother Cosmas Damian. A wax figure of St. John of Nepomuk, to whom the building is dedicated, graces the altar—don't just walk by the church, step inside.

9. **Ignaz-Günther-Haus.** This memorial house is a tribute to the 18th-century Bavarian rococo artist who lived and worked out of the edifice during his lifetime. Restoration was completed in 1977, and it is now maintained by the Munich Stadtmuseum (see below). The Madonna out front is a Günther replica, and an exhibit inside displays some of his other works.

Directly across the street is the:

10. **Münchener Stadtmuseum.** Housed in the old, 15th-century city Arsenal, the building is turreted in front. Exhibits vary seasonally, often featuring one of the countless local artists in Munich's cultural history. Several displays, however, are permanent and are reviewed in Chapter 6.

Continue down the street veering left into Sebastianplatz and admire the old houses lining the street. Follow the platz to Prälat-Zistl-Strasse. Continue a half-block to the Viktualienmarkt and:

☕ **TAKE A BREAK**   at the **Münch'ner Suppenkücke** (no phone). This place is a Munich legend, a true "soup kitchen" at what is called "the stomach of the city." Müncheners can be seen here on the coldest days devouring hearty soups such as Goulashsuppe, sausage and sauerkraut, and Krustis (sandwiches). Or, buy some bread and fruit at one of the many stands, sit back, and enjoy the fountains and statues that surround you.

3 Walking Tour 3: Schwabing

Start: Wedekindplatz.
Finish: Englischer Garten.
Time: 2½ hours with minimal stopovers.
Best Times: Morning to mid-afternoon while students bustle to and from class.
Worst Times: Monday through Friday from 7:30 to 9am and 4:30 to 6pm.

Schwabing, incorporated into the city in 1890, can be perceived as Munich's hipper younger sibling. As an artistic center, its golden era was from 1890 to 1914, with a short-lived revival after World War II when it was the legendary center of the bohemians in Germany. Thomas Mann, Herman Hesse, Rainer M. Rilke, Karl Kraus, and Frank Wedekind were some of the better-known authors who lived in the area.

The tour begins in the section of Schwabing behind the Münchener Freiheit station known as Old Schwabing. Movie theaters, music venues, even a handful of cabarets give it the markings of cosmopolitanism.

1. **Wedekindplatz,** once the community market, derives its name from playwright Frank Wedekind, well known for his Lulu plays. The plays provided the basis for the 1929 Louise Brooks film, *Pandora's Box,* and for Alban Berg's opera, *Lulu.* The platz is the focal point of the neighborhood.

Head west down Fellitzschstrasse, pass the Freihehit rail station crossing to Leopoldstrasse. Immediately to the right is:

2. **Leopoldstrasse,** the most famous street in Schwabing, the best known Jugendstil (or art-nouveau) district in all of Munich. *Jugend,* a Schwabing magazine, lent the name to the art movement that swept Central Europe at the turn of the century, urging an imminent modernization of art from Old World nostalgia to newer, fresher perspectives.

Take a left on Wilhelmstrasse, travel south for two blocks, then take a right on:

Walking Tour 3: Schwabing

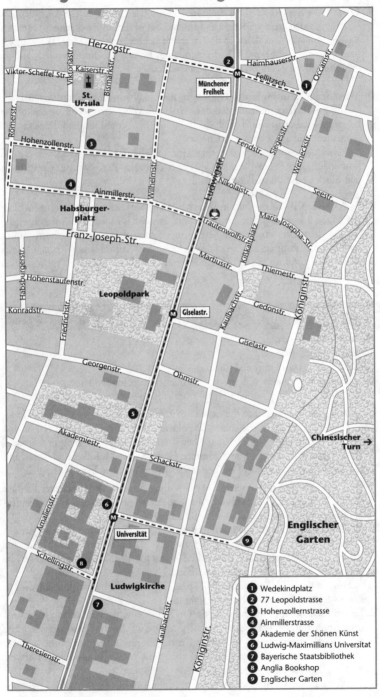

1. Wedekindplatz
2. 77 Leopoldstrasse
3. Hohenzollernstrasse
4. Ainmillerstrasse
5. Akademie der Shönen Künst
6. Ludwig-Maximillians Universitat
7. Bayerische Staatsbibliothek
8. Anglia Bookshop
9. Englischer Garten

3. Hohenzollernstrasse. This is a further study of Jugendstil. The facades that adorn the buildings lining this street are fine examples of the bright and geometric qualities that typify the Jugendstil. Look also for the little, quirky fashion boutiques that give the street its fame. Turn left on Römerstrasse, travel south a block, then head back east on:

4. Ainmillerstrasse. Jugendstil's artistic unshackling laid the foundation for an awakening of consciousness that provided a basis for many of the eager manifestos set forth by the Blaue Reiter (Blue Rider) school. Appropriately, Vassily Kandinsky, the premiere artist associated with the movement, lived down the street. You will find many of the finest examples of Jugendstil on the east end of the street—including the facade at no. 22 that sports Adam and Eve lying at the base of the tree of knowledge.

☕ **TAKE A BREAK**   at the **Cafe Roxy** Leopoldstrasse 48 (☎ **089/349-393**). The cafe-bar best represents the oft-maligned maturation of Schwabing's bohemia. Iris Berber, owner and star of German TV, presides over the neo-deco interior, Italian cuisine, and an affectedly urbane crowd. It's chic, it's hip, and the best place to relax in the neighborhood.

Head south down Leopoldstrasse until you approach the:

5. Akademie der Shönen (Academy of Fine Arts). The building, erected at the end of the 19th century, enthusiastically recalls the stylings of the Italian Renaissance. The academy is best known for the "secession" staged by its students in the 1890s, the artistic and political ripples of which were felt throughout authoritarian Central Europe. Continue south on Leopoldstrasse and you will enter the:

6. Ludwig-Maximilian Universität (University of Munich) campus. Frederich von Gärtner engineered the construction of the edifice, one of the aesthetically finest in all of Munich. Gärtner relieved Leo von Klenze (Alte Pinakotek) as Bavaria's court architect, and the relative flamboyance of this structure is compared favorably if not complementary to Klenze's more staid approach. Across the street, three smaller buildings complete the complex: a conference building, the twin-spired St. Ludwig's Church, and the:

7. Bayerische Staatsbibliothek (Bavarian State Library). This mammoth library is one of the largest in all of Europe. It stands where the Schwabing Gate of medieval Munich once cast its shadow. Check out its proportional staircase within. Before leaving campus duck down Schellingstrasse and drop in at:

8. Anglia English Bookshop, Schellingstrasse 3. The student district's liveliest street resides south of the university in a suburb of Schwabing known as Maxvorstadt, after the Munich elector whose expansion north of the city gates gave birth to this part of town. Munich has emerged as Germany's publishing district, and the bookstores throughout Schwabing will satiate the broadest appetites of knowledge-hungry readers.

Head back north up Leopoldstrasse, returning to the university's center. Take a left on Veterinärstrasse, directly across the street from Gärtner's famed building. Those without inhibition may want to begin disrobing. You're being routed to the:

9. ✪ Englischer Garten. Munich's most famous park, full of nude sunbathers. The Chinese Tower is the most recognizable landmark of the gardens. The wooden tower, trimmed with gold leaf, was destroyed during World War II but reemerged in the 1950s to the delight of imbibers at its beer garden—a Munich tradition revered even by upstart Schwabingers.

8 Shopping

Frankly, people come to Munich for the beer, not the shopping. However, as you ramble from *Biergarten* to *Bierhalle,* it's possible to encounter some beautiful (and expensive) shops and a number of rather intriguing retailers.

1 The Shopping Scene

Munich offers some of the foremost shops and boutiques in Europe. The city has an extensive pedestrian shopping area in its city center. **Kaufingerstrasse** and **Neihauserstrasse,** the principal shopping streets, extend from the Haubtbahnhof (rail station) to Marienplatz, then north to Odeonplatz. For more upscale shopping, head to **Maximilianstrasse.** The street houses numerous chic boutiques and fashion houses that rival any on Fifth Avenue.

For funkier wares, head to Schwabing, the former bohemian quarter of Munich. **Schellingstrasse** and **Hohenzollernstrasse** are home to many unusual galleries and hip boutiques. Shops in the downtown area are generally open from 9am to 6pm during the week. Stores may stay open until 8:30pm on Thursday. On Saturday, the shops generally close around 2pm. The smaller neighborhood stores usually open their doors from 8:30am to 12:30pm and reopen from 3 to 6pm. On the first Saturday of the month, *Ianger Samstag,* the downtown stores are open until 4pm from April to September and until 6pm from October to March.

2 Shopping A to Z

ANTIQUES

Munich is not a center for antique buyers, as not a lot remains after the World War II bombings, and anything really valuable is snapped up instantaneously by the prosperous bourgeoisie. There is some estate-sale stuff "from Grandmother's cupboard" but little of major consequence. In fact, many pieces come from England or France.

Seidl Antiquitäten

Siegelstrasse 21. ☎ **089/34-95-68.** U-Bahn: Münchener Freiheit.

Within a trio of rooms inside a building that's an antique in its own right, you'll find a wealth of porcelain (especially Nymphenburger and Meissen) and silver, much of it acquired from many generations of estate sales. There's also a scattering of antique furniture and oil paintings from many different eras. It's open Monday through Friday from 10am to 1pm and 3 to 6pm.

Squirrel

Schellingstrasse 54. ☎ **089/272-09-29.** U-Bahn: U3 or U6 to Universität.

This unusual shop is a delightful alternative for dedicated antique buyers tired of the endless estate-sale junk found in many antique stores. Established 20 years ago by its charming owner, Urban Geissel and his wife Gisela, it inventories a collection of luggage made by English and French purveyors to the aristocrats and millionaires of the Jazz Age. There are suitcases and steamer trunks from Louis Vuitton, whose *LV* logo was inaugurated about 20 years after the company's establishment in 1878; some antique pieces by Hérmès; and examples from English makers such as Finnegan's and Harrod's. Although they tend to be heavy, they're still serviceable, and richly imbued with the nostalgia of the great days of oceangoing travel. An expenditure of 500 DM ($350) buys a worthy suitcase from circa 1910 to 1925; 22,000 DM ($15,400) buys one of tailored crocodile with silver clasps. The place is open Monday through Friday from 11am to 6pm, Saturday from 11am to 2pm.

Kunsthandlung Timberg

Maximilianstrasse 15. ☎ **089/29-52-35.** U-Bahn: Odeonsplatz or Max-Weber Platz.

In the central shopping mall, this outlet—almost a miniature museum—has the city's best collection of new and antique Meissen porcelain. Look for an old or new Meissener coffee set with the blue-and-white onion design. Any purchase here can be packed and shipped safely—they are experienced in doing just that. Open Monday through Friday from 9:30am to 6pm and on Saturday from 9:30am to 1pm.

Philographikon Galerie Rauhut

Pfisterstrasse 11. ☎ **089/22-50-82.** U-Bahn or S-Bahn: Marienplatz.

This important gallery represents one of the most celebrated success stories of Munich's art world. It was established in 1978 by Mr. Rauhut, a television producer who transformed his hobby of collecting and categorizing rare engravings and manuscripts into a career. Within a century-old building near the Marienplatz, you'll find six rooms scattered over two floors devoted to one of the most comprehensive collections of antique art in Munich. Prices range from 30 DM ($21) for a 19th-century steel engraving, to pre-Gutenberg illuminated manuscripts (sold, depending on circumstances, as individual sheets or as entire folios) worth hundreds of thousands of deutsche marks. Other curiosities include antique maps; botanical prints from English, French, and German sources; and a series of rare prints by a Swiss-born engraver, Karl Bodmer, whose depictions in the 1820s of Native Americans are increasingly valuable on both sides of the Atlantic. It's open Monday to Friday from 10am to 6pm, Saturday from 10am to 2pm.

ARTS

Ileana Boysen (Ellenbogen)

Frauenstrasse 12. ☎ **089/29-27-98.** S-Bahn: Isartor.

This gallery, owned by a Romanian-born art historian, is across from one of Munich's best-known outdoor vegetable markets. It sells original art-nouveau stained-glass windows, carefully extracted from old houses and public buildings in Belgium, Germany, France, England, and Austria, with a scattering from 19th-century America as well. Hours are Monday through Friday from 11am to 6pm and on Saturday from 11am to 2pm.

Galerie für Angewandte Künst München

Pacellistrasse 8. ☎ **089/29-01-470.** U-Bahn: Karlsplatz.

This is the largest, most visible, and most historic art gallery of its type in Germany, established by the Bavarian government in the 1840s as a showcase for local artists. Housed within two interconnected buildings, one a *Jugendstil* monument and the other "of no artistic importance," it contains an upscale art gallery, where merchandise begins at 2,000 DM ($1,400), and a sales outlet, the Ladengeschäft, where attractive, carefully conceived crafts objects are sold at prices that begin at 40 DM ($28). Works by more than 400 artists are displayed and sold here, with the gallery's focus on sculpture in all kinds of media, crafts objects, textiles, and woven objects. It's open Monday through Friday from 9:30am to 6pm, Saturday from 9:30am to 2pm.

BOOKS

Anglia/Words'Worth

Schellingstrasse 3. ☎ **089/28-36-42.** And Schellingstrasse 21. ☎ **089/280-9141.** U-Bahn: U3 or U6 to Universität.

Few competitors in Munich cooperate with each other as gracefully as these two independent stores whose inventory consists exclusively of English-language periodicals and books. Their stock runs the gamut from 19th-century English and American classics to recent releases dealing with radical politics, with art books and offbeat modern literature thrown in as well. Words'Worth is a bit larger than Anglia. One corner is devoted to a display of tea caddies and marmalades, profits from which go directly to Britain's National Trust. Both stores are open Monday through Friday from 9am to 6pm, Saturday from 10am to 2pm, and both will cheerfully refer you to the other if they don't have what you're looking for.

Hugendubel

Marienplatz 22. ☎ **089/23-891.** U-Bahn or S-Bahn: Marienplatz.

Not only is this Munich's biggest bookstore, but it also enjoys the most central location. It sells a number of English-language titles, both fiction and nonfiction, and also offers travel books and helpful maps. Open Monday through Friday from 9am to 6:30pm and on Saturday from 9am to 2pm.

CHINA, SILVER & GLASS

Georg Jensen

Amiraplatz 1. ☎ **089/2916-1084.** U-Bahn: Odeonsplatz.

This is the only outlet in Munich for the silver patterns of the most famous silversmith in Denmark. Many of the patterns were first produced shortly after World War I and helped to alter forever the way the Scandinavians interpreted modern design. Inventory includes hollowware, jewelry, cutlery, clocks, and wristwatches. It's open Monday through Friday from 9:30am to 6pm, Saturday from 9:30am to 2pm.

Kunstring Meissen

Briennerstrasse 4. ☎ **089/28-15-32.** U-Bahn: Odeonsplatz.

This establishment's close links to the porcelain factories of Meissen and Dresden stretch back to the coldest days of the Cold War (the 1950s), when it was able to maintain itself as Munich's exclusive distributor of the products manufactured behind the so-called Iron Curtain. With the collapse of the Soviet regime and the advent of free market for the former GDR, Kunstring's exclusive access became a thing of the past. Despite that, the shop still contains one of Munich's largest inventories of the elegant porcelain that has intrigued artists, aristocrats, and everyday homeowners since the 18th century. *Note:* With two of the most impeccable pedigrees in the German-speaking world, neither Meissen nor Dresden have adopted the assembly-line methods used by many of their more industrialized modern-day competitors, a fact that makes their products beloved by traditionalists and connoisseurs. Anything you buy can be shipped, although if you're looking for the more esoteric objects, there might be a delay if Kunstring doesn't have the object in stock. Kunstring is open Monday through Friday from 9:30am to 5pm and Saturday from 9:30am to 2pm.

✪ Rosenthal

Dienerstrasse 17. ☎ **089/22-26-17.** U-Bahn or S-Bahn: Marienplatz.

Established in 1879 in the Bavarian town of Selb near the Czech border, Rosenthal is one of the three or four most prestigious names in German porcelain. Although traditional patterns are still made, most of the line now focuses on contemporary design in patterns nearer to those of Royal Copenhagen than to the more tradtional approach of Nymphenburg, Sevrès, or Limoges. Prices for Rosenthal patterns are preestablished by the manufacturer, and are rigidly maintained at constant levels throughout Germany. Therefore, although there are no price breaks at this factory outlet (owned and operated by Rosenthal itself), you will find here the widest array of Rosenthal patterns available in Germany. In addition to porcelain, the line includes furniture, glass, and cutlery, all scattered over two floors of spotlessly maintained showrooms. It's open Monday through Friday from 9:30am to 8:30pm, Saturday from 9:30am to 2pm.

✪ Nymphenburger Porzellanmanufaktur

Nordliches Schlossrondell 8. ☎ **089/179-19-70.** Bus: 41.

At Nymphenburg, about 5 miles northwest of the heart of Munich, you'll find one of Germany's most famous porcelain factories on the grounds of Schloss Nymphenburg. You can visit its exhibition and sales rooms, Monday through Friday from 8:30am to noon and 12:30 to 5pm. Shipments can be arranged if you make purchases. (This is a bit of a trek; there's also a more central branch in Munich's center at Odeonsplatz 1 ☎ **089/28-24-28;** U-Bahn: U1 to Rotkreuzplatz, then tram no. 12 toward Amalienburgstrasse.)

CHOCOLATE & CONFISERIE

Confiserie Kreutzkann

Maffeistrasse 4. ☎ **089/29-32-77.** Tram: 19.

This is one of Munich's most famous purveyors of elaborate chocolates, pastry, and the artistically shaped and colored almond paste, marzipan, first established in 1861. If you want to consume your high-calorie treats on the spot, there's a cafe on the premises where you can order coffee, priced at 4 DM ($2.80), to go with whatever appeals to you. It's open Monday to Saturday from 8am to 6:30pm.

Confiserie Reber

Herzogspitalstrasse 9. ☎ **089/26-52-31.** U-Bahn: Stachl.

Pralines, chocolates, and marzipan are the products of this famous and nostalgia-laden store. It has been here since 1876, and many locals remember coming here on childhood outings with their grandparents. About eight bite-size morsels (100 grams) cost 7.20 DM ($5.05). There's a cafe on its street-level premises that has a reputation for chocolate-slathered cakes filled with Cointreau-flavored whipped cream. Slices of this sell for 5.40 DM ($3.80), and can be consumed with coffee, or for chocoholics, with hot chocolate.

CRAFTS & FOLKLORE

Bayerischer Kunstgewerbeverein (Bavarian Association of Artisans)
Pacellistrasse 6–8. ☎ **089/29-01-470.** U-Bahn: Karlspatz.

At this showcase for Bavarian artisans, you'll find excellent handcrafts: ceramics, glass, jewelry, wood carvings, pewter, and Christmas decorations. Open Monday through Friday from 9:30am to 6pm and on Saturday from 9:30am to 2pm.

Firma Kraus
Rindermarkt 10. ☎ **089/260-41-96.** U-Bahn: Marienplatz.

In a cramped but cozy shop near the Marienplatz, this family-run outfit (Manfred and Inge Kraus established the place in 1978) sells a worthy assortment of carved wooden figures inspired by both religious and secular subjects. Inventories include carved versions of saints, angels, virgins, and crucifixes as well as depictions of hunters, farmers, and milkmaids. Most of the merchandise comes from the German-speaking Alps, although some pieces are imported from Italy, especially Florence. Prices range from 18 DM to 20,000 DM ($12 to $14,000), depending on the complexity of the piece. Open Monday through Friday from 10am to 5pm and Saturday from 10am to noon.

Haertle
Neuhauser Strasse 15. ☎ **089/23-11-790.** U-Bahn: Marienplatz or Stachus.

Although much of what it sells is crafted from wood, don't look for carvings of the saints or depictions of woodcutters and alpine farmers. Instead you'll find racks of nostalgic, and in some cases, kitschy wooden implements for the home and kitchen. Much is rustic, charming, and crafted in Bavaria, though the regional merchandise is offset with racks of porcelain, glassware, and gift items. The shop has thrived at its location in Munich's historic core for at least a century. Open Monday through Friday from 9:30am to 6:30pm, Thursday until 8:30pm, and Saturday from 9:30am to 2pm.

◌ Ludwig Mory
Marienplatz 8. ☎ **089/22-45-42.** U-Bahn or S-Bahn: Marienplatz.

This is the most famous purveyor of Bavarian beer steins in Munich, based in a richly folkloric, one-room premise near the cathedral, and basking in a reputation that has been building since the 1830s. After seeing this place, you'll never want to drink Budweiser from a can again. Fashioned from pewter, and to a lesser degree, ceramic, sometimes lidded, sometimes without, the steins range from 45 DM ($31.50) for an honest but unpretentious souvenir of your stay in Munich to a richly decorative work of art that might round off a private collection, priced at 1,200 DM ($840). It's open Monday through Friday from 9am to 6pm, Saturday from 9am to 1pm.

Otto Kellnberger Holzhandlung
Heiliggeistrasse 8. ☎ **089/22-64-79.** U-Bahn or S-Bahn: Marienplatz.

Established just after World War II, this is a small but choice emporium of traditional woodcarvings that, from a position in the Altstadt near the Marienplatz, evoke the bucolic charms of remote alpine Bavaria. Inventory includes all the folkloric charm and some of the folkloric kitsch you might have found if you had made the trek to remote Oberammergau, but with a lot less time, trouble, and expense. It's open Monday through Friday from 9:30am to 6:30pm and Saturday from 10am to noon.

Prinoth

Guido Schneblestrasse 9A. ☎ **089/56-03-78.** U-Bahn: U4 or U5 to Laimerplatz.

Most of the woodcarvings sold here are produced in small workshops in the South Tyrol, that folklore-rich part of Austria that was annexed to Italy after World War I. The selection is wide-ranging and broad, and since the setting lies 3 1/2 miles west of Munich's tourist zones, prices are substantially reasonable compared to shops closer to the Marienplatz. Open Monday to Friday from 9am to 6pm.

✪ Wallach

Residenzstrasse 3. ☎ **089/22-08-71.** U-Bahn or S-Bahn: Marienplatz.

Established more than a century ago, Wallach is the largest emporium in Munich for Bavarian handcrafts, both new and antique, as well as the evocative, sometimes kitschy folk art. You'll find antique butter churns, hand-painted wooden boxes and trays, painted porcelain clocks, wooden wall or mantelpiece clocks, and doilies whose use faded with antimacassars, but which are charming nonetheless. Most of the store's street level is devoted to handcrafted folklore. One floor above street level, you'll find dirndls, lederhosen, loden coats and traditional Bavarian garments for men, women, and children. Look also for fabrics sold by the meter, and such homewares as bedsheets and towels, many patterned in Bavarian themes. The store is open Monday through Friday from 10:30am to 6pm (Thursday until 8:30pm) and Saturday from 10:30am to 4pm.

DEPARTMENT STORES

Hertie

Bahnhofplatz 7. ☎ **089/55-120.** U-Bahn: Hauptbahnhof.

This is our favorite Munich department store, a sprawling four-story-plus-basement emporium of all aspects of the good life as interpreted by Teutonic tastes. A fixture near the main railway station since the turn of the century, it has survived wars and revolutions with predictable mercantile style. It's open Monday through Friday from 9am to 6:30pm (Thursday until 8:30pm) and Saturday from 9am to 2pm.

Kaufhof

Marienplatz. ☎ **089/23-18-51.** U-Bahn or S-Bahn: Marienplatz.

This is the Munich branch of a chain of upscale department stores that was originally established in Cologne during the late 19th century. Scattered over five floors of what's the most prestigious address in town, it came to Munich in 1972, and is today one of the largest department stores in town. Wander freely among displays that are art forms in their own right, with inventory devoted to men's, women's, and children's clothing, housewares, and virtually everything else you might think of as well. It's open Monday through Friday from 9am to 6:30pm (Thursday until 8:30pm) and Saturday from 8:30am to 2pm. There's a smaller branch of this well-respected emporium at Karlsplatz 2 (☎ **089/51250;** U-Bahn: Karlsplatz) that maintains the same hours and accepts the same credit cards.

Ludwig Beck am Rathauseck

Am Marienplatz 11. ☎ **089/23-69-10.** U-Bahn or S-Bahn: Marienplatz.

This is Munich's major department store. Most merchandise is intended for local residents; however, visitors will also be interested in this four-floor shopping bazaar, which sells handmade crafts from all over Germany, both old and new. Items include decorative pottery and dishes, etched glass beer steins and vases, painted wall plaques depicting rural scenes, and decorative flower arrangements. There's unusual kitchenware, colored flatware, calico hot pads and towels, and a collection of casually chic leather-trimmed canvas purses. The shop also offers fashions, textiles, and even jazz recordings. Within the same block the store has opened two more outlets, including Wäsche-Beck, selling lingerie, linens, and curtains, and Strumpf-Beck, featuring the town's largest selection of stockings and hosiery. Open Monday through Friday from 9:30am to 6:30pm and on Saturday from 9am to 2pm.

FASHION
MEN & WOMEN

Bogner Haus
Residenzstrasse 15. ☎ **089/290-70-40.** U-Bahn or S-Bahn: Marienplatz.

Founded by Willy Bogner, former Olympic champion downhill racer, this store stocks well-made women's clothing upstairs, men's clothing on the street level, and clothing suited for whatever sport happens to be seasonal at the time of your visit in the cellar. Somewhere in the store, you'll find whatever you need to be appropriately clad for any occasion. One of its best is the Fire & Ice Department, in the cellar, where garments for young men and women aged 16 to 20 are chosen with the kind of flair that might please some of the most demanding people in your life—your children. The store is open Monday through Wednesday and Friday from 9:30am to 6:30pm, Thursday from 9:30am to 7:30pm, and Saturday from 9:30am to 2pm.

✪ Dirndl-Ecke
Am Platzl 1/Sparkassenstrasse 10. ☎ **089/22-01-63.** U-Bahn or S-Bahn: Marienplatz or Isartor.

One block up from the famed Hofbräuhaus, this shop gets our unreserved recommendation as a stylish place specializing in high-grade dirndls, feathered alpine hats, and all clothing associated with the alpine regions. Everything sold is of fine quality—there's no tourist junk. Other merchandise includes needlework hats, beaded belts, and pleated shirts for men. You may want to buy the stylish capes, the silver jewelry in old Bavarian style, the leather shoes, or the linen and cotton combinations, such as skirts with blouses and jackets. Bavarian clothing for children is also available. Open Monday through Friday from 9am to 6pm and on Saturday from 9am to 1pm.

Frankonia
Maximilianplatz 10. ☎ **089/290-00-20.** U-Bahn: Karlsplatz or Odeonsplatz.

This store has Munich's most prestigious collection of traditional Bavarian dress (called *Tracht*). If you see yourself dressed hunter style, this place can outfit you well. There's a fine collection of wool cardigan jackets with silvery buttons. Open Monday through Friday from 9am to 6:30pm and on Saturday from 9am to 2pm.

Loden-Frey
Maffeistrasse 7–9. ☎ **089/21-03-90.** U-Bahn or S-Bahn: Marienplatz.

The twin domes of the Frauenkirche are visible above the soaring glass-enclosed atrium of this shop's showroom. Go here for the world's largest selection of Loden clothing and traditional costumes, as well as for international fashions from top European designers such as Armani, Valentino, and Ungaro. Open Monday through Friday from 9am to 6pm, except on Thursday when hours extend to 8:30pm, and on Saturday from 9am to 2pm.

Exatmo
Franz-Josef-Strasse 35. ☎ **089/33-57-61.** U-Bahn: Giselastrasse.

Only a district like Schwabing could sustain a business like this one. One of the most unusual clothiers in Munich operates from a showroom complete with mock-medieval murals. Among the racks of clothing are garments inspired by the puffy sleeves and dramatic flair of 17th-century fasions as popularized by the Three Musketeers—you can dress yourself as a fencing champion even if you don't know a thrust from an *en garde*. Virtually everything in stock is manufactured from linen or leather. Ever since it was founded, the store has purchased old pieces of linen, such as bedsheets from army surplus inventories across Europe, for reconfiguration into jackets, vests, and ruffled shirts that hang beautifully, styles that might have been appreciated by the Elizabethans. It's open Monday through Friday from 9am to 6:30pm, Saturday from 10am to 2pm.

Red/Green of Scandinavia

Kauflingerstrasse 9. ☎ **089/260-04-89.** U-Bahn or S-Bahn: Marienplatz.

This shop near the Marienplatz will sell you anything you need to appear relaxed, casual, and at home on someone's private yacht or on the local golf links. Most of the inventory comes from Denmark, and since everything was designed to withstand the blustery winds or the clear sunlight of the Baltic, they're fully capable of gracefully accessorizing whatever outdoor activity (or *après-sport* fireside chit-chat) you're about to engage in. Garments for men, women, and children are all available. It's open Monday through Friday from 10am to 6pm, Saturday from 10am to 2pm.

MEN

The Mercer

Amalienstrasse 40. ☎ **089/28-24-18.** U-Bahn: U3 or U6 to Universität.

It's one of the best-stocked men's clothing stores in town, with a roster of loyal clients that range in age from 35 to around 50. Much of the merchandise is patterned on British models, with displays devoted to such English manufacturers as Grenson shoes, Smedley, Austin Reed, and Charles Hill neckties. If you're male and discover that your wardrobe isn't adequate, this place can right some of those wrongs. It's open Monday through Friday from 11am to 6:30pm, Saturday from 10:30am to 2pm.

Moshammer's

Maximilianstrasse 14. ☎ **089/22-69-24.** U-Bahn: Isartor.

This store could be your first resource in a search for appropriate menswear. Merchandise is continental, and the staff seems aware of their own prestige and the glamor of their address. In other words, although a visit won't necessarily leave you with a warm and fuzzy feeling of Gemütlichkeit, you might at least learn how high some of the prices can be in an upscale Münchener menswear store. It's open Monday through Friday from 10am to 6pm, Saturday from 10am to 2pm.

Uli Knecht

Residenzstrasse 19–20. ☎ **089/2916-0406.** U-Bahn: Odeonsplatz.

This is the men's division of the same retailer recommended below, the kind of place where a business executive could clothe himself for either the office, the golf course, a hunting lodge, or an amorous weekend getaway. Designers represented on the two floors of showroom include Ralph Lauren, Armani, an Italian designer named Antonio Fusco, and such German outfitters as Closed and Strenesse. It's open Monday to Friday from 10:30am to 6pm, Saturday from 9am to 2pm, closed Sunday.

WOMEN

Furore

Franz-Joseph Strasse 41. ☎ **089/34-39-71.** U-Bahn: U3 or U6 to Giselastrasse.

This elegant store's merchandise revolves around a range of fashionable undergarments (brassieres, bustiers, slips, etc.) with tasteful designs, in some cases filmy and subtly erotic, in silk, cotton, and a limited roster of synthetics by Spain-born André Sard. Part of the displays are devoted to the homewear collection, sheets, towels, and decorative accessories of New York design superstar Donna Karan. Furore was the first store in Germany to distribute her designs. The store is open Monday through Friday from 10am to 6:30pm, Saturday from 10am to 2pm.

Maendler
Theatinerstrasse 7. ☎ **089/291-33-22.** U-Bahn: Odeonsplatz.

The genius of this store revolves around its division into a series of boutiques, each scattered over two floors that are well known to virtually every well-dressed woman in Bavaria. You may prefer to wander around the store, appreciating the creative vision of Joop, Claude Montana, New York New York, and Jil Sander, but a quick consultation with any of the staff poised near the store's entrance can point you in the right direction. Looking for that special something for your dinner with the city's mayor or the president of Germany? Ask to see the formal evening wear of English designer David Fielden. Looking for something more experimental, daring, and avant-garde? Head for this outfit's branch, **Rosy Maendler,** Maximiliansplatz 12 (same phone). There you'll find a more youthful version of the same store, and garments by Madonna's favorite designer, Jean-Paul Gaultier, whose exhibitionistic and/or erotic leather and rubber clothing will cause a stir on either side of the Atlantic. Both shops are open Monday through Friday from 9:30am to 6:30pm, Saturday from 9:30am to 2pm.

Uli Knecht
Residenzstrasse 15. ☎ **089/22-15-10.** U-Bahn: Odeonsplatz.

Its employees are quick to tell you that Uli Knecht is not a designer, but rather, a clever and successful retailer with a gift for distributing the creations of some of the best-known clothiers in the world. This branch for women, two doors down from the Uli Knecht store for men, covers two floors laden with garments that include sportswear, a thin scattering of formalwear, and a heavy emphasis on upscale, elegant, and highly wearable clothing that includes everything from business suits to cocktail dresses. It's open Monday through Friday from 9:30am to 7:30pm, Saturday from 9:30am to 2:30pm.

FOOD

✪ Dallmayr
Dienerstrasse 14–15. ☎ **089/21-350.** Tram: 19.

What Fauchon is to Paris, and Fortnum & Mason is to London, the venerable firm of Dallmayr is to Munich. Gastronomes as far away as Hamburg and Berlin sometimes telephone orders for exotica not readily available anywhere else, and its list of prestigious clients reads like a Who's Who of German industry and letters. Wander freely among racks of foodstuffs, some of which are too delicate to survive shipment abroad, others that can be shipped anywhere. The shop is open Monday through Friday from 9am to 6:30pm, Saturday from 9am to 1pm. The restaurant associated with this store is separately recommended in Chapter 5.

Zerwick Gewölbe
Ledererstrasse 3. ☎ **089/22-68-24.** U-Bahn or S-Bahn: Marienplatz.

The amazing thing about this place is that it has survived in a form that's more or less evocative of the Middle Ages, when it was originally established (1206). It's the oldest purveyor of venison and game in Bavaria, with so much history associated with it that it's easy to forget its modern, workaday function as a supplier of wursts, pâtés, terrines, roasts, and cutlets (most of which are made from venison, wild boar, pheasant, and game birds) to private homes and restaurants around the city. Most temporary visitors stop in for a simple platter of food, priced at around 8 DM ($5.60), perhaps preceded by a steaming bowl of one of the *Tagessuppes* (soups of the day) that are dispensed from an *Imbiss* (snack bar) set up in one corner. Look for this upscale and very historic delicatessen and butcher shop near the landmark restaurant Haxnbauer, on a small street near the Marienplatz. It's open Monday through Friday from 9:30am to 6pm, Saturday from 9:30am to 3pm.

The English Shop

Franziskanerstrasse 14. ☎ **089/48-84-00.** U-Bahn: Rosenheimerplatz.

Some visitors compare its ambience to something that might have been described by Charles Dickens; others relish its products as reminders of the English and Irish food they grew up on. It might remind you of the kind of 19th-century food shop you'd expect on the High Street of a medium-sized town in the English Midlands, except that its location in the heart of historic Munich sometimes causes some culture shock. Irish-born William Smith is the shopkeeper, receiving shipments of English butter and cheese, bacon, Scottish eggs and kippers, biscuits, and beer every Friday. Looking for an English Stilton or Double Gloucester to consume with a pint of Newcastle Brown Ale or a Cornish meat pie? You'll find them here, surrounded with goodly doses of Pickwickian nostalgia. There's also a collection of American-made Pringles potato chips and Pop-Tarts—the inventory is designed to appeal to the tastebuds of Munich's English-speaking population. It's open Monday through Friday from 10am to 6:30pm, Thursday from 10am to 8:30pm, Saturday from 10am to 2pm.

JEWELRY & WATCHES

Andreas Huber

Weinstrasse 8. ☎ **089/29-82-95.** U-Bahn or S-Bahn: Marienplatz.

This store sells all the big names in Swiss and other European wristwatches, as well as clocks. They offer some jewelry, but their specialty is timepieces. Open Monday through Friday from 9:30am to 6pm and on Saturday from 9:30am to 1pm.

Gebruder Hemmerle

Maximilianstrasse 14. ☎ **089/22-01-89.** U-Bahn: Odeonplatz or Max-Weber Platz.

This is *the* place for jewelry. The original founders of this stylish place made their fortune designing bejeweled fantasies for the Royal Bavarian Court of Ludwig II. Today, in a shop paneled in southern baroque pastel-painted wood, you can buy some of the most desirable jewelry in the capital. All pieces are limited editions, designed and made in-house by Bavarian craftspeople. The company also designs its own wristwatch, the Hemmerle, and distributes what is said to be one of the world's finest watches, the Breguet. Open Monday through Friday from 9:30am to 6pm and on Saturday from 9:30am to 1pm.

Carl Jagemann's

Residenzstrasse 3. ☎ **089/22-54-93.** U-Bahn: Marienplatz.

Its reputation for quality and honesty goes back to 1864, as does some (but not all) of the merchandise it sells. It's one of the Altstadt's largest purveyors of new and antique timepieces of all types, ranging from wristwatches to grandfather clocks, from the severely rectilinear to rococo kitsch. There's also a collection of new and antique jewelry. It's open Monday through Friday from 10am to 6pm, and Saturday from 10am to 2pm.

KITCHENWARE

Biebl

Karlsplatz 25. ☎ **089/59-79-36.** U-Bahn: Karlsplatz (for both outlets).

Set in the pedestrian zone of Munich's inner core, this is one of the most reputable and fairly priced emporiums of razor-sharp German steel in Munich. They're quick to debunk the myth that anything at all that's made in the town of Solingen, in the Ruhr Valley near the French border, is of flawless quality. Instead, they stress the impeccable quality of implements made by such Solingen-based companies as Trident Wuesthof or Henckels (for kitchen knives); Dovo (for scissors), and W.M.S. (for table cutlery). Some aspects of this place might remind you of a warehouse for surgical implements, but the choice is so overwhelming, and the prices so fair, that it's one of the best-recommended stopovers in this survey. Many excellent individual knives can be had for 20 DM ($14). Even the best rarely exceed 55 DM ($38.50) each. Look for the opening, sometime during the lifetime of this edition, of an even bigger nearby branch of this outfit on the corner of the Karlsplatz, on Neuhauser Strasse 47 (☎ **089/54-90-090**). The newer branch will also inventory a collection of pots, pans, and cooking utensils. Both outlets are open Monday through Friday from 9:15am to 6:15pm, Saturday from 9:15am to 2pm.

MARKETS

In addition to those listed below, a traditional market, the **Auer Dult,** is held three times a year in the Mariahilfplatz. Antiques dealers, food, and Bavarian bands are present; it's a great place to find bargains. Take tram 7, 15, 25, or 27.

Christkindlmarkt

Marienplatz. U-Bahn: Marienplatz.

One of the most visible and tradition-laden in Munich, this December Christmas market is the focal point of visits from all over Europe and Germany—only the Christmas market in Nürnberg is more famous. Hundreds of stalls offer Christmas ornaments, handmade children's toys, carved figures, and nativity scenes. The scene is full of local color, with the stallkeepers in their woolen coats, hats, and gloves, the scene enhanced by frequent snowfalls. Opening hours vary with the enthusiasm of the merchants. In most cases, the stalls are open from 10am to 7:30pm on Monday through Saturday, although as Christmas approaches, many open on Sunday as well.

Elisabethmarkt

Elisabethplatz. Tram: 18.

This is Schwabing's smaller and less dramatic version of Munich's premier outdoor market, the Viktualienmarkt. It's held every Monday to Saturday from 7am to about 11am, although some diehard merchants manage to hold out until 1:30pm. Completely decentralized, each individual vendor operates exclusively on his or her own account. Stalls tend to be more laden with bounty in spring, summer, and fall, but a few hardy souls maintain a presence here even in the depths of winter.

FLEA MARKETS

The famous Münchener Flohmarkt recently lost its site to bulldozers, an event that has caused lots of upset and uproar. By the time you get there, however, a new site may have been selected. Check the papers for notices of occasional flea markets, which are often set up in sports areas or convention centers.

Grossmarkthalle

Thalkirchen. U-Bahn: U3 to Thalkirchen.

This is Munich's equivalent of Paris's Rungis (formerly Les Halles). Buyers from virtually every restaurant in Munich make an early morning pilgrimage to this industrial-looking complex in the city's southern suburbs. Purveyors arrive with lorries from as far away as Italy; buyers congregate from throughout Bavaria and beyond. Be warned, though, that there's an entrance fee of 5 DM ($3.50) for you to admire the way business is conducted, and buying is wholesale only—homemakers who do show up usually bring bushel baskets or wheeled carts to haul away impressive quantities of peaches, apples, or whatever. Open Monday through Saturday from 5am to 10:30am.

Viktualienmarkt

U-Bahn or S-Bahn: Marienplatz.

Unless you happen to be living within a place where you have access to a kitchen, it's doubtful that you'll want to be hauling groceries back to your hotel room during your stay in Munich. That doesn't detract, however, from the allure of wandering through the open-air stalls of the city's most prominent food market, the Viktualienmarkt, a few minute's walk south of the Marienplatz. It's composed of hundreds of independently operated merchants who maintain whatever hours they want, often closing up their cramped premises whenever the day's inventory is sold out. Most economy-minded shoppers, however, show up, shopping basket in hand, around 8am, to stock their larders before noon. By 5pm, only the hardiest of merchants remain in place, and by early evening, the kiosks are locked up tight. On the premises are a worthy collection of leaf lettuces, wine, meats, cheeses, and all the bounty of the German agrarian world.

MUSIC

Hieber Musikhaus

In the Rathaus, Landschaftstrasse (without number). ☎ **089/2900-8040.** U-Bahn or S-Bahn: Marienplatz.

This is the largest music store in Munich, and with a history going back to 1884, it's also one of the oldest. Its stockpiles of librettos for operas by Wagner, Mozart, Puccini, and Verdi are among the most extensive anywhere, and in many cases, they inventory German-language translations even of operas originally written in Italian or French. You'll have to use a bit of ingenuity to determine which building contains whatever it is you're looking for, but in the process of educating yourself, you're likely to run into at least one or two musicians employed by the city's many orchestral groups. Looking for a musical instrument? Check out the company's inventories at Liebfrauenstrasse 1 (☎ **089/290-08-40**). Looking for keyboards and an idiosyncratic collection of secondhand sheet music that's either antique or appropriately dog-eared and annotated by anonymous musicians of yesteryear? Head for the company's branch on the Mazaristrasse 1 (☎ **089/290-08-00**). All three are within a short walk from each other, and all maintain the same hours: Monday through Friday from 9am to 6:30pm (Thursday until 7:30pm), Saturday from 9am to 2pm.

TOYS

Obletter's
Karlsplatz 8. ☎ **089/231-86-01.** U-Bahn: Karlsplatz.

Established in the 1880s, this is one of the largest emporiums of children's toys in Munich, with five floors of inventory containing everything from folkloric dolls to computer games. Some of the most charming are replicas of middle European antiques, some of which look suspiciously capable of coming alive beneath someone's Christmas tree, à la *Nutcracker Suite*. It's open Monday through Friday from 9am to 5pm (Thursday until 8:30pm), Saturday from 9am to 2pm.

Münchener Poupenstuben und Zinnfiguren Kabinette
Maxburgstrasse 4. ☎ **089/29-37-97.** U-Bahn: Karlsplatz.

This is the kind of store you either thrill to or find impossibly claustrophobic. With a 150-year history of management by matriarchs of the same family, it's one of the best sources in Germany for a miniature world where houses, furniture, birdcages, and people are cunningly crafted from pewter or carved wood, and which look deceptively similar to the real thing. Some of the figures are made from 150-year-old molds that are collectors' items in their own right. Anything in this place would make a great gift not only for a child but for an adult with a nostalgic bent. Ilse Schweizer is the present owner. It's open Monday through Friday from 10am to 6pm, Saturday from 10am to 1pm.

WINE

Geisel's Vinothek
Schützenstrasse 11. ☎ **089/5513-7140.** U-Bahn: Hauptbahnhof.

Other than Dallmayr, which does this kind of thing on a much bigger scale, this is the most sophisticated wine shop in Munich. Set adjacent to the Excelsior Hotel, with displays that celebrate grapes and winemaking in one way or another, it doubles as a restaurant (recommended separately in Chapter 5). Its inventory includes wines from Germany, Austria, Italy, and France, with bottles ranging from 14 DM ($9.80) to as much as 1,400 DM ($980) for a vintage *Château Petrus*. Many worthy bottles sell for under 30 DM ($21). Because the chef here is a passionate advocate of wines from western France, there's an especially strong selection of Bordeaux. Most of the selections offered by the glass at the bar are regularly sold by the bottle at the wine shop, allowing you to taste before you buy the whole bottle.

Munich After Dark

Munich is a major performing arts center, and has a lively nightlife as well. Munich is home to no less than four major orchestras plus a world-class opera company, and a ballet company. Many theaters are scattered throughout the city, offering everything from comic opera to modern German drama.

Munich's nightlife varies with the weather. When the weather is fair, and the night air balmy, the Biergartens and Biersteins are brimming with cheer. During the winter months, patrons of the beer gardens turn to Munich's beer halls, such as the illustrious Hofbräuhaus, where thirsty Müncheners quaff beer and share in the typical Bavarian sing-song. Beer gardens and beer halls usually empty around midnight; then the club scene cranks up. Munich's club scene is quite eclectic. It is possible to find almost any type of club, from country-western bars to ultra-techno dance halls. Many clubs rave until the wee hours of the morning. The district of Schwabing is an ideal destination for avid clubbers, home to the numerous cabarets and funky dance clubs.

1 The Performing Arts

Nowhere else in Europe, other than London and Paris, will you find so many musical and theatrical performances. And the good news is the low cost of the seats—so count on indulging yourself and going to several concerts. You'll get good tickets if you're willing to pay anywhere from 15 DM to 75 DM ($10.50 to $52.50). Pick up a *Monatsprogramm* for information and schedules.

If you speak German, you'll find at least 20 theaters offering plays of every description: classic, comic, experimental, contemporary— take your pick. The best way to find out what current productions might interest you is to go to a theater-ticket agency: The most convenient one is at Marienplatz at the entrance to the S-Bahn.

Besides the organizations listed below, Munich is home to the **Bavarian State Radio Orchestra (Bayerischer Rundfunk Münchener Rundfunkorchestra),** Roberto Abbado, musical director; the **Bavarian Radio Orchestra (Bayerischer Rundfunk Symphonieorchester),** Loren Mazel, musical director; and the **Graunke Symphony Orchestra,** directed by Kurt Graunke.

OPERA & CLASSICAL MUSIC

✪ Bavarian State Opera

Max-Joseph-Platz 2. ☎ **089/21-85-01.** Tickets 10 DM–250 DM ($7–$175), including standing room. U-Bahn or S-Bahn: Marienplatz.

The Bavarian State Opera is one of the world's great opera companies. The Bavarians give their hearts, perhaps their souls, to opera. The home of the company is the restored **Nationaltheater,** and the productions are beautifully mounted and presented. The world's greatest singers perform here. Hard-to-get tickets may be purchased Monday through Friday from 10am to 6pm, plus one hour before each performance (during the weekend, only on Saturday from 10am to 1pm). The **Opera Festival,** in July and August, ranks with those in Salzburg and Bayreuth.

The opera shares its home with a younger company, the **Bavarian State Ballet.** For ticket information, call **089/2185-1919.**

Münchener Philharmoniker (Munich Philharmonic)

Rosenheimer Strasse 5. ☎ **089/48-09-80.** Tickets 23 DM–120 DM ($16.10–$84). S-Bahn: Rosenheimer Platz. Tram: 18 to Gasteig. Bus: 51.

This famous orchestra was founded in 1893, and has been under the baton of many famous conductors; it's directed today by Sergiu Celibidache. The orchestra performs in Philharmonic Hall at the Gasteig Kulturzentrum, the largest of the center's performance halls. The concert season begins in mid-September and runs until July.

MAJOR PERFORMANCE VENUES

There are theaters and performance halls all over town. The **Residenz Theater** (Max-Joseph-Platz, ☎ **089/22-57-54**) is the home of the **Bayerisches Staatsschauspiel** (State Theater). Concerts are given in the **Herkulessaal** (in the Residenz, ☎ **089/29-06-71**). The **Staatstheater am Gärtnerplatz** (☎ **089/201-67-67**) offers a varied program of operetta, ballet, and musicals.

✪ Altes Residenztheater (Cuvilliés Theater)

Residenzstrasse 1. ☎ **089/2185-1920.** Opera tickets, 30 DM–250 DM ($21–$175); play tickets, 10 DM–71 DM ($7–$49.70). U-Bahn: U3, U4, U5, or U6 to Odeonsplatz.

A part of the Residenz (see "Museums and Palaces" in Chapter 6), this theater is a sightseeing attraction in its own right. The Bavarian State Opera and the **Bayerisches Staatsschauspiel (State Theater)** perform small-scale works here in keeping with the tiny theater's intimate character. Box-office hours are the same as those for the Nationaltheater. The theater is celebrated as Germany's most outstanding example of a rococo tier-boxed theater. Seating an audience of 550, it was designed by court architect François de Cuvilliés in the mid-18th century. During World War II the interior was dismantled and stored. After the war it was reassembled in the reconstructed building. For an admission of 3 DM ($2.10), visitors can look at the theater Monday through Saturday from 2 to 5pm and on Sunday from 10am to 5pm.

Deutsches Theater

Schwanthalerstrasse 13. ☎ **089/5523-4360.** Tickets, 35 DM–100 DM ($24.50–$70), higher for special events. U-Bahn: Karlsplatz.

The regular season of the Deutsches Theater goes throughout the year. Musicals are popular, but operettas, ballets, and international shows are performed as well. During Carnival, in January and February, the theater becomes a ballroom; seats are removed and replaced by tables and chairs for more than 2,000 guests. There are costume balls and official black-tie festivities, famous throughout Europe.

☉ Gasteig Kulturzentrum

Rosenheimer Strasse 5. ☎ **089/48-09-80.** S-Bahn: Rosenheimer Platz. Tram: 18. Bus: 51.

The Gasteig Cultural Center opened in 1985 amid much controversy. A huge glass-and-brick arts center, it is the home of the Munich Philharmonic and also shelters the Richard Strauss Conservatory and the Munich Municipal Library. Gasteig stands on the bluffs of the Isar River in the Haidhausen district. You can purchase tickets to events at the ground-level Glashalle on Monday through Friday from 10am to 6pm and on Saturday from 10am to 2pm.

Münchener Kammerspiele

Maximilianstrasse 26–28. ☎ **089/2372-1328.** Tickets 10.50 DM–47.50 DM ($7.35–$33.25). U-Bahn: Marienplatz. S-Bahn: Isartorplatz. Tram: 19 to Maximilianstrasse.

Contemporary plays as well as classics from German or international playwrights, ranging from Goethe to Brecht and Shakespeare to Goldoni, are performed here. The season lasts from early October to the end of July. You can reserve tickets by phone Monday through Friday from 10am to 6pm, but you must pick them up at least two days before a performance. The box office is open Monday through Friday from 10am to 6pm and on Saturday from 10am to 1pm, plus one hour before performances.

The theater also has a second smaller venue called **Werkraum,** where new productions—mainly by younger authors and directors—are presented. The location is at Hildegardstrasse 1 (call the number above for more information).

2 The Club & Music Scene

NIGHTCLUBS

Bayerischer Hof Night Club

In the Hotel Bayerischer Hof, Promenadeplatz 2–6. ☎ **089/212-09-94.** Cover 18 DM ($12.60) Fri–Sat. Tram: 19.

This nightclub in the cellar of the Bayerischer Hof offers sophisticated entertainment. It's a piano bar until 10pm, when a partition opens, revealing a bandstand where an orchestra plays to a dancing crowd until 3 or 4am. Entrance to the piano bar is free, but there's a cover charge to the nightclub on Friday and Saturday nights. Drinks begin at 15.50 DM ($10.85); meals run 35 DM–40 DM ($24.50–$28). It's open daily from 6pm.

Night Flight

Franz-Joseph Strauss Airport, Wartungsallee 9. ☎ **089/9759-7999.** Cover 5 DM–12 DM ($3.50–$8.40). S-Bahn: S8 to Flughafen.

It's one of only two or three nightclubs in Europe that dramatize the landings and takeoffs from an airport as part of a visual thrill. To reach it, you'll have to either drive 25 miles north of the city or take a 30-minute ride on the S-Bahn. The site is on the periphery of the Munich Airport, in an industrial-looking building midway between three enormous hangars. You can drink at three different bars, dance, and listen to the loud music that changes according to the night of the week. There's even a restaurant, serving main courses from 16 DM to 20 DM ($11.20 to $14), and drinks that cost from 6.50 DM ($4.55). In summer, there's an outside terrace where virtually everything at the airport can be seen with eerie clarity. Friday nights, with techno-rap as the theme, draw the youngest audience. Other nights, the crowd ranges from 25 to a youthful 40. It's open Tuesday through Saturday from 9pm to at least 3am, and in some cases, until 8am the following morning.

Welser Kuche

Residenzstrasse 27. ☎ **089/29-65-65.** U-Bahn: U3 to Odeonsplatz.

Welser Kuche recreates a hearty medieval feast. Meals begin every night of the week at 8pm, and guests must be prepared to stick around for three hours as they are served by *Magde* and *Knechte* (wenches and knaves) in 16th-century costumes. In many ways this is a takeoff on the many medieval Tudor banquets that are so popular with tourists in London. Food is served in hand-thrown pottery, and guests eat the medieval delicacies with their fingers, aided only by a stiletto-like dagger. Many recipes are authentic—they are based on a 16th-century cookbook discovered in 1970. You can order a 6- or 10-course menu, called a *Welser Feast,* for 69 DM or 79 DM ($48.30 or $55.30), respectively. On Tuesday only, a *Bürgermahl* of five courses costs 59 DM ($41.30). The place can be good fun if you're in the mood; but it's likely to be overflowing with tourists, so reservations are recommended. It's open daily from 7pm to 1am.

CABARET

Rationaltheater

Hesseloherstrasse 18. ☎ **089/33-50-40.** Tickets 26 DM–30 DM ($18.20–$21). U-Bahn: Münchener Freiheit.

Rationaltheater is a political cabaret, in existence since 1963. Some critics claim that its satire is so pointed that it has the power to topple governments. The show is performed Tuesday through Saturday, starting at 8:30pm. Tickets must be reserved by phone, beginning at 10am.

JAZZ

Jazzclub Unterfahrt

Kirchenstrasse 96. ☎ **089/448-27-94.** Cover 15 DM–28 DM ($10.50–$19.60) Tues–Sat, 5 DM ($3.50) Sun jam session. U-Bahn or S-Bahn: Ostbahnhof.

This is Munich's leading jazz club, lying near the Ostbahnhof in the Haidhausen district. Within a Gemütlich ambience of pinewood paneling and flickering candles, the 120-seat club presents live music Tuesday through Sunday from 9pm to 1am. In one corner is an art gallery where a changing collection of paintings and sculptures is sold. Sunday night there's a special jam session for improvisation. Beer begins at 4.80 DM ($3.35); snacks run 6.50 DM–10 DM ($4.55–$7).

Schwabinger Podium

Wagnerstrasse 1. ☎ **089/39-94-82.** No cover. U-Bahn: U3, U4, U5, or U6 to Münchener Freiheit.

This club offers varying nightly entertainment. Some evenings are dominated by oldies and rock 'n' roll. Beer begins at 5.80 DM ($4.05). It's open Sunday through Thursday from 8pm to 1am and on Friday and Saturday from 8pm to 2am.

COUNTRY

Rattlesnake Saloon

Schneeglöckchenstrasse 91. ☎ **089/150-40-35.** Cover 10 DM–15 DM ($7–$10.50). S-Bahn: S1 to Fasanerie.

One of Munich's two country-western saloons, it's a down-home homage to the redneck charms of hound dogs, battered pickup trucks, and cowboy hats and boots. It offers a roster of rib-sticking platters (rib-eye steaks, barbecued pork, chili) to wash down the steins of Spaten beer that go so cheerfully with the live country music. Whence come the swains who will serenade your arrival with country-cousin melodies? From Munich, England, Canada, and even in some cases, Nashville, Tennessee. Regardless of how authentic the twang in the music might be, there are many charming aspects to an evening here, and someone will invariably rise to the challenge of conducting a rodeo-style line dance lesson for anyone who's interested in learning. Rattlesnake is open Wednesday through Sunday from 7pm to 1am. Beer costs 5.50 DM ($3.85).

Oklahoma

Schäftlarnstrasse 156. ☎ **089/723-43-27.** Cover 10 DM–12 DM ($7–$8.40). U-bahn: U3 or U6 to Implerstrasse, then bus 31 or 57.

Except for having no restaurant, this is the twin of the Rattlesnake Saloon, with the same owner and the same emphasis. Live bluegrass and country/western music is performed, often by Europeans, decked out in the requisite cowboy boots and honky-tonk references. Come for an insight into how the Teutonic world interprets the Nashville experience, and be prepared for a few doses of kitsch. The place sings honky-tonk and cowboy blues Tuesday through Saturday from 7pm to 1am. The beer of choice is Spaten, which costs from 5.50 DM ($3.85) per mug.

DANCE CLUBS & DISCOS

La Scala Music Bar

Oskar-von-Miller Ring 3, at Gabelsbergerstrasse. ☎ **089/23-58-58.** U-Bahn: Odeonsplatz.

Inaugurated in 1993, an apricot-colored reinvention of an older bar on the same site, this place is known for a sophisticated electronic amplification system that makes recorded music sound wonderful. Featured is modern jazz, African-American music, rock and soul, techno, acid jazz, and, during slow periods, easy listening. Clients tend to be well-dressed German-speaking equivalents of yuppies of all ages. There's a range of exotic cocktails that includes what seems to be everybody's favorite, "Sex on the Beach," priced at 15.50 DM ($10.85). In summer, the venue moves to an outdoor terrace a few feet above the traffic of the street outside. Italian-inspired platters cost from 15 DM–25 DM ($10.50–$17.50) each. It's open Wednesday through Saturday from 8pm to 3am. There's a cover charge of 10 DM ($7) that applies from Thursday to Saturday.

Max Emanuel Brauerei

Adalbertstrasse 33. ☎ **089/271-51-58.** 10 DM–13 DM ($7–$9.10) cover charge, including the first drink. U-Bahn: U3 or U6 to Universität.

Beer hasn't been brewed here since the 1920s, when the place was originally transformed into a showcase for the consumption of beer-hall-style food and Löwenbräu beer. Bombed into oblivion during World War II, it was rebuilt in 1948, and continues to serve robust food and steins of beer every day from 11am to 1am. Three nights a week, however, the cavernous floor above street level reverberates with either salsa music (Wednesday and Friday from 9pm) or 1950s-style rock and roll (Sunday beginning at 8pm). During salsa night, most of Munich's Latino population, from everywhere from Puerto Rico to southern Chile, make it a point of honor to show up to show off their merengue steps. Sunday nights the site can be just as much fun, in a convertible-Chevy and saddle-shoes kind of way. After your first drink (which is included in the price), a stein of Löwenbräu costs 4.90 DM ($3.45).

Schwabinger Podium

Wagnerstrasse 1. ☎ **089/39-94-82.** No cover charge. U-Bahn: Karl-Preig-Platz.

No one will really care if your German is halting, since the music is usually so loud that no one will be able to hear you anyway. The setting is urban, underground, smoky, crowded, and often raucous—a setting the place's fans wouldn't change even if they could. There's some kind of live music every night, and a crowd that seems well versed in the musical scenes of London and Los Angeles.

Wunderbar

Hochbrückenstrasse 3. ☎ **089/29-51-18.** Cover 7 DM ($4.90). U-Bahn or S-Bahn: Marienplatz.

In 1995, this once-staid cellar bar reinvented itself, changed its musical direction, and reconfigured itself into a dance bar. The result is an animated watering hole with music that includes recent releases of hip-hop, Brit-pop, and house music, all presented in an industrial-looking environment with lots of chrome and dark gray accents. Beer costs 5.50 DM ($3.85), long drinks from 12.50 DM ($8.75), and whisky sours, which a lot of the well-dressed clients seem to order, go for 13.50 DM ($9.45) each. The age of clients ranges from 18 to 35. It's open nightly from 8pm to 4am.

3 The Bar & Cafe Scene

Alter Simpl

Türkenstrasse 57. ☎ **089/272-30-83.** Tram: 18. Bus: 53.

Once a literary cafe, Alter Simpl takes its name from a satirical review of 1903. There's no one around anymore who remembers that revue, but Alter Simpl is still on the scene, made famous by its legendary owner, Kathi Kobus. Lale Andersen, who popularized the song "Lili Marlene," frequented the cafe when she was in Munich. (She always maintained that the correct spelling of the song was "Lili Marleen," as pointed out repeatedly in her autobiography—she died while promoting the book.) Today it attracts locals, including young people, counterculturists, and *Gastarbeiter* ("guest workers," or foreign workers). The real fun occurs after 11pm, when the iconoclastic artistic ferment becomes more reminiscent of Berlin than Bavaria. Drinks begin at 7 DM ($4.90), with a beer costing 4.70 DM ($3.30) and up, and light meals costing 10 DM–20 DM ($7–$14). It's open Monday through Saturday from 7pm to 3 or 4am.

Cafe Extrablatt

Leopoldstrasse 7, Schwabing. ☎ **089/33-33-33.** U-Bahn: U3 or U6 to Universität.

Owned by a prominent Munich newspaper columnist, Michael Grater, this cafe manages to capture the nocturnal essence of Schwabing. You'll enter a sprawling, sometimes smoky room, where photographs of celebrities adorn the walls, a commodious bar extends across one wall, and warm-weather tables on the sidewalk attract many of Munich's writers, artists, and counterculture fans. A simple *Tagesmenu* will fend off starvation for around 15 DM ($10.50), while a large beer costs around 5.50 DM ($3.85). Open Monday through Thursday from 7am to midnight, Friday and Saturday from 9am to 1am, and Sunday from 9am to midnight.

Cafe Puck

Türkenstrasse 33. ☎ **089/280-22-80.** U-Bahn: U3 or U6 to Universität.

This is a convivial, dark-paneled hangout that manages to combine aspects of a cafe, a restaurant, and a bar. Its main focus changes according to whatever time of the day or night you happen to drop in, but you can always be assured of an insight into hip Munich, and a cross-cultural sampling of clients, from locals who come to dine to students who use it as a beer- and wine-drinking hangout. Menu items change daily, and are likely to include samplings from the culinary traditions of Germany, North America, Mexico, or China. Platters of food range in price from 13.50 DM to

23 DM ($9.45 to $16.10), and full-fledged American breakfasts—which can even include pancakes with maple syrup—are served every day between 9am and 6pm. These are sometimes requested late in the afternoon as a kind of status symbol by anyone recovering from too many drinks consumed the night before. One particular favorite is a pork steak *teller* that's actually a meal in itself.

The atmosphere is convivial and infectious, encouraged by the foam and suds of Spaten and Franziskaner, but if you get bored, you'll find a selection of German and English-language newspapers to read. It's open daily from 9am to 1am.

Cocorico
Schellingstrasse 22. ☎ **089/28-43-72.** U-Bahn: U3 or U6 to Universität.

At first glance, the place might appear like a more-elaborate-than-usual snack bar, where a French-inspired menu lists a selection of crêpes—both salted and sweet— as well as salads, sandwiches, and light platters of food designed to go with wine or beer. Prices range from 5.15 DM to 16 DM ($3.60 to $11.20). Many clients seem to use the cafe as a rendezvous point for meeting friends, and the informality of the cuisine and service contributes to the appealing atmosphere of chitchat and banter that flows across the candlelit tables. Open Monday through Friday from 10am to midnight, Saturday from noon to 6pm.

Havana Club
Herrnstrasse 30. ☎ **089/29-18-84.** S-Bahn: Isartor.

It's a lot less *Cubano* than its name suggests—it's named after a brand of rum. Gloria Estefan once appeared during a sojourn in Munich; most of the rest of the time, how-ever, it functions as a singles bar where rum-based cocktails, ranging in price from 13 DM to 20 DM ($9.10 to $14) each, help lubricate the rolling good times. The only food served is salty, snacklike fare, usually peanuts. It's open Monday through Thursday from 6pm to 1am, Friday and Saturday from 7pm to 2am.

Nachtcafe
Maximilianplatz 5. ☎ **089/59-59-00.** No cover. Tram: 19.

It hums, it thrives, and it captures the nocturnal imagination of everyone: No other nightspot in Munich attracts such an array of soccer stars, film celebrities, literary figures, and, as one employee put it, "ordinary people, but only the most sympatheti-cally crazy ones." Waves of patrons appear at different times of the evening—at 11pm when live concerts begin, at 2am when the restaurants close, and at 4am when diehard revelers seek a final drink in the predawn hours. There are no fewer than four indoor bars (and an additional three on an outdoor terrace in summertime), and lots of tiny tables. The decor is updated 1950s; the music jazz, blues, and soul. Beer costs 7 DM ($4.90), drinks run 12 DM ($8.40), and meals go for 18 DM to 40 DM ($12.60 to $28). It's open daily from 9pm to 6am.

O'Reilly's Irish Pub
Maximilianstrasse 29. ☎ **089/29-33-11.** U-Bahn or S-Bahn: Marienplatz.

Too constant a diet of Bavarian folklore can tax even the heartiest of beer drinkers, so for a worthy (Gaelic) alternative, head for a venue near the Marienplatz that's awash with Guinness, Irish stew and—on some evenings—Gaelic music. You'll find it in a historic vaulted cellar close to the Vier Jahreszeiten hotel, where tiled floors and an all-Irish staff help keep the noise reverberating until late at night. The best-known brands of beer from England, Ireland, the Czech Republic, and Germany are available. If you're hungry, you can order filet steaks, Irish stew, burgers, and mixed grills. Beer costs from 4 DM to 6.50 DM ($2.80 to $4.55), main courses from 16.50 DM to 33 DM ($11.55 to $23.10). Hours are Monday through Thursday from 4pm to 1am, Friday and Saturday from 4pm to 3am, and Sunday from noon to 1am.

Pusser's

Falkenturmstrasse 9. ☎ **089/22-05-00.** No cover. U-Bahn: Marienplatz.

Associated with a well-designed chain of bars and restaurants based in Annapolis, Maryland, this establishment celebrates the nostalgia and grog that helped keep the British navy afloat throughout the 18th and 19th centuries. Set on two levels of a prewar building near the Marienplatz, it combines aspects of both a bar and a restaurant. Look for the fishing boat from Tortola (British Virgin Islands) suspended from the ceiling. Menu items are international, but with a Caribbean flair (black bean soup, grilled fish in Mexican salsa), and even include some Italian dishes. Main courses range from 18 DM to 25 DM ($12.60 to $17.50). Everybody's favorite is a half-pound of peel-it-yourself shrimp for 29 DM ($20.30).

Despite its international outlook, Pusser's is much more of a local hangout than you might expect, with a clientele from around the Altstadt. In the cellar bar a pianist performs every day from 9pm until closing, and the most popular drink is a rum-based Painkiller in a special mug that holds a whopping 16 ounces of Caribbean kick. It's open Monday through Saturday from 4pm to 3am, Sunday from 6pm to 3am.

Schultz

Barerstrasse 47. ☎ **089/271-47-11.** U-Bahn: U3 or U6 to Universität.

Schultz is a New York–style bar in Schwabing, popular with theater people who crowd in for smoke-filled chatter. The food is uncomplicated. The decor, as they say here, is "unobvious and understated." Beer starts at 4.50 DM ($3.15); drinks run 14 DM ($9.80) and up. Open daily from 5pm to 1am.

Schumann's

Maximilianstrasse 36. ☎ **089/22-90-60.** Tram: 19.

Located on Munich's most desirable shopping street, Schumann's doesn't waste any money on decor. It doesn't have to, as it depends on the local *beau monde* to keep it fashionable. Schumann's is known as a "thinking man's bar"—Charles Schumann, author of three bar books, wanted a bar that would be the artistic, literary, and social focus of the metropolis. Popular with the film, advertising, and publishing worlds, his place is said to have contributed to a remarkable renaissance of bar culture in the city. Drinks run 9 DM–30 DM ($6.30–$21). Beer is 5.50 DM ($3.85). It's open Sunday through Friday from 5pm to 3am and closed on Saturday.

Shalom

Leopoldstrasse 130. ☎ **089/36-66-62.** No cover. U-Bahn: U3 or U6 to Münchener Freiheit.

You might be reminded of a 1980s singles bar in a large urban North American city. Within a room suitable for only 300 persons, there's a surprisingly small bar where bodies are sometimes four and five deep, clamoring for a drink. Most crowded are Thursday through Saturday, when most of the clients are divorced, almost-divorced, or nominally unattached in one way or another. A small dance floor rocks and rolls to Latino merengue, French dance tunes, or North American disco. It's open every night from 9pm to 4am. Beer costs around 8 DM ($5.60).

Shamrock

Trautenwolfstrasse 4. ☎ **089/33-10-81.** No cover. U-Bahn: Universität.

Despite differences in language, culture, and the way beer is brewed, the Germans and the Celts seem to get along famously, at least at this rollicking Irish pub near the university. It features the brews of both countries, including Kilkenny and Guinness, which usually sell for between 5.50 DM and 5.90 DM ($3.85 and $4.15) per mug. A modest assortment of food is served (nothing to write home about), such as baguette-style sandwiches and stuffed pita pockets, but most clients come here to drink. Try to schedule your visit for anytime between 9pm and midnight, when some kind of music (not necessarily Irish) is presented. It's open Monday through Thursday from 5pm to 1am, Friday from 5pm to 3am, Saturday from 11am to 3am, and Sunday from 11am to 1am.

Tomato

Siegesstrasse 19. ☎ **089/34-83-93.** U-Bahn: U3 or U6 to Münchener Freiheit.

Its large-screen TV and its emphasis on American-style football might remind you of the sports bars you left behind at home, even though this one speaks with a distinctive Teutonic accent. It has thrived in this site since 1975, partly because it screens U.S. sporting events as well as rugby and soccer. Despite its name, there are almost no references inside to the tomato the place is named after. Owned and operated by the Paulaner brewery, whose beer is showcased, the place is open Sunday through Thursday from 7:30pm to 1am, and from 7:30pm to 3am on Friday and Saturday. Beer costs 5.50 DM ($3.85).

Türkenhof

Türkenstrasse 78. ☎ **089/280-02-35.** No cover. U-Bahn: U3 or U6 to Universität. Bus: 53 (all night).

With its 150-year-old setting in what was originally a butcher shop, this place looks a little like a traditional beer hall. But you'll quickly realize by the animated dialogue and the youthful energy of many of the patrons that it's much more than a venue for conventional Bavarian schmaltz. One of the owners is Greek, a fact that accounts for the relatively cosmopolitan food. Within an oversized room whose humming conversations reverberate against the walls, you can hoist a stein of five kinds of Augustiner beer, the only brand sold in this brewery-sponsored place. Salads and platters of food are relatively inexpensive, priced from 10 DM to 18 DM ($7 to $12.60).

4 Beer Halls

The Bierhalle is a traditional Munich institution, offering food, entertainment, and, of course, beer.

Augustinerbrau

Neuhäuserstrasse 27. ☎ **089/5519-9257.** U-Bahn or S-Bahn: Karlsplatz. Tram: 19.

On the principal pedestrians-only street of Munich, this beer hall offers generous helpings of food, good beer, and mellow atmosphere. Dark-wood panels and ceilings in carved plaster make the place look even older than it is. It's only been around for less than a century, but beer was first brewed on this spot in 1328, as the literature about the establishment claims. The long menu changes daily, and the cuisine is not for dieters: It's hearty, heavy, and starchy, but that's what customers want. Half a liter of beer begins at 5.20 DM ($3.65); meals cost from 20 DM to 39 DM ($14 to $27.30). It's open Monday through Saturday from 11am to midnight.

✪ Hofbräuhaus am Platzl

Am Platzl 9. ☎ **089/22-16-76.** U-Bahn or S-Bahn: Marienplatz.

The Hofbräuhaus is a legend among beer halls. Visitors with only one night in Munich usually target the Hofbräuhaus as their number-one nighttime destination. Owned by the state, the present Hofbräuhaus was built at the end of the 19th century, but the tradition of a beer house on this spot dates from 1589. In the 19th century it attracted artists, students, and civil servants, and it was called the Blue Hall because of its dim lights and smoky atmosphere. When it grew too small to contain everybody, architects designed another, in 1897. This was the 1920 setting for the notorious meeting of Hitler's newly launched German Workers Party when a brawl erupted between the Nazis and their Bavarian enemies.

Today 4,500 beer drinkers can crowd in here on a given night. Several rooms are spread over three floors, including a top-floor room for dancing. With its brass band (which starts playing at 11am), the ground-floor Schwemme is most typical of what you probably expected—here it's eternal Oktoberfest. In the second-floor restaurant, strolling musicians, including an accordion player and a violinist, entertain. Dirndl-clad servers place mugs of beer at your table between sing-alongs. Every night the Hofbräuhaus am Platzl presents a typical Bavarian show in its Fest-Hall, starting at 8pm and lasting until midnight. The entrance fee is 8 DM ($5.60), and the food is the same as that served in other parts of the beer palace. A liter of beer costs 9.90 DM ($6.95); meals run 9 DM to 25 DM ($6.30 to $17.50). It's open daily from 9am to midnight.

Mathäser Bierstadt

Bayerstrasse 5. ☎ **089/59-28-96.** U-Bahn or S-Bahn: Karlsplatz (Stachus).

Mathäser Bierstadt is a rowdy "beer city," filled both afternoons and evenings with happy imbibers. To reach the Bierhalle, walk through to the back, then go upstairs. Featured is a brass band oompahing away. The largest Bavarian tavern, the Mathäser contains tables of drinkers joining in the songs. Even at midafternoon the place is often packed, making you wonder if anybody is working in the entire city. In addition to the main hall, there is a rooftop garden and a downstairs tavern. Löwenbräu kegs spill out onto the sidewalk for stand-up sausage and kraut nibblers. Specialties of the house include knuckles of veal and pork. At certain times of the year you can order soups made with fresh white asparagus.

Daily the Mathäser holds a special program featuring a big brass band and yodeling. It's also famous for its Bavarian breakfasts with Weisswurst and beer. A liter of beer begins at 9.90 DM ($6.95); meals are 9 DM–25 DM ($6.30–$17.50). Open daily from 8am to 11:30pm.

Platzl's Theaterie

Am Platzl 1. ☎ **089/23-70-30.** U-Bahn: Marienplatz. Tram: 19.

Platzl's Theaterie faces its more famous competitor, the Hofbräuhaus. Every night, it presents a Bavarian folk program in the large beer-hall area. The women dancers wear dirndls; the men dress in lederhosen, loden jackets, and felt hats. Together they perform the *Schulplattler,* the thigh-slapping folk dance of the Bavarian Alps. The price for a four-course meal and a show is 132 DM ($92.40). Platzl draft beer from a keg is placed at the table; half a liter begins at 5.10 DM ($3.55). Open Tuesday through Saturday from 6:30pm to midnight.

Waldwirtschaft Grosshesslohe

George-Kalb-Strasse 3. ☎ **089/79-50-88.** Tram: 7.

This popular summertime rendezvous has seats for some 2,000 drinkers. The gardens are open daily from 11am to 10pm (they have to close early because neighborhood residents complain). Music, from Dixieland to English jazz to Polish band music, is played throughout the week. Entrance is free and you bring your own food. It's located above the Isar River in the vicinity of the zoo. A liter of beer costs 10 DM ($7).

5   Gay & Lesbian Clubs

Much of Munich's gay and lesbian scene takes place in the blocks between the Viktualienmarkt and Gärtnerplatz, particularly on Hans-Sachs-Strasse.

New York

Sonnenstrasse 25. ☎ **089/59-10-56.** No cover Mon–Thurs, 10 DM ($6.60) Fri–Sun, including first drink. U-Bahn: U1, U2, U3, or U6 to Sendlingertorplatz.

The strident rhythms and electronic sounds might just have been imported from New York, Los Angeles, or Paris. The sound system is accompanied by laser-light shows. This is Munich's premier gay (male) disco. Most clients, ranging in age from 20 to 35, wear jeans. Beer begins at 6.50 DM ($4.55), and drinks are 16.50 DM ($11.55) and up. It's open daily from 11pm to 4am.

Moritz

Klenzestrasse 43. ☎ **089/201-67-76.** No cover. U-Bahn: U2 to Frauenhoferstrasse.

This is one of Munich's most stylish gay bars. It sprawls over mirror-ringed premises outfitted with red leather armchairs and marble-topped tables. Full meals, including Thai dishes, cost around 50 DM ($35), and are served until midnight. A beer costs from 4.50 DM ($3.15). Despite a clientele that tends to be 70% gay and male, the place prides itself on a convivial welcome for straight clients.

Stadtcafé

St. Jakobsplatz 1. ☎ **089/26-69-49.** No cover. U-Bahn or S-Bahn: Marienplatz.

It considers itself the communications center of gay Munich, an intellectual beacon that attracts creative people. By Munich nightlife standards, it closes at a relatively early hour; night owls drift on to other late-night venues. Expect lots of chitchat from table to table, and there's sure to be someone scribbling away at his or her unfinished story (or unfinished novel). Glasses of wine cost from 6 DM to 14 DM ($4.20 to $9.80), depending on the vintage; coffee and beer cost from 5 DM ($3.50). It's open Monday through Friday from 10am to 1am; Friday through Sunday from 10am to 2am.

Soul City

Maximiliansplatz 5. ☎ **089/59-52-72.** Cover 7 DM–12 DM ($4.90–$8.40). U-Bahn: Karlsplatz.

It's the most popular and animated gay disco in Munich. There are enough nooks and crannies for quiet dialogue, and a sound system that's among the best in the city. It's open every night from 10pm to at least 6am. Lesbians make up a respectable proportion of the clients, although gay men comprise the majority. Don't even try to phone this place—whenever staff members are there, they're usually so busy monitoring the crowd that there's barely time to answer the phone. Beer costs from 4.50 DM ($3.15).

Teddy Bar

Hans-Sachsstrasse 1. ☎ **089/260-33-59.** No cover. U-Bahn: Sendlingertor. Tram: 18 or 25.

Teddy Bar is a small, cozy, gay bar decorated with teddy bears. It draws a congenial crowd, both foreign and domestic. From October to April, there's Sunday brunch from 11am to 3pm. Beer costs 4.50 DM ($3.15); drinks run 11 DM ($7.70). The bar is open Sunday through Thursday from 6pm to 1am and stays open on Friday and Saturday nights until 3am.

10 Excursions from Munich

Within an hour of Munich lie mountains, lakes, spas, and medieval towns that truly typify Bavaria. The landscape is dotted with castles, including the fairy-tale castles of Ludwig II, as well as villas and alpine resorts (see Chapter 11).

A short drive from Munich delivers visitors to the heart of Starnberg's "Five Lakes Region." **Starnberger See** and **Ammersee** are preferred weekend destinations for Müncheners. This region affords an enormous assortment of sports: sailing, windsurfing, waterskiing, cycling, golf, hiking, and skiing, to name a few. The **Tegernsee** region is also a popular destination. The picturesque spa town of **Bad Tölz** is known for its healing waters and clear mountain air. The environs of Munich are as rich in culture and history as natural beauty, as well as **Dachau,** symbol of Germany's cultural nadir.

1 Starnberger See

17 miles SW of Munich

This large lake southwest of Munich is a favorite with Müncheners on holiday. If you take a cruise on the lake, you can observe how the terrain changes from low-lying marshlands on the north to alpine ranges towering above the lake in the south. For information on various lake cruises, contact the **Staatliche Schiffahrt** (☎ 08151/ 12-023) at Dampfschiffstrasse 5, in Starnberg. Cruises are frequent in the summer months.

Around the 40-mile shoreline you can see no fewer than six castles, including the Schloss Berg, where Ludwig II was sent after he was certified insane in 1886. Across the lake from Berg stands the castle of Possenhofen, the home of Ludwig's favorite cousin, Sissi. It was here the king drowned under mysterious circumstances— local legend asserts that he was trying to swim to Possenhofen. Many historians suggest he was murdered. A cross on the water marks the spot where his body was found. A Votivkapelle (a memorial chapel to Ludwig) is on the shore above the cross. It is reached by walking up the hill from the village of Berg, into the Hofgarten and along the wall of the Schloss Berg (no connection with the hotel of the same name recommended below), which lies 3 miles southeast of Starnberg and is not open to the public.

Excursions from Munich

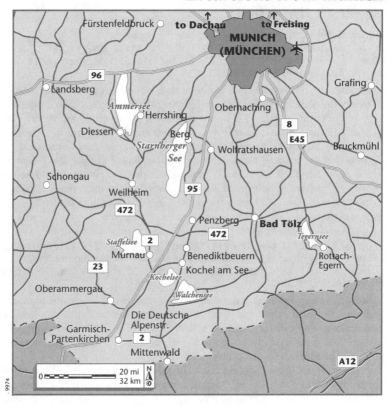

ESSENTIALS

GETTING THERE

BY TRAIN   The suburban train (S6) is a 40-minute ride from Marienplatz in the heart of Munich.

BY CAR   From Munich, motorists can take Autobahn 95 toward Garmisch to the Starnberg exit.

VISITOR INFORMATION

For information contact the tourist office (☎ **08151/13-008**) at Kirchplatz 3, Berg, June through October, Monday through Friday from 8am to 6pm and Saturday from 9am to 1pm; November through May, Monday through Friday from 8am to 6pm.

OUTDOOR ACTIVITIES

Although Starnberger See is full of history and culture, most Müncheners head to the lake for sunshine and water sports. On sunny days, the lake is crowded with speedboats, paddleboats, and windsurfers, all of which can be rented from **Surf Tools** (☎ **08151/89-333**).

WHERE TO STAY & DINE

Dorint Hotel Leoni am Starnberger See

Ortsteil Leoni, Assenbucher Strasse 44. D-82335 Berg. ☎ **08151/5080.** Fax 08151/506140. 70 rms, 3 suites. MINIBAR TV TEL. 235 DM–265 DM ($164.50–$185.50) double; 325 DM–395 DM ($227.50–$276.50) suite. AE, DC, MC, V.

Comfortable and low-slung, this hotel rises three stories from a position between the edge of the lake and a rolling Bavarian hillside. Built in the early 1970s, it has a cozy country-cousin decor, and the public rooms offer big-windowed views of the lake, its swimmers, and its sailboats. The bedrooms are outfitted in a dignified 19th-century *Landhaus* style. On the premises are a rustic bar, the Dorfstubl, and two restaurants, the informal Damfersteg and the more formal König Ludwig. A swimming pool has direct access to a swimming pier that juts into the lake. A sauna, solarium, and steam bath round out the facilities. In summer, when the place is most popular, a *Biergarten* serves frothy mugs of beer in a setting a few feet from the edge of the water.

Strandhotel Schloss Berg

Seestrasse 11, D-82335 Berg. ☎ **08151/50-101.** Fax 08151/50105. 40 rms, 10 suites. MINIBAR TV TEL. Winter 195 DM–200 DM ($136.50–$140) double; 260 DM ($182) suite. Summer 165 DM–195 DM ($115.50–$136.50) double; 240 DM ($168) suite. Rates include breakfast. AE, DC, MC, V.

Set within about 500 yards of the town's famous castle (which is privately owned and cannot be visited), this hotel is the most luxurious and comfortable in town. It occupies two separate buildings, one a 1994 remake of an older building, the other an all-new chalet-style structure erected at the same time, both separated from one another by a parking lot and copses of trees.

Rooms on the upper end of the prices listed above are in the older building, whose windows overlook the lake. Bedrooms are comfortable, conservatively decorated, and eminently appropriate for weekend getaways from Munich. Our favorite hangout here is the bar, a skillfully paneled prelude to a Bavarian-style restaurant that charges 24 DM ($16.80) to 30 DM ($21) for a full meal.

2 Tegernsee

30 miles SE of Munich

This alpine lake and the resort town on its eastern shore have the same name. Although small, this is one of the loveliest of the Bavarian lakes, with huge peaks seemingly rising right out of the water. The lake, its string of resort towns, including the elegant resorts of Rottach-Egern, and ritzy health clinics are popular year-round.

ESSENTIALS

GETTING THERE

BY TRAIN　The station of Tegernsee is a one hour and 20 minute ride from Munich's Hauptbahnhof. To reach the hotels in Rottach-Egeren, you must take a taxi from the station.

BY CAR　From Munich take the A8/A9 Autobahn toward Salzburg. At exit 97 (Holzkirchen) veer south and follow the signs to Tegernsee.

VISITOR INFORMATION

For information, contact the tourist office (☎ **08033/18-01-40**) at Haus de Gastes, Hauptstrasse 2, April through October, Monday through Friday from 8am to 5pm,

Saturday and Sunday from 10am to noon and 3 to 5pm; November through March, Monday through Friday from 8am to noon and 1 to 5pm, Saturday and Sunday from 10am to noon and 3 to 5pm.

WHAT TO SEE & DO

In the town of Tegernsee, the two major sights span some 12 centuries. The oldest of these is the Benedictine monastery. Built in the 8th century, it was turned into a castle and village church by Bavarian king Maximilian I in the 19th century. The other attraction is a contemporary church, a fine example of modern German church architecture, designed by Olaf Gulbransson of Munich.

Because of the small size of the lake, it freezes over early in winter, making it an attraction for skaters.

WHERE TO STAY
VERY EXPENSIVE

✪ Bachmaier Hotel am See

Seestrasse 47, D-83700 Rottach-Egern. ☎ **08022/2720.** 206 rms, 60 suites. MINIBAR TV TEL. Summer 290 DM–1,110 DM ($203–$777) double; 1,000 DM–2,000 DM ($700–$1,400) suite. Winter 255 DM–870 DM ($178.50–$609) double, 700 DM–1,700 DM ($490–$1,190) suite. Half board included. AE, DC, MC.

Expanded massively since its original construction in 1827 as a farmhouse, this posh resort is the most elegant beside the Tegernsee, set in the heart of town. Today, eight additional buildings supplement the original, generously proportioned *Gartenhaus*. It is almost like a village of minihotels, ringed with terraced gardens. Decors of public rooms include an eclectic blend of Biedermaier, Directoire, and Louis XV styles. On the premises are all the amenities of a major summer resort, including a swimming pool, a bathing pier, and a state-of-the-art sport and fitness center contained within its own building. On-site restaurants include two folkloric bistros, a main dining room, and an upscale dining area referred to as the Gourmet Restaurant. Virtually everyone who has ever checked in here does so on the half-board plan, including former clients Helmut Kohl, Tom Jones, Englebert Humperdinck, and many of Munich's influential movers and shakers.

EXPENSIVE

Bachmaier-Alpina

Valepper Strasse 24, D-83700 Rottach-Egern. ☎ **08022/2041.** Fax 08022/27-27-90. 15 rms, 8 suites. MINIBAR TV TEL. 250 DM ($175) double; 405 DM ($283.50) suite. AE, DC, MC. Closed late Oct to mid-Dec and Mar–Apr.

This is the inexpensive, three-star sibling of the more glamorous, better located Bachmaier Hotel am See, described below. It was built in the mid-1980s, in a comfortable but uninspired style derived from the modern chalets of Switzerland, and it's inland from the lake, within a quiet residential neighborhood. Bedrooms are simple but comfortable. Although there are very few grace notes and extra facilities on site, guests are welcome to enjoy the sprawling physical plant of the Bachmaier, 2 miles west of the hotel. Although the Alpina serves no meals other than breakfast, guests who pay a surprisingly reasonable supplement of 25 DM ($17.50) per person per day can arrange half board in the main dining room of the Bachmaier.

Parkhotel Egerner Hof

Aribostrasse 19, D-83700 Rottach-Egern. ☎ **08022/6660.** Fax 08022/66-62-00. 68 rms, 18 suites. MINIBAR TV TEL. 308 DM–420 DM ($215.60–$294) double; 420 DM–555 DM ($294–$388.50) suite. Half board 45 DM ($31.50) supplement per person per day. AE, DC, MC, V.

Its detractors suggest that this hotel maintains a constant struggle to become a more modern version of the town's five-star aristocrat, the Bachmaier. Despite that, many urbanites from Munich prefer this 1992 contender's four-star comfort and alert staff. Although there's no lake view—the hotel is surrounded by meadows and trees—and the hotel is a 20-minute walk south of the town center, there's a lot to be recommended here. Bedrooms are traditionally cozy and warm, and it has three charming restaurants. Most clients on half-board plans head for the Sankt-Florian, the hotel's equivalent of a main dining room. Most nonresidents, however, opt either for a meal in the Dichterstube (dinner only), or the Hubertus-Stüberl (lunch and dinner). Both of these latter choices are separately recommended in "Where to Dine," below. A visit to any of these might be preceded with a drink at the hotel's cozy bar.

MODERATE

Haltmair am See

Seestrasse 33–35. D-83700 Rottach-Egern. ☎ **08022/2750.** Fax 08022/27564. 30 rms, 2 suites. TV TEL. Summer 180 DM–195 DM ($126–$136.50) double; 230 DM ($161) suite. Winter 170 DM–180 DM ($119–$126) double; 200 DM ($140) suite. Rates include breakfast. No credit cards.

Unpretentious, with a bit less experience in dealing with non-German clients than any of the other hotels recommended here, this hotel has a 100-year-old architectural core that was expanded in the mid-1980s. The decoration is almost obsessively Bavarian, with lots of alpine accessories and dark wood paneling in the bedrooms. It's near the center of the town, across the street from the edge of the lake. Other than a worthy buffet breakfast, no meals are served.

INEXPENSIVE

⑤ Gastehaus Maier-Kirschner

Seestrasse 23, D-83700 Rottach-Egern. ☎ **08022/67-110.** Fax 08022/67-11-37. 34 rms, 11 suites. TV TEL. Summer 160 DM–180 DM ($112–$126) double; 240 DM ($168) suite. Winter 120 DM–140 DM ($84–$98) double; 200 DM ($140) suite. Rates include breakfast; 15 DM ($10.50) extra for occupants of suites. AE.

This is one of the best bets in town for comfortable, reasonably priced accommodations with a personal touch. The site has an ancient history, going back to 1350, when a farmhouse was recorded here; however, such antique vestiges you may notice date from 1870 when the site became a local farmer's homestead. After a fire in 1900, the place was rebuilt into a guesthouse that was expanded over the years. There's an amply proportioned central hallway, and paneled public rooms that invite guests to linger over newspapers and coffee. Bedrooms contain simplified reproductions of antique baroque furniture and have comfortable armchairs. No meals, other than breakfast and midafternoon coffee and snacks, are served. Only the Seestrasse separates this hotel from the edge of the lake.

Gasthof zur Post

Nördliche Hauptstrasse 17–19, D-83700 Rottach-Egern. ☎ **08022/66-780.** Fax 08022/667-8162. 70 rms. TV TEL. 150 DM ($105) double. MC, V.

The oldest hotel in town, a place that originally served as the village post office, was built in the 1860s, with an elaborately ornamented four-story facade accented with balconies. The interior is beautifully crafted, with wooden ceilings and furniture whose natural grain glows with a patina acquired over the years. The owners, the Wittman family, are descendants of the original founders, and work hard to maintain their folkloric guesthouse. Accommodations are equivalent to what you'd find in a woodsy chalet hotel in Switzerland, clean and comfortable, and without unnecessary frills. On the premises are three dining rooms (Post Stübl, Postillion, and Nebenzimmer), all of which serve Bavarian and German food; main courses cost from 18 DM–22 DM ($12.60–$15.40). Dining hours are daily from 11:30am to 2pm and 6 to 9:30pm.

WHERE TO DINE

Dichterstube/Hubertus-Stüberl

In the Parkhotel Egerner Hof, Aribostrasse 19. ☎ **08022/6660.** Reservations recommended. In the Dichterstube, main courses 42 DM–47 DM ($29.40–$32.90), fixed-price dinner 136 DM ($95.20). In the Hubertus-Stüberl, main courses 22 DM–32 DM ($15.40–$22.40). AE, DC, MC, V. Daily noon–2pm (Hubertus-Stuberl only) and 6–10pm (both restaurants). CONTINENTAL (in Dichterstube)/BAVARIAN (in Hubertus-Stüberl).

Reaching these two well-recommended restaurants requires a 20-minute pedestrian trek or a very brief drive south of the town center; however, it's worth the effort, considering the quality of the food. The less expensive of the two, Hubertus-Stüberl, is outfitted like the interior of a hunting lodge, with all the requisite folklore and references to "the Hunt." There, menu items include cream of garlic soup with croûtons, goulash soup, carpaccio of bonito with a paprika-flavored vinaigrette, smoked filet of trout with horseradish sauce, and such main courses as ragoût of venison with chive-flavored polenta and veal schnitzel "in the style of the Tegernsee" with roasted potatoes.

Meals are more formal, more ambitious, and more expensive in the Dichterstube, site of the best cuisine in town. The seven-course set-price menu is a veritable banquet that requires serious gastronomic attention. Ordering à la carte might be wise for persons with less hearty appetites. Depending on the season, menu items might include a galette of wild rice with tartare of salmon and caviar; braised zander with a ragoût of crabs; glazed John Dory with chicory sauce; lobster salad with avocados and orange-pepper marmalade; and such desserts as a stuffed chocolate cake with champagne-flavored mousse and lemon-flavored sorbet.

3 Ammersee

24 miles W of Munich

Smaller and less popular than Starnberger See, Ammersee is a bit more rustic and wild than its cousin. In the past, Ammersee was thought too far from the city for excursions. For that reason, it was never overdeveloped and retains much of its natural splendor. Although it does have its share of summer homes and hotels, its shores are not quite as saturated or overcrowded as Starnberger See.

ESSENTIALS

GETTING THERE

BY TRAIN   The suburban train (S5) is a 40-minute ride from Marienplatz in the heart of Munich.

BY CAR   Take the A96 Autobahn west toward Lindau. Get off at the Herrsching/ Wessling exit (Highway 2068) and follow signs to Herrsching.

OUTDOOR ACTIVITIES

To experience the lake on a more personal level, try windsurfers, paddleboats, or rowboats. All can be rented at Stummbaum (☎ **08152/1375**) at Summerstrasse 22, in Herrsching.

AROUND THE LAKE

For a magnificent tour of the lake, take one of the steamship cruises. Boats depart hourly from 9am to 6pm. For information on various trips, contact **Staatliche Schiffahrt** (☎ 081/43-229) at Landsberger Strasse 81 in Ammersee.

The village of **Herrsching** with a population of 10,000 is home to an enormous villa with fabulous turrets, facades, and pagoda roofing, the **Kurpark Schlösschen** (☎ 08152/4250). It was constructed in the late 19th century as a summer getaway for the artist Ludwig Scheuermann. It is now home to the municipal cultural center and the venue for many summer evening concerts. The small fishing village of **Diessen,** popular for its pottery and its church, the Marienmünster, is a short ferry ride from from Herrsching. Also a short trip from Herrsching, and well worth the time, is the ancient monastery of **Andechs.** Set high on Heiliger Berg (holy mountain), this Benedictine monastery draws multitudes of pilgrims and beer aficionados. The pilgrims visit for the religious relics from the Holy Land; the less devout make the journey for the stupendous beers and cheeses produced by the monks. The monastery is open daily from 6:30am to 6pm. To reach the monastery from Herrsching, take the MVV or the Omnibusverkehr Rauner. Visitors may also hike the nearly 2 miles to the top.

WHERE TO STAY

Hotel Promenade

Summerstrasse 6, D-82211 Herrsching. ☎ **08152/1088.** Fax 08152/5981. 11 rms. MINIBAR TV TEL. 168 DM–208 DM ($117.60–$145.60) double. Breakfast included. AE, MC, V. Closed Dec 20–Jan 20.

This is a small, businesslike hotel, with a staff that speaks almost no English, occupying a site directly in the center of the town. Built in 1988, and with fewer than a dozen bedrooms, it has a blandly modern decor, a bar, and a restaurant that serves Croatian and international food. Its position directly beside the lake permits sweeping views from the balconies of some of its bedrooms, and there's a lakeside terrace in case your room happens to face the wrong direction.

Piushof

Schönbichlstrasse 18, D-82211 Herrsching. ☎ **08152/1007.** Fax 08152/8328. 20 rms, 1 suite. MINIBAR TV TEL. 175 DM ($122.50) double; 320 DM ($224) suite. Rates include breakfast; 35 DM ($24.50) supplement, per person, for half board. AE, MC, V.

This is the best hotel in Herrsching, a local, three-star icon of Bavarian-inspired decor built around a core that was originally constructed in 1903 as a farmhouse. A hotel since 1975, it was named after the grandfather of the Bavarian/Austrian family (the Mosers) that own it today. Bedrooms are outfitted with Bavarian schmaltz, and are clean and very comfortable. The hotel is popular for its location in the heart of the hamlet, and for the well-prepared food and generous portions served by its restaurant (The Piushof). Main courses cost from 18 DM ($12.60) to 36 DM ($25.20). Lunch is served from noon to 2pm, dinner from 6 to 9pm, every day except Sunday night and all day Monday. The specialties include a species of trout, *Ammersee Renke,* that thrives in the nearby lake, prepared simply in lemon-butter sauce with herbs.

WHERE TO DINE

Andechser Hof

Zum Landungssteg 1. D-82211 Herrsching. ☎ **08152/8579.** Main courses 15 DM–35 DM ($10.50–$24.50). AE, DC, MC, V. Daily 11am–10pm. BAVARIAN.

This is one of the best-known dining spots in town, the kind of place that offers beer and an array of snacks throughout the afternoon and substantial platters of Bavarian food for dinner. The setting is a solid 1905 building renovated into its present form with loads of references to the Bavarian experience and Bavarian decor. A *Biergarten* adjacent to the hotel offers such specialties as ragoût of beef, or pork schnitzel with fresh vegetables of the day.

Don't overlook the possibility of an overnight stopover here. There's a total of 21 clean rooms full of nostalgic charm, all with private bath, phone, and TV, renting for 230 DM ($161) for a double.

4 Dachau

10 miles NW of Munich

In 1933 what had once been a quiet little artists' community outside Munich became a tragic symbol of the Nazi era. In March, shortly after Hitler became chancellor, Himmler and the SS set up the first German concentration camp on the grounds of a former ammunition factory. Countless prisoners arrived at Dachau between 1933 and 1945. Although the files show a registry of more than 206,000, the exact number of people imprisoned here is unknown.

ESSENTIALS
GETTING THERE
BY TRAIN   The suburban train (S2) is a 20-minute ride from Marienplaz in the heart of Munich.

BY CAR   The best road for motorists is a country road, B12. Motorists can also take the Stuttgart Autobahn, exiting at the signposted Dachau turnoff.

TOURING THE CAMP
Entering the camp, you are faced by three memorial chapels—Catholic, Protestant, and Jewish—built in the early 1960s. Immediately behind the Catholic chapel is the Lagerstrasse, the main camp road lined with poplar trees, once flanked by 32 barracks, each housing 208 prisoners. Two barracks have been rebuilt to give visitors insight into the horrible conditions endured by the prisoners.

The museum is housed in the large building that once contained the kitchen, laundry, and shower baths, where the SS often brought prisoners for torture. Photographs and documents show the rise of the Nazi regime and the superpower of the SS; there are also exhibits depicting the persecution of Jews and other prisoners. Every effort has been made to present the facts. The tour of Dachau is a truly moving experience. Admission is free, and the camp is open Tuesday through Sunday from 9am to 5pm. The English version of a documentary film, *KZ-Dachau*, is shown at 11:30am and 3:30pm. All documents are translated in the catalog, available at the museum entrance.

5 Freising

20 miles N. of Munich

Freising, one of Bavaria's oldest towns, grew up around a bishopric founded in the 8th century. By the 12th century, under Bishop Otto von Freising, the see had begun a spritual and cultural boom. It was the bitter rivalry between Bishop Otto and Henry the Lion that launched the city of Munich. The bishop owned a profitable toll bridge over the Isar until Henry the Lion destroyed it and built his own bridge, wresting control of the lucrative salt route from the bishop, and founding his settlement, Munichen. The quarrel had repercussions down to the beginning of the 19th century—until 1803 Munich was forced to pay compensation to Freising for Henry's action.

ESSENTIALS
GETTING THERE
BY TRAIN   Take line 1 of the S-Bahn to Freising, a 25-minute ride.

BY CAR   Freising is northeast of Munich on the Bll.

VISITOR INFORMATION   The tourist information office is at Marienplatz 7 (☎ 081/61-54-122).

WHAT TO SEE & DO

All the main sights are within walking distance of the Banhof. The Altstadt contains a number of restored canons' houses with fine baroque facades, along the Hauptstrasse and in the Marienplatz-Rindermarkt area. The Gothic **St. George's Parish Church** with its lovely baroque tower, was built by the same architect who designed Munich's Frauenkirche. Opposite, in the former Lyzeum of the prince-bishops is the **Asamsaal,** a room decorated by the father of the famous Asam brothers, with a fine stucco and fresco ceiling. Tours are offered occasionally; check the tourist office for information.

Southwest of the Alstadt on a gentle hill is the **Staatsbrauerei Weihenstephan,** the world's oldest brewery. The monks of the Benedictine monastery of Weihenstephan were granted the privilege of brewing and serving their own beer in 1040, a tradition that still continues. Guided tours, including beer tasting, are conducted on the hour from 9am to 2pm, except at noon, from Monday to Thursday, costing 3 DM ($4.25).

Mariendom
Domberg.

The cathedral is a twin-towered romanesque basilica, constructed between 1160 and 1205, and located on the Domberg, a low hill above the Altstadt. The building is rather plain on the outside, but the interior was lavishly ornamented in the baroque style by the Asam brothers in 1723–24. Egid Quirin Asam designed the interior, and Cosmas Damian Asam created the ceiling fresco of the *Second Coming,* with its floating figures and swirling clouds. A notable early medieval sculpture is the famous *Bestiensäule* (Beast Column), an entwined mass of men and monsters. The church's principal feature is the large romanesque crypt, one of the oldest in Germany, which has survived in its original form.

The 15th-century **cloister** on the east side of the cathedral was decorated with frescoes and stucco-work by Johann Baptist Zimmerman. To the west of the church is the **Dombibliothek,** a library that dates from the 8th century. In the 18th century the library acquired a lively ceiling fresco designed by François Cuvilliés.

The **Diözesanmuseum** is the largest diocesan museum in Germany, and contains a comprehensive collection of religious art, including the famous *Lukasbild,* an exceptional Byzantine icon. The museum's exhibits document the history of the Catholic Church over nine centuries. It's open Tuesday through Sunday from 10am to 5pm; there is an admission charge.

6 Bad Tölz

31 miles S of Munich

Situated where the rolling foothills become the mountains of the Alps, the historic spa town of Bad Tölz offers something for all travelers. Flanking both sides of the Isar River, the town is divided into two distinct sectors. On one side stands the historic medieval town, complete with chapels, turrets, and walls. The town, older than Munich, offers fine examples of medieval and baroque art and architecture.

Other than spa treatments, the major attraction is **Stadtpfarrkirche,** a church built in 1466. It's an exquisite example of late German Gothic architecture. On the opposite side of the Isar lies the modern spa whose iodized water is known throughout the world for its soothing and healing powers. Its treatments revolve around the iodine-rich springs of Bad Tölz. Various treatments may also include climatic and terrain therapy.

ESSENTIALS
GETTING THERE

BY TRAIN   The train is a one-hour ride from Munich's Haubtbahnhof.

BY CAR   From Munich, motorists can take the Autobahn A8 or A9 toward Salzburg. Exit at Holzkirchen and follow signs southward toward Bad Tölz.

VISITOR INFORMATION

For information, contact the **Kurverwaltung** (☎ 08041/70-071), at Ludwugstrasse 11 in Bad Tölz, Monday through Friday from 9am to noon and 2 to 5:30pm; Saturday from 9am to noon.

OUTDOOR ACTIVITIES

Bad Tölz location in the foothills of the Alps makes it a prime spot for hikers. However, the terrain is also suited for bicycle tours, tennis, and golf. The Isar River offers various water sports, including boating, swimming, and fishing. The winter snows make Bad Tölz ideal for downhill and cross-country skiers and snowboarders.

WHERE TO STAY
MODERATE

Kurhotel Eberl

Buchenerstrasse 17. D-83646 Bad Tölz. ☎ **08041/4050.** Fax 08041/41796. 31 rms, 3 suites. TV TEL. 245 DM–265 DM ($171.50–$185.50) double; 285 DM–305 DM ($199.50–$213.50) suite. Rates include half board. No credit cards. Closed December.

Set in a meadow about a quarter-mile west of the resort's center, this is a white-fronted, timber-studded replica of the kind of modern chalet you're likely to see a lot of in Switzerland. Built in 1984, its public rooms are lavishly finished with rough-textured beams and timbers for a look that—at least from the inside—might make you think that the hotel is older than it is. Bedrooms are conservatively and comfortably outfitted with pale colors and exposed wood, and many have balconies. This is the kind of hotel where guests, most of whom are German, check in with the intention of eating all their evening meals on site. Because only residents are allowed in the *stübe*-like dining room and the lounges—the hotel is otherwise closed to the public—some aspects of this place might remind you of a private club. Although the town's public spa facilities are nearby, the hotel has its own indoor swimming pool, saunas, and array of spa facilities such as massages and mudpacks—these can be bought as part of an all-inclusive health and rest regime.

INEXPENSIVE

Ⓢ Alexandra

Kyreinstrasse 33, D-83646 Bad Tölz. ☎ **08041/78-430.** Fax 08041/784-399. 23 rms. TEL. 90 DM–138 DM ($63–$96.60) double. Rates include breakfast. MC.

Built in 1982 of dark-stained wood, and lavishly accented with flower boxes, this hotel was named after the then-infant daughter of the owner. Set near the town center, on the opposite side of the riverfront promenade from the banks of the Isar, it offers an all-Bavarian decor with fine interior woodwork. Bedrooms are unpretentious, and outfitted—as you guessed—with reproductions of Bavarian furniture. Other than breakfast, no meals are served. Overall, it's a worthwhile and relatively inexpensive hotel choice.

Haus an der Sonne

Ludwigstrasse 12, 83646 Bad Tölz. ☎ **08041/6121.** Fax 08041/2609. 23 rms. TEL. 110 DM–147 DM ($77–$102.90) double. Rates include breakfast. Half board 21 DM ($14.70) extra per person. AE, DC, MC, V.

This is a cozy, unpretentious hotel whose country baroque ocher-colored facade is a 10-year-old copy of 18th-century models. In summer, café tables are set on the pavement outside, and throughout the year, members of the Wosar family provide a well-managed, cozy retreat amid a warmly paneled setting. On the premises is a sauna and whirlpool and a cellar-level guest's lounge with its own fireplace. Bedrooms contain modern pinewood furniture, some pieces accented with painted panels that evoke old Bavaria. About five have their own TV sets, and all have radios.

Jodquellenhof-Alpamare

Ludwigstrasse 13–15, D-83646 Bad Tölz. ☎ **08041/5090.** Fax 08041/509-441. 81 rms. TV TEL. 145 DM–210 DM ($101.50–$147) double. Half board 50 DM ($35) extra per person per day. AE, DC, MC, V.

This is Bad Tölz's equivalent of a "grand hotel," with a longer history than any other hotel in town. Originally built in 1860, and modernized, both inside and out, many times since then, it helped launch Bad Tölz into the full-fledged resort you see today. If you opt to stay here, however, don't expect 19th-century authenticity: Although from the outside the green and white premises still look vaguely Mediterranean, the hotel has, both commercially and architecturally, kept up with the times. Unlike some spa hotels in other parts of Germany whose greatest appeal is to older, more staid clients, Jodquellenhof attracts a family clientele, many of whom check in with children as part of their annual holiday. The hotel is located within a verdant park that it shares with Alpamare, a water amusement area with a Disneyesque collection of water slides, Jacuzzis, three indoor swimming pools, and two outdoor swimming pools. Parents and children can pad over to Alpamare, dressed in swimsuits and bathrobes, in any weather, directly from their rooms. Entrance to Alpamare, open daily to residents of this hotel between 7am and 9pm, is free for guests, but costs 50 DM ($35) per person for nonresidents. Also on the premises is an array of spa facilities, including soaking tubs filled with thermally heated water, and all the mudpacks, massage, and health or beauty treatments you'd expect. There's a pleasant hotel bar, and a dining room whose business mostly derives from feeding hotel guests who sign up for meal plans.

Bedrooms at this place, incidentally, are outfitted in a neutral, rather bland style, all with balconies.

Kolbergarten

Fröhlichgasse 5. D-83646 Bad Tölz. ☎ **08041/9067.** Fax 08041/9069. 15 rms. MINIBAR TV TEL. 150 DM–160 DM ($105–$112) double. AE, DC, MC, V.

The finest and most lavish hotel in Bad Tölz, it's set within a historic zone on the east bank of the Isar that's sometimes used for outdoor concerts and parades. It was built in 1905 by the famous *Jugendstil* architect Gabriel von Seidel, who added many more folkloric touches, including lavishly ornate eaves, than are usual in his work. The interior has a turn-of-the-century dignity, always with a noteworthy emphasis on humanity, warmth, and charm. Bedrooms are as authentic and antique-laden as anything you'll find in Bad Tölz.

The hotel's restaurant, Ladurner, is an upscale oases of well-prepared cuisine dedicated to the traditions of South Tyrol, a German-speaking alpine region annexed by Italy from Austria after World War I. Meals are served at lunch and dinner every day except Tuesday. Main courses cost from 16 DM to 34 DM ($11.20 to $23.80), set-price menus from 40 DM to 50 DM ($28 to $35).

Because of its limited number of bedrooms (although you'll probably appreciate the sense of intimacy this provides), management funnels their overflow to their larger and slightly less expensive sibling hotel, the Posthotel Kolberbräu, which is separately recommended below.

Posthotel Kolberbräu

Marktstrasse 29, D-83646 Bad Tölz. ☎ **08041/76-880.** Fax 08041/9069. 45 rms. TV TEL. 120 DM–140 DM ($84–$98) double. Rates include breakfast. Half board 23 DM ($16.10) supplement per person per day. AE, DC, MC, V.

This hotel belongs to the same owner as the Kolbergarten (see above) but is in a less congested setting. Because of its position in the center of town, it makes no attempt to surround itself with landscaping. What you'll find is a cozy, old-fashioned hotel whose identity is firmly anchored in the commercial life of Bad Tölz. It has an imposing neoclassical facade whose foundations date from the 1600s. Its bistro, whose interior contains a labyrinth of small dining areas, is one of the most consistently crowded in town, and is separately recommended below. Its bedrooms are more prosaic than those at the more aristocratic Kolbergarten, and have the kind of cozy, old-fashioned Teutonic decor that nobody dislikes, but nobody thrills to either. Ten of them contain private balconies.

Tölzer Hof

Rieschstrasse 21, D-83646 Bad Tölz. ☎ **08041/8060.** Fax 08041/80-63-33. 84 rms, 2 suites. MINIBAR TV TEL. 98 DM–112 DM ($68.60–$78.40) double; 220 DM–250 DM ($154–$175) suite. Half board 28 DM ($19.60) extra per person per day. AE, MC, V.

Built in 1984 in a plain design of white stucco, blackened timber balconies, and terracotta roof tiles, this hotel is a worthy middle-bracket choice with almost no emphasis on old-timey nostalgia. That suits many escapist Müncheners just fine, as they settle into rooms outfitted in a style that looks like a slightly more luxurious version of a bachelor's pad, complete with the kind of low-slung couches and coffee tables you don't feel guilty about putting your feet on. You'll be happiest here if you understand in advance that this is a decidedly middle-bracket hotel, honest, unassuming, and with an efficiency so pronounced that it almost verges on the Spartan. The hotel's most unusual feature is a glass-sided greenhouse in the parking lot near the entrance, site of the reception desk and a café. There's a sauna on the premises and a swimming pool within walking distance.

WHERE TO DINE
MODERATE

✪ Altes Fahrhaus

An der Isarlust 1. D-83646 Bad Tölz. ☎ **08041/6030.** Reservations recommended. Main courses 38.50 DM–47 DM ($26.95–$32.90); fixed-price dinner 85 DM–135 DM ($59.50–$94.50). No credit cards. Wed–Sun 11:30am–2:30pm and 6pm–midnight. Closed November. CONTINENTAL.

More than anything else in Bad Tölz, this Bavarian-style turn-of-the-century building is defined as a *restaurant avec chambres* where the overnight accommodations, although comfortable, are less significant than the restaurant. Set 2 miles south of the resort's center, adjacent to the right bank of the Isar River, it's a 2-acre compound whose centerpiece was adapted for use by the present owners around 1980.

The owner is Ely Reiser, who closely supervises (or prepares herself) everything coming out of her kitchens. The food is the best in the region, often a destination for Munich-based gastronomes searching for a respite from city life. Menu items change with the seasons, but might include a salad of green asparagus with strips of braised goose liver; bouillon of venison with ravioli or a filet of venison baked in herbs with a pepper-flavored cream sauce; filet of turbot in champagne sauce; and filet of veal with red wine sauce, noodles, and exotic mushrooms. Because the menu changes almost every day, even the owner is reluctant to define one particular house specialty, although one superb dish that's usually available is a well-seasoned rack of lamb, served with eggplant, gratin of potatoes, and zucchini in a mustard sauce. Dessert might be a Grand Marnier soufflé with rhubarb.

On the premises are five bedrooms, each with its own terrace overlooking the river, TV, telephone, and minibar. With breakfast included, doubles cost 180 DM ($126). These rooms are not recommended for overnights on Monday or Tuesday, as the restaurant that justifies their existence is closed on those nights.

INEXPENSIVE

Restaurant Posthotel Kolberbräu

Marktstrasse 29. ☎ **08041/76-880.** Main courses 11 DM–30 DM ($7.70–$21); fixed-price menus 28 DM–31 DM ($19.60–$21.70). AE, DC, MC, V. Daily 11am–2pm and 5–9pm. GERMAN/BAVARIAN.

This is the kind of no-nonsense, high-volume restaurant that virtually everyone in town has visited at least once in his or her lifetime. A civic rendezvous point, lots of deals have been made here over steins of beer and hearty Germanic food. Much of the business generated by this place occurs during the lunch and dinner hours noted above, but throughout the afternoon the place remains open for coffee, pastries, beer, wine, and an abbreviated roster of warm food and platters.

The Bavarian Alps

If you walk into a rustic alpine inn along the German-Austrian frontier and ask the innkeeper if he or she is German, you'll most likely get the indignant response, "Of course not! I'm Bavarian." And the innkeeper is undoubtedly right, because even though Bavaria is a *Land* of Germany, some older inhabitants can still remember when Bavaria was a kingdom, even though it was by then part of the German Reich (1871–1918).

The huge province includes not only the Alps but also Franconia, Lake Constance, and the capital city of Munich. However, we'll take this opportunity to explore separately the mountains along the Austrian frontier, a world unto themselves. While the Alps are a winter vacationland, you'll find that the resorts and villages boast year-round attractions. The area's hospitality is famous, and the picture of the plump, rosy-cheeked innkeeper who has a constant smile on his or her face is no myth.

Munich is the gateway to the region for those arriving by plane. From Munich, autobahns lead directly to the Bavarian Alps. If you're beginning your tour in Garmisch-Partenkirchen in the west, you should fly to Munich. However, if you'd like to begin your tour in the east, at Berchtesgaden, then Salzburg in Austria has better plane connections.

The Bavarian Alps are both a winter wonderland and a summer playground. Skiing is the best in Germany. It's centered around the chief resort, Garmisch-Partenkirchen, famed as the site of the fourth Winter Olympics in 1936 and the World Alpine Ski Championships in 1978. A normal snowfall in January and February measures from 12 to 20 inches. This leaves about 6 feet of snow in the areas served by ski lifts. Of course, the great Zugspitzplatt snowfield can be reached in spring or autumn by a rack railway. The Zugspitze at 9,720 feet above sea level is the tallest mountain peak in Germany. Ski slopes begin at a height of 8,700 feet, and you can ski all summer.

The second great ski district in the Alps is Berchtesgadener Land. Alpine skiing is centered on Jenner, Rossfeld, Götschen, and Hochschwarzeck, with consistently good snow conditions until March. There is a cross-country skiing center and many miles

What's Special About the Bavarian Alps

Great Towns and Villages

- Berchtesgaden, favorite hideaway of Ludwig I, one of the scenic highlights of the Alps.
- Garmisch-Partenkirchen, Germany's top alpine resort, famed for skiing and mountain climbing.
- Oberammergau, a village of great charm, site of a noted passion play.
- Mittenwald, straight out of The Sound of Music, an alpine village extraordinaire.

Religious Shrine

- Kloster Ettal, one of the finest examples of German rococo architecture.

Top Attractions

- Königssee, outside Berchtesgaden, one of the most scenic bodies of water in Europe.
- Obersalzberg, site of Kehlstein, Hitler's "Eagle's Nest," one of Europe's great panoramas.
- Chiemsee, known as the "Bavarian Sea," with two islands, Herrenchiemsee and Frauenchiemsee.

Palaces

- Neues Schloss, on Herrenchiemsee, Ludwig II's fantastic attempt to rival the grand palace of Versailles.
- Schloss Linderhof, outside Oberammergau, a French rococo palace, architectural fantasy of Ludwig II.

Special Event

- Passion play, at Oberammergau, launched in 1634, the world's "longest running show," but staged only once a decade.

of tracks kept in first-class condition, natural toboggan runs, one artificial ice run for toboggan and skibob-runs, and ice-skating and ice-curling rinks.

In summer, alpine hiking is a major attraction—climbing mountains, enjoying nature, watching animals in the forest—lucky hikers sometimes see an ibex or other endangered species firsthand. One of the best areas for hiking is the 4,060-foot Eckbauer, lying on the southern fringe of Partenkirchen (the tourist office there will supply maps and details). Many visitors come to the Alps in summer just to hike through the Berchtesgaden National Park, bordering the Austrian province of Salzburg. The 8,091-foot Watzmann Mountain, the Königssee (Germany's cleanest, clearest lake), and parts of the Jenner (the pride of Berchtesgaden's four ski areas), are within the boundaries of the national park, which has well-mapped trails cut through protected areas, leading the hiker along spectacular flora and fauna. Information about hiking in the park is provided by the National Park Information Post Königssee in the former railway station at Königssee (☎ 08652/62-222).

Mountain biking in summer is a sport for the entire family. Uphill rides are exciting, gravel paths are not a problem, and downhill rides are a real challenge. The tourist office at Berchtesgaden (see below) will provide details of where to ride and where to rent bikes.

If you'd like to go swimming in an alpine lake—not to everyone's body temperature—there are many "lidos" in the Bavarian Forest.

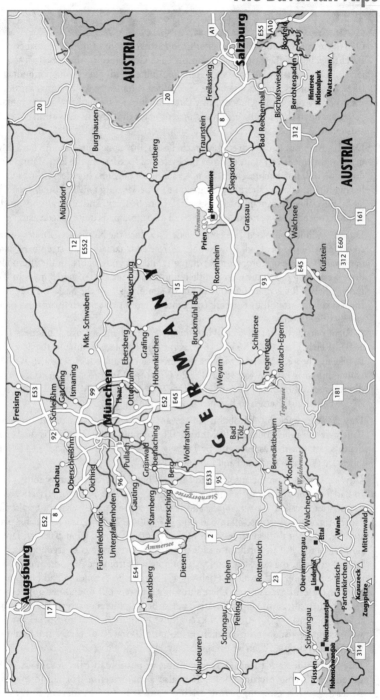

1 Exploring the Region by Car

One of the most scenic drives in all of Europe stretches for some 300 miles between Berchtesgaden in the east and Lindau on Lake Constance in the west (see Chapter 10). Die Deutsche Alpenstrasse (German Alpine Road) goes through mountains, lakes, black forests, and "castles in the sky." When commercial reality hasn't intruded, it's evocative of a Disney fantasy. In winter, driving can be perilous, and mountain passes are often shut down. We always prefer to take the drive in early spring or early autumn.

Day 1   After our last stopover in Munich, head south along Autobahn A8 (and drive in the right lane if you want to avoid the hysterical speeders on the left). Turn south on Route B20 for Berchtesgaden, 98 miles southeast of Munich. After settling in and having lunch, take an afternoon excursion to Obersalzburg and Kehlstein (you can go by bus). The Kehlstein road was blasted from bedrock, and a lift ascends to the summit, once Hitler's famed Eagle's Nest. The panorama is quite spectacular.

Day 2   While still based in Berchtesgaden, explore the Königssee 3 miles to the south (a two-hour boat ride). This long, narrow lake, famed for its steep banks and dark waters, is one of Europe's most dramatic and romantic sights. In the afternoon, drive west along the alpine road and then north on Route B20 some 12 miles to Bad Reichenhall. This is one of Germany's most famous spas on the Saalach River. The town was built around its Kurpark (spa center), and it's filled with luxury and moderately priced hotels.

Right outside town in a tasteful baroque style, Kirchberg-Schlössl, Thumseestrasse at Bad Reichenhall (☎ **08651/2760**), is the leading place to dine in the area. Try its pike in a beer sauce served with the inevitable sauerkraut or filet of zander. A three-course lunch is offered for 38 DM ($26.60) from 11am to 3pm. A four-course dinner is served from 6pm to midnight for 79 DM ($55.30). Main courses begin at 27 DM ($18.90). Return to Berchtesgaden for the night.

Day 3   Get back on Autobahn A8 toward Munich but turn off at Prien am Chiemsee, 53 miles southeast of Munich. The premier attraction here is the Neues Schloss, a fantastic castle begun by Ludwig II in 1878 on the island of Herrenchiemsee. You can find food and lodging at Prien.

Day 4   Get back on the autobahn to Munich, but take a cross-country route (472) to Bad Tölz, one of Bavaria's leading spas, although lacking in major attractions. Its spa quarter is called *Kurverwaltung* and it makes a good place to take a break. The Hotel Am Wald, Austrasse 39 in Bad Tölz (☎ **08041/78-830**), is a reasonable place to dine, with meals beginning at 28 DM ($19.60). It serves good Bavarian fare—nothing fancy, but fit fortification for this breezy part of the country. Standing on its own grounds, the hotel lies about a 10-minute walk from the Altstadt, or old town.

Leave Bad Tölz and go along Highway 472 for another 5 miles to Bad Heilbrunn, another typical Bavarian spa. There's not much to see, but in another 4 miles you reach Benediktbeuern, Upper Bavaria's oldest Benedictine monastery. Records trace it back to the year 739. After a look, continue along for 4 miles to Kochel am See, with its alpine vistas, and from there take Route 20 for 20 miles to Mittenwald on the Austrian frontier. Plan an overnight stay.

Day 5   You'll want to spend as much time as possible in Mittenwald—Goethe called it a "living picture book." It is also a major center for violin making. At least give it a morning before driving northwest for 12 miles on Route 2 to Garmisch-Partenkirchen, two towns combined. After checking in, head for the major attraction, the Zugspitze, the highest peak in Germany (more about this later). Wear warm clothing.

Day 6   Leaving Garmisch-Partenkirchen, head north for 12 miles to Oberammergau. Along the way you'll pass Kloster Ettal, founded by Ludwig the Bavarian in 1330. Its original 10-sided church is a stunning example of the Bavarian rococo style. Some 6 miles to the west is Schloss Linderhof, one of "Mad King" Ludwig's royal residences, built on the grounds of his hunting lodge between 1874 and 1878. These two attractions will take up most of your day, but you'll still arrive in the little old woodcarver's village of Oberammergau, 7 miles northeast of Linderhof, in time to wander and walk about. Later enjoy a hearty Bavarian dinner before turning in to your alpine bed.

2 National Park Berchtesgaden

This national park occupies the southeast corner of Germany, comprising a large portion of the state of Bavaria, and bordering Austria's province of Salzburg. The park was established in 1978 by a decree from the Bavarian government. It is a lush expanse of 84 square miles, with altitudes ranging from 1,800 feet at lowland Königssee to the Watzman, towering nearly 9,000 feet.

Nature finds sanctuary in the park, which facilitates the preservation of the natural ecosystems indigenous to the area. Conservation goals take precedence, so visitor recreation is tempered with a desire to keep impact on the park low, but a successful median can be obtained through the visitor's education of the ecosystem's fragility.

Limestone dominates most of the rock bed, suggesting that this was once a highly aquatic region. Formed by sediment deposited on the ocean floor 200 million years ago, the rock folded and lifted. Although most of the accompanying sandstone has eroded away, the limestone remains. Of course, several alpine lakes dot the landscape, the most significant of which is the Königssee. The steep moutain valleys and moraines suggest recent glacial recession was responsible for many of the grand landscapes found in the park.

Atlantic and continental influences characterize the climate. A substantial annual rainfall fosters the heavy tree vegetation of the region. The valleys receive approximately 60 inches of rainfall a year; the mountains are doused by approximately 110 inches annually.

Vegetation is affected by altitudinal gradient. Nearly half of the vegetation is remnants of deciduous forests, such as mixed mountain forests dominated by spruce, pines, and beeches. Nearly a third of the vegetation sprouts on rock debris and in crevices. The rest is comprised of alder and dwarf pine bushes, alpine meadows, and other surfaces such as lakes and a glacier. The mixed mountain forest thrives below 4,500 feet; the coniferous forest above it exist in an altitude of up to 5,500 feet, and above that, wind-dwarfed bushes and alpine meadows predominate. Once the forest was exploited for salt mines; it's now overpopulated and overgrazed by game.

In spring, summer, and autumn many different rare species of plants flower. They are protected, and don't live long once picked, so please leave them for the next person to enjoy. The flora coexist with a variety of alpine animals such as the chamois, ibex (reintroduced in 1930), the marmot, snow hare, alpine salamander, golden eagle, ptarmigon, black grouse, caipercaillie, alpine chough, black woodpecker, and the three-toed woodpecker. Other animals, the wolf, lynx, bear, and golden vulture, once thriving inhabitants, have not survived. Refer to the box on flora and fauna in this chapter for more specifics on vegetation and wildlife.

SPORTS & OUTDOOR ACTIVITIES IN & AROUND THE PARK

The park is open to visitors all year long and offers many recreational opportunities—hiking being the most obvious. A Jenner cable car reaches a park border at 5,500 feet—one way to expedite a hike. The park offers 115 miles of clearly marked and well-maintained paths and climbing routes and eight mountain huts and restaurants with catering during the summer months. The **Alpine Association,** located at the entrance of the park's Kurgarten, Maximilianstrasse 1 (☎ **08652/2207**), can provide you with literature and direct you to maps and passes.

Other summertime activities include ballooning, through **Outdoor Club Berchtesgaden,** Ludwig-Ganghofer-Strasse 20¹/₂ (☎ **08652/5001**). Summer curling can be played every Tuesday evening at 7pm on the asphalt surface of the ice rink Eisstadion, Berchtesgaden. Cycling and mountain biking give outdoor enthusiasts an opportunity to enjoy the outdoors and exercise simultaneously. Maps are available from the **Kurdirektion** (the local tourist office) and bikes can be rented at the train station (☎ **08652/5074**). Licensed anglers will find plenty of fishing opportunities at Lake Hintersee and the rivers Ramsauer Ache and Königsseer Ache. Passes are available from the **Ramsau tourist office** (☎ **08657/98-89-20**). Hang gliding (with permission) is available from Mount Jenner through **Sport Roberto** (☎ **08652/3218**). Horseback riding lessons are available to beginners through advanced riders at **Blasi Hof,** Reichenhallerstrasse 128, Hallthurm, near Berchtesgaden (☎ **08651/4520**). Rides can be arranged for 25 DM ($17.50) per hour. Practice your kayaking technique on one of the many rivers (water level permitting) in the area such as the Ramsauer, Königisser, Bischofswiesener, and Berchtesgadener Aches. Beautiful valleys provide scenic paragliding opportunities. Contact **Berchtesgadener Gleitschirm-flieger** e.V., Königsseestrasse 15 (☎ **08652/2363**). Go whitewater rafting with the **Outdoor-Club Berchtesgaden** (☎ **08652/5001**).

Of course there's plenty to do outdoors during the winter as well. In addition to some of the greatest alpine and cross-country skiing in all of Europe (☎ **08652/96-72-97** for current snow conditions), visitors can go ice-skating at the rink in Berchtesgaden (☎ **08652/61-405**) from October through February or on the Hintersee Lake once it's sufficiently frozen. A nice way to spend a winter's night is huddled with a companion in the back of a horse-drawn sled (☎ **08652/3453**).

3 Berchtesgaden

98 miles SE of Munich, 11 miles SE of Bad Reichenhall, 14 miles S of Salzburg

Ever since Ludwig I of Bavaria chose this resort as a favorite hideaway, the tourist business in Berchtesgaden, situated below the many summits of Watzmann Mountain (8,900 feet at the highest point), has been booming. According to legend, the mountain peaks were once a king and his family who were so evil that God punished them by turning them into rocks. The king has evidently not been completely silenced, however, because the Watzmann has been responsible for the deaths of several mountain climbers on the mile-high cliff on its eastern wall.

Berchtesgaden is an old alpine village with ancient winding streets and a medieval marketplace and castle square. Since the name of the village has often been linked with the führer and the Nazi hierarchy, many visitors mistakenly believe they are seeing one of Hitler's favorite haunts. This impression is erroneous. Hitler's playground was actually at Obersalzberg, on a wooded plateau about half a mile up the mountain. Berchtesgaden is very much a quiet Bavarian town.

Impressions

My memories of winter days in Berchtesgaden are ones of glorious sunshine, crisp air and a ring of sparkling mountains: a deep drink of blue fire from a chalice of ice.
—Hugo von Hofmannstal (1874–1929)

ESSENTIALS
GETTING THERE

BY TRAIN The Berchtesgaden Bahnhof lies on the Munich–Freilassing rail line. Twelve trains a day arrive from Munich (trip time: 1¹/₂ hours). For rail information and schedules, call **08652/5473**. Berchtesgaden has three mountain rail lines—the Obersalzbergbahn, Jennerbahn, and Hirscheckbahn—that connect the mountain plateaus around the resorts. For more information, contact **Berchtesgadener Bergbahn AG** (☎ **08652/95810**) and **Obersalzbergbahn AG** (☎ **08652/2561**).

BY BUS Long-distance bus service from Passau as well as from Bad Reichenhall is provided by **RBO Regionalbus Ostbayern GmbH in Passau** (☎ **0851/73-435**). Regional bus service to alpine villages and towns around Berchtesgaden is offered by **Regionalverkehr Oberbayern RVO at Berchtesgaden** (☎ **08652/5473**).

BY CAR Access by car is via the A8 Autobahn from Munich in the north or Route 20 from the south. The drive from Munich takes about two hours.

VISITOR INFORMATION

For tourist information, contact the **Kurdirektion,** Königssee Strasse 2 (☎ **08652/967-0**), open Monday through Friday from 8am to 5pm, Saturday from 9am to noon.

WHAT TO SEE & DO

The **Stiftskirche** (Abbey Church), dating from 1122, is adjacent to the Königliches Schloss Berchtesgaden. The church is mainly romanesque, with Gothic additions. One of its ancient twin steeples was destroyed by lightning and rebuilt in 1866. The church interior contains many fine works of art; the high altar has a painting by Zott dating from 1669. In the vestry is a small silver altar donated by Empress Maria Theresa of Austria.

Schlossplatz, partially enclosed by the castle and Stiftskirche, is the most attractive plaza in town. On the opposite side of the square from the church is a 16th-century arcade that leads to Marktplatz, with typical alpine houses and a wooden fountain from 1677 (restored by Ludwig I in 1860). Some of Berchtesgaden's oldest inns and houses border this square. Extending from Marktplatz is the Nonntal, lined with more old houses, some built into the rocks of the Lockstein Mountain that towers above.

Königliches Schloss Berchtesgaden

Schlossplatz 2. ☎ **08652/2085.** Admission 7 DM ($4.90) adults, 3 DM ($2.10) children 6–16, free for children 5 and under. Easter–Sept, Sun–Fri 10am–1pm and 2–5pm; Oct–Easter, Mon–Fri 10am–1pm and 2–5pm. Bus: 9539.

Berchtesgaden grew up around a powerful Augustinian monastery whose monks introduced the art of woodcarving, for which the town is noted to this day. When the town became part of Bavaria in 1809, the abbey was secularized and eventually converted to a palace for the royal family of Wittelsbach. Now it is a museum, mostly devoted to the royal collection of sacred art, including wood sculptures by the famed artists Veit Stoss and Tilman Riemenschneider. You can also explore a gallery of 19th-century art. There's a collection of Italian Renaissance furniture from the 16th century and three armoires displaying many pistols and guns of the 17th and 18th centuries, plus swords and armor. Precious porcelain and hunting trophies are also shown.

Salzbergwerk Berchtesgaden

Bergwerkstrasse 83. ☎ **08652/60-020.** Admission 18 DM ($12.60) adults, 9 DM ($6.30) children. May–Oct 15, daily 8:30am–5pm; Oct 16–Apr, Mon–Sat 12:30–3:30pm. Bus: 9539.

At the eastern edge of town are the salt mines once owned by the Augustinian monastery. Operations began here in 1517. The mines contain two types of salt, one suitable only for salt licks for cattle and other animals. The deposits are more than 990 feet thick and are still processed today from four galleries or "hills." Older children will especially enjoy the guided tours that begin with a ride into the mine on a small wagonlike train after donning protective miner's clothing. After nearly a half-mile ride, visitors leave the train and explore the rest of the mine on foot, sliding down a miner's slide and riding on the salt lake in a ferry. The highlight of the tour is the "chapel," a grotto containing unusually shaped salt formations illuminated for an eerie effect. The 1^1/$_2$-hour tour can be taken any time of the year, in any weather.

WHERE TO STAY
EXPENSIVE

✪ Hotel Geiger

Berchtesgadenstrasse 111, D-83471 Berchtesgaden. ☎ **08652/9653.** Fax 08652/96-54-00. 45 rms, 3 suites. MINIBAR TV TEL. 180 DM–300 DM ($126–$210) double; 320 DM–600 DM ($224–$420) suite. Rates include continental breakfast. V. Parking 8 DM ($5.60). Bus: 9539.

A traditional chalet inn on Berchtesgaden's upper fringes, the Geiger is a genuine antique—a gabled, extravagantly ornate hotel looks like what every tourist imagines a German hotel to be. The hotel has more amenities and style than any other in town, including the Fischer (see below). From its terraces, guest rooms, and breakfast rooms, you can enjoy panoramic views of the mountaintops. This remarkable retreat is owned by the Geiger family, who created the hotel more than a century ago.

Biedermeier enthusiasts will revel in the sitting rooms, completely furnished in that style. Any Geiger family member will give you the history of any furnishing, especially the painting in the paneled drawing room of *Silent Night* (it upset everyone by depicting Mary as awaiting the birth of Jesus on a Bavarian farm). The comfortable rooms are also furnished with antiques. Prices are based on whatever bath facilities you request and whether you have a balcony.

Dining/Entertainment: Dining is a true event here (see "Where to Dine," below). Guests like to gather in the drawing room for after-dinner coffee and cognac in front of the fireplace.

Services: Room service, massage, laundry.

Facilities: Open-air pool, indoor pool, sauna, solarium, fitness room.

MODERATE

✪ Hotel Fischer

Königsseer Strasse 51, D-83471 Berchtesgaden. ☎ **08652/9550.** Fax 08652/6-48-70. 54 rms. TV TEL. 104 DM–125 DM ($72.80–$87.50) double. Half board available for stays of three days or more, 208 DM–250 DM ($145.60–$175) double. Rates include buffet breakfast. MC, V. Closed Nov to mid-Dec and mid-Mar to Apr 5.

A short uphill walk from the Berchtesgaden railway station, in a spot overlooking the town, this hotel was built in the late 1970s in the Bavarian style. It is the second-ranking address in town, and, although comfortable in every way, it doesn't match the Geiger for charm. Fronted with dark-stained wooden balconies against a cream-colored facade, it rambles pleasantly along the hillside. The bedrooms are cozy and traditional, each with a regional theme. On the premises is an indoor swimming pool, a sauna, a solarium, and an alpine-style restaurant and bar.

Vier Jahreszeiten

Maximilianstrasse 20, D-83471 Berchtesgaden. ☎ **08652/9520.** Fax 08652/50-29. 59 rms. TEL. 160 DM–260 DM ($112–$182) double. Rates include buffet breakfast. AE, MC, V. Free parking outside, 9 DM ($6.30) in the garage. Bus: 9539.

An old inn with modern extensions, the Vier Jahreszeiten has been in the hands of the Miller family since 1876. It's in the heart of the village and has a colorful and distinguished restaurant (see "Where to Dine," below). The inn has been remodeled and improved over the years and now offers a good level of comfort, making it a formidable rival of the Fischer. Some of the newer units, with tiny sitting rooms and balconies, resemble suites. Most of the accommodations have minibars and TVs. In addition to the main dining room, there's a terrace for summer dining and viewing. The hotel offers an indoor pool, a sauna, and a solarium.

Wittelsbach

Maximilianstrasse 16, D-83471 Berchtesgaden. ☎ **08652/96-380.** Fax 08652/66-304. 29 rms, 3 suites. MINIBAR TV TEL. 160 DM–200 DM ($112–$140) double; from 280 DM ($196) suite. Rates include buffet breakfast. AE, DC, MC, V. Closed Nov–Dec 15. Parking 8 DM ($5.60). Bus: 9539.

The Wittelsbach, a hotel that dates from the 1890s, has been stylishly modernized and now offers well-furnished rooms in the heart of Berchtesgaden. The rooms are quiet and sunny; most have balconies with fine views of the mountains. Breakfast is the only meal served.

INEXPENSIVE

Watzmann

Franziskanerplatz 2, D-83471 Berchtesgaden. ☎ **08652/2055.** Fax 08652/51-74. 38 rms (16 with shower). 56 DM–68 DM ($39.20–$47.60) double without shower, 88 DM–144 DM ($61.60–$100.80) double with shower. AE, DC, MC, V. Closed Nov to Dec 25. Free parking. Bus: 9540 or 9541.

Built as part of a brewery 300 years ago, the Watzmann has been altered and expanded many times since. Today it is your best budget bet in town, although it doesn't have the style or amenitites of the properties previously considered. Set opposite the church on the main square, it has a large outdoor terrace, a cozy Bavarian-inspired decor, and dozens of turn-of-the-century artifacts. Everyone seems to stop throughout the day or night for a beer, coffee, or lunch. Inside, you'll find huge carved wooden pillars, oak ceilings, wrought-iron chandeliers, and hunting trophies. The doors of the simply furnished guest rooms are painted with floral murals.

WHERE TO DINE

Demming-Restaurant Le Gourmet

Sunklergässchen 2, D-83471 Berchtesgaden. ☎ **08652/9610.** Reservations required. Main courses 22.80–35 DM ($15–$23.10). AE, DC, MC, V accepted for hotel guests only. Daily 11:30am–2pm and 5:30–8:30pm. Closed Nov 1–Dec 15. Bus: 9539. BAVARIAN/INTERNATIONAL.

The Demming Hotel contains one of the town's best restaurants. Formerly a wealthy private house, it looks over a panoramic view of mountains and forests. Many locals regard dining here as something of an event. Only fresh ingredients are used in the well-prepared dishes, including hearty mountain fare, such as roast beef with chive sauce, and an array of veal and fish dishes. Sometimes we wish the chef could be less timid in his cookery, but what you get isn't bad unless you're seeking zesty flavors.

The hotel rents plainly furnished but comfortable bedrooms, costing 160 DM ($112) for a double.

Hotel Geiger

Berchtesgadenstrasse 111. ☎ **08652/96-55-55.** Reservations required. Main courses 21 DM–38 DM ($14.70–$26.60). V. Daily noon–2pm and 6:30–9pm. Bus: 9539. BAVARIAN/ INTERNATIONAL.

Even if you don't stay here, you may want to visit for a meal, as the hotel has the finest cuisine in Berchtesgaden. Its owner makes guests feel well cared for in a cultivated atmosphere featuring hearty cuisine. Trout and game are specialties. Begin perhaps with a parfait of goose liver with a mango purée or lentil soup with sausages. At Christmas an old German favorite—a soup of baked apples with croûtons—is served. For a main course, consider filet or saddle of veal on risotto with fresh truffles, salmon trout with vegetables, or "From Mother Nature's kitchen"—that is, spinach ravioli and small cakes made with red beets and served with Bavarian bleu cheese sauce. Desserts include old German favorites such as gingerbread mousse with a mulled claret pear.

DAY TRIPS
✪ KÖNIGSSEE

This "jewel in the necklace" of Berchtesgaden is one of Europe's most scenic bodies of water. Its waters appear to be dark green because of the steep mountains that jut upward from its shores. Low-lying land on the northern edge of the lake contains a parking lot and a few charming inns and bathing facilities, but the rest of the lake is enclosed by mountains, making it impossible to walk along the shoreline. The only way to explore the waters, unless you're like one of the mountain goats you may catch sight of above, is by boat. Electric motorboats (no noisy power launches allowed) carry passengers on tours around the lake in summer, and occasionally even in winter. The favorite spot on Königssee is the tiny flat peninsula on the western bank. It was the site of a basilica as early as the 12th century. Today the Catholic Chapel of St. Bartholomew is still used for services (except in winter). The clergy must arrive by boat since there's no other way to approach the peninsula. The adjacent buildings include a fisher's house and a restaurant, which was once a favored hunting lodge of the Bavarian kings. Here you can sample trout and salmon caught in the crisp, clean waters. At the southern end of the lake you come to the Salet-Alm, where the tour boat makes a short stop near a thundering waterfall. If you follow the footpath up the hillside, you'll reach the summer pastures used by the cattle of Berchtesgaden Land.

Just over the hill is Lake Obersee, part of Königssee until an avalanche separated them eight centuries ago. If you prefer a shorter trip, you can take the boat as far as St. Bartholomew and back. To reach the lake from Berchtesgaden by car, follow the signs south from the town (only 3 miles). It's also a pleasant hour's walk or a short ride by electric train or bus from the center of town.

For information about excursions, call **08652/96-36-18.** An entire tour of Königssee requires about two hours. There are boats in summer every 15 minutes, so getting off one boat and climbing aboard another is easy if you want to break up the tour.

During the summer, the first boat departs every morning at 7:15am and the last boat leaves at 5:30pm. In winter, boats leave about every 45 minutes. A round-trip fare for a lake tour is 21 DM ($14.70) for adults and 11 DM ($7.70) for children.

✪ OBERSALZBERG

The drive from Berchtesgaden to Obersalzberg at 3,300 feet is along one of Bavaria's most scenic routes. Here Hitler settled down in a rented cottage while he completed *Mein Kampf*. After he came to power in 1933, he bought Haus Wachenfeld and had it remodeled into his residence, the Berghof. Obersalzberg became the center of holiday living for Nazis such as Martin Bormann and Hermann Göring.

At Obersalzberg, you can walk around the ruins of Hitler's **Berghof.** Here the 1938 meeting between Hitler and British Prime Minister Neville Chamberlain resulted in the Munich Agreement. Chamberlain came away hailing "peace in our time," but the Nazi dictator felt he had merely given the prime minister his "auto-graph," and continued preparations for World War II. The Berghof was destroyed in 1952 by Bavarian government authorities at the request of the U.S. Army—the Americans did not want a monument to Hitler. One of the only fully remaining structures from the Nazi compound is a guesthouse, the General Walker Hotel, used by U.S. troops stationed in Europe. Wear good walking shoes and be prepared to run into some VERBOTEN! signs.

Hitler built the **bunkers** and air-raid shelter in 1943. Three thousand laborers completed the work in nine months, connecting all the major buildings of the Obersalzberg area to the underground rooms. Many readers have expressed their dis-appointment when reaching this site, apparently thinking they would tour Hitler's sumptuously decorated private apartments. A bunker is open for a visit, part of Hitler's air-raid-shelter system. Newly opened are prison cells used by the *Reichssicherheitsdienst* (State Security Police) and considered a last refuge for Hitler and other high officials of the Third Reich. Entrance to the bunker and prison cells is 5 DM ($3.50); they're open daily from 9am to 5pm. Guided tours in English are conducted daily from mid-May to mid-October, starting at the Berchtesgaden tourist office and offered by Berchtesgaden Mini Bus Tours (☎ **08652/64-971;** see "Organized Tours," below).

A major point of interest to visitors is the **Kehlstein,** or Eagle's Nest, which can be reached only by a thrilling bus ride up a 4¹/₂-mile-long mountain road, blasted out of solid rock and considered an outstanding feat of construction and engineering when begun in 1937 under the leadership of Bormann, who intended it as a 50th birthday gift for Hitler. The Eagle's Nest was not, as the name may suggest, a mili-tary installation. It was a site for relaxation, a tea house, and was not popular with Hitler, who rarely visited it. To reach the spot, you must enter a tunnel and take a 400-foot elevator ride through a shaft in the Kehlstein Mountain. The building, with solid granite walls and huge picture windows, houses a mountain restaurant. Called the Kehlsteinhaus, the restaurant is open from the end of May to the end of Octo-ber. Buses from the Hintereck parking lot in Obersalzberg run to the Eagle's Nest about every half hour. The ticket price includes the elevator ride to the top. You can also explore the rooms of the original tea house, which include Eva Braun's living room. Below is the Obersalzberg area where Hitler's Berghof once stood, and nearby is the site of Martin Bormann's house and the SS barracks. To the north you can see as far as Salzburg, Austria, and just below the mountain, to the west, is Berchtesgaden, with its rivers dwindling off into threads in the distance.

For information about trips to Kehlstein, call **08652/5473.** RVO buses (local buses based in Berchtesgaden) run from the Berchtesgaden Post Office to Obersalzberg–Hintereck, and from Hintereck special buses go to the Kehlstein parking lot. By local bus the round-trip journey from Berchtesgaden to Obersalzberg costs 7 DM ($4.90). From Obersalzberg (Hintereck) the special mountain bus and elevator ride through the rock costs 20 DM ($14). If you're hearty, instead of taking the elevator, you can walk up the final stretch to the Eagle's Nest from the summit parking lot in about 30 minutes. The Kehlstein line operates daily from mid-May to mid-October, during which there are full catering services offered at Kehlsteinhaus. The Kehlstein road is closed to private vehicles.

Obersalzberg is becoming an important health resort; the ruins of Bormann's Gusthof Farm are now the Skytop Lodge, a popular golfing center in summer and a ski site in winter.

Organized Tours

The best way to see the area is not on your own but with the services of the American-run **Berchtesgaden Mini Bus Tours,** Hanielstrasse 5 (☎ **08652/64971**), in Berchtesgaden. Tours take visitors to the Eagle's Nest, Obersalzberg, and the bunker system, the Salt Mines, and the Königssee. Tours cost 5 DM–40 DM ($3.50–$28). There's an information and ticket booth at the Berchtesgaden tourist office across the street from the train station. One of the most popular tours is the "Sound of Music" tour to nearby Salzburg.

Where to Stay

⑤ Hotel Zum Türken

D-83471 Berchtesgaden-Obersalzberg. ☎ **08652/2428.** Fax 08652/4710. 17 rms (13 with shower or bath). 100 DM ($70) double without shower or bath, 170 DM ($119) double with shower or bath. AE, DC, MC, V. Rates include continental breakfast. Closed Tues. Free parking. Obersalzberg bus from Berchtesgaden.

In Obersalzberg, the Hotel zum Türken is legendary. It stands today in the alpine style, with terraces and views for hotel guests only. On its facade is a large painted sign of "The Turk," and the foundation is stone, with the windows framed in shutters. A large handmade sign is written across the hillside, with a rather ominous pronouncement, pointing the way to the "Bunker." The story goes that the original building here was erected by a veteran from the Turkish war. At the turn of the century it was acquired by Karl Schuster, who turned it into a well-known restaurant that drew many celebrities of the day, including Brahms and Crown Prince Wilhelm of Prussia. However, anti-Nazi remarks he made in the 1930s led to trouble for Herr Schuster, who was arrested. In time, Bormann used the building as a Gestapo headquarters, and air raids and looting in April 1945 nearly destroyed the Türken. Many tourists erroneously think that the Türken was Hitler's famed Berghof.

Herr Schuster's daughter, Therese Partner, was able to buy the ruin from the German government for a high price in 1949. She opened a cafe and rooms for overnight visitors. Today, the Türken is run by Frau Ingrid Scharfenberg, granddaughter of Karl Schuster. Pleasantly furnished units are rented, and a self-service bar is on the ground floor. The rooms have no private phones, but there is an international pay phone in the main hallway.

4 Chiemsee

Prien am Chiemsee: 53 miles SE of Munich, 14 miles E of Rosenheim, 40 miles W of Salzburg

Known as the "Bavarian Sea," Chiemsee is one of the Bavarian Alps' most beautiful lakes, in a serene landscape. In the south the mountains reach almost to the water. Many resorts line the shores of the large lake, but the Chiemsee's main attractions are on its two islands, Frauenchiemsee, with its interesting local customs, and Herrenchiemsee, site of Ludwig II's palace that was meant to recreate Versailles.

ESSENTIALS
GETTING THERE

BY TRAIN The Prien Bahnhof is on the major Munich–Rosenheim–Freilassing–Salzburg rail line, with frequent connections in all directions. Ten daily trains arrive from Munich (trip time: one hour). For information, call **08051/19-419.**

BY BUS Regional bus service in the area is offered by RVO Regionalver-kehr Oberbayern, Betrieb Rosenheim (☎ **08031/62-006** for schedules and information).

BY CAR Access by car is via the A8 Autobahn from Munich.

VISITOR INFORMATION

For tourist information, contact the **Kur und Verkehrsamt,** Alte Rathausstrasse 11, in Prien am Chiemsee (☎ **0851/69-050**), open Monday through Friday from 8:30am to 6pm, Saturday from 9am to noon.

GETTING AROUND

By Steamer From the liveliest resort, Prien, on the west shore, you can reach either Frauenchiemsee or Herrenchiemsee via lake steamers that make regular trips throughout the year. The round-trip fare to Herrenchiemsee is 9.50 DM ($6.65), 11 DM ($7.70) to Fraueninsel. The steamers, operated by **Chiemsee-Schiffahrt Ludwig Fessler** (☎ **08051/6090**), make round-trips covering the entire lake. Connections are made from Gstadt, Seebruck, Chieming, Übersee/Feldwies, and Bernau/Felden. Large boats leave Prien/Stock for Herrenchiemsee at the island of Herreninsel from May to September, daily about every 20 minutes between 9am and 5pm. The last return is at 7:25pm.

BY BUS There is also bus service from the harbor to the DB station in Prien (Chiemsee–Schiffahrt) and around the lake by RVO.

WHAT TO SEE & DO
FRAUENCHIEMSEE

Frauenchiemsee, also called Fraueninsel, is the smaller of the lake's two major islands. Along its sandy shore stands a fishing village whose boats drag the lake for pike and salmon. At the festival of Corpus Christi, these boats are covered with flowers and streamers, the fishers outfitted in Bavarian garb, and the young women of the village dressed as brides; as the boats circle the island, they stop at each corner for the singing of the Gospels. The island is also the home of a Benedictine nunnery, founded in 782. The convent is known for a liqueur called *Kloster Likör.* Sold by nuns in black cowls with white-winged headgarb, it's supposed to be an "agreeable stomach elixir."

HERRENCHIEMSEE

Herrenchiemsee (also called Herreninsel), at Herrenchiemsee 3 (☎ **08051/3069**), is the most popular tourist attraction on the lake because of the fantastic castle,

✪ **Neues Schloss,** begun by Ludwig II in 1878. Never completed, the castle was to have been a replica of the grand palace of Versailles that Ludwig so admired. A German journalist once wrote: "The Palace, a monument to uncreative megalomania and as superfluous as the artificial castle ruins of the 19th century, is an imposing postlude of feudal architectural grandeur nonetheless." One of the architects of Herrenchiemsee was Julius Hofmann, whom the king had also employed for the construction of his fantastic alpine castle, Neuschwanstein. When money ran out and work was halted in 1886, only the center of the enormous palace had been completed. Surrounded by woodlands of beech and fir, the palace and its formal gardens remain one of the most fascinating of Ludwig's adventures, in spite of their unfinished state.

The palace entrance is lit by a huge skylight over the sumptuously decorated state staircase. Frescoes depicting the four states of existence alternate with Greek and Roman statues set in niches on the staircase and in the gallery above. The vestibule is adorned with a pair of enameled peacocks, Louis XIV's favorite bird.

The state bedroom is brilliant to the point of gaudiness, as practically every inch of the room has been gilded. On the dais, instead of a throne stands the richly decorated state bed, its purple-velvet draperies weighing more than 300 pounds. Separating the dais from the rest of the room is a carved wooden balustrade covered with gold leaf. On the ceiling a huge fresco depicts the descent of Apollo, surrounded by the other gods of Olympus. The sun god's features bear a strong resemblance to Louis XIV.

The Great Hall of Mirrors is unquestionably the most splendid hall in the palace and the most authentic replica of Versailles. The 17 door panels contain enormous mirrors reflecting the 33 crystal chandeliers and the 44 gilded candelabra. The vaulted ceiling is covered with 25 paintings depicting the life of Louis XIV.

The dining room is a popular attraction for visitors because of the table nicknamed "the little table that lays itself." A mechanism in the floor permitted the table to go down to the room below to be cleared and relaid between courses. Over the table hangs an exquisite chandelier of Meissen porcelain, the largest in the world and the single most valuable item in the palace.

You can visit Herrenchiemsee at any time of the year. From April to September 30, tours are given daily from 9am to 5:30pm; off-season, daily from 10am to 4:30pm. Admission (in addition to the round-trip boat fare) is 7 DM ($4.90) for adults, 4 DM ($2.80) for students, and free for children under 15.

WHERE TO STAY & DINE

⑤ Bayerischer Hof

Bernauerstrasse 3, D-83209 Prien am Chiemsee. ☎ **08051/6030.** Fax 08051/62-917. 47 rms. TV TEL. 160 DM ($112) double. Rates include buffet breakfast. V. Closed Nov and last week of Jan. Parking 10 DM ($7).

The Estermann family will welcome you to the Bayerischer Hof. The rustic aspects of the decor create the illusion that this relatively severe modern hotel is indeed older and more mellow than it is. Of particular note is the painted ceiling in the dining room, where regional meals are served. The rest of the hotel is more streamlined—modern, efficient, and quite appealing.

Yachthotel Chiemsee

Harrasser Strasse 49, D-83209 Prien am Chiemsee. ☎ **08051/6960.** Fax 08051/51-71. 97 rms, 5 suites. MINIBAR TV TEL. 240 DM–310 DM ($168–$217) double; 340 DM–470 DM ($238–$329) suite. Rates include buffet breakfast. AE, DC, MC, V. Free parking.

The best place to stay on the lake is the Yachthotel Chiemsee, on the western shore of the "Bavarian Sea." Launched in 1989, the hotel has more style and flair than its

The Fairy-Tale King

Often called "Mad" King Ludwig (although some Bavarians hate that label), Ludwig II was born in 1845, the son of Maximilian II. He was born in Munich, and Munich is his final resting place.

Only 18 years old when he was crowned king of Bavaria, handsome Ludwig initially attended to affairs of state, but he soon grew bored and turned to the pursuit of his romantic visions. He transformed his dreams into some of the region's most elaborate castles, nearly bankrupting Bavaria in the process.

The "dream" king was born at Nymphenburg, the baroque palace, set in a great park that was the summer residence of the Bavarian rulers. In the Marstall Royal Stables there, you can still see the richly decorated and gilded coaches and sleighs in which young Ludwig loved to travel, often at night, with his spectacular entourage. His crown jewels can be admired in the treasury in the Königsbau wing of the Residence in the heart of Munich.

A bisexual loner who never married, Ludwig often filled his time with music, and he was both a great fan and a benefactor of Richard Wagner. The king had Wagner's operas mounted for his own pleasure, and watched them in royal and solitary splendor.

At Linderhof, the first romantic palace that he built, he went so far as to reconstruct the Venus grotto from the Munich opera stage design for *Tannhäuser*. Near Oberammergau in the Graswang Valley, Linderhof was the smallest of Ludwig's architectural fantasies, his favorite castle, and the only one completed at the time of his death. To construct his own Versailles, he chose one of Germany's most beautiful lakes, Chiemsee. He called the palace Herrenchiemsee in homage to Louis XIV, the Sun King. Today visitors can enjoy the castle's Versailles-style Hall of Mirrors and its exquisite gardens.

Nestled in a crag high above the little town of Hohenswangen is the most famous of the royal designer's efforts, the multiturreted Disneyland-like Neuschwanstein. From a distance the castle appears more dreamlike than real, and it's the most photographed castle in Germany. The king's study, bedroom, and living room sport frescoes of scenes from Wagner's operas *Tristan and Isolde* and *Lohengrin*.

Finally, Ludwig's excesses became too much, and he was declared insane in 1886 when he was 41 years old. Three days later he was found drowned in Lake Starnberg on the outskirts of Munich—he may have committed suicide, or he may have been murdered. On the bank of the lake is a memorial chapel dedicated to him. He is buried with other royals in the crypt beneath the choir of St. Michael's Church.

competitors. It offers attractively furnished rooms, all with king-size beds and balconies or terraces opening onto the water.

Dining/Entertainment: A choice of restaurants—complete with a lakeside terrace and a marina—await you, although you can order from the same menu in all three. The most elegant room of all, patronized for its view if not its food, is the Seepavillion. The Seerestaurant is slightly more rustic but still with an elegant flair, and the Zirbelstüberl goes alpine Bavarian all the way.

Services: Room service (7am to midnight), laundry, baby-sitting.

Facilities: Sailing (a two-masted yacht with a skipper is available for sailing Apr–Oct), rowing, squash, tennis, riding, golf (nearby), horse-drawn carriage trips; spa department, beauty care center, sauna, solarium, health and fitness center, outdoor whirlpool, indoor pool.

5 Garmisch-Partenkirchen

55 miles SW of Munich, 73 miles SE of Augsburg, 37 miles NW of Innsbruck

In spite of its urban flair, Garmisch-Partenkirchen, Germany's top alpine resort, has kept some of the charm of an ancient village, especially in Partenkirchen. Even today you occasionally see country folk in traditional costumes, and you may be held up in traffic while the cattle are led from their mountain-grazing grounds down through the streets of town.

ESSENTIALS
GETTING THERE

BY TRAIN   The Garmisch-Partenkirchen Bahnhof is on the Munich–Weilheim–Garmisch–Mittenwald–Innsbruck rail line with frequent connections in all directions. Twenty trains per day arrive from Munich (trip time: 1 hour and 22 minutes). For rail information and schedules, call **08821/19-419**. Mountain rail service to several mountain plateaus and the Zugspitze is offered by the **Bayerische Zugspitzenbahn** at Garmisch (☎ **08821/7970**).

BY BUS   Both long-distance and regional buses through the Bavarian Alps are provided by **RVO Regionalverkehr Oberbayern** in Garmisch-Partenkirchen (☎ **08821/51-822**).

BY CAR   Access is via the A95 Autobahn from Munich; exit at Eschenlohe.

VISITOR INFORMATION

For tourist information, contact the **Verkehrsamt,** on Richar-Strasse-Platz (☎ **08821/1806**), open Monday through Saturday from 8am to 6pm, Sunday from 10am to noon.

GETTING AROUND

An unnumbered municipal bus services the town, depositing passengers at Marienplatz or the Bahnhof, from which you can walk to all centrally located hotels. This free bus runs every 15 minutes.

WHAT TO SEE & DO

The symbol of the city's growth and modernity is the **Olympic Ice Stadium,** built for the 1936 Winter Olympics and capable of holding nearly 12,000 people. On the slopes at the edge of town is the much larger **Ski Stadium,** with two ski jumps and a slalom course. In 1936 more than 100,000 people watched the events in this stadium. Today it's still an integral part of winter life in Garmisch—the World Cup Ski Jump is held here every New Year.

Garmisch-Partenkirchen is a center for winter sports, summer hiking, and mountain climbing. In addition, the town environs offer panoramic views and colorful buildings. The pilgrimage **Chapel of St. Anton,** on a pinewood path at the edge of Partenkirchen, is all pink and silver, inside and out. Its graceful lines are characteristic of 18th-century style. The Philosopher's Walk in the park surrounding the chapel is a delightful spot to wander, just to enjoy the views of the mountains around the low-lying town.

This area of Germany has always attracted the German romantics, including the "Fairy-Tale" king, Ludwig II. Perhaps with Wagner's music sounding in his ears, the king ordered the construction of a hunting lodge in the style of a Swiss chalet, but commanded that the interior look like something out of *The Arabian Nights*. It's still there. The lodge, **Jagdschloss Schachen,** can only be reached after an arduous climb. The tourist office will supply details. Tours at 11am and 2pm daily often leave from the Olympic Ski Stadium heading for the lodge—but check that first.

WHERE TO STAY
EXPENSIVE

Alpina Hotel

Alpspitzstrasse 12, D-82467 Garmisch-Partenkirchen. ☎ **08821/7830.** Fax 08821/71-374. 30 rms, 1 suite. MINIBAR TV TEL. 240 DM–290 DM ($168–$203) double; 330 DM ($231) suite. Rates include buffet breakfast. AE, DC, MC, V. Parking 15 DM ($10.50).

In this Bavarian hostelry, only three minutes from the Hausberg ski lifts, guests have all sorts of luxury facilities, including a garden with wide lawns and trees and an open patio. But, even so, this is not the town's leading hotel, an honor going to such classics as the Grand Hotel Sonnenbichl or the more traditional Posthotel Partenkirchen. Alpina has many winning features. Its facade is graced with a wide overhanging roof and Tyrolean-style entranceway and windows. Each of the guest rooms sports a personalized decor: Yours may have a snow-white sofa, chairs, walls, lamps, and carpet, with original paintings as accents; or it might feature sloped pine ceilings, a Spanish bedspread, and matching armchairs.

Dining/Entertainment: The open tavern dining room has two levels, and there's an extensive brick wine cellar offering a wide choice. Bavarian and international dishes are served in a beamed rustic dining room and on the sun terrace.

Services: Room service, laundry, dry cleaning.

Facilities: Covered pool with recreational terrace, open-air pool, sun terrace.

Grand Hotel Sonnenbichl

Burgstrasse 97, D-82467 Garmisch-Partenkirchen. ☎ **08821/7020.** Fax 08821/70-21-31. 90 rms, 3 suites. MINIBAR TV TEL. 350 DM ($245) double; 650 DM–1,000 DM ($455–$700) suite. Rates include continental breakfast. AE, DC, MC, V. Free parking. Take Route 23 toward Oberammergau.

The finest hotel in the area is on the hillside overlooking Garmisch-Partenkirchen, 1 mile from the city center and 2 miles from the Bahnhof, with views of the Wetterstein mountain range and the Zugspitze from its front rooms (those in the rear open onto a rock wall). The hotel was built in 1898 by the family of Georg Bader. After World War II it was used as a military hospital. Some of the bedrooms are showing wear and tear, and, although usually spacious, some do not have a complete tub bath. The decor is more or less art nouveau.

Dining/Entertainment: The hotel serves excellent food. You can have light, modern cuisine in the elegant gourmet restaurant, the Blauer Salon, or Bavarian specialties in the Zirbelstube. Afternoon coffee and fresh homemade cake are served in the lobby or on the sunny terrace. Drinks are available in the Peacock Bar.

Services: Room service, laundry, dry cleaning.

Facilities: Pool, sauna, solarium, fitness and massage rooms, beauty farm.

Obermühle

Mühlstrasse 22, D-82467 Garmisch-Partenkirchen. ☎ **800/528-12-34** in the U.S., or 08821/70-40. Fax 08821/70-41-12. 87 rms, 4 suites. MINIBAR TV TEL. 250 DM–325 DM ($175–$227.50) double; 320 DM–350 DM ($224–$245) suite. Rates include buffet breakfast. AE, DC, MC, V. Free parking. Take Route 24 (Zugspitzstrasse) toward Griesen.

This hotel is situated within a 5- to 10-minute walk from Garmisch's center, in a quiet, isolated spot much favored by repeat guests. The Wolf family, the owners, have operated a hotel on this spot since 1634, although the present building was constructed in 1969. They still maintain the traditional hospitality that has characterized their family for so long. Although a bit more sterile than either the Posthotel Partenkirchen or Alpina, the mountain panoramas from its beer garden and terrace are compensating factors. Most rooms have balconies with views of the Alps. Nearby are miles of woodland trails crisscrossing the nearby foothills. The rooms often have style and comfort, some with traditional Bavarian character.

Dining/Entertainment: Bavarian and international dishes are featured in the excellent restaurant. The garden and cozy Weinstube might be places you'll choose to wander through also.

Services: Room service, laundry, baby-sitting.

Facilities: Indoor pool set below a wooden roof shaped like a modified Gothic arch (at least it's pointed), sauna, solarium.

✪ Posthotel Partenkirchen

Ludwigstrasse 49, D-82467 Garmisch-Partenkirchen. ☎ **08821/51-067.** Fax 08821/78-568. 56 rms, 3 suites. MINIBAR TV TEL. 300 DM–350 DM ($210–$245) double. AE, DC, MC, V. Rates include continental breakfast. Town bus.

After many stages in its development—it was once a posting inn—the Posthotel Partenkirchen has emerged as one of the town's most prestigious hotels, and has the added asset of an unusually fine restaurant (see "Where to Dine," below). Here you'll experience old-world living, with personalized service offered by the owners. The picturesque facade has decorative murals around the front entrance and window boxes planted with red geraniums. The U-shaped rooms are stylish, with hand-decorated or elaborately carved furnishings. The balconies are sun traps, overlooking a garden and parking for your car, and offer a view of the Alps.

Dining/Entertainment: Of the two dining rooms, the larger is known for its decor: a wooden beamed ceiling, wrought-iron chandeliers, and huge arches that divide the room, making it more intimate. In the rustic Weinlokal Barbarossa, there are nooks for quiet before- or after-dinner drinks. Musicians provide background music.

Services: Room service, laundry.

Facilities: Golf, tennis, swimming, hiking, mountain climbing, skiing, cycling, hiking, horseback riding, paragliding.

MODERATE

Hotel Hilleprandt

Riffelstrasse 17, D-82467 Garmisch-Partenkirchen. ☎ **08821/2861.** Fax 08821/74-548. 17 rms, 1 suite. TV TEL. 140 DM–156 DM ($98–$109.20) double; 180 DM ($126) suite. Rates include buffet breakfast. MC, V. Free parking. Town bus.

In a tranquil location, this cozy chalet is close to the Zugspitz Bahnof and the Olympic Ice Stadium. Its cutout wooden balconies, attractive garden, and backdrop of forest-covered mountains give the impression of an old-time alpine building; however, a complete renovation in 1992 brought in streamlined modern comfort. Guests enjoy a fitness room, a sauna, a pleasant breakfast room, and the accommodating personality of owner, Klaus Hilleprandt, who is also the chef, serving excellent Bavarian food. Each room opens to a private balcony.

✪ Reindl's Partenkirchner Hof

Bahnhofstrasse 15, D-82467 Garmisch-Partenkirchen. ☎ **08821/58-025.** Fax 08821/73-401. 65 rms, 23 suites. MINIBAR TV TEL. 160 DM–190 DM ($112–$133) double; 320 DM–550 DM ($224–$385) suite. Breakfast 18 DM ($12.60) extra. AE, DC, MC, V. Closed Nov 11–Dec 12. Town bus. Parking 12 DM ($8.40).

Reindl's opened in 1911, and from the beginning it attracted a devoted following. Maintaining high levels of luxury and hospitality, owners Bruni and Karl Reindl have kept this a special Bavarian retreat. The annexes, the Wetterstein and the House Alpspitz, have balconies, and the main four-story building has wraparound verandas, giving each room an unobstructed view of the mountains and town. The well-furnished rooms have all the amenities, including safes.

Dining/Entertainment: The place is also known for Reindl's much honored restaurant (see "Where to Dine," below).

Services: Room service, laundry.

Facilities: Covered pool, sauna, sun room, health club, open terrace for snacks, two attractive gardens.

✪ Romantik-Hotel Clausing's Posthotel

Marienplatz 12, D-82467 Garmisch-Partenkirchen. ☎ **08821/7090.** Fax 08821/70-92-05. 42 rms, l suite. TV TEL. 160 DM–200 DM ($112–$140) double; from 450 DM ($315) suite. AE, DC, MC, V.

This hotel with its florid pink facade is full of history, and the events that happened here are a part of Garmisch's very identity. Set in the heart of town, it was originally built in 1512 as a tavern. During the Thirty Years' War, it was a haven for refugees when nearby Munich was ravaged and besieged. In 1891, it was sold to a prosperous beer baron from Berlin, whose claim to fame came from his invention of a new brand of beer, *Berliner Weissen,* with hints of yeast and raspberry flavoring, which quickly became one of the most popular brands in Garmisch.

In the early 1990s, the interior was radically upgraded without losing the establishment's antique sense of *Gemütlichkeit.* What had been unused space beneath the eaves was transformed into what are now the inn's best accommodations. All the rooms successfully mingle antique charm with the modern, well-insulated comforts you'd expect.

The most glamorous restaurant here is the Stüberl, a paneled enclave of warmth and carefully presented cuisine. The Verandah offers simple platters, drinks, and glassed-in comfort in winter, open-air access to the bustling Marienplatz in summer. Bavarian schmaltz is the venue at the Post-Hörnd'l, where live music is presented every evening throughout the year between 7 and 11:30pm.

INEXPENSIVE

Ⓢ Gästehaus Trenkler

Kreuzstrasse 20, D-82467 Garmisch-Partenkirchen. ☎ **08821/3439.** Fax 08821/1562. 10 rms (5 with shower). 77 DM–85 DM ($53.90–$59.50) double without shower, 91 DM–95 DM ($63.70–$66.50) double with shower. Rates include continental breakfast. No credit cards. Free parking. Eibsee bus: 1.

For a number of years Frau Trenkler has made travelers feel well cared for in her guesthouse, which enjoys a quiet central location. She rents five doubles with showers and toilets and five doubles with hot and cold running water. The rooms are simple but comfortably furnished.

Ⓢ Gasthof Fraundorfer

Ludwigstrasse 24, D-82467 Garmisch-Partenkinchen. ☎ **08821/2176.** Fax 08821/71-073. 30 rms. TV TEL. 124 DM–144 DM ($86.80–$100.80) double; 160 DM–280 DM ($112–$196) family room for two to five. Rates include buffet breakfast. AE, MC, V. Free parking. Town bus.

The family-owned Gasthof Fraundorfer is directly on the main street of the town, just a five-minute walk from the old church. Its original style has not been updated, so it retains the character of another day. There are three floors under a sloping roof, with a facade brightly decorated with window boxes of geraniums and decorative murals depicting a family feast. You'll be in the midst of village-centered activities here, near interesting shops and restaurants. The guest rooms are furnished with traditional alpine styling, some with four-poster beds. Some larger units are virtual apartments, suitable for up to five guests. Owners Josef and Barbel Fraundorfer are proud of their country-style meals. There's Bavarian yodeling and dancing every night except Tuesday. Dinner reservations are advisable.

In addition, the owners operate the Gästehaus Barbara in back, with 20 more beds. A typical Bavarian decor includes a *Himmelbett* ("heaven bed"). A double in their new house costs 150 DM ($105).

Haus Lilly

Zugspitzstrasse 20a, D-82467 Garmisch-Partenkirchen. ☎ **08821/52-600.** 8 rms. 100 DM ($70) double; 150 DM ($105) triple or quad. Rates include buffet breakfast. No credit cards. Free parking. Town bus.

This spotlessly clean guesthouse, a 15-minute walk from the Bahnhof, wins prizes for its copious breakfasts and the personality of its smiling owner, Maria Lechner, whose English is limited but whose hospitality is universal. Each cozy room includes free access to a kitchen, so in-house meal preparation is an option for guests wanting to save money. Breakfast offers a combination of cold cuts, rolls, cheese, eggs, pastries, and coffee, tea, or chocolate.

WHERE TO DINE
EXPENSIVE

Posthotel Partenkirchen

Ludwigstrasse 49, Partenkirchen. ☎ **08821/51-067.** Reservations required. Main courses 22 DM–50 DM ($15.40–$35); fixed-price menus 32 DM–76 DM ($22.40–$53.20). AE, DC, MC, V. Daily noon–2pm and 6–9:30pm. Eibsee bus 1. CONTINENTAL.

The Posthotel Partenkirchen is renowned for its distinguished continental cuisine—in fact, its reputation is known throughout Bavaria. The interior dining rooms are rustic, with lots of mellow, old-fashioned atmosphere. You could imagine meeting Dürer here. Everything seems comfortably subdued, including the guests. Perhaps the best way to dine here is to order one of the fixed-price menus, which change daily, depending on the availability of seasonal produce. The à la carte menu is extensive, featuring game in the autumn. You can order fresh cauliflower soup followed by main dishes such as Schnitzel Cordon Bleu or mixed grill St. James. The Weinerschnitzel served with a large salad is the best we've had in the resort.

✪ Reindl's Restaurant

In the Partenkirchner Hof, Bahnhofstrasse 15. ☎ **08821/58-025.** Reservations required. Main courses 27 DM–41 DM ($18.90–$28.70); fixed-price meals 50 DM ($35) at lunch, 120 DM ($84) at dinner. AE, DC, MC, V. Daily noon–2:30pm and 6:30–11pm. Closed Nov 11–Dec 12. Town bus. CONTINENTAL.

One of the best places to eat in Partenkirchen is Reindl's, a first-class restaurant in every sense of the word. It is the only hotel in town that competes successfully with Posthotel Partenkirchen. The seasonal menu comprises *cuisine moderne* as well as regional Bavarian dishes. Some famous French wines and champagnes—Romanée Conti, Château Lafite Rothschild, and Château Petrus—are offered. The chef de cuisine is Marianne Holzinger, daughter of founding father Karl Reindl. She has worked in the kitchens of Die Ente vom Lehel in Wiesbaden, The Breakers in Palm Beach, and Aubergine in Munich. The restaurant is known for honoring each "food season": For example, if you're here in asparagus season in spring, a special menu samples the dish in all the best-known varieties.

As a good opening to a fine repast, we suggest the scampi salad Walterspiel with fresh peaches, lemon, and tarragon or homemade goose-liver pâté with Riesling jelly. Among main dishes, we recommend coq au Riesling (chicken in wine) with noodles or veal roasted with Steinpilzen, a special mushroom from the Bavarian mountains. Among the fish dishes, try wild salmon with white and red wine and butter sauce. For dessert, you can select Grand Marnier sabayon with strawberry and vanilla ice cream or something more spectacular—a Salzburger Nockerl for two.

MODERATE

⑤ Alpenhof

Am Kurpark 10. ☎ **08821/59-055.** Reservations recommended. Main courses 17.50 DM– 42 DM ($12.25–$29.40); fixed-price lunch 24.50 DM–28.50 DM ($17.15–$19.95). DC, MC, V. Daily 11:30am–2pm and 5:30–9:30pm. Closed three weeks in Nov. Town bus. BAVARIAN.

The Alpenhof is widely regarded as the finest restaurant in Garmisch outside the hotel dining rooms (see above). The cuisine here is neatly grounded in tradition, with a flavorful use of ingredients. In summer, try for an outside table; in winter, retreat to the cozy interior, which is flooded with sunlight from a greenhouse extension. Renate and Josef Huber offer a variety of Bavarian specialties, as well as trout "any way you want," salmon grilled with mousseline sauce, and ragoût of venison. For dessert, try a soufflé with exotic fruits. An exceptional meal for 28.50 DM ($19.95)—the best for value at the resort—is presented daily.

INEXPENSIVE

⑤ Flösserstuben

Schmiedstrasse 2. ☎ **08821/2888.** Reservations recommended. Main courses 12 DM– 32.50 DM ($8.40–$22.75). AE, MC. Daily 11am–2:30pm and 4:30–11pm (or as late as 1:30am, depending on business). Town bus. GREEK/BAVARIAN/INTERNATIONAL.

Regardless of the season, a bit of the Bavarian Alps always seems to flower amid the wood-trimmed nostalgia of this intimate restaurant that lies close to the town center. On certain evenings, the weathered beams above the dining tables are likely to reverberate with laughter and good times. You can select a seat at a colorful wooden table or on an ox yoke–inspired stool in front of the spliced saplings that decorate the bar. Moussaka and souvlaki, as well as sauerbraten and all kinds of Bavarian dishes, are abundantly available.

Riessersee

Reiss 6. ☎ **08821/95-440.** Main courses 9.80 DM–33.80 DM ($6.85–$23.65). Daily 11:30am– 2pm and 6–9pm. No credit cards. BAVARIAN.

On the shores of a small lake with emerald-green water, this restaurant is reached after a lovely 2-mile stroll from the center of town. A café-restaurant, it is the ideal place for a leisurely lunch or afternoon tea or coffee, the latter served with cakes, ice cream, and chocolates. It makes a particularly good place to stop over after your exploration of the Zugspitze. The zither music played on Saturday and Sunday will soothe your nerves after such an adventure. You may like the place so much you'll stick around for one of the good-tasting dishes that feature Bavarian fish or game specialties. Caviar and lobster are available on occasion, and you can order some of the best-tasting veal dishes here at all times.

The Natural World of the Alps

Many alpine animals such as the lynx, otter, and alpine ibex have all but disappeared during this century from the Bavarian Alps. Other endangered animals include wildcats, susliks, certain nesting birds, toads, and fish.

An effort undertaken to reintroduce species eradicated from their habitats by hunters and farmers has been an unqualified success. Brown bears have been sighted in increased numbers over recent years, along with migrating elk. Wolves have not reemerged since their ultimate annihilation in the 1950s (attempts in the U.S. to reintroduce wolves in the American Rocky Mountains has been mired in controversy). Without any check on their numbers by their natural enemies, the deer and stag population has enjoyed such exponential growth that hunting in some regions has become necessary to keep the population in check and preserve the natural balance.

Other species continue to thrive in the alpine environment. Unobtrusive hikers will find the Alps teeming with creatures—the chamois gracefully bounding up alpine heights, golden eagles in circling flight, the griffon vulture floating with its intimidating 9-foot wing spread. A hiker might even be befriended by a marmot or an alpine chaugh basking in a sunny meadow. Never threaten the gentle marmot or you might learn why it's nicknamed the whistle pig. The hill country and lower mountain ranges are often home to badgers, martens, and hares. Hedgehogs are rare, one of the endangered species of rodents.

Ornithologists literally have a field day in the Bavarian Alps. The range of birds is immense. Great white herons guide you on a teasing trail—they pause for respite along the Danube's banks long enough for you to catch up to them, only to depart in flight to another sanctuary 20 meters downstream. Storks, marsh warblers, gray geese, spoonbills, and terns can also be sighted. The streak of blue you see may be a blue kingfisher, diving for insects in the rippling of streams and rivers. The distinctive red and black wings of the gray alpine wall creeper distinguish it from the gray cliff faces it ascends. The spotted woodpecker, goldfinch, redstart, thrush,

6 Exploring the Alps

From Garmisch-Partenkirchen, you can see the tallest mountain peak in Germany, the ✪ **Zugspitze,** at the frontier between Austria and Germany. Its summit towers 9,720 feet above sea level. Ski slopes begin at a height of 8,700 feet. For a panoramic view of both the Bavarian and the Tyrolean (Austrian) Alps, go all the way to the peak. The Zugspitze summit can be reached from Garmisch by taking the cogwheel train to Zugspitzeplatz. The train leaves Zugspitzeplatz daily every hour between 8:35am and 2:35pm. Travel time from Garmisch is 75 minutes. The Eibsee cable car (Eibsee-Seilbahn) may be taken from Eibsee, a small lake at the foot of the mountain. It makes the 10-minute run at least every half hour from 8:30am to 4:30pm (in July and August, until 5:30pm).

The cable car to the Zugspitze summit (Gletscherbahn), a four-minute ride, departs from Sonn Alpin to the summit at least every half hour during the operating hours of the cogwheel train and the Eibsee cable car. The Zugspitze round-trip is 72 DM ($50.40) for adults and 42 DM ($29.40) for children 4 to 16; children under 4 ride free. More information is available from the Bayerische Zugspitzbahn, Olympiastrasse 27 in Garmisch-Partenkirchen (☎ **08821/7970**).

and bluelit barter sing all winter, but the finch, lark, and song thrush save their voices for spring. Keen eyes only will spot falcons, buzzards, and other birds of prey. Don't forget to watch for nocturnal birds like the tawny owl if you're hiking at night.

Of course, if you spend the entire time with your head in the clouds, you'll miss what's underfoot. Edelweiss are the harbingers of spring. They blossom ahead of most wildflowers, often cropping up amid a blanket of snow, enjoying a short and fragile life. The season for mountain wildflowers varies depending on spring temperatures and snowpack. Most wildflowers blossom by the end of July or early August. Many are protected; it is against the law to pick them or take the plants. More than 40,000 plant species are threatened by extinction worldwide, and the Alps are no exception. In any case, the snowdrop, the pink meadow saffron, and the gorgeous colors of the mountain rose and gentian are finest in their natural setting in flowering alpine meadows. You can, however, pick the bluebills, pinks, cornflowers, buttercups, daisies, and primroses that blossom in such abundance.

You might even find a snack along your trail—wild raspberries, strawberries, bilberries, blackberries, cranberries, flap mushrooms, chanterelles, and parasol mushrooms are often found. However, edible varieties can be easily confused with inedible or poisonous varieties—know what you're picking and be careful. Autumn in the mountains brings an array of colors and splendor with the turning of the leaves. Those interested in finding out more about the flora of Bavaria can visit an alpine garden or an instructional guided path.

An ongoing effort is being made to conserve the area's valuable biotopes—high-altitude forests, water marshes, and the specialized plant life of steep cliffs and mountain banks. Nature reserves buffer the detrimental impact of agriculture and forestry, and outside their domains, farmland has been reallocated to include low-yield cultivation and extended pastures. But it's also important that hikers be sensitive to their ecological impact as they enjoy nature in the Alps.

The ✪ **Alpspitz** region is a paradise for hikers and nature lovers in general. From early spring until late fall, its meadows and flowers are a delight and its rocks evoke a prehistoric world. At altitudes of 4,600 to 6,300 feet, the Alps present themselves in a storybook fantasy. Those who want to explore the northern foot of the Alpspitz can take the Alpspitz round-trip by going up on the Alpspitz cable car, over the Hochalm, and back down on the Kreuzeck or Hausberg cable car, allowing time in between for hikes lasting from half an hour to an hour and a half. Snacks are served at the Alpspitz cable car's top station or at the more rustic Hochalm Chalet.

The Alpspitz cable car to Osterfelderkopf, at a height of 6,300 feet, makes its nine-minute run at least every hour from 8am to 5pm. The round-trip cost is 35 DM ($24.50) for adults and 21 DM ($14.70) for children 4 to 14.

The Hochalm cable car from the Hochalm to Osterfelderkopf makes its four-minute run at least every hour during the operating hours of the Alpspitz cable car. A single ride costs 6 DM ($4.20) for adults and 4 DM ($2.80) for children.

The Alpspitz round-trip with the Osterfelder cable car, the Hochalm cable car, and Kreuzeck or the Kreuzwankl/Hausberg cable car is 40 DM ($28) for adults and 24 DM ($16.80) for children.

These fares and times of departure can fluctuate from season to season. Therefore, for the latest details, check with the tourist office, the Kurverwaltung, on Richard-Strauss-Platz (☎ **08821/1806**), open Monday through Saturday from 8am to 6pm and on Sunday from 10am to noon only, or else call **08821/7970.**

From Garmisch-Partenkirchen, many other peaks of the Wetterstein range are accessible as well, via the 10 funiculars ascending from the borders of the town. From the top of the **Wank** (5,850 feet) to the east, you get the best view of the plateau on which the twin villages of Garmisch and Partenkirchen sit. This summit is also a favorite with the patrons of Garmisch's spa facilities because the plentiful sunshine makes it ideal for the *Liegekur* (deck-chair cure).

HIKING IN THE BAVARIAN ALPS

When winter snows melt, hikers take to the mountains in the shadow of the Zugspitze. The timid prefer gentle strolls around blue-green alpine lakes, whereas the more adventurous head for the naked glaciers just as in a Stallone movie. Hiking remains a national pastime in Bavaria, even if it doesn't enjoy the cult status it did in the 1920s heyday of Leni Riefenstahl and her mountain films.

Everybody seems to hit the trails, from preschoolers to those living comfortably on pensions at Bavarian farmhouses. The tourist office in Garmisch-Partenkirchen will help you find trails of varying degrees of difficulty. After that, you just follow the signs.

One of the best places to begin is the 4,060-foot peak **Eckbauer** that lies on the southern fringe of Partenkirchen. The smallest of the Wetterstein mountain chain, its easy trails are recommended to first-time alpine hikers. Hikers take a chairlift to the top, where, in the real Bavarian style, they can refresh themselves with a glass of buttermilk at the Bergasthof. In less than an hour you can walk back down through a forest. If it's lunchtime, stop at the terraced restaurant of the Forsthaus Graseck hotel, which opens onto a gorge.

An interesting hike is through the **Partnachklamm Gorge,** lying between the Graseck and Hausberg peaks. The gorge was created by the Partnach River. An open-sided tunnel has been drilled along it. After taking the cable car to the first station on the Graseck route, follow the paths along the sides of the slope to the right and trail the river as it cascades over the rocks. The path circles around by crossing the gorge, and returns you to the point where you entered. Many readers have found this one of their most memorable sightseeing adventures in Bavaria. The experience of walking along a rocky ledge just above a rushing river and often behind small waterfalls, while looking up at 1,200 feet of rocky cliffs, always fills one with awe. At the end of this sometimes wet tunnel walk, you can take a horse and buggy back to the chairlift.

The highest trails are on the Alpspitze between Osterfelderkopf at 6,720 feet up and the final point of the Alpspitzbahn at 12,460 feet. The Zugspitzbahn, the rail line between Garmisch-Partenkirchen and Eibsee, at the base of the Zugspitze, offers a brochure outlining seven trails most favored by hikers. You don't have to be an Olympic athlete to try them. Some hikes will take four to five hours, and a few are suitable for the entire family.

7 Oberammergau

59 miles SW of Munich, 12 miles N of Garmisch-Partenkirchen

In this alpine village the world-famous passion play is presented; performances are generally given every 10 years. The next one is scheduled for the year 2000, May through October. Surely the world's longest-running show (in more ways than one), it began in 1634 when the town's citizens took a vow to present the play in gratitude for being spared from the devastating plague of 1633. Lasting about eight hours, the play is divided into episodes, each introduced by an Old Testament tableau connecting predictions of the great prophets to incidents of Jesus's suffering. The actors in the play are still the townspeople of Oberammergau.

Oberammergau stands in a wide valley surrounded by forests and mountains, sunny slopes, and green meadows. It has long been known for the skill of its woodcarvers. Here in this village right under the Kofel, farms are still intact, as well as first-class hotels, cozy inns, and family boarding houses.

Numerous hiking trails lead through the mountains around Oberammergau to hikers' inns such as the Kolbenalm and the Romanshohe. You can, however, simply go up to the mountaintops on the Laber cable railway or the Kolben chairlift. Oberammergau also offers opportunities to tennis buffs, minigolf players, cyclists, swimmers, hang-gliding enthusiasts, and canoeists. The recreation center, **Wellenberg,** with its large alpine swimming complex with open-air pools, hot water and fountains, sauna, solarium, and restaurant, is one of the Alps's most beautiful recreation centers. The Ammer Valley, with Oberammergau in the (almost) center, is a treasure trove for explorers, who use it as a base for visiting Linderhof Castle, the Benedictine monastery at Ettal, or the fairy-tale Neuschwanstein and Hohenschwangau castles.

ESSENTIALS
GETTING THERE

BY TRAIN   The Oberammergau Bahnhof is on the Murnau–Bad Kohlgrum–Oberammergau rail line, with frequent connections in all directions. Through Murnau all major German cities can be reached. Daily trains arrive from Munich (trip time: 2 hours) and from Frankfurt (trip time: 7 hours). For rail information and schedules, call **08821/19-419.**

BY BUS   Regional bus service to nearby towns is offered by **RVO Regionalverkehr Oberbayern** in Garmisch-Partenkirchen (☎ **08821/51-822**). An unnumbered bus goes back and forth between Oberammergau and Garmisch-Partenkirchen.

BY CAR   Oberammergau is 1 1/2 hours from Munich and 5 1/2 hours from Frankfurt. Take the A95 Munich–Garmisch–Partenkirchen Autobahn and exit at Eschenlohe.

VISITOR INFORMATION

For tourist information, contact the **Verkehrsbüro,** Eugen-Papst-Strasse 9A (☎ **08822/10-21**), open Monday through Friday from 8:30am to 6pm and Saturday from 8:30am to noon.

WHAT TO SEE & DO

If you visit Oberammergau in an "off" year, you can still see the **Passionspielhaus,** Passionwiese, the modern theater at the edge of town where the passion play is performed. The roofed auditorium holds 4,700 spectators, and the open-air stage is a wonder of engineering, with a curtained center stage flanked by gates opening onto the so-called streets of Jerusalem. The theater and production methods are contemporary, but the spirit of the play is marked by the medieval tradition of involving the entire community in its presentation—all those without speaking parts seem to be included in the crowd scenes. The impressive auditorium is open to the public daily from 10am to noon and 1:30 to 4pm. Admission is 4 DM ($2.80) for adults and 2.50 DM ($1.75) for children and students.

Aside from the actors, Oberammergau's most respected citizens include another unusual group, the woodcarvers, many of whom have been trained in the village woodcarver's school. In the **Pilatushaus,** Ludwigthomstrasse (☎ **08822/1682**), you can watch local artists at work, including woodcarvers, painters, sculptors, and potters. Hours are Monday through Friday from 10:30am to 5:30pm. You'll see many examples of these art forms throughout the town, on the painted cottages and inns and in the churchyard. Also, when strolling through the village, watch for the houses with frescoes by Franz Zwink (18th century), named after fairy-tale characters, such as "Hansel and Gretel House" and the "Little Red Riding Hood House."

The **Heimatmuseum,** Dorfstrasse (☎ **08822/94-136**), has a notable collection of Christmas crèches, all hand-carved and hand-painted, from the 18th through the 20th centuries. It's open May 15 to October 15, Tuesday through Saturday from 2 to 6pm; off-season, only on Saturday from 2 to 6pm. Admission is 3 DM ($2.10) for adults and 1.50 DM ($1.05) for children.

NEARBY ATTRACTIONS

✪ Schloss Linderhof

Until the late 19th century, a modest hunting lodge stood on a large piece of land, 8 miles west of the village, owned by the Bavarian royal family. In 1869 "Mad Ludwig" struck again, this time creating a French rococo palace in the Ammergau Mountains. Unlike Ludwig's palace at Chiemsee, Schloss Linderhof was not meant to copy any other structure. And unlike his castle at Neuschwanstein, its concentration of fanciful projects and designs was not limited to the palace interior. In fact, the gardens and smaller buildings at Linderhof are, if anything, more elaborate than the two-story main structure. It is his most successful venture, and the only one that was completed.

The most interesting palace rooms are on the second floor, where ceilings are much higher because of the unusual roof plan. Ascending the winged staircase of Carrara marble, you'll find yourself at the West Gobelin Room (music room), with carved and gilded paneling and richly colored tapestries. This leads directly into the Hall of Mirrors. The mirrors are set in white and gold panels, decorated with gilded woodcarvings. The ceiling of this room is festooned with frescoes depicting mythological scenes, including *The Birth of Venus* and *The Judgment of Paris.*

The king's bedchamber is the largest room in the palace and is placed in the back, overlooking the Fountain of Neptune and the cascades in the gardens. In the tradition of Louis XIV, who often received visitors in his bedchamber, the king's bed is closed off by a carved and gilded balustrade.

In the popular style of the previous century, Ludwig laid out the gardens in formal parterres with geometrical shapes, baroque sculptures, and elegant fountains. The front of the palace opens onto a large pool with a piece of gilded statuary in its center, from which a jet of water sprays 105 feet into the air.

The park also contains several other small but exotic buildings, including the Moorish Kiosk, where Ludwig often spent hours smoking chibouk and dreaming of himself as an Oriental prince. The magic grotto is unique, built of artificial rock, with stalagmites and stalactites dividing the cavelike room into three chambers. One wall of the grotto is painted with a scene of the Venus Mountain from *Tannhäuser.* The main chamber is occupied by an artificial lake illuminated from below, and in Ludwig's time it had an artificial current produced by 24 dynamo engines. A shell-shaped boat, completely gilded, is tied to a platform called the Lorelei Rock.

The fantasy and grandeur of Schloss Linderhof, D-82488 Ettal-Linderhof (☎ **08822/3512**), is open to the public throughout the year and makes a day trip from Munich, as well as from Oberammergau. It's open April to September, daily from 9am to 5:30pm; from October to March, the grotto and Moorish Kiosk are closed, but the castle is open daily from 10am to 12:15pm and 12:45 to 4pm. Admission is 7 DM ($4.90) for adults, 4 DM ($2.80) for students 16–24, and free for children 15 and under.

Buses run between Oberammergau and Schloss Linderhof seven times per day from 9am; the last bus leaves Linderhof at 5:35pm. A round-trip passage costs 7 DM ($4.90).

✪ Kloster Ettal

In a lovely valley sheltered by the steep hills of the Ammergau, Kloster Ettal, on Kaiser-Ludwig-Platz at Ettal (☎ **08822/740**), was founded by Ludwig the Bavarian in 1330. Monks, knights, and their ladies shared the honor of guarding the statue of the Virgin, attributed to Giovanni Pisano. In the 18th century, the golden age of the abbey, there were about 70,000 pilgrims every year. The minster of Our Lady in Ettal is one of the finest examples of Bavarian rococo architecture in existence. Around the polygonal core of the church is a two-story gallery. An impressive baroque facade was built from a plan based on the designs of Enrico Zuccali. Inside, visitors stand under a vast dome, admiring the fresco painted by John Jacob Zeiller in the summers of 1751 and 1752. The abbey lies along the road between Garmisch-Partenkirchen and Oberammergau. Admission is free, and it's open daily from 8am to 6:30pm (closes at 4:30pm in winter).

Ettal stands 2 miles south of Oberammergau. Buses from Oberammergau leave from the Rathaus and the Bahnhof once per hour during the day, with round-trip passage costing 4.50 DM ($3.15). Call **8821/51-822** for information.

SHOPPING

The region's woodcarvings have always been sought after, and many an example has graced the mantelpieces, *étagères,* and what-not shelves of homes around the world. Know before you buy that even some of the most expensive pieces might have been roughed in by machine prior to being finished off (fine carved details) by hand. Most subjects are religious, deriving directly from 14th-century originals which, usually because of their exposure to the elements, war, or whatever, have not stood the test of time very well. To cater to the demands of modern tourism, there's been an increased emphasis lately on secular subjects, such as drinking or hunting scenes. Competition for sales is fierce. Many objects are carved in hamlets and farmhouses throughout the region.

There's a woodcarving school in town, whose conditions of study might remind you of the severity of the medieval guilds. Students who labor over a particular sculpture are required to turn it in to the school after its completion, where it's either placed on permanent exhibition or sold during the school's once-a-year sell-offs. These occur very briefly, usually over a two-day period in July, and cannot be considered a steady or reliable source of supply for temporary visitors, who usually do better at any of the trio of shops recommended below.

Peter Zwink
Schnitzlergasse 4. ☎ **08822/857.**

Long before the days of electricity, every self-respecting Bavarian home would have at least one, and often several, clocks whose designs have ever since been associated with the rustic rococo traditions of the region. If you want a cuckoo clock, you'll be able to find a selection here, but the staff may hurry to tell you that this tradition belongs to the Black Forest, farther to the north. Look instead for mantel clocks and floor clocks carved with baroque-style designs, many of them cunningly crafted from pine, maple, or basswood. Some of the clocks need to be wound only once a year, a tradition that families carry out as part of their New Year's Day rituals. It's open from 9am to noon, and from 2 to 6pm, but closed all day Wednesday and on Saturday afternoon.

Josef Albl
Devrientweg 1. ☎ **08822/6433.**

Established sometime after World War II, this taciturn but prestigious woodcarver specializes in bas-reliefs, some of which are as complicated as anything you're likely to find within the region. Although the traditional art forms that have come down from the Middle Ages depict religious subjects, many carvings made today are of secular scenes from Bavarian life, especially hunting scenes. Prices for some of the touristy simple pieces sell for as little as 20 DM ($14), although pieces you might want commissioned can stretch into the tens of thousands of dollars. It's open from 9am to 1pm and 2 to 6pm, daily except Saturday afternoon and all day Sunday.

Tony Baur
Dorfstrasse 27. ☎ **08822/821.**

This store contains the most sophisticated collection of woodcarvings in Oberammergau. Established around 1980, it employs a small cadre of carvers who usually work from their homes to create carvings inspired by medieval originals, often fully rounded examples of religious subjects. Outgoing and personable, the sales staff is quick to admit that the rough forms of many of the pieces are done by machine, with most of the intricate work completed by hand. Most pieces are crafted from maple, pine, or linden (basswood), with special emphasis on religious and huntsman's motifs. Prices range from 40 DM ($28) to a recent high of 14,600 DM ($10,220) for pieces of museum quality. Although carvings can be left in their natural grain, sometimes using elaborately contrasting areas of light and dark wood, some of the most charming are polychromed, and in some instances, partially gilded. It's open Monday to Friday from 9am to 6pm, Saturday from 9am to 5pm. From Easter to October, it also opens every Sunday, from 10am to 5pm.

WHERE TO STAY & DINE
MODERATE

Hotel Restaurant Böld
König-Ludwig-Strasse 10, D-82487 Oberammergau. ☎ **08822/3021.** Fax 08822/71-02. 57 rms. TV TEL. 180 DM–200 DM ($126–$140) double. Rates include continental breakfast. AE, DC, MC, V. Free parking outside, 10 DM–15 DM ($7–$10.50) in the garage. Bus: 30.

This inn has steadily improved in quality and now is among the town's premier choices. Only a stone's throw from the river, the well-designed chalet hotel offers comfortable public rooms in its central core and well-furnished guest rooms in its contemporary annex. All rooms have private bath and satellite TV; most units also open onto balconies. A sauna is offered for guests' relaxation, as are a solarium and whirlpool. The restaurant features both international and regional cuisine. In the bar, you'll find a tranquil atmosphere, plus attentive service. Raimund Hans and family are the hosts.

Parkhotel Sonnenhof
König-Ludwig-Strasse 12, D-82487 Oberammergau. ☎ **08822/9130.** Fax 08222/3047. 72 rms, 2 suites. TV TEL. 190 DM–280 DM ($133–$196) double; 320 DM–460 DM ($224–$322) suite. Rates include buffet breakfast. AE, DC, MC, V. Free parking.

Short on charm and alpine rusticity, this modern hotel still has a lot going for it and a lot of seasoned Oberammergau devotees. First, it's far enough away from the crowds that descend in summer—often in tour buses—to offer guests peace and tranquility. It is, however, within walking distance of the center. The hotel overlooks the Ammer River and a beautiful Pfarrkirche (parish church). Every room has a bedroom balcony with an alpine vista, often of Oberammergau's mountain, the Kobel. The bedrooms, although devoid of old-fashioned charm, are well maintained and filled with first-class comforts. The hotel has more amenities than most in the area—an indoor pool, sauna, and such extra features as a bowling alley. It's also a family favorite, with a children's playroom. Two restaurants offer many international dishes, although the Bavarian specialties are what's good here.

INEXPENSIVE

⑤ Alte Post

Dorfstrasse 19, D-82487 Oberammergau. ☎ **08822/9100.** Fax 08822/910-100. 32 rms (28 with bath). TV TEL. 120 DM ($84) double without bath, 140 DM ($98) double with bath. Rates include continental breakfast. AE, MC, V. Closed Oct 25–Dec 19. Parking 6 DM ($4.20). Bus: 30.

A provincial inn in the village center, the Alte Post is built in chalet style—wide overhanging roof, green-shuttered windows painted with decorative trim, a large crucifix on the facade, and tables set on a sidewalk under a long awning. It's the village social hub. The interior has storybook charm, with a ceiling-high green ceramic stove, alpine chairs, and shelves of pewter plates. The rustic guest rooms have wood-beamed ceilings and wide beds with giant posts; most have views.

The main dining room is equally rustic, with a collection of hunting memorabilia, and there's an intimate drinking bar. The restaurant serves excellent Bavarian dishes.

⑤ Hotel Café-Restaurant Friedenshöhe

König-Ludwig-Strasse 31, D-82487 Oberammergau. ☎ **08822/3598.** Fax 08822/43-45. 14 rms. TEL. 100 DM–160 DM ($70–$112) double. Rates include buffet breakfast. AE, DC, MC, V. Closed Oct 27–Dec 14. Free parking. Bus: 30.

The hotel name means "peaceful height." Built in 1906, the villa enjoys a beautiful location, and is one of the better inns in town, although not in the same league as Böld or Parkhotel Sonnenhof. It was reconstructed into a pension and café in 1913, and before that it hosted Thomas Mann, who stayed and wrote here. The guest rooms, furnished in tasteful modern style, are well maintained. TVs are available on request.

The Bavarian and international cuisine is known for its taste and the quality of its ingredients. The hotel offers a choice of four dining rooms, including an indoor terrace, with a panoramic view, and an outdoor terrace.

Hotel Schilcherhof

Bahnhofstrasse 17, D-82487 Oberammergau. ☎ **08822/4740.** Fax 08822/37-93. 20 rms. 109 DM–139 DM ($76.30–$97.30) double. Rates include buffet breakfast. AE, MC, V. Closed Nov 20–Christmas. Parking 10 DM ($7). Bus: 30.

An enlarged chalet with surrounding gardens, the Schilcherhof has a modern wing with good-value rooms. In summer, the terrace overflows with beer and festivities. Five minutes away lies the passion-play theater; also nearby is the Ammer River, which flows through the village. In summer you need to reserve well in advance to get a room. Although the house is built in the old style, with wooden front balconies and tiers of flower boxes, it has a fresh look.

Schlosshotel Linderhof

Linderhof 14, D-82488 Ettal. ☎ **08822/790.** Fax 08822/4347. 29 rms. MINIBAR TV TEL. 120 DM–160 DM ($84–$112) double. Additional bed 45 DM ($31.50) extra. Rates include breakfast. AE, DC, MC, V. Free parking.

This hotel was originally constructed about a century ago as one of the outbuildings of the famous palace. Designed with gables, shutters, and half-timbering in the style of a Bavarian chalet, it has been tastefully enlarged and renovated by members of the Maier family. Bedrooms are dignified and high-ceilinged, tasteful and comfortable, in a style that suggests 19th-century gentility.

Much of its business derives from its cozy restaurant, which extends onto a stone terrace accented with parasols and potted flowers. An array of fixed-price menus focus on such hearty regional food as pork schnitzels with mixed salad and cream of tomato soup. Food orders are accepted daily from 8am to 8pm.

⑤ Turmwirt

Ettalerstrasse 2, D-82487 Oberammergau. ☎ **08822/3091.** Fax 08822/14-37. 22 rms. MINIBAR TV TEL. 140 DM–180 DM ($98–$126) double. Rates include buffet breakfast. AE, DC, MC, V. Bus: 30.

A cozy Bavarian-style hotel, the Turmwirt offers many rooms with private balconies opening onto mountain views. A lodging house stood on this spot in 1742, and the present building was constructed in 1889. It has been altered and renovated many times over the past few decades. It's an intricately painted, green-shuttered country house, with a well-maintained homelike interior. The owners are three generations of the Glas family, who often present Bavarian folk evenings. The town center is an invigorating five-minute walk from the hotel.

Wolf Restaurant-Hotel

Dorfstrasse 1, D-82487 Oberammergau. ☎ **08822/3071.** Fax 08822/10-96. 32 rms. TV TEL. 110 DM–180 DM ($77–$126) double. Rates include buffet breakfast. AE, DC, MC, V. Free parking. Bus: 30.

An overgrown Bavarian chalet, the Wolf Restaurant-Hotel is at the heart of village life. Its facade is consistent with others in the area: an encircling balcony, heavy timbering, and window boxes spilling cascades of red and pink geraniums. Inside it retains some local flavor, although certain concessions have been made: an elevator, conservative room furnishings, a dining hall with zigzag paneled ceiling, and spoke chairs. The hotel is also equipped with a lift, sauna, solarium, and outdoor pool. Only five singles are available.

The Hafner Stub'n is a rustic place for beer drinking as well as light meals. Dining here can be both economical and gracious. There's always a freshly made soup of the day, followed by a generous main course, such as Wiener schnitzel or roast pork with dumplings and cabbage.

8　Mittenwald

66 miles S of Munich, 11 miles SE of Garmisch-Partenkirchen, 23 miles NW of Innsbruck

A picturesque village of traditional Bavarian houses with balconies and overhanging eves, the year-round resort of Mittenwald lies in a pass in the Karwendel Range. Especially noteworthy and photogenic are the painted walls of the houses—even the baroque church tower is covered with frescoes. On the square stands a monument to Mathias Klotz, who introduced violin making to Mittenwald in 1684. The town is a major international center for this highly specialized craft.

In the countryside around Mittenwald, the Wetterstein and Karwendel ranges offer constantly changing scenic vistas. In the winter, the town is a skiing center, and in the summer an even more popular range of outdoor activities invite the visitor.

ESSENTIALS
GETTING THERE
BY TRAIN   Mittenwald is reached by almost hourly train service, since it lies on the express rail line between Munich and Innsbruck (Austria). From Munich, trip time is $1^{1}/_{2}$ to 2 hours, depending on the train. It takes about 5 to 6 hours by train from Frankfurt. Call **08821/19-419** for information.

BY BUS   Regional bus service from Garmisch-Partenkirchen and nearby towns is frequently provided by **RVO Regionalverkehr Oberbayern** at Garmisch. Call **08821/51-822** for schedules and information.

BY CAR   Access by car is via the A95 Autobahn from Munich.

VISITOR INFORMATION
For tourist information, contact the **Kurverwaltung und Verkehrsamt,** Dammkarstrasse 3 (☎ **08823/33-981**), open Monday through Friday from 8am to noon and 1 to 5pm; Saturday, 10am to noon.

WHAT TO SEE & DO
The **Geigenbau- und Heimatmuseum,** Ballenhausgasse 3 (☎ **08823/2511**), has exhibits devoted to violins and other stringed instruments, from their invention through various stages of their evolution, as well as a violin workshop, which is open Monday through Friday from 10 to 11:45am and 2 to 4:45pm, and on Saturday and Sunday from 10 to 11:45am, charging an admission of 2.50 DM ($1.75) for adults and 1 DM (70¢) for children. The museum is closed from November 1 to December 20.

Mittenwald has good spa facilities, with large gardens landscaped with tree-lined streams and trout pools. Concerts during the summer are held in the music pavilion.

Some 80 miles of hiking paths wind up and down the mountains around the village. Chairlifts make the hiking trails readily accessible. Of course, where there are trails there is mountain biking. A cycling map is available through Mittenwald's administration office. Besides hiking or biking through the hills on your own, you can take part in organized mountain-climbing expeditions. Horse and carriage trips or coach tours from Mittenwald to nearby villages are available; contact the tourist office (see above) for information. You can always go swimming to cool off on a hot summer's day. The Lautersee and Ferchensee are brisk waters that even in summer might be forfeited by the faint-hearted for the heated adventure pool in Mittenwald.

In the evening you are treated to typical Bavarian entertainment, often consisting of folk dancing and singing, zither playing, and yodeling, but you also have a choice of concerts, dance bands, discos, and bars.

WHERE TO STAY
MODERATE
⑤ Berghotel Latscheneck
Kaffeefeld 1, D-82481 Mittenwald. ☎ **08823/1419.** Fax 08823/10-58. 12 rms. TV TEL. 200 DM–230 DM ($140–$161) double. Rates include continental breakfast. No credit cards. Closed Apr 18–May and Nov 25–Dec. Free parking.

Set against a craggy backdrop of rock and forest a short walk above the center of town, this chalet is ringed with green shutters, wraparound balconies, and a flagstone-covered sun terrace. Guests are never far from a vista, since large, weatherproof windows flood the wood-trimmed interior with sunlight. The guest rooms are modern and attractively furnished.

During chilly weather an open fireplace warms and brightens the eating areas (open only to guests). The Kranzberg ski lift nearby makes the place attractive to skiers. A covered pool and a sauna can provide a relaxing prelude to a quiet evening.

Hotel Post

Obermarkt 9, D-82481 Mittenwald. ☎ **08823/1094.** Fax 08823/10-96. 90 rms, 5 suites. TV TEL. 140 DM–240 DM ($98–$168) double; 220 DM–300 DM ($154–$210) suite. Rates include buffet breakfast. No credit cards. Closed Nov 22–Dec 17. Parking 8 DM ($5.60).

The Post is the most seasoned and established chalet hotel in the village, and it's been here since 1632, when stagecoaches carrying mail and passengers across the Alps stopped here to refuel. Although it doesn't offer the tranquility or the scenic views of Berghotel Latscheneck, it nevertheless is Mittenwald's finest address. A delightful breakfast is served on the sun terrace, with a view of the Alps. On a cool day, take time out to enjoy a beer in the snug lounge-bar with an open fireplace. For a night of hearty Bavarian specialties, head for the wine tavern or the Poststüberl, the latter nestled under low beams. The decor, with its deer antler collection and wood paneling, is full of alpine charm. Guest rooms are furnished in a comfortable although standard way. Available to guests are an indoor pool, massage facilities, and sauna.

Rieger Hotel

Dekan-Karl-Platz 28, D-82481 Mittenwald. ☎ **08823/5071.** Fax 08823/925-0250. 45 rms. TV TEL. 185 DM–239 DM ($129.50–$167.30) double. Rates include buffet breakfast. AE, DC, MC, V. Closed Oct 21–Dec 17. Parking 8 DM–10 DM ($5.60–$7).

The Rieger is attractive, whether snow is piled up outside or the window boxes are cascading with petunias. After the Post and Berghotel Latscheneck, the Rieger ranks number three in town. The living room has a beamed ceiling, wide arches, and a three-sided open fireplace. The indoor pool has a picture-window wall. Add to this a room for sauna and massages (segregated by sex except on Monday, family time, when both sexes join the crowd). The guest rooms are pleasant and comfortable, with a certain amount of Bavarian charm.

INEXPENSIVE

Alpenrose

Obermarkt 1, D-82481 Mittenwald. ☎ **08823/5055.** Fax 08823/37-20. 20 rms, 2 suites. MINIBAR TV TEL. 124 DM–185 DM ($86.80–$129.50) double; 185 DM ($129.50) suite. Rates include buffet breakfast. AE, DC, MC, V. Free parking.

A particularly inviting place to stay is the Alpenrose, in the village center at the foot of a rugged mountain. The facade is covered with decorative designs; window boxes hold flowering vines. The inn's basic structure is 14th century—it was once part of a monastery—although additions and improvements have been made over the years. The present inn is comfortable, with suitable plumbing facilities. The hotel's rooms are divided between the Alpenrose and its annex, the Bichlerhof; they're modernized but often with Bavarian traditional styling.

The tavern room, overlooking the street, has many ingratiating features, including coved ceilings (one decoratively painted), handmade chairs, flagstone floors, and a square tile stove in the center. In the Josefikeller, beer is served in giant steins, and in the evening musicians gather to entertain guests. The dining room provides excellent meals, including Bavarian specialties.

⑨ Gästehaus Franziska

Innsbruckerstrasse 24, D-82481 Mittenwald. ☎ **08823/92-030.** Fax 08823/3893. 14 rms, 4 suites. MINIBAR TEL. 98 DM–138 DM ($68.60–$96.60) double; 158 DM–178 DM ($110.60–$124.60) suite. Rates include buffet breakfast. AE, V. Closed Nov 11–Dec 13. Free parking.

When Olaf Grothe built this guesthouse, he named it after the most important person in his life—his wife, Franziska. Both have labored to make it the most personalized guesthouse in town by furnishing it tastefully and giving sympathetic attention to their guests' needs. Each room and suite is furnished in traditional Bavarian style. All have balconies opening onto mountain views; the suites also have safes and tea or coffee facilities. Breakfast is the only meal served, but there are plenty of restaurants nearby. It's extremely difficult to obtain bookings between June 20 and October 2.

Gästehaus Sonnenbichl

Klausnerweg 32, D-82481 Mittenwald. ☎ **08823/92-230.** Fax 08823/58-14. 20 rms. MINIBAR TV TEL. 110 DM–150 DM ($77–$105) double. Rates include buffet breakfast. No credit cards. Closed Nov–Dec 15.

One of the more modest hostelries in town, this inn nevertheless offers good value and comfort. Lodged into a hillside, the chalet has a view of the village set against a backdrop of the Alps. The rooms are freshly decorated in vivid natural colors. The guesthouse is often completely booked, so reserving well in advance is a good idea. Breakfast is the only meal served.

WHERE TO DINE

⑨ Restaurant Arnspitze

Innsbruckerstrasse 68. ☎ **08823/2425.** Reservations not required. Main courses 25 DM–38 DM ($17.50–$26.60); fixed-price meal 36.50 DM ($25.55) at lunch, 76.50 DM ($53.55) at dinner. AE. Thurs–Mon noon–2pm and daily 6–9pm. Closed Oct 25–Dec 19. Bus: RVO. BAVARIAN.

Housed in a modern chalet hotel on the outskirts of town, the Restaurant Arnspitze is the finest dining room in Mittenwald. Although you can also eat well at the inns previously recommended, over the years we've found the menus at this place more enticing than all the others. The restaurant is decorated in the old style; the cuisine is solid, satisfying, and wholesome. You might order sole with homemade noodles or veal steak in creamy smooth sauce, then finish with one of the freshly made desserts. There's an excellent fixed-price lunch.

9 Neuschwanstein & Hohenschwangau

The 19th century saw a great classical revival in Germany, especially in Bavaria, mainly because of the enthusiasm of Bavarian kings for ancient art forms. Beginning with Ludwig I (1786–1868), who was responsible for many Greek revival buildings in Munich, this royal house ran the gamut of ancient architecture in just three short decades. It culminated in the remarkable flights of fancy of Ludwig II, often called "Mad King Ludwig," who died under mysterious circumstances in 1886. In spite of his rather lonely life and controversial alliances, both personal and political, he was a great patron of the arts.

The name "Royal Castles" is limited to the castles of Hohenschwangau (built by Ludwig's father, Maximilian II) and Ludwig's Neuschwanstein. Ludwig's other extravagant castles, Linderhof (near Oberammergau) and Herrenchiemsee (Chiemsee), are described earlier in this chapter.

In 1868, after a visit to the great castle of Wartburg, Ludwig wrote to his good friend, composer Richard Wagner: "I have the intention to rebuild the ancient castle ruins of Hohenschwangau in the true style of the ancient German knight's castle." The following year, construction began on the first of a series of fantastic edifices, a series that stopped only with Ludwig's untimely death in 1886, only five days after he was deposed because of alleged insanity.

ESSENTIALS
GETTING THERE

BY CAR From Munich, motorists can take the E533 toward Garmisch-Partenkirchen. At the end of the autobahn, the road becomes Route 95 for its final run into Garmisch. From Garmish, continue west on Route 187 to the junction with Route 314, at which point you cut north to Füssen, where the castles are signposted.

BY TOUR BUS **Panorama Tours** offers an 8¹/₂ hour day tour from Munich to Neuschwanstein and Hohenschwangau that also includes Linderhof and a brief stopover in Oberammergau. For information see "Organized Tours" in Chapter 6, or call (☎ **089/59-15-04** daytime, 0177-20-33-037 after hours).

VISITOR INFORMATION

Information about the castles and the region in general is available at the **Kurverwaltung,** Rathaus, Münchenerstrasse 2 in Schwangau (☎ **08362/81-98-0**). Open Monday through Friday from 8am to 5pm.

VISITING THE ROYAL CASTLES

There are often very long lines in summer, especially in August. With 25,000 people a day visiting, the wait in peak summer months can range from 4 to 5 hours for a 20-minute tour.

✪ NEUSCHWANSTEIN

At Neuschwansteinstrasse 20 (☎ **08362/81-035**), this was the fairy-tale castle of Ludwig II. Construction went on for 17 years until the king's death, when all work stopped, leaving a part of the interior not completed. From 1884 to 1886 Ludwig lived in the rooms on and off for a total of only about six months.

The doorway off the left side of the vestibule leads to the king's apartments. The study, like most of the rooms, is decorated with wall paintings showing scenes from the Nordic legends (which also inspired Wagner's operas). The theme of the study is the Tannhäuser saga, painted by J. Aigner. The only fabric in the room is hand-embroidered silk, used in curtains and chair coverings, all designed with the gold and silver Bavarian coat-of-arms.

From the vestibule, you enter the throne room through the doorway at the opposite end. This hall, designed in Byzantine style by J. Hofmann, was never completed. The floor is a mosaic design, depicting the animals of the world. The columns in the main hall are the deep copper red of porphyry. The circular apse where the king's throne was to have stood is reached by a stairway of white Carrera marble. The walls and ceiling are decorated with paintings of Christ in heaven looking down on the 12 apostles and six canonized kings of Europe.

The king's bedroom is the most richly carved in the entire castle—it took 4¹/₂ years to complete this room alone. Aside from the mural depicting the legend of Tristan and Isolde, the walls are decorated with panels carved to look like Gothic windows. In the center is a large wooden pillar completely encircled with gilded brass sconces. The ornate bed is on a raised platform with an elaborately carved canopy. Through the balcony window you can see the 150-foot waterfall in the Pollat Gorge, with the mountains in the distance.

The fourth floor of the castle is almost entirely given over to the Singer's Hall, the pride of Ludwig II and all of Bavaria. Modeled after the hall at Wartburg, where the legendary song contest of Tannhäuser supposedly took place, this hall is decorated with marble columns and elaborately painted designs interspersed with frescoes depicting the life of Parsifal.

The castle can be visited year-round, and in September visitors have the additional treat of hearing Wagnerian concerts along with other music in the Singer's Hall. For information and reservations, contact the tourist office, Verkehrsamt, Schwangau, at the Rathaus (☎ **08362/81-980**). The castle is open (guided tours only) April to September, daily from 9am to 5:30pm; off-season, daily from 10am to 4pm. Admission is 10 DM ($7) for adults, 7 DM ($4.90) for students and seniors over 65; children 15 and under enter free.

To reach Neuschwanstein involves a steep half-mile climb from the parking lot for Hohenschwangau Castle (see below). This is about a 25-minute walk for the energetic, an eternity for anybody else. To cut down the climb, you can take a bus to Marienbrücke, a bridge that crosses over the Pollat Gorge at a height of 305 feet. From that vantage point you, like Ludwig, can stand and meditate on the glories of the castle and its panoramic surroundings. If you want to photograph the castle, don't wait until you reach the top, where you'll be too close to the edifice to photograph it properly. It costs 3 DM ($2.10) for the bus ride up to the bridge or 2.50 DM ($1.75) if you'd like to take the bus back down the hill. Marienbrücke is still not at the castle. From the bridge it's a 10-minute walk to reach Neuschwanstein. This footpath is very steep and not easy for elderly people to negotiate—or for anyone who has trouble walking up or down precipitous hills.

The most traditional way to reach Neuschwanstein is by horse-drawn carriage, costing 7 DM ($4.90) for the ascent, 3.50 DM ($2.45) for the descent. Some readers have objected to the rides, though, complaining that too many people are crowded in.

✪ HOHENSCHWANGAU

Not as glamorous or as spectacular as Neuschwanstein, the neo-Gothic Hohenschwangau Castle, Alpseestrasse 24 (☎ **08362/81-127**), nevertheless has a much richer history. The original structure dates back to the 12th-century Knights of Schwangau. When the knights faded away, the castle began to do so too, helped along by the Napoleonic Wars. When Ludwig II's father, Crown Prince Maximilian (later Maximilian II), saw the castle in 1832, he purchased it and in 4 years had it completely restored. Ludwig II spent the first 17 years of his life here and later received Richard Wagner in its chambers, although Wagner never visited Neuschwanstein on the hill above.

The rooms of Hohenschwangau are styled and furnished in a much heavier Gothic mode than those in the castle built by Ludwig. Many are typical of the halls of knights' castles of the Middle Ages in both England and Germany. There's no doubt that the style greatly influenced young Ludwig and encouraged the fanciful boyhood dreams that formed his later tastes and character. Unlike Neuschwanstein, however, this castle has a comfortable look about it, as if it actually were a home at one time, not just a museum. The small chapel, once a reception hall, still hosts Sunday mass. The suits of armor and the Gothic arches here set the stage for the rest of the room.

Among the most attractive chambers is the Hall of the Swan Knight, named for the wall paintings depicting the saga of Lohengrin—before Wagner and Ludwig II. Note the Gothic grillwork on the ceiling with the open spaces studded with stars.

Hohenschwangau is open April to September, daily from 8:30am to 5:30pm; October to March, daily from 10am to 4pm. Admission is 10 DM ($7) for adults and 7 DM ($4.90) for children 6 to 15 and seniors over 65; children 5 and under enter free. Several parking lots nearby enable you to leave your car there while visiting both castles.

WHERE TO STAY & DINE NEARBY

Hotel Lisl and Jägerhaus

Neuschwansteinstrasse 1–3, D-87643 Hohenschwangau. ☎ **08362/88-70.** Fax 08362/81-107. 51 rms. MINIBAR TV TEL. 280 DM ($196) double. AE, DC, MC, V. Closed Jan to mid-Mar. Free parking. Bus: Füssen.

This graciously styled villa with an annex across the street was seemingly made to provide views as well as comfort. Both houses sit in a narrow valley, surrounded by their own gardens. Most rooms have a view of at least one of the two royal castles and some rooms open onto views of both Schlosses. In the main house, two well-styled dining rooms serve good-tasting meals. The restaurant features an international as well as a local cuisine.

Hotel Müller Hohenschwangau

Alpseestrasse 16, D-87645 Hohenschwangau. ☎ **08362/8-19-90.** Fax 08362/81-99-13. 43 rms, 2 suites. TV TEL. 200 DM–260 DM ($140–$182) double; 300 DM–400 DM ($210–$280) suite. Rates include continental breakfast. AE, DC, MC, V. Closed Nov–Dec 20. Free parking. Bus: Füssen.

The yellow walls, green shutters, and gabled alpine detailing of this hospitable inn are enough incentive for you to stay here. However, its location near the foundation of Neuschwanstein Castle makes it even more alluring. An enlargement and upgrading in 1984 left the basic Bavarian lines intact yet added extra modern conveniences. On the premises are a well-maintained restaurant lined with burnished pinewood, a more formal evening restaurant with views over a verdantly planted sun terrace, lots of rustic accessories, and comfortable rooms. Nature lovers usually enjoy hiking the short distance to nearby Hohenschwangau Castle.

Appendix

A Glossary

Altstadt   old part of a city or town
Anlage   park area
Apotheke   pharmacy
Bad   spa
Bahn   railroad, train
   Bahnhof   railroad station
   Bergbahn   funicular (cable railway)
   Hauptbahnhof   main railroad station
   Seilbahn   cable car
   Stadtbahn (S-Bahn)   commuter railroad
   Strassenbahn   streetcar, tram
   Untergrundbahn (U-Bahn)   subway, underground
    transportation system in a city
Baroque   ornate, decorated style of art and architecture
in the 18th century; characterized by elaborate gilding and
ornamentation
Bauhaus   style of functional design for architecture and objects,
originating in the early 20th century in Germany
Berg   mountain
Biedermeier   solid, bourgeois style of furniture design and
interior decoration in the mid-19th century
Der Blaue Reiter   group of nonfigurative painters, founded in
Munich in 1911 by Franz Marc and Wassily Kandinsky
Brücke   bridge
Brunnen   spring or well
Burg   fortified castle
Damm   dike, embankment
Dom   cathedral
Domplatz   cathedral square
Drogerie   shop selling cosmetics, sundries
"Evergreen"   alpine traditional music
Fleet   canal
Gasse   lane
Gastarbeiter   foreign worker
Gasthof   inn
Gemütlichkeit (adj. gemütlich)   comfort, coziness, friendliness
Graben   moat

Gutbürgerliche Küche (German) home-cooking
Hotel Garni hotel that serves no meals or serves breakfast only
Insel island
Jugendstil art nouveau
Kai quay
Kaufhaus department store
Kloster monastery
Kneipe bar for drinking, may serve snacks
Konditorei cafe for coffee and pastries
Kunst art
Marktplatz market square
Messegelände exhibition center, fairgrounds
Neue Küche cuisine moderne, novelle cuisine
Neustadt new part of city or town
Oper opera
Platz square
Rathaus town or city hall
  Altes Rathaus old town hall
  Neues Rathaus new town hall (currently used as such)
Ratskeller restaurant in Rathaus cellar serving traditional German food
Reisebüro travel agency
Rococo a highly decorative development of baroque style
Schauspielhaus theater for plays
Schloss palace, castle
See lake (*der See*) or sea (*die See*)
Spielbank casino
Stadt town, city
Steg footbridge
Strasse street
Teich pond
Tor gateway
Turm tower
Ufer shore, riverbank
Verkehrsamt tourist office
Weg road
Weinstube wine bar or tavern serving meals

B Menu Terms

SOUPS (SUPPEN)

Erbsensuppe pea soup
Gemüsesuppe vegetable soup
Guiaschsuppe goulash soup
Kartoffelsuppe potato soup
Linsensuppe lentil soup
Nudelsuppe noodle soup

MEATS (WURST, FLEISCH & GEFLÜGEL)

Aufschnitt cold cuts
Brathuhn roast chicken
Bratwurst grilled sausage
Deutsches beefsteak
  hamburger steak
Eisbein pigs' knuckles
Ente duck
Gans goose
Hammel mutton
Kalb veal
Kaltes geflügel cold poultry
Kassler rippchen pork chops

Lamm lamb
Leber liver
Nieren kidneys
Ragout stew
Rinderbraten roast beef
Rindfleisch beef

Sauerbraten sauerbraten
Schinken ham
Schweinebraten roast pork
Truthahn turkey
Wiener schnitzel veal cutlet
Wurst sausage

FISH (FISCH)

Aal eel
Forelle trout
Hecht pike
Karpfen carp
Krebs crawfish

Lachs salmon
Makrele mackerel
Rheinsalm Rhine salmon
Schellfisch haddock
Seezunge sole

EGGS (EIER)

Eier in der schale boiled eggs
Mit speck with bacon
Rühreier scrambled eggs

Spiegeleier fried eggs
Verlorene eier poached eggs

SALADS (SALAT)

Gemischter salat mixed salad
Gurkensalat cucumber salad

Rohkostplatte raw vegetable platter

SANDWICHES (BELEGTE BROTE)

Käsebrot cheese sandwich
Schinkenbrot ham sandwich
Schwarzbrot mit butter
  pumpernickel with butter

Wurstbrot sausage sandwich

VEGETABLES (GEMÜSE)

Artischocken artichokes
Blumenkohl cauliflower
Bohnen beans
Bratkartoffeln fried potatoes
Erbsen peas
Grüne bohnen string beans
Gurken cucumbers
Karotten carrots
Kartoffelbrei mashed potatoes
Kartoffelsalat potato salad
Knödel dumplings
Kohl cabbage

Reis rice
Rote Rüben beets
Rotkraut red cabbage
Salat lettuce
Salzkartoffeln boiled potatoes
Sauerkraut sauerkraut
Spargel asparagus
Spinat spinach
Steinpilze boletus mushrooms
Tomaten tomatoes
Vorspeisen hors d'oeuvres
Weisse Rüben turnips

DESSERTS (NACHTISCH)

Blatterteiggebäck puff pastry
Bratapfel baked apple
Käse cheese
Kompott stewed fruit
Obstkuchen fruit tart

Obstsalat fruit salad
Pfannkuchen sugared pancakes
Pflaumenkompott stewed plums
Torten pastries

FRUITS (OBST)

Ananas pineapple
Apfel apple

Apfelsine orange
Banane banana

Birne pear
Erdbeeren strawberries
Kirschen cherries

Pfirsich peach
Weintrauben grapes
Zitrone lemon

BEVERAGES (GETRÄNKE)

Bier beer
Ein dunkles a dark beer
Ein helles a light beer
Milch milk
Rotwein red wine

Schokolade chocolate
Eine tasse kaffee a cup of coffee
Eine tasse tee a cup of tea
Tomatensaft tomato juice
Wasser water

CONDIMENTS & TABLE ITEMS

Brötchen rolls
Brot bread
Butter butter
Eis ice
Essig vinegar
Gabel fork
Glas glass
Löffel spoon

Messer knife
Pfeffer pepper
Platte plate
Sahne cream
Salz salt
Senf mustard
Tasse cup
Zucker sugar

COOKING TERMS

Gebacken baked
Gebraten fried
Gefüllt stuffed
Gekocht boiled

Geröstet roasted
Gut durchgebraten well done
Nicht durchgebraten rare
Paniert breaded

Index

ACCOMMODATIONS

FROMMER'S COMPLETE TRAVEL GUIDES

*(Comprehensive guides to destinations around the world, with
selections in all price ranges—from deluxe to budget)*

FROMMER'S FRUGAL TRAVELER'S GUIDES

(The grown-up guides to budget travel, offering dream vacations at down-to-earth prices)

Australia from $45 a Day	India from $40 a Day
Berlin from $50 a Day	Ireland from $45 a Day
California from $60 a Day	Italy from $50 a Day
Caribbean from $60 a Day	Israel from $45 a Day
Costa Rica & Belize from $35 a Day	London from $60 a Day
Eastern Europe from $30 a Day	Mexico from $35 a Day
England from $50 a Day	New York from $70 a Day
Europe from $50 a Day	New Zealand from $45 a Day
Florida from $50 a Day	Paris from $65 a Day
Greece from $45 a Day	Washington, D.C. from $50 a Day
Hawaii from $60 a Day	

FROMMER'S PORTABLE GUIDES

(Pocket-size guides for travelers who want everything in a nutshell)

Charleston & Savannah	New Orleans
Las Vegas	San Francisco

FROMMER'S IRREVERENT GUIDES

(Wickedly honest guides for sophisticated travelers)

Amsterdam	Miami	Santa Fe
Chicago	New Orleans	U.S. Virgin Islands
London	Paris	Walt Disney World
Manhattan	San Francisco	Washington, D.C.

FROMMER'S AMERICA ON WHEELS

(Everything you need for a successful road trip, including full-color road maps and ratings for every hotel)

California & Nevada	Northwest & Great Plains
Florida	South Central &Texas
Mid-Atlantic	Southeast
Midwest & the Great Lakes	Southwest
New England & New York	

FROMMER'S BY NIGHT GUIDES

(The series for those who know that life begins after dark)

Amsterdam	Los Angeles	New York
Chicago	Miami	Paris
Las Vegas	New Orleans	San Francisco
London		